Vulnerable Populations

Volume 2

Vulnerable Populations

Sexual Abuse Treatment for Children,
Adult Survivors, Offenders, and
Persons with Mental Retardation

Volume 2

Suzanne M. Sgroi, M.D.

Lexington Books
D.C. Heath and Company/Lexington, Massachusetts/Toronto

Library of Congress Cataloging-in-Publication Data
(Revised for volume 2)

Vulnerable populations.

Vol. 2 has subtitle: Sexual abuse treatment for children, adult survivors, offenders, and persons with mental retardation.
    Includes bibliographies and index.
    1. Child molesting—Treatment.   2. Sexually abused children—Mental health.   3. Adult child abuse victims—Mental health.   4. Psychotherapy.   5. Mentally handicapped—Sexual behavior.   6. Child Abuse, Sexual—psychology.   7. Mental Retardation—psychology. 8. Psychotherapy.   9. Sex Offenses.   I. Sgroi, Suzanne M., 1943–   .
    RC560.C46V85   1988   616.85′83   87–29893
    ISBN 0–669–16336–8 (v. 1 : alk. paper)
    ISBN 0–669–16338–4 (pbk. : v. 1 : alk. paper)
    ISBN 0–669–20942–2 (v. 2 : alk. paper)
    ISBN 0–669–20943–0 (pbk. : v. 2 : alk. paper)

Published simultaneously in Canada

Printed in the United States of America
Casebound International Standard Book Number: 0–669–20942–2
Paperbound International Standard Book Number: 0–669–20943–0
Library of Congress Catalog Card Number 87–45325

The paper used in this publication meets the minimum requirements of American National Standard for Information Sciences—Permanence of Paper for Printed Library Materials, ANSI Z39.48–1984. ∞™

Year and number of this printing:

89 90 91 92 10 9 8 7 6 5 4 3 2 1

To A. Nicholas Groth, Ph.D.,
Friend and Colleague,
"Nick."

You have traversed hundreds of thousands of miles—
teaching, consulting, and helping others to learn to work
with sexual offenders. A pioneer in your field, you were the
first to advocate widely for humane and enlightened
treatment for men (and women) who rape and molest
children and adults. In doing so, you have helped countless
victims, past and present. You have assisted an untold
number of children who will never know the trauma of
sexual victimization by your contributions to our knowledge
about treating offenders and preventing future abuse.

Go gently as you journey, Nick. Our gratitude, affection,
and respect go with you.

Contents

Prologue

A society may be judged by the manner in which it treats the members of various vulnerable populations. They are: children, the elderly and persons with physical handicaps, mental illnesses, and mental retardation. A truly caring society will recognize its vulnerable populations and take steps to provide them with special care and protection from abuse and exploitation. Although we lack the capacity to prevent all harm that might occur, we do have the resources and the knowledge to do so much that is affirming, nurturing, healing, and empowering. A society's willingness to cherish its vulnerable populations may be a measure of its humanity. And we can learn to do so much more. . . .

Acknowledgments

This book could not have been finished without the unswerving loyalty and generous professional support given by Jamshid A. Marvasti, M.D., during the entire time when it was being written. I also owe many thanks to Alma Fitzsimmons, R.N., Phyllis Cramer, and Norah Sargent, M.A., for helping me to staff two offices during the same time period. Norah's help with editing and preparing the entire manuscript as well as that of Sister Judith A. Carey with the chapters dealing with persons with mental retardation are greatly appreciated as well.

Introduction

In 1981, when I was writing the Introduction to *Handbook of Clinical Intervention in Child Sexual Abuse,* it seemed that the beginning of a new decade provided a powerful and compelling metaphor for change. If the 1960s was a decade of discovery and recognition of the various forms of child maltreatment, some might characterize the 1970s as a period of landmark legislative and governmental influence upon a newly developed area of profound social concern. What, then, of the 1980s? Surely it is now apparent that the decade that is ending has been a time in which the societal response to sexual abuse of children has been a widespread demand for rapid remedies and simple solutions. The glare of nationwide publicity and "hype" that began in 1984 as a result of reports of sexual abuse of small children in day-care centers and nursery schools was unprecedented and totally unexpected. How disturbing to discover that inadequacies in investigative approaches and gaping deficits in services would be so mercilessly illuminated by that spotlight! With media attention focused elsewhere, professionals in the field continue to work hard in a milieu of high expectations and increasing demands.

As this book reflects, there is no simple, universal solution to any aspect of sexual abuse of a member of any vulnerable population. Yet people want concise remedies for complex, multidetermined problems. In March 1989, at the third national annual child abuse conference sponsored by the Children's Hospital of Philadelphia, Dr. Jan E. Paradise spoke movingly of the difficulties inherent in resisting the technological imperative to perform a test just because the equipment and the technology to do so are available. She was referring to the use of the culposcope in performing medical examinations when sexual abuse of female children is suspected. Although most child victims of sexual abuse have no telltale physical signs when a medical examination is performed, there is great pressure to find physical evidence to document the complaint when sexual victimization of young children is suspected. The culposcope is an instrument that can be used to illuminate, magnify, and photograph the external genito-urinary and anal regions of children who are being examined medically. A physician who collects observational data and photographs with this instrument has a powerful and persuasive advantage when presenting medical evidence in court.

However, an illuminated and magnified view of a child's perineum can, at best, tell us only that evidence of trauma does or does not exist. What if the abuser was a child molester who gently rubbed or manipulated the child's body in a way that did not cause trauma? Culposcopy cannot detect and photograph fingerprints on a little girl's (or a little boy's) bottom. How genital trauma (if it can be documented) might have been caused and who caused it are still questions that can be answered only by weighing the credibility of an allegation that a particular person sexually abused the child. Medical experts for the defense can (and do) make countering arguments that the trauma documented by the culposcope did not result from sexual abuse. Rarely, if ever, does the culposcope document compelling medical evidence of child sexual abuse that could not be seen by the naked eye when the child was examined. Yet even when all agree that child sexual abuse did occur, the identity of the abuser can be contested fiercely.

The culposcope, nevertheless, when properly used, is a valuable tool, especially for examining young children who lack verbal capacity to describe clearly and consistently what happened to them. Should it be used for medical examinations of *all* children whom we suspect may have been sexually abused? Herein lies the technological imperative to use an instrument or perform a test just because it is available. The answer is that indications and standards for a new procedure must be formulated and tested with repeated usage. By the end of the 1990s, the advantages and limitations of the culposcope will be much better documented and the indications (and lack thereof) for its use more widely accepted and understood.

Meanwhile, in the field of offender treatment, there is a growing technological imperative to perform psychological tests on offenders of both sexes and to perform penile plethysmography on male offenders (by attaching a strain gauge to the penis of an offender and recording his penile erectile response to various stimuli). The former reflects a deeply held wish or belief that people who commit sexual crimes against children will have recognizable psychological profiles that differentiate them from the rest of humanity. As it turns out, sexual abusers of children can be male or female, white or black, tall or short, bright or dull, kind or cruel, well educated or ignorant, spiritually devout or irreligious, generally law abiding or criminal, and so on. In other words, many of us who work with sexual offenders against children are increasingly impressed by the overwhelmingly human characteristics of this troubled population. No one could deny that people have psychological motivations for committing sexual crimes against children. But anyone could sexually abuse a child; there are no psychological profiles that differentiate persons who have committed such offenses from those who have not. In the words of Walt Kelly's Pogo, "We have met the enemy and they are us!"

The technological imperative to perform penile plethysmography reflects a different belief: the offender's response to treatment can be assessed reliably in this way. There is no doubt that we can measure how various stimuli influence a man's penile erectile response under laboratory conditions. It is also possible to demonstrate how behavioral conditioning influences a male offender's arousal pattern (as measured by penile plethysmography) while he is being tested. What has not been demonstrated, however, is the extent to which generating these data and comparing them during the treatment period has predictive value regarding treatment outcomes. Why is it that a capacity to generate such data strengthens the credibility of some treatment providers? Perhaps it is because so little data on treatment of victims or offenders has been collected, analyzed, and published. In the 1990s, it will be incumbent upon us all to collect more clinical data pertaining to treatment of cases of child sexual abuse. In order for the data to be meaningful, however, we must also become more precise in our definitions of progress in treatment and treatment outcomes. Only then will our research efforts be in the service of learning how to do a better job of providing treatment rather than satisfying a technological imperative to collect data regardless of its relevance simply because we can.

Largely unnoticed during the 1980s were treatment initiatives that addressed therapy and reeducation for victims and abusers alike. Volume 2 of *Vulnerable Populations* focuses on these initiatives, some of them reflecting years of work in the field. The first four chapters address treatment of sexually abused children and adolescents. Dr. Jamshid Marvasti, a child psychiatrist, breaks new ground in chapter 1, "Play Therapy with Sexually Abused Children," by providing long-needed guidelines for this infrequently discussed therapy modality. Chapter 2, coauthored by David Hussey, a psychiatric social worker, and Dr. Mark Singer, a clinical psychologist, addresses another timely topic, treatment of sexually abused adolescents in an inpatient psychiatric unit. In chapter 3, Kerry Christensen Homstead, Ed.D, and Lynn Werthamer, M.S.W., share valuable insights and experience gained in providing cyclic time-limited group therapy for sexually abused adolescent girls. In the next chapter, Francis J. Pescosolido, M.S.W., provides helpful information for treatment of sexual victimization issues in adolescent boys, an oft-neglected but still vulnerable population.

The next section of the book focuses on clinical work with adult survivors of child sexual abuse. In chapters 5 and 6, I describe stages of recovery and peer group therapy approaches for adult survivors. Both chapters draw heavily on experience gained in working with women adult survivors at New England Clinical Associates, a private office devoted to working with various types of child sexual abuse clients. Chapter 7 deals with the impact of childhood sexual abuse on the spirituality of the adult survivors; Norah M. Sargent, M.A., draws on a combined background in clinical work and spirituality in offering treatment suggestions.

The next section of this volume introduces yet another vulnerable population, persons with mental retardation. In 1985, I was asked by Dr. Amy B. Wheaton, then acting commissioner of the Connecticut Department of Mental Retardation, to develop a curriculum to train persons with mental retardation to avoid sexual victimization. Although I was initially hesitant to comply, I changed my mind when an extensive search failed to uncover a published curriculum that can be used with persons who function in the lower than normal range of measured intelligence. Chapter 8 is a teaching guide for a curriculum developed after extensive field testing. Chapter 9 presents the curriculum itself, which is adaptable for persons with mild, moderate, and severe levels of mental retardation. These could not have been published without the assistance of Dr. Wheaton and the contributions of Sister Judith A. Carey, an educational psychologist whose expertise in working with persons with mental retardation provided an invaluable contribution. Chapter 10, "Evaluation and Treatment of Sexual Offense Behavior in Persons with Mental Retardation," came to be written in response to questions raised during numerous evaluations in subsequent years. Persons with mental retardation are an extremely vulnerable population, especially with regard to sexual victimization. In the next decade, it is probable that we will see much greater interest and many more contributions in this area.

One new phenomenon of the 1980s was the birth of private offices and treatment centers that specialize in working with cases of child sexual abuse. Some of these endeavors were short-lived; others have been more durable. The difficulties in sustaining such free-standing private programs while delivering affordable treatment services are many and challenging. Chapter 11, "The Chesapeake Institute," describes a private program in Maryland that provides high-quality treatment services to many types of child sexual abuse clients. The coauthors, Linda Canfield Blick and Thomas S. Berg (both psychiatric social workers) have provided a detailed description of their program and its treatment philosophy.

The last section of this volume focuses on offender treatment. In chapter 12, Dr. A. Nicholas Groth, with the help of Frank Oliveri, once again illuminates the topics of sexual offenders and sexual offense behavior. Chapter 13, by Margaret C. Vasington, M.A., is a compelling contribution that addresses the treatment of personal victimization issues in convicted sexual offenders. Finally, in chapter 14, I have described an approach to community-based treatment for sexual offenders against children, with a focus on time-limited cyclic peer group therapy as the primary therapy modality.

This book is a state-of-the-art contribution. None of the approaches described in any of the chapters represents a simple or final solution. As the field evolves, we need to keep on learning and working and trying other ways. Since so much of our work with victims and offenders is enhanced by the use of metaphor, it may be useful to end this introduction by reflecting on the lessons to be learned from Charles Lamb's "Dissertation on Roast Pig." Many of the people with whom we have worked at the New England Clinical Associates office have enjoyed the following version of that timeless tale.

In pre-historic times, there lived a barbaric clan who had tamed fire to the extent of learning to build hearths to warm their rude huts. These savages were so primitive that, in winter, they brought their domestic animals into their own huts so that all could keep warm. Although they had learned to domesticate chickens and goats and pigs, they had not yet learned to use fire to cook food. Accordingly, the clan would slaughter the domestic animals and eat their flesh raw.

One day, the leader of the village, a man reknowned for his wisdom and prowess in hunting, decided to lead everyone on a hunt for fresh meat. The headman left behind his young son, admonishing him to tend the fire carefully so that a newly-farrowed litter of pigs in the hut would not freeze. The boy tended the fire faithfully for a long time until he became bored and restless. Forgetting his father's warnings, he piled wood on the hearth and left the hut. When he returned, he discovered that the hut had caught on fire; despite frantic efforts, he could not put it out and the hut burned to the ground. The larger animals all escaped although they were scorched by the fire. Poking disconsolately in the wreckage, the boy accidentally touched the charred body of one of the piglets, all of which had perished in the flames. Yelping in pain, he thrust his burned hand into his mouth. Some of the roasted skin and flesh of the piglet, which had been stuck to his hand, thereby found its way into his mouth. The boy now was distracted by this new experience. By chance, he was the first person in his clan to taste the delights of roast pig! Fearfully, he broke apart the smoking carcass and tasted another piece. It was wonderful! Throwing caution to the winds, he began to cram pieces of scorched pork into his mouth, eating it as fast as he could.

Unbeknownst to the boy, his father had returned. As he surveyed the wreckage of his hut, the headman began to weep and curse and beat his breast while demanding an explanation from his son. However, the boy paid no attention to his father and continued to gorge himself. In a rage, the father cuffed the boy aside and bent down to see what he had been doing. Thrusting his hand into the place where the piglets had been lying, he also burned his hand. History repeated itself. The headman also thrust his hand into his mouth and in a similar fashion, tasted roast pig for the first time. Wiser and more experienced than his son, the headman immediately divined what had taken place. Sitting down in the midst of the smouldering wreckage, the headman ate and ate and ate. His son crept quietly back and parent and child sat side by side, devouring roast pig.

After a long time, the headman stopped gorging himself. He stood up, paced around the perimeter of his ruined hut and became very thoughtful. Then, with grunts and scowls and stern admonitions, he spoke seriously to his son. He told the boy that, under no circumstances, must anyone learn of their discovery. With great solemnity, the savages kept their secret and told no one about the new use of fire which had been revealed to them. However, the other people in the clan could not help noticing as time went on, that the headman's hut burned down with frightening regularity—just about as often as the sow gave birth to a new litter of piglets.

When I tell this story to clients, I like to conclude by remarking, "People keep on doing things the hard way when they don't know any better. Different solutions are possible. It isn't necessary to keep on using the same solutions, over and over again. We can learn different solutions. It's okay to learn to solve problems in a different way."

This holds true for treatment interventions with vulnerable populations. We can learn more creative ways to work with sexually abused children, adult survivors, offenders, and persons with mental retardation, while still retaining the useful lessons of the past. Good luck to us all!

1
Play Therapy with Sexually Abused Children

Jamshid A. Marvasti

Definition of Play

The clinical use of play can be divided into a play diagnosis phase followed by a play therapy phase (although in many situations it is difficult to differentiate the two). In play diagnosis the interviewer's focus is on identifying significant events in the child's life and assessing their impact on personality and feelings. In a subsequent play therapy phase, the therapist's focus is on correcting any abnormalities identified in play diagnosis.

Play Diagnosis

In play diagnosis, the interviewer builds a relationship with the child by encouraging him or her to interact with dolls, toys, and other play material that aid in identifying the child's principal emotional conflicts. Once those conflicts are identified, the toys are used again in play therapy but this time as an aid in helping the child find better solutions for these conflicts. Play diagnosis is a technique to enable a child to reveal internal conflicts, fantasies, wishes, and perceptions of the world. Generally children use repression, projection, displacement, and symbolization as the main ego defense mechanisms during play. The child displaces the emotions of anger, hate, and love onto the dolls and toys. During play diagnosis the child is encouraged by the therapist to displace his or her feelings and traumas onto the dolls and toys. Through this play, the therapist may observe the child's self-view and the role that he or she assumes in the family. The child may be the family scapegoat, a parentified child, or a Cinderella. The child's view of others may also be noticed in play, especially his or her perception of family members and their interpersonal relationship, and the family's dynamics. The child's defense mechanisms and method of dealing with emotional conflicts may also be manifested in play diagnosis.

During the second play session, Jimmy arranged the family dolls inside the dollhouse. Then the mother doll brought a new puppy home, which became the center of attention. Later a monster from outside came and kidnapped the new puppy. This play was a reflection of the child's resentment toward his new baby sister. The child displaced his resentment and anger onto the monster and by using displacement was able to express his conflict with his new baby sister. The child also used symbolization by substituting a new puppy for his new baby sister.

Displacement is a powerful defense mechanism used during play; the child is able to reveal his or her internal world without fear because these activities are "done" by the dolls, not by the child. It is the doll who is afraid of an Indian, not the child. It is the dinosaur who is full of anger, rage, and murderous wishes, not the child. It is the monster who takes the father and throws him out of the home, not the child.

Five-year-old Mary was living with her mother. The parents were divorced, and Mary visited her father on weekends at his home. There were some allegations of sexual abuse, drug dealing, and violence in her father's home. During play sessions a "Bonnie Baby" lived in a home with her "Bonnie Mother." Once in a while, the mother brought the "Bonnie Baby" to another home to "have fun." But Bonnie Baby "didn't like the other home" or the "animals' house" as Mary called it. Bonnie was somewhat reluctant to go to the other home and hid herself in the closet in her mother's house. The therapist commented that "Bonnie Baby" was not happy about going to the other house, which Mary said was "full of scary things." The therapist took another puppet and asked Mary's puppet, "What is going on with this Bonnie Baby?" Mary's puppet said that she was afraid to visit that house. The therapist's puppet said, "Oh, she should have a reason to be afraid. I wish that she would tell us what is scary there." Mary's puppet said, "It is scary, but she can't talk now; Bonnie Baby cannot talk now." During this play session, there was some indication that Mary was reluctant and fearful of going into her father's home. However, in earlier interviews with the child and her mother, the child mentioned that she liked to see her father, and the mother agreed that the child "had fun" with her father during the visitation period.

The mother later said she was puzzled that her daughter frequently wet the bed after visiting her father and speculated that she probably missed him.

However, during the subsequent play sessions, there was no indication that Mary missed her father.

During play sessions, the therapist tries to understand the symbolic meaning of the child's play. Children use play to express their wishes, traumas, and internal world. With the help of ego defense mechanisms, it is possible for their play to be free from censorship of the superego and free from reality principles. As Piaget (1962) confirmed, play is the child's assimilation of reality to ego needs; for example, dead people can be alive and children can fly. In play, a child reshapes reality to self-needs. Play obviously is the opposite of work. Work is assimilation of self to the needs of the environment.

Probably Freud (1920) was the first to consider observing and interpreting play as a means for understanding the emotional condition of children. He described the play of an 18-month-old child, a "good little boy" who had the habit of throwing his toys in the corner and crying "Gone!" One day, after repeating the same play, the child added another dimension: he repeatedly threw a reel out of his crib and called "Gone!" but then pulled it back. Upon its return, the child called "There!" with pleasure in his voice. Freud considered this repetition of an object's disappearance and, "Gone!" and "There!" as a game the child invented for the purpose of ego mastery of the traumatic experience of his mother's temporary departure. The child became an active participant in the play, contrary to his real-life experience in which he was a passive victim. Freud believed that in play, children repeat whatever has made a great impression on them in real life. They abreact and make themselves master of the situation. The universality of certain games and play, such as Peek-a-Boo, may indicate the child's attempt to deal with separation anxiety and object consistency. It follows that a child who is a victim of trauma, especially incest, may try to master the trauma through play and the repetition of that play. When the trauma is excessive, the child repeats the events during the play in order to digest the overwhelming trauma gradually. This play, which is centered around the traumatizing situation, is repeated over and over for the possible purpose of ego mastery.

Play Therapy

The second part of play is play therapy. In play therapy, the therapist "undoes" the displacement, projection, and symbolization observed in the play diagnosis phase. In play diagnosis the therapist encourages the child to express himself or herself by using displacement and other ego defense mechanisms. In play therapy, however, the reverse should occur: displacement should be broken and projection "undone." The similarities between the doll's feelings and the child's feelings will be explained to the youngster. For example, the therapist may say, "Jimmy, I wonder if you feel the same way as this doll?" Or, "Now this is you, Mary, who are angry at your mother, just like the doll." The therapist relates the child's play to his or her conflicts and fears and helps the child find a better solution, not for the doll necessarily but for the child.

In play therapy, ventilation of feelings is beneficial, but it is only a small part of therapy. Real therapy starts when the defense mechanisms are broken and the child verbally reveals real concern about his or her conflicts. The therapist connects the content of the play to the child's own life and explains the similarities between the doll's life and the child's life. In other words, the therapist helps the child face reality:

> Natasha created a scenario that she repeated during several sessions of play therapy. A monster found a little elephant in the street and brought it to the dollhouse to be cared for. Eventually the therapist felt that the little elephant was, in a symbolic way, the child; and the monster was, most likely, her mother. In one of the sessions when Natasha was playing a powerful role, she threw the monster and the dinosaur out of the dollhouse and said, "I got rid of all the monsters. I got rid of all dinosaurs." The therapist interrupted Natasha and said, "But there is still one monster left that we haven't dealt with and that is, possibly, your mother."

In this case, the therapist's comment about the monster was a stepping-stone for the child to begin the real work of dealing with her mother.

The interpretation of the child's play is also an important part of therapy, especially with older children. It formulates the problem, or conflict, into words in order to promote the child's understanding of his or her own feelings. In legal situations, especially with children who are sexually abused, a verbal statement by the child during play may be valuable. Obviously the justice system wants to hear the child's statement about the abuse, but statements made during play concerning a father doll who puts his finger in the daughter doll's vagina may not be very valuable to a judge as evidence. Interpretation by the therapist will be necessary if the statement is to be used in the legal process (Marvasti 1986a).

Therapeutic Interpretation of the Child's Play

One issue in play therapy is the content of the play and its symbolic meaning. When a child plays a scenario in which a car becomes disabled on a lonely road at night in the middle of a snowstorm and "No one is around to help," the child may be indirectly describing a cold environment and feelings of abandonment, helplessness, and depression. It is important to pay attention to the child's nonverbal communication—body language, dreams, and play. A verbal statement generally arises from the conscious level of the mind; however, play, dreams, and body language probably represent the unconscious.

> Mary was a victim of father-daughter incest. She verbally expressed to her therapist, "It didn't bother me too much. It doesn't bother me anymore; he is my father anyway. I can forgive and forget and that is what I did." Later, however, when the therapist invited the child to play, the child played out a scenario of Indians, cowboys, dinosaurs, and monsters who constantly fought and expressed revenge and resentment. There was no indication of forgiveness or forgetting each other's behavior. The content of play obviously showed that the child was full of anger and desired revenge; however, her verbal statement contradicted her unconscious wishes and fantasies.

After encouraging the child to play, the therapist may observe both the content of the play and the characters the child uses (dinosaurs and monsters or kings and princesses). It is important to identify the child's main conflict; in some ways, play rather than verbal statements may better indicate the child's true feelings. Children may have learned that it is undesirable to express negative feelings verbally. It is evident in our culture that children are not allowed to talk about their hate and anger; however, in play, children may act out their most undesirable feelings with the help of displacement and projection.

The Child's Perception of an Event: Objective versus Subjective Reality

During play the child is generally preoccupied by psychic reality, or subjective reality, rather than objective reality. Psychic reality is the child's perception of events in his or her environment, and objective reality is what is actually happening. The investigator's intervention in child sexual abuse cases is designed to try to find the objective reality as much as possible. A child's psychic reality might be different or, because of wishfulness, might be a distortion of objective reality. In play, the child and therapist are dealing with the child's psychic reality, and for years, play therapists were concerned primarily with the child's perception of the events. For example, if the child perceived that he or she was responsible for the parents' divorce or the father's death, the therapist would deal with the child's psychic reality and try to help him or her to overcome the emotional trauma of that perception or misperception. However, in the last several years, child sexual abuse cases have modified this pattern. The justice system has imposed an emergency mandate to identify the objective reality as soon as possible: Who did it? How was it done? When did it happen? During play diagnosis, however, it is desirable to understand the child's perception and interpretation of events, which may be different from objective reality (Marvasti 1987).

> Jimmy was taken by his mother to a dentist and then came to a psychotherapist's office for play therapy. During play, he created a scenario whereby a father doll forced a hammer into the mouth of his child and punished him. Although it was the mother who took the child to the dentist, the child's play revealed that he felt he was sent to the dentist by his father as punishment for having angered him earlier that day.

The child's perception and interpretation of sexual abuse are the most important elements in determining the impact of the abuse and its contribution to psychopathology in the child.

> Michelle, a 4-year old child, was molested almost every other night by her father. Her mother worked at night and slept during the day. She was a depressed woman who was unable to give enough attention or affection to her child. After the disclosure of incest, the father was prohibited from living in the home. During the play session, the therapist felt that the child interpreted the sexual molestation as a sign of affection and attention. The child was angry at her mother because she did not come to her bed every other night to kiss her, touch her, and fondle her as her father had done. This interpretation became evident when the child played out a scenario with the dollhouse: a monster came and took the father doll out of the home and put him in jail. Later the girl doll went to the monster and asked him if he could give back her father and take the mother instead.

This example revealed that Michelle's interpretations of sexual abuse were markedly different from the interpretation of adults and the justice system (Marvasti 1986b).

Children not only play out the frustrating events that they experience; they may also express through play their preoccupation with someone else's statement, story, or explanation of an event.

> A divorced husband was accused of sexually abusing his daughter while he was bathing her. Allegations implied that he put his finger

in her vagina and kissed her breasts while she was in the tub. The child was sent to a clinician for an evaluation. During the first play session, the child took the father doll and put his finger around the genital part of the child doll and kissed her breasts. The therapist could have reported the details of the play session to authorities as evidence of the alleged abuse. However, by chance, the therapist became aware of the child's conversation with her mother immediately before she arrived at the therapist's office. The child asked her mother, "Why can't I visit Daddy anymore?" The mother explained in detail that her father was accused of putting his finger in her vagina and kissing her breasts while he was giving her a bath. In the play session, the child played out her preoccupation, the cause of her frustration and deprivation, in the way that she was told.

This example illustrates how important it is for the play diagnostician to be skilled and experienced. Any play scenario may need to be questioned and challenged.

In order to interpret a particular scenario correctly, the therapist needs to develop a close interpersonal relationship with the child through multiple play sessions. An abused child who is told repeatedly by the offender that he or she is lying about the sexual abuse incident may set up the same scenario in play therapy by making a doll lie about an event in the dollhouse. The same is true if the child is instructed by the offender to lie about someone else. The child may very well play out the same scenario in play therapy, having the doll lie or accusing the doll of lying. Long-term therapy in the context of a trusting relationship can reveal the objective reality.

During play diagnosis with sexually abused children, details of the victimization may direct us toward objective reality.

Sheila, a 6-year-old girl, was forced to masturbate and lick an adult's penis until ejaculation. The defense attorney argued that the child might have seen her mother in bed with her boyfriend during sexual activity, or she may have seen an X-rated movie. However, in the first interview with the therapist, the child was asked to described the details of the incident in regard to taste, color, and feel. She called semen the "milky, warm, white, sticky thing spit off his thing. It had a yucky taste; it was sticky between my fingers." These are details the child could not learn by watching her mother in bed or an X-rated movie.

In order to identify objective reality correctly, the play therapist must have a deep interest in children and enjoy playing with them. He or she should know the child's culture, including favorite cartoons, heroes, and movie stars. These are especially important in working with teenagers. For example, the teen who arrives with red and green hair is not necessarily psychotic but simply manifesting an expression of an adolescent subculture.

Therapeutic Principles and Goals in Play Therapy

The therapeutic principles and goals in play therapy are the same as in any other kind of therapy:

1. Establishing a therapeutic relationship that allows expression of child's feelings.
2. Providing corrective emotional experiences during the therapy session in the context of the child's play.

The following case example is illustrative.

> Junie, a 7-year-old child, felt that the therapist would punish and abandon her if she showed anger during play therapy. It was evident that this feeling prevailed at home. Through the use of dolls, however, the therapist showed that it was all right to express anger, and even the "monster" doll has a right to get angry. Also, when the therapist took a toy gun and started to shoot at the bad guy, the child, somewhat surprised, looked at the therapist and said, "Is it all right to be angry in front of you?" As therapy progressed, the child eventually expressed many negative feelings toward her parents and classmates. When the therapist asked why she had never said these things before, she replied that her parents did not allow her to express feelings of anger and told her that anger was shameful.

3. Allowing or inviting the ventilation of pent-up emotions.
4. Suggestion or persuasion.
5. Developing awareness.

During play therapy, the therapeutic changes may take place gradually as the child:

- Identifies with the therapist as a healthy person.
- Develops a positive interpersonal relationship with the therapist.
- Gains knowledge of the insight into the emotional trauma.
- Reworks the trauma.

- Resolves the developmental crisis that results from incest and sexual trauma, a dysfunctional family structure, or a combination.
- Increases self-esteem, self-image, self-confidence, and trust in others.
- Increases autonomy.
- Improves coping skills and learns a problem-solving approach.
- Grieves the loss of parents and/or friends or the loss of virginity.
- Increases his or her ability to postpone gratification.
- Learns to practice impulse control.
- Improves reality testing.

Projective Technique in Play Diagnosis

Mutual Storytelling Technique

In this method (developed by Gardner 1971), the child is asked to tell a self-created story to the therapist. Then the therapist surmises its psychodynamic meaning and creates a responding story. In mutual storytelling the therapist creates a story with the same characters, setting, and events of the child's story but with healthier adaptations and resolutions of the conflicts.

I have used a story completion game with children to obtain information about the child's feelings, motives, and preoccupations. In this technique, the clinician begins to tell a story and asks the child to add to it. Eventually the therapist and child together create a complete story.

Jimmy, an adopted child, came to therapy because of alleged sexual abuse. He claimed that he was not concerned about his biological parents. In a story completion session, the therapist began, "Once upon a time there was a boy who was walking on the street and . . ." Jimmy added, "and he was looking for someone." The therapist added, "and maybe it is an important person for . . ." The child mentioned, "for him, and it is a very, very important person." The child went on with the story and had the "boy" go to the gas station and ask for the address of a family. After searching all over town, he eventually found the house and the family. He knocked on the door, but no one answered. A neighbor came out and asked what he was doing there. The boy replied that he just wanted to see the people who lived in the house for a second. The neighbor asked why, and the boy said that he wanted to ask them why they gave their son up for adoption.

At times, the therapist might wish to make the story have a happy ending.

Drawing a Picture

Children may project their trauma, wishes, and internal conflict through drawing and artwork.

> Janet apparently was sexually abused by her uncle on the night that she stayed with him and her aunt. The next day she was brought to the police station, but she was mute and would not talk to anyone about the incident. She was unwilling to talk at the therapist's office; however, she seemed interested in drawing and coloring. The therapist and child both started to draw a picture. The therapist asked the child if she could draw a picture of the things that she loved and a picture of the things that she was afraid of. Eventually the therapist asked the child to draw things that she was not able to talk about. The child drew a picture of a girl who was lying down on the couch and a man who had his hand on the girl's genital area. When the therapist asked what this man was doing, the child became quiet. Eventually the therapist asked the child if she could write a story about this man and girl. The child wrote, "Uncle Jimmy put me on the sofa and hurt me."

A child's drawing of himself or herself or the family may be a valuable source of information because the child's portrayal of the human figure is more or less a projection of his or her characteristics. In psychological assessment of a child, diagnosticians commonly ask the child to draw his or her home and family (elaborated as Kinetic Family Drawing by Burns and Kaufman 1970). In Kinetic Family Drawing, the child is asked to draw members of her family "doing" something. The House-Tree-Person (HTP) also is being used as a projective technique (Hammer 1960).

Winnicott's Squiggles Game has been developed by Winnicott (1971a) for diagnostic purposes. In this game the clinician draws a formless scribble on a paper and asks the child to convert it into a recognizable form. This is repeated with the child starting with the scribble and so on, each taking a turn. The clinician also encourages the child to talk about the forms created.

Exploring Dreams and Fantasies

Other projective information can be obtained when children talk about their dreams, nightmares, and fantasies. Many clinicians ask children what they would ask for if they could have three wishes granted.

> Sabrina, who was allegedly sexually abused by her father, had never disclosed her victimization. During one session, the therapist asked

her about her three wishes. The child said that one of her wishes was to go to an island, where she could talk about her secret without anyone going to jail.

Role Reversal Play

In this technique, the child "becomes" the therapist and the therapist "becomes" the child. The child asks questions, and the therapist answers using the child's life history as a model. The clinician may ask many questions and ask the child to help him or her with "my problems." The clinician can then assess the child's problem-solving ability and insights.

Jennifer asked the therapist to "become" the patient, and she herself sat in the doctor's chair and "became" the doctor. She said, "Tell me about your life." During this play, the therapist said that he had been sexually abused by his father. He did not know what to do because part of him liked his father, and part of him was angry at the father.

Therapist: Tell me, Doctor, what should I do?
Child: I can understand that you like and hate your dad, but you should try to forget him .
Therapist: I can't; he's my father. How could I forget him? He comes to my mind all the time.
Child: When he comes to your mind, count sheep.
Therapist: I did all of these things, but still he comes to mind.
Child: Tell me how long you kept it a secret.
Therapist: For a long time. But what do you think I felt when I kept this a secret for a long time?
Child: That keeping the secret was more painful for you than many other things.

The clinician thus discovered that the secrecy of the sexual abuse was more traumatic to the child than had previously been suspected. The child's use of the defense mechanisms of denial and suppression also was revealed by this technique.

Use of Props

The child can use costumes, puppets, and dolls to project internal feelings.

Beth is a 6-year-old girl who was allegedly abused by one of her family members. During the play session, she put one puppet on her right hand and another on her left hand. She called the right hand puppet a "cute child" and the left puppet a "bad guy." The "bad guy" told the "cute child," "If you open your mouth, I will kill you." Eventually the therapist introduced his puppet, and a three-way conversation continued. Near the end of the session, the therapist removed the puppet from his hand and asked the child, "Beth, can you tell me in your real life if you know anyone who is like your left-hand puppet?" And Beth looked at the therapist and said, "Yes, Uncle Jimmy," The therapist then suggested that the child put the puppets away and talk about her own life and the child readily agreed.

> *Therapist:* Is it scary to live in the same house as Uncle Jimmy?
> *Child:* Yes, it is scary. He tells me not to talk even about my fear.
> *Therapist:* I am glad that you are talking to me about your fear.
> *Child:* He said he may kill me if I talk.
> *Therapist:* He should be afraid of your talking.
> *Child:* Yes, he may go to jail as he told me.

Psychodrama

This technique is especially effective in group play therapy with children. Generally the scenario of the psychodrama is created or "written" by the therapist together with the children. Then they enact the psychodrama.

In a group therapy session with children who were sexually abused, the therapist arranged a psychodrama about a family who lived in the woods. One day the police came to arrest a member of the family. One of the children played the role of the police officer, and the others played the roles of the family members. They began to discuss why "our daddy should be arrested." The police officer explained that Daddy had sexually abused one of the children. Mother said, "No, my child is lying." The father said, "I never touched her." The officer called for a judge, and both of them came into the home, and told the parents, "We know who is lying and who is telling the truth. Shame on you." During this psychodrama, the therapist interfered several times by asking questions and making clarifications. For example, the therapist asked the children how they felt about their fathers, thus, bringing up the feelings of abused children toward their fathers. The therapist asked, "How does this child feel when her father is being taken to jail." And one child answered, "I feel bad and guilty." The therapist asked, "Why?" The child answered, "Because she put her dad in jail." The therapist commented, "Only the judge can put people in jail; no one else."

Despart Fable Test

Some diagnosticians have used the Despart Fable Test with children, although the scientific value of this test is not yet proved. There are a number of the Despart Fables.

The Bird Fable is designed to ascertain whether the child is emotionally dependent (that is, fixated on his or her parents) or independent:

> A daddy and mommy bird and their little birdie are asleep in the nest on a branch. All of a sudden, a big wind blows and shakes the tree. The nest falls on the ground, and the three birds awaken with a start. The daddy flies quickly to a pine tree and the mother to another pine tree. What is the little bird going to do? He knows how to fly a little already.

The goal of the Funeral Fable is to investigate hostility, death wishes, guilt feelings, and self-punishment:

> A funeral procession is going through a village street, and people ask, "Who is it that is dead?" Somebody answers, "It's somebody in the family who lives in this house." Who is it?

A child who has no conception of death can be told instead: "Somebody in the family took a train and went away, and will never come back. Who is it? [Enumerate the members of a family.]"

Practical Issues in Play Therapy

The Playroom and Play Materials

The playroom should be in close proximity to the waiting room, where the parents usually stay. The ideal playroom has a clear view of the waiting room through a window or one-way mirror, beneficial for children who exhibit severe separation anxiety, especially during the first session. The playroom should not be too far from the bathroom, because young children frequently want to use it during the session. Play materials should include dolls, a dollhouse, puppets, and other toys (which, preferably, are unbreakable). A family of dolls is encouraging to a child's play therapy. If there is a need for more than one dollhouse, as in the case of a child of divorced parents, a cardboard box or even a picture drawn by the child may represent one of the houses. A fairly large selection of simple dolls is very useful: three or four male dolls who might represent a father or stepfather, an uncle, or a doctor and several female dolls who might represent a mother, stepmother, teacher, or other important family members. Anatomically correct dolls should

it might provide an opportunity to reveal more of his wishes or fears regarding sexual behavior with adult authority figures.

Another example is Robert, a 5-year-old child who was expelled from three different day-care centers because he repeatedly asked other boys to come to the bathroom where he would touch their penises. He also asked them to touch his penis in compulsive play. During the play session, the therapist asked Robert if he knew why he came to see the therapist.

> *Robert:* No, I don't know why.
>
> *Therapist:* Robert you came to see me because I want to help you. Children who have problems come to see me. Do you know what your problem is, Robert?
>
> *Robert:* I don't have any problem.
>
> *Therapist:* Robert, have you been expelled from day care three times?
>
> *Robert:* Yes.
>
> *Therapist:* Do you know why you were expelled?
>
> *Robert:* Yes, because I touched them there.
>
> *Therapist:* Robert, you know that day care does not like you to touch others' penises in the bathroom. They expelled you because they think that you forced children to touch your penis and you forced them to let you touch theirs. Other kids' parents do not like that.
>
> *Robert:* Do you touch children's penises?
>
> *Robert:* No, not at all. The only penis that I touch is my penis, and I touch it when I am alone and in the privacy of a room.
>
> *Robert:* Is my bedroom a private room?
>
> *Therapist:* Yes, that is a private room.
>
> *Robert:* Okay.

This time it was the therapist who initiated the discussion regarding sexual behavior. Once again, the therapist reminded the child about appropriate boundaries and limits. Then he reinforced the sexual education principle that masturbation is a private behavior. Robert's query if his bedroom was a private room was answered affirmatively by the therapist. Thus the limit setting inherent in the explanation that day-care personnel and "other kids' parents" do not want children to force others to comply with interactive sexual behaviors was followed by communicating implicitly that masturbation was permissible for Robert in the privacy of his bedroom.

At the beginning of the play session, the therapist should explain to the child why he or she is in the therapist's office. Otherwise the child may manifest preoccupation with the question through play.

Jackie: [putting a car inside a castle in the first therapy session]. This little car is here to be fixed.
   Therapist: How does this little car feel being in this castle?
   Jackie: The little car is afraid. She's in a strange place—doesn't know why she's here.
The therapist then explained that the little car was there for a purpose just like little children who visit a doctor's office. Later, the therapist explained that children came to his office to talk and play about the things that were bothering them.

Separation Anxiety from Parents

If the child shows separation anxiety from his or her parent, it is advisable to allow the parent to stay with the child for a short time during the first session. In other cases, the child may be sensitive to the noise of the office door; if it is closed or opened, the child fears that his or her mother may be leaving. Other children may run toward the window frequently to look out to see if their parents' cars are still there.

   It is sometimes possible to allow the parents to be in the playroom until the child becomes less anxious and develops a relationship with the therapist. The therapist can leave the consultation room and the waiting room doors open so that the child sees his or her parent, from a distance. Bringing the parents to the playroom obviously decreases the child's anxiety, but it may increase the therapist's anxiety. In any event, the parents' presence undoubtedly influences (usually in an inhibitory fashion) the child's capacity to play freely. The parents should be told not to comment or participate in any conversation during the play session, if possible.

Play Therapy Techniques

Structured Play Therapy

In both play diagnosis and play therapy the therapist finds out as much information as possible about the child and the alleged victimization. Structuring the play is very important; it enables the therapist to guide the child directly or indirectly into areas of play that reveal more information about the alleged abuse.

   Laura was allegedly abused at day care. The mother was also suspicious of her ex-husband. The child had visited her father every other weekend since her parents' divorce. In an individual session with the therapist, the mother explained that the child would not talk to anyone—including the mother, the police, or protective services—about the incident.

The therapist, armed with this knowledge, decided to have a structured play session. Three dollhouses were arranged near each other, and the child was invited to play. The therapist asked the child to help him name these three dollhouses. Eventually the therapist directed the child to name one the father's house, one the mother's house, and one day care. A few dolls were added, and the therapist used a hand puppet to communicate his thoughts about them. Addressing the dolls, he eventually asked how they felt when they went to day care or to their father's home. Near the end of the first session, the child brought up a "bad guy" from day care who took off the clothes of the girl doll. Still using the puppet, the therapist said to the child's doll, "I wish this girl would tell someone about what happened to her in day care." The child's doll answered, "It is not time yet."

In this case, the therapist had obtained enough information about the child's situation before the first session. He arranged the play material to resemble the child's environment and structured the play to be centered around the happenings at day care, the father's home, and the child's home. The therapist limited the session to making a story about the family of dolls and the three dollhouses. He presented only a few relevant play materials, thereby directing the play around identifying the child's feelings toward her immediate environment.

Obviously the theme of the child's play in this kind of play therapy differs from an unstructured one in which the child may prefer to use cowboy and Indian dolls and create a fight between them, while the G.I. Joe doll may eventually enter the battle and side with the cowboys.

Release Therapy

Levy (1938) developed the technique of release therapy used for the treatment of children who have experienced overwhelming traumatic events. Levy provided the child with play materials, directed the child to recreate the traumatic event, and eventually helped the child to ventilate emotions through play. The child was not forced into a set play pattern but indirectly was encouraged to play out the traumatic events that he or she had experienced. Only a few toys were made available to the child, so, again indirectly, the child was encouraged to use those play materials that were connected in some way to his or her trauma. This type of play is based on psychoanalytic philosophy of repetition compulsion. Given the opportunity and the right play materials, a child replays a traumatic incident over and over until he or she is able to digest it and assimilate its associated negative feelings, emotions, and thoughts.

Levy's release therapy is similar to Solomon's (1938) technique of active play therapy. Active play therapy, utilized with the impulsive and acting-out child, enables the child to express rage, fear, and other negative emotions through play. Solomon believed that this had an abreactive effect and was beneficial because the child was able to act out negative feelings without experiencing any negative consequences from adults. Eventually the therapist redirected the mental energy that the child used earlier for acting-out behavior and reshaped it to socially appropriate and play-oriented behavior. Although this kind of release therapy has been used with sexually abused children, especially with rape victims, the child needs sufficient ego resources and support to be able to reexperience the traumatic and anxiety-producing memory and events.

> Sharon, a 7-year-old victim of rape, was able to remember partially the incident of rape; however, her mounting anxiety and anger prevented her from discussing the traumatic events. In one of the sessions, the therapist arranged to have only clay and two baseball bats and no other play materials available. The therapist made a penis from clay and asked the child what she would like to do with the baseball bat and penis. Sharon did not answer. She became tense and avoided eye contact with the clay. The therapist took the bat and started to hit the penis, until its shaped changed. Any time the shape changed, the therapist took the clay and shaped it back to a penis and continued hitting it. Sharon gradually decreased her anxiety and started to help the therapist by commenting on the shape of the clay and at times handing the bat to the therapist. Eventually the therapist invited her to join the "beating game." At the end of the session, the therapist became an observer while Sharon actively hit the penis and reshaped the clay into a penis over and over.

Nondirective Play Therapy

In this modality of therapy, an extension of Rogerian psychotherapy, there is total permissiveness. The therapist is a nonparticipant observer who encourages the child to use any play material for as long as desired. The therapist will neither criticize nor approve, and there is no interpretation or confrontation. The therapist merely reflects the child's feelings.

The philosophy of nondirective therapy is based on the drive for self-realization in human beings, which motivates all behavior in children and adults. Given the opportunity to play freely, any child will play through his or her own emotional conflicts and arrive at a solution.

Axline (1947), who introduced this technique, provides eight basic principles that are guidelines for therapists involved in nondirective play therapy:

1. The therapist must develop a warm, friendly relationship with the child, in which good rapport is established as soon as possible.
2. The therapist accepts the child exactly as he or she is.
3. The therapist establishes a feeling of permissiveness in the relationship so that the child feels free to express feelings completely.
4. The therapist is alert to recognize the feelings the child is expressing and reflects those feelings back in such a manner that the child gains insight into his or her behavior.
5. The therapist maintains a deep respect for the child's ability to solve problems if given the opportunity. The responsibility to make choices and to institute change is the child's.
6. The therapist does not attempt to direct the child's actions or conversation in any manner. The child leads the way; the therapist follows.
7. The therapist does not attempt to hurry the therapy along. It is a gradual process, recognized as such by the therapist.
8. The therapist establishes only those limitations necessary to anchor the therapy to the world of reality and to make the child aware of his or her responsibility in the relationship.

Axline stressed that it is important to identify and recognize the child's feelings and reflect these feeling back to the child. She defines reflection as mirroring feeling and affect and as such recognizes that it is restricted within the metaphor the child offers. She thus differentiates between reflection of the feeling and interpretation of the child's play.

Psychoanalytic Play Therapy

In this kind of play therapy, play is used for more than abreaction, and ventilation may be a very small part of this kind of therapy. Neither is play simply recreation; rather, it is a medium of interpretation and a means of promoting observation and establishing contact. Melanie Klein (1932) explained that children's play can be considered to be similar to adult free association because play activities are free from the censorship of reality.

Once a relationship has been established, the analyst will try to understand and interpret the symbolism in child psychoanalysis of the child's play and dreams and will make the unconscious elements conscious. The systematic uncovering of the unconscious material may be the cornerstone of child psychoanalysis. The modality of therapy, which takes 4 to 5 years, is indicated only in some neurotic children and is not appropriate therapy for a child with sexual trauma but no long-standing neurotic conflicts.

Holistic Play Therapy with Sexually Abused Children

Regardless of the type and modality of play therapy used and regardless of the therapist's school of thought, there is need for a holistic approach to therapy with sexually abused children. I have used a mixture of supportive therapy, release therapy, and structured and nonstructured therapy, all based on the psychoanalytic theory of child development. This eclectic and psychodynamically oriented play therapy has emerged as a desirable form of therapy for sexually abused children.

The following concepts in psychodynamic theory are key:

1. Ego Defense Mechanisms: Displacement, projection, reaction formation, symbolization, and repression, all basic elements in defense mechanisms, are clear in children's play. Children project their repressed feelings (unconscious and conscious material) onto the dolls and toys without full knowledge of having done so. Fantasy often reveals underlying repressed material, and children are unaware that during play they are disclosing their own wishes and feelings when they are talking about the doll's wishes and feelings.

2. The Unconscious: Children who have experienced traumatic, and therefore anxiety-producing, events tend to repress these experiences and the emotions associated with them into their unconscious. It requires a tremendous amount of mental energy to keep this material repressed in the unconscious. One of the goals of child therapy is to establish an appropriate and comfortable milieu in which the patient can discover and bring up the repressed unconscious material in a gradual way. This gradual way is indicated by the child and should proceed at the child's pace rather than at the therapist's speed. Recovering the unconscious material in this gradual manner greatly reduces the chance of producing severe anxiety in a child.

3. Resistance: As introduced by Freud, resistance is a barrier, that is, any defensive behavior that prevents a child from recalling and/or revealing unconscious material. A certain amount of resistance in the beginning of treatment is acceptable and natural; however, once trust has developed between the child and the therapist, the therapist may gradually confront the child's resistance.

4. Transference: This is a process whereby a child projects feelings for significant people in his or her past onto the therapist. In play therapy, the child has an option to displace feelings on to the dolls, and the guise

of play will protect him or her from discovering forbidden impulses and emotions. Similarly the child may displace hate and love (that he or she feels toward parents) on to the therapist. As Freud (1905) mentioned, transferences are new editions of impulses and fantasies with a special peculiarity: "They replace some earlier person by the person of the physician."

5. Countertransference: This concept involves those unresolved conflicts from the therapist's childhood, which he or she projects onto the patient and their therapeutic relationship. Although the therapist can use transference to help the child gain insight into her or his feelings, countertransference can be a strong barrier to therapy if the therapist is unaware of it. Probably anyone who works with sexually abused children and their families, especially when a family member is the offender, will react emotionally, and the therapist is not immune. Incest may evoke unconscious feelings that are a barrier in dealing with these families and with the sexually abused child. Personal psychoanalysis and psychotherapy or intensive supervision by a qualified therapist may be beneficial.

Play Process

After obtaining sufficient information about the background of the patient and family and the details of the incident of victimization, the therapist arranges for an individual session with the child. Sometimes the parents are at a loss as to how they will explain the need for therapy to the child, and the therapist may be of assistance to them in formulating a plan. Obviously, the child should be told in advance about the meeting with the therapist. The therapist keeps in mind the most important aspect of therapy: establishing a relationship with the child. This relationship has elements of genuineness; it requires the therapist to have the capacity to be aware of his or her own feelings, assets, and liabilities in regard to interpersonal relationships with children. The therapist needs to be aware of the barrier of countertransference. It is necessary for the therapist to have empathy and a genuine desire to understand the child's feelings. The therapist's ability to place himself or herself in the child's world and perceive this world from the child's prospective is most helpful.

First Stage

In the first stage of play therapy, the child is met in the waiting room and brought into a playroom. An attempt is made to decrease the child's separation anxiety. During the first session, the therapist may ask the child if she knows why she came to see the therapist. The therapist attempts to clarify any confusion or misperceptions, perhaps by saying, "I am a doctor who sees children who are unhappy at home or school or because something happened to them that is bothering them or something happened to them that their parents are concerned about it. I see them here, I play and talk with them, and I try to understand them and help them."

There is no general procedure for play with sexually abused children: it should be individualized on the basis of each child's needs and reactions. There are, however, common points typically indicated in play therapy with sexually abused children. During the first sessions, the therapist may remind the child that he is aware that someone from protective services and from the police department may have talked to her. He should observe the child in regard to her reaction to this statement and also should have prior knowledge about the child's reaction during previous interviews. The therapist must place himself on the child's level. His reaction to and behavior toward the child in a play session should be natural so that the child feels the play is spontaneous.

The therapist can begin by sitting on a low stool or on the floor, at the child's eye level. He may invite the child to explore the playroom and point out the play materials. The therapist should remember that the first stage, especially the first session, of therapy focuses on decreasing the child's anxiety, decreasing the child's fear of the therapist and fear of abandonment by her parent, and establishing the relationship. During the first session, the therapist may obtain some diagnostic information in regard to the child's behavior—for example, the level of her anxiety, her restlessness, her mood, her politeness, her attitude, and her assertiveness.

It is important that the therapist does not promise to child protective services, the parents or anyone else, that he has the capacity or that it is his goal to validate the sexual abuse incident in a short period of time. Our experience reveals that sometimes it may take fifteen to twenty sessions before the child is able to identify and talk about the victimization. The therapist follows the child's pace rather than his own pace or his desire for finding and validating the sexual abuse complaint. The child should be told about and invited to interact with any toys or dolls she wants. The therapist may say, "You and I get together here, and we play and talk the way that we want. This is your time, and we can play or talk or paint or whatever you wish to do." If the therapist is aware of a patient's past history of aggressive and acting-out behavior, he should remind her of the limits, rules, and regulations of the playroom.

Based on the therapist's choice of treatment approach, he may arrange for structured play therapy or do nondirective play therapy. During nondirective therapy, the therapist follows the child around the playroom. If the child is attracted to the dollhouse, the therapist may introduce the family of dolls and actively participate in play, encouraging the child to project and displace her feelings onto the dolls and toys in order to discover the child's conflicts. The therapist needs to inform the child that although the purpose of meeting the therapist is to look at elements bothersome to the child, it is up to the child to bring up these things when she feels comfortable.

During this first stage of play, the therapist intensively observes the child's play. If the child does not want to play but does want to read a book or draw a picture by herself, she should be allowed to do so. The therapist sits near the child and is attentive to her drawing. If the child says that she wants to talk instead of play, the therapist respects the child's desire, and they talk.

The child may interact with the dolls and dollhouse, use puppets, or play with clay or in the sandbox. The therapist joins the child and at times participates; however, in the beginning, the therapist is somewhat passive, asking the child to give him the role that the child wants him to play. The purpose of this passivity is to decrease contamination of the child's play. Play in the dollhouse may reveal psychodynamic knowledge and interpersonal relationship information about the child's family or may show the child's wishes, fears, and desires in regard to her environment.

> Paula, in one of the sessions of play therapy, arranged a family dolls in the dollhouse: a mother and father who slept in one room and two children. One day a snake came, threw the father out of the home, and married the mother. Then every night, the snake came into the girls' room and kissed them. Later, the kissing changed to biting, and the children were afraid. The children did not dare to tell their mother about it because the snake told them, "If you open your mouth and talk, I will die, and your mother will be unhappy the rest of her life."

Paula was coming to therapy because of sexual abuse by her stepfather. She projected her family life into her play by portraying how her mother married her stepfather (the snake) and threw her biological father out of the house. In reality, every night the stepfather went to the girls' bedroom and kissed them goodnight. Gradually the goodnight kiss changed to the sexual molestation of Paula. The stepfather told Paula that if she disclosed "their sweet secret," he would divorce her mother, and her mother would not be able to survive financially without him.

At this stage, it would be premature for the therapist to consider whatever the child is expressing through play as verification of experiences that the child has gone through. For example, if the girl doll wished to stay in the daddy doll's bedroom and put the mommy doll in the attic, that play does not indicate that the child has actually gone through this experience and has slept in her father's bed. As we know, children may project their fears, wishes, and preoccupations onto the dolls and toys.

During diagnostic play, the therapist obtains information about the child's level of anxiety, her activity, her object relationships, her impression about herself, and her level of aggression, control, and inhibition. He also may obtain some information about the child's knowledge of sexuality. As the child continues to develop the relationship with her therapist, she creates and explores a situation that allows her to express her unconscious emotions. Eventually the child feels comfortable enough to present through play the traumatic events that she has experienced.

The therapist tries to create a permissive atmosphere for the child to express her feelings, regardless of how negative they are. The therapist is not judgmental nor does he overreact to the child's statements or to the "doll's" aggression. The therapist is building an unconditional relationship with the child, which allows the child to be free, and to explore her feelings and express them through the media of play. The therapist may then gradually focus on the child's feelings as expressed through play by commenting on the doll's feelings and trying to help the child to understand the doll's feeling. At this stage, it is desirable for the therapist to avoid giving any advice or making any judgmental statement.

> Paula created a scenario during the play session. She arranged for a family dolls to stay in the dollhouse. The father doll woke up and told the mother doll, "You didn't make breakfast for any of us." One by one the children woke up and asked the mother doll, "You haven't made breakfast yet?"
>
> *Therapist:* These dolls should be very hungry.
> *Paula:* Yes, they are hungry.
> *Therapist:* And not only hungry. Maybe they are also angry.
> *Paula:* You think they are angry?
> *Therapist,* Why not? Many children get angry at their mother when their breakfast is not ready.
> *Paula:* Yes. These dolls are angry at their mom because she doesn't make anything for them.
> *Therapist:* What do you think is going on in this dollhouse? When there is no food, it seems that there is no mom.
> *Paula:* Yeah.
> At this time Paula took the father doll, and he yelled at the mother doll, "No wonder I'm divorcing you. You didn't make anything for us. Lazy bum!"

The therapist allowed the child to play as she wanted. He did not direct her play nor did he suggest that the dolls represented her own family. He did, however, comment that the "father" doll and the "children" dolls must be hungry and also angry. He helped Paula to understand why the dolls might feel both hungry and angry. Paula could proceed at her own pace, and the therapist's interpretations and clarifications were directed at the dolls rather than at Paula herself.

If the child avoids playing with dolls or with the scenario the therapist desires, the therapist needs to wait patiently. In the case of a sexually abused child, the therapist is interested in validating the sexual abuse and may be under pressure to do so from the family or from child protective services; however, the child's desires and needs should be respected. A therapist may indirectly and gently encourage the child toward the subject matter he wishes to explore. A further example of Paula's case is illustrative.

> When the family was fighting in the dollhouse, the therapist took a puppet and asked the girl doll, "Is there anything bothering you in this home?" The therapist then asked the child to take the girl doll in her hand and continue the communication. The child took the girl doll.
>
> *Child's puppet:* Yes, a lot of things are bothering me.
>
> *Therapist's puppet:* I wish you would tell me about what is bothering you. Many dolls told me that when they talked about their feelings, they feel better.
>
> *Child's doll:* I can't talk, I can't talk.
>
> *Therapist's puppet:* I believe that you have a reason for why you cannot talk. I wish that you would tell me the reason why you cannot talk.
>
> *Child's puppet:* I can't talk. I can't talk. Don't ask, don't ask.

The therapist continued for a few more minutes to encourage the doll to talk and explore the barrier but eventually felt that the "doll" was too afraid to talk. The therapist then brought a doctor doll to the scene and told the child's doll. "This is a doctor doll. Children go to him and talk to him about what is bothering them. They tell him things that they don't dare tell their parents." The child still continued to express her fear through the doll that "I can't talk. I don't talk. Don't ask." The therapist stopped encouraging the doll to talk and tried to explore other aspects of the family dynamics. Because of the child's extreme anxiety, the therapist felt that encouraging the child to talk about what was bothering her was not appropriate at this time. The child might need to project more of her feelings through the doll, so the therapist tried to explore the interpersonal relationship of family members with each other, especially the mother-father relationship.

In diagnostic play, the therapist may identify the child's perception of herself or her environment and the people around her. She may reveal the dynamics of her family relationships in a variety of ways. For example, she may not involve the Father doll in play, or there may be a "secret" in the dollhouse. People may not talk to each other; family members may scapegoat one of the dolls; the girl doll takes care of her mother (role reversal); or the doll is punished because the parents think that she lies.

When children are involved in the justice system, the police sometimes are either represented as princes or monsters when they take the father out of the house and jail him in the dollhouse game. The child may play that the parents are dead and the child alone and abandoned. During sandbox play, the child may bury the offender in the sand, or make a jail and put the offender in, gradually discharging her anger.

If the child did not come willingly to the office, it may show up in the play. This was the case with Jimmy, who during the first play session in the doll house, brought a doll to the doll doctor's office. The doctor doll immediately sent the doll back home, called the doll's parents, and told them, "Don't push him anymore."

The first stage may be summarized as follows: introduce the therapist, playroom materials, and rules and regulations; decrease the child's separation anxiety and "stranger anxiety" and do some diagnostic work. The first stage should be primarily devoted to making the child feel comfortable in the therapist's office, with less priority given to diagnostic information.

Second Stage

By this stage, rapport and a trusting relationship have developed. The child has tested the therapist enough and found him to be a reliable person who is not judgmental and does not punish the child for talking about negative feelings. The therapist does not comment on or overreact to the doll's feelings of hate and/or murderous wishes and does not ignore the child. The therapist is warm, can show empathy, is reliable, and can be trusted.

The therapist has learned a certain amount of information about the child's family condition, interpersonal relationships, fears, and perceptions of the traumatic incidents she has experienced. But even at this stage, therapists should not expect to discover that the child's main trauma is sexual victimization. Unfortunately, this may be a preconceived idea on the part of some therapists. The therapist should be aware that the child knows what hurt her. Possibly she may express that the more significant trauma was separation from a parent or her parents' divorce. She may suffer from guilt feelings and feel that she caused her parents' separation or the financial problems brought about by the father's removal from the home.

The therapist continues to comment on the doll's feelings and tries to help the child become aware of the doll's feelings, occasionally shifting from the doll's to the child's feelings. For example, the therapist may say, "If I was this doll, I would get angry at my dad also." Later the therapist might ask the child, "Mary, how about you?" If the child acknowledges some of her feelings, the therapist continues the conversation: "I'm very interested in knowing more about you and your feelings about your dad, especially when he does something that gets you angry at him." This is an invitation for the child to continue talking about her aggression, and if the child wishes to continue, the therapist listens in a nonjudgmental way. However, if the child changes the subject and returns to play, the therapist may comment and follow the child: "Oh, you prefer to play rather than talk about your anger toward your dad. I can understand how uncomfortable you could feel when you think about your anger toward your dad. We can play now, but whenever you feel comfortable, you may start to talk to me about it."

The therapist sets therapeutic goals and every few sessions reevaluates the progress. Therapeutic goals may include increasing the child's ability to verbalize feelings; increasing the child's capacity for experiencing pleasure and fun; decreasing the child's parentified behavior; helping the child to become a child again through play sessions; and enabling the child to participate in age-appropriate activity and play.

During this second stage, the child victim of incest may play out a variety of themes with family dolls, such as fear of being punished, fear of abandonment by parents, repetitive play of self-punishment and guilt, repetitive cleaning of the dollhouse by dolls (or the therapist's office by child), a hostile mother-daughter relationship, fear of losing the family, divided loyalty toward parents, or fear of authority. The therapist should be sensitive to the child's message and react appropriately:

> Seven-year-old Sherry in the second session of play therapy told a story of a girl doll who went to "other lands" and met a lot of people one by one. The doll wished to know if these people liked her, and she asked these questions "thousands of times" any time she met someone. The therapist speculated that the child wanted to know how the therapist felt about her. He appropriately responded to the child's wishes, and the child confirmed the therapist's speculation.

A number of stumbling blocks may be encountered in the second stage of play therapy with incest victims. Oversexualized behavior toward the therapist may make the therapist uncomfortable, causing him to suppress the exploration of sexuality with the child. At times, an oversexualized child may attempt to touch the therapist's genital area, which may cause the therapist to have second thoughts about the offender's claim (that the child initiated the sexual act). Sometimes the child's overt sexuality may sexually stimulate the therapist, creating guilt and shame in the therapist. This is especially so in the therapists who consider themselves and the child as nonsexual beings. Oversexualized behavior may touch the repressed sexuality in the therapist and stimulate either excitement or distress.

Second, the child may act out instead of talking and expressing feelings verbally. Acting out occurs when unconscious material is being presented through action rather than words. It may be manifested by aggressive or sexual responses, both within the therapeutic session or outside. Acting out is considered a barrier and a resistance in therapy since it acts as a substitute for words and prevents the patient from gaining insight into feelings and behavior.

The child might present a pseudohealthy attitude expressed by superficial coping skills, pleasant mood, and pretending to feel in control. This may lead the unskilled therapist to believe that the child is not in need of therapy. Or the child may recant the abuse: "It didn't happen; maybe it was a dream that I had." Such statements may deceive the therapist and divert attention from incest to other subjects. A therapist who allows diversion is actively participating in the conspiracy of silence with family members. One of the therapist's tasks is to affirm the incest.

Finally, emergence of other serious psychopathology (such as schizophrenia) may cloud the incest issues. During the session, the child may talk about bizarre and strange events, mixing reality with fantasy, and may even hallucinate or develop delusional thinking and ideas. Therapists might then ignore the issues of incest or sexual abuse and/or consider it part of a delusional system. In this situation, it is appropriate that the child be seen by a psychiatrist for treatment of psychopathology, while the original therapist continues the play sessions for the purpose of validating the alleged sexual abuse. Communication between the two therapists is essential.

In summary, the second stage is mainly a diagnostic stage, although therapy is also a component. The therapist obtains enough information about how the child's family functions, her interpersonal conflicts, her role in the family, her object relationship, the quality of her relationship with the therapist, the nature of the sexual abuse, and the child's perception of the abuse. A therapeutic alliance has developed, and the therapist has obtained some idea about the main traumatic events from the child's point of view. Most important, the therapist has attempted to see the world as the child sees it.

Third Stage

By now the therapist knows enough about the child's main conflict and has identified information about the child's feelings and problems. In the third stage, the therapist becomes more active and, if needed, somewhat challenging to the child. The therapist is certain of the child's trust in him, rapport has been developed, and he is able to direct the child, through persuasion, to bring up anxiety-producing subjects and can request that the child talk about them. As in any other stage of therapy, when the child's anxiety increases, the therapist should be empathic and try to decrease the child's anxiety or slow down her speed of exploring the anxiety-producing material. It is important to remember that the goal is therapy without torture.

The therapist may explore the doll's ambivalent feelings toward parental figures, especially the abusive parent. Then the child and the therapist explore the doll's wishes and desires in regard to the doll's family. Positive feelings toward the abusive parent and negative feelings toward the non-abusive parent are also explored. When appropriate, the therapist and the child may discuss the child's feelings and relationship with the therapist.

Julie came a few minutes late for the session and was very upset. She told the therapist, "This damn car was out of order, and I arrived late."

Therapist: Julie, it seems that you are very eager to come to your session here, where we talk and play together.

Julie: Yes, I enjoy being here. ·

Julie later brought up her dream about a man with black hair and black eyes and a mustache who came to their home and rented a room. He later married the mother in that home and lived with the children forever. The therapist, who had developed a close relationship with Julie, asked her, "Do you know anyone in reality who looks like the man in your dream?"

Julie: No I don't know anyone with black eyes, black hair, and black mustache.

Therapist: Do I have black eyes, black hair, and black mustache?

Julie: (laughing) Oh God, that was you! I knew you would find him for me.

The therapist later commented that some children become close to their therapist, wish that the therapists would marry their mothers and become their fathers or that the therapist would stay in their home. The therapist mentioned that these are the very honest and ordinary feelings that children may have and said, "It is good to talk about it and explore it, even if it may never happen."

Gradual improvement in a child's feelings about her victimization could be reflected in any play in this third stage.

A 6-year-old child was playing a scenario wherein a wolf bit and destroyed the children and the rest of the family in the dollhouse. This pattern of play was repeated, and there were definite indications of hopelessness, victimization, and helplessness.

After a few months of therapy, the play gradually changed. This time there were people from the neighborhood who came to help whenever the wolf entered the home. The neighbors knew that this family needed help when a child picked up the telephone and called a neighbor, specifically, a farmer with a gun. The play obviously no longer showed the hopeless and helpless theme that was present at the beginning. Sometimes the wolf ran away and sometimes the family, with the help of the farmer, killed the wolf.

The use of the telephone in this play session was important. At the beginning of therapy, the therapist had given his telephone number to the child and had asked him to call whenever things were seriously bothering him. Although the child had not used the telephone during the few months of therapy, the importance of having the permission to do so was evident in this play. Also, the child was able to work out her lack of trust in adults and was able to seek and ask for help.

In one of the sessions, the therapist brought up a discussion about the wolf, using a puppet to ask the child why the wolf had this tendency to eat and scare children. The child's puppet answered that she did not know. The therapist's puppet asked. "Let's asked the wolf." After some discussion, it was noticed that the wolf was not a wolf. He was a "nice boy"; however, he had lost his parents and become a wolf. The therapist interpreted that the child's feeling of abandonment by her parents gave her so much anger and aggression that she felt like a wolf who wanted to destroy her parents. However, her fear of retaliation by her parents and her quilt feelings presented themselves by portraying her as a victim of the wolf in the dollhouse.

During play therapy, the therapist frequently enters into an intense emotional interchange with the child. The child victim manifests feelings and behavior in the playroom similar to those she expressed toward her parents. The therapist encourages the child to talk out her difficulty in her relationship with the therapist. For example, the child in the previous case said, "I am afraid you would touch me there. I am afraid you would hate me one day."

At the third and fourth stages of therapy, the therapist may interpret the child's actions, play, and talk. Interpretation of the play is withheld until its symbolic meaning is clear; sometimes it becomes hardly necessary because the child may already comprehend it.

Jerry arranged the family dolls. The son, the main character in the dollhouse, had a special power: he was able to "see everything" and was guarding and protecting the home. He could move the houses around and could fly. Magical fantasy and omnipotent feelings were present during this session. Later the father doll punched the son "without reason." A monster arrived and took the father and put him on the edge of the roof "to scare him a lot."

Therapist's puppet: It seems that the monster is angry at Father. I wonder who else is angry at him in this house.

Jerry: No, no anger. Let's see the rest.

Therapist's puppet: I wish someone would tell me what this father did to make the monster angry.

Jerry: The monster's job is to kill people, scare them.

Therapist's puppet: But I saw the anger in the monster. It is all right to be angry; even me, a small puppet gets angry. Sometimes I feel my anger may kill someone.

Jerry's play revealed his main ego defense mechanisms; repression, denial, and avoidance, which made it difficult for him acknowledge his anger. He continued his play by admitting that the monster was "hungry" rather than "angry" and "eats people." His play revealed a regression toward the oral state, especially as oral aggression connecting anger to the mouth; biting, chewing and swallowing dominated the session. Eventually, he admitted that the monster was angry at the father.

Therapist's puppet: Let's remember what Father did before the monster came to eat him.

Jerry: He punched that son, but he deserves it. He is a bad boy.

Therapist's puppet: How does the son feel?

Jerry: He feels all right.

Therapist's puppet: Let's ask his mouth— how his mouth feels, the mouth that was punched.

Jerry: His mouth is painful, his hiney is painful, but he is all right.

Therapist's puppet: His mouth is painful, his hiney is painful.

Jerry: Oh; the monster is coming.

Therapist's puppet: Oh; anger is coming. I wonder if the mouth and hiney called the monster to come.

Jerry: Hello mouth, Hello hiney. This is the monster. What can I do for you?

After this exchange in the play, the monster started to fly around the son. At times, Jerry put the monster and the son together; they touched each other, the son held the monster, sat on him and flew. A repetitive play of attachment and detachment between the son and monster occurred. The therapist felt that it was the appropriate time for commenting on the monster's and son's connection as Jerry was putting the doll representing the son over the monster doll, making them one entity. The therapist commented,

"Now that the monster and son are friends and together, it seems that they are one person: a son who is angry at his father, and he gives his anger to the monster to take care of it."

In summary, the third stage is mainly a therapy stage, although the gathering of diagnostic information still plays a part. There will be improvement in the child's feelings and behavior. Ventilation of pent-up emotions, promotion of self-worth, corrective interpersonal experiences, and examination of maladaptive patterns have occurred. The therapist's trust has been tested by the child. Toys and play material are still important, although the child is able to verbalize some feelings. This stage is a transition state—from dolls to words—and toward the end of this stage, words are the main vehicle of expression, which is the beginning of the fourth stage.

Fourth Stage

Some of the child's defense mechanisms are gradually broken, and the doll's life becomes connected to the child's life or the doll's feelings and behaviors create a bridge to the child's feelings and behaviors. During this process, the defense mechanism of attributing negative feelings to dolls is removed, and the child is exposed to her own feelings and the reality of her life situation. The child is encouraged to verbalize extensively her life event's and to bring up the way that she is coping with her victimization and family problems. The work involves helping the child to accept her limitations, mourn her losses, and eventually get in touch with the reality of her life. Later in this stage there will be the process of termination and separation from the therapist and mourning for the "nice time" that the child had with him. The child needs to be reminded that she had the capacity to develop a close relationship with the therapist and she could build similarly satisfying close relationships with peers, friends, or family members.

The child has found a better solution for her emotional conflict. She has developed an aptitude for problem solving. She has self-confidence in her power to heal and is aware that although she cannot ignore the problems of daily life, she does have coping mechanisms. If needed, she can get help from others. She has explored in detail the incidents of abuse, and she has given the total responsibility for her victimization to the offender. She has explored her guilt feelings and self-blaming attitude and has partially or totally overcome them. She has also overcome her misperception of "self-damage" due to the sexual abuse. She has reconciled her positive feelings toward the offender with her negative feelings about him and has accepted her anger. In the ultimate stage, she forgives the offender for his offense and leaves it behind her.

In the fourth stage, the therapist also experiences separation from the patient. He has developed a close relationship with the child and may also experience a loss of this relationship and mourn it. The therapist may express to the child his difficulty in separating from the child: "It is also difficult for me not to see you anymore." The therapist may explain that it is natural for attachment to be pleasurable and for detachment to involve some pain. The therapist may explain to the child that he may think about the child from time to time, in the same way the child may think about him, and "that is life."

The therapist summarizes the child's progress over the treatment period and asks the child to express her perception of her progress and her feelings about play therapy and about the therapist. A certain amount of regression may be seen in the child during this stage as the termination and separation may be somewhat painful to her. The termination should not be abrupt; the child may need to be prepared for it, and sometimes it may take a few months to terminate completely. The sessions, which may have been once a week, gradually decrease to once every two weeks or once every month. It may be helpful for the child to have a calendar on which to mark off a few months ahead of time the day of the last session.

> Chantell, an 8-year-old child, had difficulty going through separa-
> tion from her therapist. In her last session of play therapy, she talked
> about her swimming teacher who told her that some kids need "to
> be pushed a little" from the diving board because they are "a little
> scared" of jumping into the water.
>   Near the end of the session, she told the therapist about her first
> session two years ago, when he sang the "six little monkeys jumping
> on the bed" for her. "I remember it all." Then she sang it, giving
> the song back to the therapist. Then she asked for a pen so that she
> could write her new address. She gave the pen back, wanting to put
> it in the therapist's pocket rather than hand it to him: "I may forget
> and take your pen home." Then she talked about the playroom rules
> and regulations—that no one can take any toys home and no one
> should break any toys during play. Then she said, "Maybe one day
> I will see you in the supermarket with your kids." She left the play-
> room with tears in her eyes.

Play Therapy with Sexually and Physically Abused Children

Children who were the subjects of physical and emotional abuse besides sexual abuse may have more psychopathology and may need more thera-peutic attention. Green (1978) described several types of psychopathology seen in physically abused children: an overall impairment of ego functioning associated with intellectual and cognitive defects; panic states resulting from inflicted feared trauma: severe distortion of object relationship with a lack of trust; impaired impulse control; low self-image; self-destructive behaviors; difficulty with separation; and difficulties in school adjustment.

In intrafamily sexual abuse, children may have role reversal situations that are expressed and presented during the individual or group play therapy. These children also have difficulty going through separation and individuation process from their parents. A type of pseudomaturity is often present.

The goals of treatment should be individualized on the basis of each child's psychopathology, coping mechanisms, ego strengths, and environmental circumstances. In children who were multiply abused (sexually and physically abused and neglected emotionally by family members), there are usually many elements that need therapeutic attention. These include possible internalization of the effect of the physical assault, identification with the aggressor, excessive feelings of rejection and neglect by parents, and a distorted and disturbed adult-child interaction. In some children who were involved in incest with their parents, a pattern of grandiosity and pseudomaturity may be seen, and a child may feel that she possesses power and requires special attention. On the contrary, in physically abused children and emotionally neglected children, a failure to meet the parents' distorted expectations, disturbed object relationship, and internalization of "bad me" along with a very poor self-esteem and self-concept may all be evidenced. Indications of depression are seen in both cases. Aggression, distrust, difficulty in impulse control, hyperactivity, and a kind of "all bad–all good" quality may be seen in an abused child's personality. During therapy the child may project this all good–all bad quality on the therapist. Some physically abused children may attempt to provoke the therapist into punishing them. Others may desire to be physically restrained and aggravate the therapist in ways that make physical restraint likely, such as by running around the room, hitting the therapist, or inflicting self-injury.

Again, the purpose of play therapy with these children is to allow them to reenact in displacement and projection the traumatic events that they experienced. It is an opportunity to help them search for a better solution and a more adaptive way of coping with their disturbance and with the abusive environment that they experienced.

In the first few sessions, Jimmy had no eye contact with the therapist. It was difficult for him to trust the therapist. He was afraid of noise outside of the office. He sat far from the therapist, and it appeared that he was afraid that he would be attacked. He was shy, tense, and overanxious about his behavior. He played checkers, constantly trying to please the therapist. He was not aggressive or assertive in checkers but allowed the therapist to win. Gradually he was able to express his feelings in play therapy sessions. During one session while playing with the dollhouse, he asked the therapist to be the father, while Snoopy would be the child. Snoopy asked: "Daddy, what are we having for supper?" and the therapist answered, "My dear son, we are having pizza." He interrupted and said, "Oh, you doctor! You don't know how to play! You should tell Snoopy, 'You fat kid! All you ever do is eat and eat. I am sick and tired of your big mouth.' The therapist replied, "Oh, what an angry father," and asked the child how Snoopy felt. The child answered, "Snoopy feels bad, feels he is nothing, feels he made his father angry." Then he cut a piece of tape and taped Snoopy's mouth. "Now he can't talk, and he can't eat."

In another session, Snoopy made a little noise when he dropped a spoon, and this woke up his mother. She started to yell at him, "You want to kill me! I worked all night, and now I wanted to sleep. You damned boy, you woke me up!" Then a monster came and took Snoopy. The therapist asked Jimmy, "What will the monster do to Snoopy?" Jimmy responded, "The monster would not eat him, but he will scare him, and in the end Snoopy's mother will kill the monster and they will live happily ever after." Several times in this session, Jimmy symbolically expressed his desire to be protected and rescued by his mother.

In another session the father and mother dolls were fighting in their bedroom. Snoopy put a pillow over his "eyes" not to hear, but it was too late. He already heard his father yelling, "When I leave you, then you and your fat boy will have to beg the neighbors for food." The mother doll yelled back, "You wouldn't be happy. You are his father. You take care of him. I want to be by myself."

When the therapist asked Jimmy how Snoopy felt, he answered, "They are not talking about Snoopy. No, no!" Later he changed his mind and said, "Snoopy is too bad a boy. His mom and dad don't want him."

The therapist tried to reverse the child's perception of the events by bringing a puppet into the play. The puppet at one time said, "No, these parents are too bad. Snoopy shouldn't live with them," in an attempt to prepare the child for possible placement in a foster home. The therapist brought several puppets and dolls to the dollhouse, and the therapist's puppet instructed them to sing: "Parents are bad, Snoopy is cute." Jimmy's desire to see his parents as "good" was discussed by the therapist's puppet. Snoopy's ambivalent feelings toward his parents were brought up by other dolls.

Some emotionally neglected and physically abused children do not know how to play. They do not know the pleasure of being a child and in the beginning of therapy may need to be encouraged to learn how to play. Others may be out of control when they are placed in the playroom, needing constant limit setting and sometimes even physical restraint. Some abused and neglected children need to test the therapist constantly. They may have difficulty in getting close to the therapist, and their anxiety may substantially increase if the therapist attempts to get close to them. They may need to sense a safe distance between themselves and an adult therapist. These children may not tolerate rewards, compliments, and praise from the therapist in the beginning; their ego distortion and their self-esteem do not allow them to tolerate praise. They are expecting and, at times, looking for punishment and abuse. Limit setting, a kind but firm approach toward these children, may be beneficial eventually. The therapist needs to be consistent in approach toward these children so they can learn new behaviors and new approaches. The children learn that aggression and temper tantrums do not help them to gain anything. They also learn that regardless of what they do, the therapist will not abuse them; thus, the children learn new patterns of getting attention from the therapist, and decrease previous patterns, of seeking negative attention from adults.

In sexually abused children, especially when the abuse has been intrafamilial, affection and sex are mixed, and children of these families may internalize this confusion. They may not be able to recognize that persons of the opposite sex can care about them, love them, and have interest in them without mixing it with sex. Some physically abused children also connect their physical abuse with love. These behaviors are reenacted in the therapeutic environment with the therapist. These feelings are expressed toward the therapist, who can help the children go through the corrective emotional experience to separate physical abuse from love and to experience a positive relationship with the adult therapist without sexualizing it or mixing it with physical pain. In some cases of physically abused and emotionally neglected children, food is a strong reinforcer. Children have learned at home to use food as a substitute for parents' love; in therapy sessions, food may be used as a reward and reinforcer, especially for children who do not learn the fun of play and are attracted only to food.

The length of therapy with sexually abused children who also have experienced physical abuse and emotional neglect will be much longer, and their improvement may be slower. The therapist needs to be consistent and available and to create a stable environment for these children. These children need to know that they are not forgotten by their therapist. They are not rejected by him or her. When the therapist goes on vacation, he or she needs to prepare the child ahead of time for this absence. When he or she cancels an appointment, he or she needs to speak to the child on the telephone. Sending a postcard from vacation is a reminder to the child that he or she is thinking of the child. These children grow up in unpredictable and unstable environments, and the therapist needs to create a very predictable and very stable one. This helps the children who already generalize their feelings of unpredictability and instability from their personal environment to all environments. These children see adults as unpredictable, impulsive, abusive, and unstable. By creating a predictable, warm, rewarding environment in the office and conveying a sense of justice and honesty, the therapist helps these children to decrease the internalization of their abusive environment and decrease the generalization of their abusive home situation to all other situations.

Many of these children need long-term intensive play therapy. If the therapist is temporarily employed by a clinic and is not available after six to nine months, he or she should not start therapy with these children. Children who have been abused sexually and physically are sensitive to abandonment and rejection. They need a minimum of one to two, and sometimes three to four, years of play therapy. These children need to be involved with a skilled therapist who has decided to take the responsibility of the treatment and is aware of the need for long-term involvement with them.

The therapist should not satisfy the "sick part" of the child—the part that forces the therapist to get angry and or reject her or him. A certain amount of anger exists in all of us and can be evoked by any child; however, if this anger is related to the child's acting-out behavior motivated by the child's "sick part" wishing to evoke that anger, the therapist should have the self-knowledge and control to refrain from becoming angry at the child. In other circumstances, there is a need for the therapist to explain to the child that such behavior would make anyone angry, including the therapist.

Therapeutic Barriers: Pitfalls for the Therapist

Selective listening, preconceived ideas, nonindividualizing therapy, formulary treatment and personalizing reactions, and selective listening are pitfalls. The therapist may hear only some of the patient's statement. In play therapy selective seeing is present. That means that the therapist sees certain aspects of the child's play but because of a possible internal conflict within the therapist is unable to see or to hear other parts of the child's play and statements.

> Five-year-old Jenni was telling her therapist about her mother's going to the hospital. The therapist, who was involved with this child because of sexual abuse by the father, tried to bring the child back to the incest issue, which happened while the mother was in the hospital. The therapist was not able to listen to the child's statement concerning the hospitalization. From the child's point of view, the

mother's hospitalization was more traumatic than the father's incest. Later, when the therapist was asked about the child's statement in regard to her mother's hospitalization, the therapist did not remember that she tried to change the subject.

Preconceived ideas and formulary treatment are considered barriers in obtaining good results in psychotherapy. A therapist with preconceived ideas has developed a set of beliefs that conveys to him or her what is traumatic to a child and what is not. Without considering the child's perception of an event, the therapist substitutes preconceived perceptions and expects the child to react to an event in the way that the therapist of "ordinary people" would respond. Eventually the therapist directs the child to react in a specific way. The therapist has a set of beliefs in treatment and by generalizing and non-individualizing the therapy ignores the uniqueness of every child's perceptions, reactions, symptom formation, and resolution and coping mechanisms. For example, if during the initial interview, a child explains the negative impact of incest on his or her life, a clinician usually accepts the child's perception. However, if another patient expressed that past incestuous experience had nothing to do with current symptoms, some therapists would consider this as a denial and repression, and the treatment goals, in a formulary way, would be designed to overcome the denial when, indeed, the patient's perception was correct. Other examples of the danger of generalizing treatment include children and adolescents who were sexually abused by family members in an alcoholic family. These families were called "alcoholic" by an alcohol counselor, and a modality of group treatment for "children of alcoholics" was suggested. These same patients were labeled by another clinician as "incest victims" whose problems were related to growing up in an "incestuous family." Although both clinicians were probably correct in their preconceived assumption, eventually it is the patient (with conscious and unconscious revelations) who indicates how she or he perceived the early environment. She or he indicates which elements contributed to symptom formation.

Both conscious and unconscious feelings may be evoked within a therapist while treating sexually abusive families. In an attempt to cope, a therapist can develop counterfeelings. If a therapist is not aware, the issue of countertransference (the therapist's displacement of feelings toward his or her family onto the patient's family) could create a serious barrier in treatment. Personalizing reactions is a frequent phenomenon that may be seen in therapists: "Because I hated my stepfather, this child may also hate her stepfather." This is an obvious barrier to understanding the child's perceptions. The common fallacy that female therapists develop more sympathy toward sexually abused girls and male therapists may have "more understanding" in regard to fathers in father-daughter incest is an example of personalizing reaction. Overidentification with a child victim or with an incest offender may have an impact on the objectivity of the therapist in dealing with incestuous families.

Conclusion

In this chapter the basic principles of play therapy with sexually abused children have been discussed. The therapeutic stages obviously overlap each other. Not every child victim of sexual abuse is in need of play therapy. When play therapy is indicated, not every child needs to complete the four stages. Sexual abuse, especially incest, occurs in dysfunctional families. The parents in these families have personality problems, and there are chronic interpersonal difficulties among the family members. Because the sexual trauma is imposed upon an already fragile ego structure, these cases may require intensive play therapy.

Play therapy may not be the only modality of treatment used for incestuous families. Generally individual therapy with each parent and group therapy for the offender are essential before any family therapy can begin. Play therapy for the child victim is only one of the components of the treatment program for these families, although in a few rare cases, because of an uncooperative parent or parents, it may be the only choice. Play therapy might help the child to tolerate the parent's psychopathology. Clinicians should remember that because of the therapist's personal feelings, skills, and capacity to develop empathy and enjoy contact with the child, the therapist as a person is the most important tool in facilitating a corrective interpersonal experience.

Winnicott (1971b) pointed out that play therapy occurs when both child and therapist are prepared to enter into the play as fully as possible: "Psychotherapy is done in the area of overlap between the playing of the patient and the playing of the therapist."

References

Axline, V. 1947. *Play Therapy*. Boston: Houghton-Mifflin.

Burns, R.C., and Kaufman, S.H. 1970. *Kinetic Family Drawing*. New York: Brunner-Mazel.

Erikson, E. 1963. *Childhood and Society*. New York: Norton.

Freud, S. 1920. "Beyond the Pleasure Principle." In *The Standard Edition of the Complete Psychological Works of Sigmund Freud,* vol. 18:3–64. London: Hogarth 1955.

Freud, S. 1905. "A Fragment of an Analysis of a Case of Hysteria." In *The Standard*

Edition of the Complete Psychological Works of Sigmund Freud, vol. 7:3–122. London: Hogarth 1955.

Gardner, R.A. 1971. *Therapeutic Communication with Children: The Mutual Storytelling Technique.* New York: Jason Aronson.

Green, A.H. 1978. "Psychopathology of Abused Children." *Journal of the American Academy of Child Psychiatry* 17: 92–103.

Hammer, E.F. 1960. "House-Tree-Person (H-T-P) Drawings as a Projective Technique with Children." In A.I.Robins and M.R. Haworth, *Projective Techniques in Children.* New York: Grune & Stratton.

Klein, M. 1932. *The Psychoanalysis of Children.* London: Hogarth Press.

Levy, D. 1938. "Release Therapy in Young Children." *Psychiatry,* I: 387–389.

Marvasti, J.M. 1986a. "Play Therapy and the Child Victim: Making the Correct Interpretation." Presented at Thirteenth National Conference on Juvenile Justice, New Orleans, January.

Marvasti, J.M. 1986b. "Using Dolls in Interviewing Sexually Abused Children." Presented at Fourth National Conference on the Sexual Victimization of Children, New Orleans, May.

Marvasti, J.M. 1987. "The Validity of Play Interview with Sexually Abused Children." Presented at the First European Congress on Child Abuse and Neglect, Rhodes, Greece, April.

Piaget, J. 1962. *Play, Dreams and Imitation in Childhood.* New York: Norton.

Solomon, J. 1938. "Active Play Therapy." *Orthopsychiatry* 8:479–498.

Winnicott, D.W. 1971a. *Therapeutic Consultation in Child Psychiatry.* New York: Basic Books.

Winnicott, D.W. 1971b. *Playing and Reality.* Harmondsworth: Penquin.

2

Innovations in the Assessment and Treatment of Sexually Abused Adolescents: An Inpatient Model

David Hussey
Mark Singer

T he Adolescent Unit at St. Vincent Charity Hospital and Health Center in Cleveland, Ohio, is a twenty-four bed inpatient psychiatric unit designed in 1986 for the care of emotionally or psychiatrically impaired adolescents. The staff is composed of professionals who have specific interests and training in working with adolescents and includes psychiatrists, nurses, social workers, counselors, special education teachers, art therapists, recreation therapists, and various other health care providers. The Adolescent Unit uses a treatment approach designed to address specific problem areas.

Traditionally adolescent inpatient psychiatric units have provided a wide range of services to patients, typically including individual and group psychotherapies, family therapy, educational classes, and art and recreation therapies. Specific problems that patients may have are addressed within the context of these generalized services. A number of problem areas common to troubled youth have been identified in the clinical and research literature and include drug and alcohol abuse, eating disorders, and sexual and physical abuse (Jessor, Chase, and Donovan 1980; Newcome and Bentler 1986; Steinhauer and Rae-Grant 1983). Recent advances in treatment suggest that each of these problem areas may be successfully approached using groups composed of members experiencing similar life events and difficulties. The idea of specialty programming is based on these advances coupled with the concept that troubled youth often have a similar nexus of problems. Thus, within the context of the inpatient adolescent psychiatric unit at St. Vincent, specific specialty programs address three major problem areas. These specific

The research portions of this chapter were supported by a grant from the Woodruff Foundation, Cleveland, Ohio. We gratefully acknowledge the work and insights of the dedicated staff of the Adolescent Unit at St. Vincent Charity Hospital. Special Thanks to Pamela Bertaud-Klier, art therapist.

programs are nested within a more generalized psychiatric program capable of addressing a wider array of problems.

Traditional service delivery systems have often separated inpatient psychiatric and chemical dependency treatment: however, a significant percentage of adolescents who present with emotional or psychiatric problems are also experiencing substance abuse problems that often go unidentified. Teenagers with emotional or psychiatric problems may use mood-altering chemicals for a number of reasons, including: as a means to modify unpleasant feelings, to alleviate depression, to reduce tension, or to aid in coping with life's pressures. In recognition of this relationship, all adolescents admitted to the unit at St. Vincent are required to have a complete substance abuse assessment as part of their overall evaluation.

During the assessment period, both the adolescent and his or her family complete a series of diagnostic interviews and questionnaires. When these assessments are completed, an interdisciplinary team meets to determine the specific treatment needs. Adolescents found to be abusing drugs or alcohol are referred to the dual diagnosis specialty program—a program designed to serve youth who have coexisting mental health and chemical abuse problems. This specialty program provides intensive educational, group, family, and individual treatment services based on a modified Twelve Step AA model.

A great deal of media attention has recently been given to eating disorders among adolescents, specifically, bulimia and anorexia nervosa. Our experience has shown, as with drug and alcohol abuse, that adolescents may use their relationship with food as a means of expressing and coping with stress. Commonly adolescents with eating disorders tend to deny or hide this problem; therefore, all adolescent patients receive a nutritional assessment at the time of admission, with special attention given to identifying a possible eating disorder. Patients suspected of having eating disorder symptoms are given a more in-depth evaluation.

Eating disorder programming is integrated within the general unit milieu. A protocol-based behavioral reinforcement approach is used either to restore or maintain a healthy target weight. Specific eating disorder therapy and support groups concentrate on important recovery issues. In addition, these youngsters are required to participate in other group therapies that address adolescent development and family issues. Their exposure to peers who do not have eating disorders encourages socialization and provides opportunities to learn new coping skills.

The known incidence of physical and sexual abuse in the general population of children and adolescents is high enough to be considered a major public health problem (Walker, Bonner, and Kaufman 1988). Research further indicates that the incidence of abuse among psychiatrically hospitalized youth is even higher than in the general population; such abuse can cause severe emotional and psychiatric trauma among its victims (Husain and

Chapel 1983; Emslie and Rosenfeld 1983). Consequently, it is imperative that hospital-based treatment programs use effective methods of screening and treating adolescent victims and their families.

Screening

Nationally, it is suspected that approximately a quarter of all women have some sort of childhood sexual experience with an adult by age 18 *(Los Angeles Times* 1985). Data on males who have been abused are less common; however, it is thought that 15 percent of men might also have had a sexually abusive experience with an adult prior to age 18 (Alter-Reid et. al. 1986). We were particularly concerned about the higher rates of abuse reported among so-called high-risk populations, which include runaways, substance abusers, and psychiatric inpatients (Alter-Reid et al. 1986). Recent studies of psychiatric inpatients have indicated that up to 81 percent of these patients have had some history of major physical or sexual assault (Jacobson and Richardson 1987).

Disclosure of physical and sexual abuse is a critical issue for the staff of adolescent psychiatric inpatient units to address. Several years ago, we became acutely aware of the alarming number of teenagers admitted to our unit who had already identified histories of physical and sexual abuse. In addition, the psychiatric literature was beginning to document the high incidence of abuse among specific populations, such as adolescents who were suicidal or had runaway histories.

It was not only the high incidence of reported abuse that was of concern to us but also the apparent lack of treatment progress in adolescent patients for whom we suspected, but could not confirm, a history of serious abuse. In an era of shortened hospital stays and declining reimbursement patterns for psychiatric admissions, we felt it necessary to intensify our inpatient evaluation and treatment components. This led us to begin to look at establishing an effective, comprehensive, systematic way to screen the adolescents admitted to our unit for histories of victimization.

Disclosure

Many mental health professionals are taught the necessity and importance of reporting abuse to their local protective service agency. While professionals are taught about reporting suspected child abuse, teaching them the process of how to facilitate such a disclosure from a frightened and embarrassed teenager is often overlooked.

In looking at disclosure dynamics, it is imperative to conceptualize them as a process rather than a one-time static event. What has become apparent to us in our work is that most first-time disclosures are inaccurate. By inaccurate we do not mean that the disclosure is false; rather it is greatly minimized and incomplete. The process of first disclosing life experiences that are perceived by the victim as less risky or less threatening is not unusual. This is due to a wide variety of reasons, which often include hesitancy, embarrassment, shame, guilt, repression, and fear of exposure and retaliation. The following case example illustrates these dynamics:

> A 17-year-old adolescent female was transferred from a substance program to St. Vincent's adolescent unit after a serious suicide attempt. Initial screening revealed a depressed, anxious youth with a long-standing history of substance abuse and poor self-esteem. Intensive assessment efforts to identify a precipitant to the suicide attempt led to the disclosure of previous sexual abuse by a neighbor (a 16-year-old male) when the patient was 12 years old. After several weeks of inpatient treatment, in which the patient appeared to be making progress, her suicidal ideation resurfaced. At that point she reported that her oldest brother had also sexually abused her. The patient expressed many reservations about returning home, though the brother no longer lived there. After two months, the patient was transferred to a long-term treatment facility. After another serious suicide attempt, she finally reported that her alcoholic father had abused her since she was 6.

Most of the law enforcement and protective service investigation models are not equipped to deal with disclosure from this process-oriented perspective. Delays in time and changes of victim accounts can hamper and impede the judicial process. Yet if we wish to facilitate disclosure, we need to be sensitive to the process of disclosure and the realization that full and accurate disclosure occurs in stages as time elapses. (See chapter 1.)

It is our experience that high-risk populations need to be screened systematically in ways that maximize and initiate the process of disclosure. In many ways, this is similar to obtaining important information about other issues that adolescents are uncomfortable about discussing with adult authority figures. "Have you ever been sexually abused?" is a good, direct question but is probably the equivalent of, "Do you do drugs?" All too often it is perceived by the adolescent as too threatening and simply met with a response of "No." In order to facilitate these types of disclosures, we need to utilize more sophisticated screening approaches that employ multiple measures of the variables thought to relate to sexual abuse. Furthermore, the method of collecting this information needs to be as nonthreatening as possible and perceived by the adolescent as something that will eventually help him or her to feel better about himself or herself and the current situation.

In a national random sample of 1,200 males and 1,300 females, Lewis found that one-third of abused adults first disclosed their sexual abuse over the telephone *(Los Angeles Times* 1985). Only 3 percent of those with histories of abuse said that it was ever reported. It was thought that a telephone survey might be a good investigative technique because of the perception of anonymity and the lack of face-to-face contact with an interviewer. This reasoning led us to believe that indirect methods of disclosure might be extremely valuable in obtaining accurate substance abuse histories. Thereafter, we also opted to use a similar method for victimization screening for adolescent patients.

Adolescent Sexual Concern Questionnaire (ASC)

The ASC is an appropriate acronym for an instrument that is designed to help detect sexual abuse. (See appendix 2–1 at the end of this chapter.) The usual way to find out if someone has been sexually abused is to ask; however, one must ask in a way that gives permission for teenagers to relate emotionally painful and confusing experiences. An understanding of disclosure dynamics, as well as the many ways in which adolescents react to past or present victimization, are important screening prerequisites.

The ASC is designed to be used in the context of a structured interview by a professional familiar with the dynamics of sexual abuse and comfortable in discussing sexuality issues. It has forty one items, each presented in a Likert-type format to minimize simple true-false responses. The items screen for physical and sexual abuse and cover a wide range of issues, including physical appearance, birth control, concerns about sex, venereal disease, AIDS, homosexuality, homophobia, and sexual deviance. The ASC is structured so that it moves from less risky to more risky items in order for the interviewer to establish a rapport with the teenagers and then choose points of emphasis for exploration. We use a same-sex interviewer (a master's-level social worker) to maximize discussion and disclosure of sensitive sexual material. The same types of critical questions are asked in several different ways to serve as a validity check on responses. The ASC is written on a sixth-grade level and is administered to patients along with several other questionnaires within the first three days of admission. The instrument is meant to be used as a guide for the interviewer and an opportunity to provide educational information to the patient. It is simple, relatively short, and not too threatening. This is the delicate balance that needs to be achieved when creating instruments that are clinically useful and possess a research capability.

If the interviewer is suspicious or concerned that the adolescent may have been abused yet such abuse has not directly been acknowledged in the interview or on the ASC, then some important steps need to be taken. Usually it is advantageous to conclude the interview with a hopeful ending that lets the teenager know that there are still concerns about victimization. Through the use of generalizations and anticipatory guidance techniques, the focus now becomes preparing the teenager for later disclosure. A statement such as, "sometimes people remember painful or confusing experiences that had been previously forgotten," allows the question of victimization to remain an open topic for further exploration. We are consistently impressed by the number of teenagers who have come back to us during the middle or later portions of their hospital stays to disclose sexual abuse histories. Frequently we will identify a staff member, such as a primary or associate nurse, to continue to explore this question in the course of hospital treatment. The growing rapport and trust that develops in the context of this important therapeutic relationship can provide the foundation for a frightened adolescent to share his or her victimization experiences. The importance of understanding the process of disclosure and leaving the door open for future disclosure cannot be overemphasized.

Aside from the ASC instrument and interview, there are other assessments that provide a cross-check for victimization screening. By virtue of having a victimization component that includes weekly educational inservices for all staff, we have developed a broad-based clinical sensitivity to these issues across disciplines. This has resulted in specific questions and behavioral observations being incorporated in other evaluations. For example, medical and nursing personnel give special attention to the reaction of patients to the history, physical, and search that are required of all patients upon admission. Social workers are careful to note family dynamics evidencing role and boundary distortions or historical clues symptomatic of abusive relationships. Sometimes the only initial clues are through the projective evaluations conducted by the art therapists in which the Draw-A-Person (DAP) and Kinetic Family Drawings (K-F-D) are extensively utilized. These and other cross-checks provide a comprehensive screening approach that maximizes inpatient assessment capabilities.

From the data we compiled, 68 of the 260 adolescents admitted to our unit were determined to have been sexually abused. The ASC was able to identify 21 patients which histories of sexual abuse that had been never been disclosed. It also identified 30 patients with previously revealed histories of sexual abuse. Another 17 patients reported histories of sexual abuse during their inpatient stay but were not first identified through the ASC. Five of these patients had previously identified histories of abuse, and 12 were first-time disclosures. The positive prediction rate for those who disclosed being sexually abused for the first time was 64 percent (21 of 33) and was 86 percent (30 of 35) for youth who had previously revealed being sexually abused. These statistics cannot account for cases that remained undisclosed; however, an overall positive prediction rate of 75 percent (51 of 68) was achieved by the ASC for patients who were able to be classified as sexually abused.

Table 2–1 displays the key screening responses for the ASC. These responses were obtained by comparing ASC responses from youth who were known to have been sexually abused with youth who had no known history of such abuse and then determining differences between the two groups through use of chi-square analyses. Statistically significant differences emerged in the following content areas:

- *Having dreams or nightmares:* Overall between-group differences were significant at the $p < .01$ level. Also significant between-group differences existed for females, with sexually abused females having more concerns about dreams or nightmares than their same-gender control group counterparts ($p < .05$).

Table 2–1
Key Screening Responses

Area of Question or Concern	Sexual Abuse (N = 68)	No Known Sexual Abuse (N = 192)
**Having dreams or nightmares	43%	31%
**Not having enough muscles	40%	23%
**Feeling ugly	40%	18%
**How far to go with sex	24%	10%
*Birth control	24%	13%
**Getting pregnant	26%	8%
*Venereal disease	18%	8%
**Being raped or sexually abused	33%	7%
**Feeling upset about sexual things you've done	24%	11%
**Feeling upset about sexual things that happened to you	39%	5%
**Having a terrible secret	21%	7%
**Being afraid of the opposite sex	22%	4%
*Having difficulty controlling sexual feelings	15%	6%
**Being touched in a private part of your body against your wishes	27%	6%
**Using sex to gain friends or money	12%	3%

* $\chi^2 p < .05.$
**$\chi^2 p < .01.$

- *Feeling ugly:* Significant between-group differences were at the $p < .01$ level. Although no reliable differences were found for females, sexually abused males were more concerned about feeling ugly than males with no known sexual abuse ($p < .01$). This finding was due to the relatively high percentages for females in both groups having endorsed concerns about feeling ugly (sex abuse group, 44 percent; control group, 40 percent). Such high percentages may have been due to the clinical population under study. For males, however, one-third of those who had been sexually abused endorsed concerns about feeling ugly, compared to 8 percent of males with no known abuse endorsing this item. In the revised version of the ASC, we attempted to broaden this concept by changing the statement from questions or concerns about "feeling ugly" to questions or concerns about "how you look."

- *How far to go with sex:* Overall group differences were at the $p < .01$ level. No differences emerged for females, but males who had been sexually abused indicated more questions or concerns on this item than males with no known abuse ($p < .05$).

- *Birth control:* Although between-group differences existed ($p < .05$), no gender-related differences were evidenced.

- *Getting pregnant:* There were no differences related to gender; overall group differences were significant at the $p < .01$ level.

- *Venereal disease:* Overall group differences were significant ($p < .05$), and reliable differences emerged between male groups, with sexually abused males having more questions and concerns about VD than control group males ($p < .05$).

- *Being raped or sexually abused:* Group differences were at the $p < .01$ level. Within genders, both sexually abused males and females endorsed more questions and concerns on this item than their controls ($p < .05$ and $p < .001$ respectively).

- *Feeling upset about sexual things you've done:* Overall group differences were significant ($p < .01$), but no reliable differences by gender were noted.

- *Feeling upset about sexual things that have happened to you:* In addition to highly significant overall group differences ($p < .0001$), equally significant differences emerged in males who had been sexually abused versus male controls ($p < .0001$) and females who had been sexually abused versus female controls ($p < .0001$).

- *Having a terrible secret:* Overall group differences were reliable ($p < .01$). Gender-related differences were present for females, with significantly more sexually abused females endorsing this item than females who were not known to have been so abused ($p < .05$).

- *Being afraid of the opposite sex:* Group differences were at the p <.01 level. When differences by gender were examined, both males and females who had been sexually abused indicated more concerns in this area than their no-known-abuse counterparts (p <.01 for both males and females). This finding raises the possibility that these sexually abused children may experience ongoing difficulties in relationships with the opposite sex.

- *Having difficulty controlling sexual feelings:* Significance was at the p <.01 level for overall group differences, with gender differences emerging only for males. Compared to males with no known sexual abuse, sexually abused males endorsed having more concerns related to this item (p <.05). One possible implication of this finding is that this expression of difficulty controlling sexual feelings could relate to impulsive sexual acts and/or to being sexually abusive to others.

- *Being touched in a private part of your body against your wishes:* In addition to overall group differences (p <.01), differences by gender were evidenced by both males and females. Compared with their respective control group gender, more sexually abused males and females endorsed this item (p <.01 for each gender).

- *Using sex to gain friends or money:* While overall group significance was achieved (p <.01), gender differences emerged only for females. Over one out of ten (13 percent) females who were sexually abused had questions or concerns about using sex to gain friends or money; however, none of the females who were not known to have been sexually abused endorsed this item (p <.001). Those expressing concerns on this item must be considered at risk for abusive and exploitative relationships or prostitution. Due to the relatively small percentage of affirmative responses and to emphasize the emotional component of sexual exploitation, this item was changed to read "using sex to gain affection" on the revised version of the ASC.

The ASC provides an important degree of programmatic integrity to victimization screening of adolescent psychiatric inpatients. Two of the key program components are documentation and uniformity in evaluating all adolescents for victimization experiences. There is clear, written documentation of the screening assessment and interview. The interviewer has noted patient reactions to critical items within the margin of the instrument itself. In addition, use of the instrument provides a degree of uniformity to the manner and scope of interviewing for victimization experiences.

Data on Our Population

We have systematically collected information for adolescents admitted to our unit over a consecutive two-year period. This information includes demographic data, drug-and alcohol-related data, psychiatric data, and victimization screening data. To date, our overall sample consists of 260 patients.

The average age of our sample is 15.6 years, with a range from 12 to 18 years. The sample contains 150 males and 110 females and is predominantly white (86 percent). Through our screening protocol, 21 of the 150 males (14 percent) and 47 of the 110 females (43 percent) were determined to have histories of sexual abuse. We believe this to be a conservative figure; our screening was probably unable to identify all adolescents who had been sexually abused due to patients' reluctance to disclose such histories. A comparison by psychiatric diagnoses of adolescents identified as sexually abused to those not so identified is contained in table 2–2.

Comparisons of drug and alcohol use between patients known to have been sexually abused (SA) and those with no evidence of abuse (NSA) yield some interesting findings. Forty-three percent of SA adolescents compared to 28 percent of NSA adolescents reported having a problem with drinking. Similar differences were evidenced between SA and NSA youth regarding a self-reported problem with drugs (40 percent versus 28 percent, respectively). Indeed, one in five SA patients reported getting professional help for drinking (one in ten NSA patients so reported).

Tables 2–3 and 2–4 display alcohol and drug abuse measures for each of the two groups of patients. Forty-four percent of SA youth in comparison to 27 percent of NSA youth indicated being drunk three times or more in the past two months; 43 percent of SA youth compared with 29 percent of NSA youth reported being high on drugs at least three times over the past two months. The average age of first drug use was identical for both groups

Table 2–2
Psychiatric Diagnoses

	Sexual Abuse (N = 68)		No Known Sexual Abuse (N = 192)	
Adjustment Disorder	44	(65%)	102	(53%)
Conduct Disorder	6	(9%)	37	(19%)
Eating Disorder	1	(2%)	11	(6%)
Neurotic Disorder	4	(6%)	6	(3%)
Thought Disorder	2	(3%)	6	(3%)
Affective Disorder	7	(11%)	23	(12%)
Other	4	(6%)	7	(4%)

Table 2–3
Times Drunk in the Past Two Months

	Sexual Abuse (N = 66)		No Known Sexual Abuse (N = 187)	
None	26	(39%)	97	(52%)
One	6	(9%)	18	(10%)
Two	5	(8%)	20	(11%)
Three	2	(3%)	12	(6%)
Four or more	27	(41%)	40	(21%)

Table 2–4
Times High on Drugs in Past Two Months

	Sexual Abuse (N = 62)		No Known Sexual Abuse (N = 187)	
None	24	(39%)	118	(63%)
One	5	(8%)	8	(4%)
Two	7	(11%)	8	(4%)
Three	5	(8%)	9	(5%)
Four or more	21	(34%)	44	(24%)

(13.2 years), and the average age of first drink was highly similar between groups (12.0 years SA; 12.3 years NSA).

Close to half (46 percent) of the SA group reported that they drank for the express purpose of getting high or drunk, with 28 percent of the NSA group stating that they drank for this purpose. It is not surprising that 37 percent of the SA group compared to 19 percent of the NSA group indicated having blackouts due to drinking. Commensurately, one out of four in the SA group in comparison to one out of ten in the NSA group reported usually starting to drink because of sad or lonely feelings.

When queried about the potential benefits of drug use, SA adolescents reported greater benefits than NSA adolescents across several categories. Greater percentages of sexually abused adolescents endorsed that the use of drugs helped them relax (82 percent SA; 64 percent NSA), helped them be friendly (49 percent SA; 32 percent NSA), helped them feel good about themselves (51 percent SA, 27 percent NSA), and helped them make friends with others who used drugs (58 percent SA; 36 percent NSA).

The data show that, in our population, adolescents who had been sexually abused had more harmful substance use patterns, had more frequently sought professional help for drinking, had a greater incidence of blackouts, and perceived getting more benefits from taking drugs than adolescents not known to have suffered from such abuse. Additionally, greater percentages of sexually abused youth self-reported having an alcohol or drug problem than NSA youth.

There are several possible explanations for the more severe patterns of substance use found among our SA adolescents. First, we know that the emotional sequelae of sexual abuse often include depression, anxiety, and anger (Alter-Reid et al. 1986). It is possible that SA youth may use mood-altering substances as a means of modifying these unpleasant feelings. Second, adolescents commonly use mood-altering substances to enhance self-esteem and to reduce feelings of loneliness and isolation. Since victimized adolescents can have difficulty in making close relationships and trusting others, the drug culture may provide them with an arena in which they have numerous "friends" yet no close interpersonal relationships. Thus by being part of the drug culture, the sexually abused adolescent can successfully avoid interpersonal closeness but still have peer group affiliations, remaining outwardly involved with others yet inwardly isolated.

Finally, as a response to stress or trauma, children may engage in coping strategies that are dissociative in nature, thereby trying to control what is occurring by creating a different reality through fantasy or repression. Children may learn to rely on the distancing tactics of dissociation when they are feeling overwhelmed by life events. Such early defenses may place the child at risk for future substance abuse, since a primary reason for using mood-altering substances is modifying one's internal experiences. Therefore, a person's style of coping with stress during childhood may be replicated on a developmental level through substance abuse during adolescence (Singer, Petchers and Hussey in press).

Treatment Philosophy

If the hallmark of disclosure is facilitating the process (the process of preparing for admitting the confusing and traumatic past), then the hallmark of treatment is to reinterpret correctly and understand the meaning of the traumatic past in a way that can minimize some of the negative effects. For the victimized adolescent, this occurs within the context of identity formation and fragmentation. The original defenses used to accommodate or adjust to the abuse have served as ego survival strategies. They now need to be transformed to integrate the meaning of the abuse into a healthier, non-fragmented identity. Residual effects of failing to do so can include low self-esteem, self-hatred, disturbed relationships, and poor impulse control.

The common features employed to accommodate the abuse include denying the abuse, altering the affective responses to it, and changing the meaning of it (Rieker and Carmen 1986). In denying the abuse, one often finds minimizing and incomplete disclosure. For adolescents, this may be reflected in the development of distancing and disassociative strategies that frequently include heavy substance abuse patterns (Singer, Petchers, and Hussey in press). The altering of affective responses can result in sudden anger and impulsive or self-destructive behaviors. It is not surprising that adolescent disclosure scenarios are replete with angry and labile teenagers who first disclose abuse in the face of extreme emotional conflict when they can no longer contain or disguise their rage associated with the abuse.

In changing the meaning of the abuse, we frequently find that someone else besides the victim has defined the meaning of the abuse. All too often it is actually the perpetrator who has determined that meaning. If not, society, the media, the newspapers, or someone else may have inaccurately defined it. Frequently, if the abuse has occurred early, the interpretation of it is from the unfair and biased perspective of current empowerment patterns. This is particularly true for males, who blame themselves for past abuse based on their present physical and emotional capabilities to resist an assault or or avoid sexual entrapment. Adolescent patients need an accurate definition of the abuse experience and the right to own their feelings. The first treatment task, then, becomes to understand the victim's processing of the victimization experience. The ongoing therapeutic task will then be to allow the victim to own and accept the feelings associated with it and to reframe the meaning of the experience in a way that can allow for healthier identity development and future growth.

The use of creative media with adolescents, particularly in a supportive group setting, can be highly effective in initiating this process. It can provide a direct or indirect method of discovering, accessing, and altering the meaning of the experience through the use of symbols, abstractions, projections, and fantasies (Wadeson 1980; Schaefer 1988). The goal is to help create a healthy identity by reclaiming the traumatic past (Rieker and Carmen 1986).

Treatment

Patients who are found to have histories of sexual abuse are referred for specific victimization treatment. The treatment they receive is in addition to and in conjunction with the regular treatment regime on the unit. The three primary contexts in which treatment takes place are individual, group, and family therapies.

Individual Therapy

The individual therapy can take several different forms depending on patient treatment requirements. Often the nursing staff person who is assigned to be the patient's primary or associate worker helps to guide the patient through the initial disclosure process with a combination of supportive and insight-oriented therapies. The initial focus is on the development of a therapeutic alliance in which victimization concerns can be identified, validated, and connected to other treatment issues responsible for the teenager's hospitalization. The other treatment issues often include depressed or suicidal behavior, substance abuse, unruliness, running away, or aggressive acting out. Frequently it is easier to engage adolescent patients in therapeutic work around these already identified behaviors that precipitated their inpatient admission. The patient's increased understanding of the meaning behind these behaviors within the context of a growing treatment relationship can lead back to an exploration of victimization issues. The technique, then, is to begin with what is manifest and apparent, identify the pain and conflict associated with it, and process the possible connection between that pain and the prior abuse.

The other form in which individual victimization therapy takes place is usually in the context of work with male victims, sexual deviancies, or sexual adjustment problems. We seldom have enough male sexual abuse victims at any one time to perform group therapy. The program manager, who is a male, master's-level social worker, and the art therapist, who is female and also has a master's degree, provide the majority of this therapy. In addition to the therapy with male victims, individual therapy also encompasses work with fire setters, perpetrators, exhibitionists, obscene telephone callers, and those struggling with sexual identity issues. This therapy most often involves males, although occasionally female perpetrators and those deemed inappropriate for group therapy are seen individually. The sessions take place two times per week, and the individually tailored treatment strategies are based on specific patient problems and needs. Because of the short-term nature of hospital stays on our unit (the average length of stay is twenty seven days), much of the work is diagnostic in nature and anticipatory of outpatient follow-up.

A 16-year-old male patient was referred for individual treatment after his initial evaluation revealed a history of exhibitionism and sexual perpetrating. The patient admitted to fondling a 4-year-old female neighbor on several occasions. The patient was involved in individual therapy with the art therapist two times per week. During the course of individual treatment, the art therapist encouraged him to look at certain themes in his artwork. She noted the prominence of a telephone receiver in one of his projects. With some prodding, the patient admitted to a long history of obscene telephone calling. Further therapeutic exploration revealed the patient's own history of sexual abuse from ages 7 through 10 by an older male peer. This was the first time the patient had disclosed his own abuse, though he had been carefully questioned several times in the past. These disclosures identified important areas for continued therapeutic work.

Group Therapy

Female patients with a history of sexual abuse are referred to the self-expression art therapy group, coled by an art therapist and the program manager. It meets two times per week for approximately one hour per session. It is important to watch the intensity level of this group because of the delicate nature of the clinical material being explored. The group is confidential in that the other adolescents on the unit are not aware of the victimization focus and abuse history of group members. It is one of three different art therapy groups that meet regularly on the unit. It is our experience that adolescents are appropriately reluctant to share widely their personal abuse experiences being broadly acknowledged with other peers. If they wish to share their abuse experiences with peers or in other group therapies, they are certainly permitted to do so. It is imperative, however, that they do not violate another self-expression group member's confidentiality. This rule helps to promote the development of group trust and cohesion and maximizes the supportive group dynamics.

The focus of the group is on feelings and perceptions, not the details of the abuse. The group leaders usually select an issue they feel is valuable or timely for the group to explore. Then they choose a task, select an art medium, and decide on a time limit for project completion. There is an introduction and initial discussion explaining the task. The group leaders frequently take part in the art projects themselves but are always attentive to the individual needs of group members. This attention to the patient's art therapy process often reveals the most important diagnostic and therapeutic information that is obtained during the hospitalization. The group members are required to share their projects during the discussion period and offer feedback to peers.

The art therapy tasks are varied and designed to address specific victimization issues. Some are diagnostic in nature and structure to facilitate further disclosure and explore key relationships. Others are of a projective or cathartic orientation utilized to access repressed affects or buried memories, and work through conflicted emotions

An abstract family collage can be a useful diagnostic as well as cathartic experience. It can be completed by using a variety of precut wooden shapes of figures. Patients are instructed to represent their families by choosing and arranging the wooden shapes to represent various family members. This three-dimensional project allows patients a symbolic way of representing family dynamics and relationships through the use of art. They are encouraged to label or identify the shapes and to use markers to add color or detail to their project. The therapists give careful attention to the process through which they develop the collage. Patients then discuss their collage within the therapeutic setting.

This project has served as a useful assessment tool particularly for exploring family role and boundary issues. Patients often represent underlying conflicts and concerns regarding family members and family process. During the course of one group therapy session, a 16-year-old female patient took her index finger and flicked the wood chip representing her stepfather across the room. Although she was extremely angry at him for sexually harassing her, she was unable to acknowledge her own disguised, negative feelings. Pointing out her behavior during this group therapy session enabled her to begin to identify and explore her negative feelings.

In addition to the use of art therapy, educational presentations, movies, and more traditional group discussions are also employed. The use of drama, poetry, and other creative media are valuable therapeutic formats for victimization treatment.

Art Journal

Art therapy journals were designed and developed by the art therapist for use in both individual and group therapy sessions. The journal contains a packet of markers and approximately twenty five sheets of drawing paper. On the top of each piece of drawing paper is a title describing a therapeutic task—for example, "Represent three positive things that you have accomplished during your hospitalization." The journal is often shared during the beginning of each group session, and patients frequently work on it during periods of anxiety or sleeplessness. It is noteworthy that many of our patients were abused at night in their bedrooms at home and still manifest significant sleep disturbances while in the hospital. An initial reason for the development of the journal was to maintain a continuity of therapeutic process between groups. Frequently, teenagers can depict confusing or painful experiences artistically or abstractly before they can process them verbally. As we began to teach patients to become accustomed to the discharge and mastery of conflicted feelings through the use of art, we realized the necessity of providing a therapeutic bridge between group sessions. The journal has served well as a bridge by providing the opportunity for continuing the use of a familiar therapeutic medium. The journal is also often shared with the primary or associate nurse in individual therapy sessions.

Art Therapy

The use of art therapy is a primary modality in our victimization component. Art therapy requires a knowledge of the creative process and the nature and language of symbolism—its form, content, and process. It also requires a knowledge of psychotherapy, including human development and interpersonal relationships and their underlying psychodynamics. It can be especially effective in treating sexual abuse since both sexuality and abuse tend to be difficult subjects to address. Sex is often a very private subject. As a society, we are curious about anything sexual, yet we can also be truly embarrassed when confronted with others' intimate knowledge or our personal sexuality. Abuse similarly involves a powerful and strong secrecy dynamic, which tends, in combination with the associated emotional trauma, to lend itself to denial, repression, and psychological burial. The task is to find an effective method of processing and reframing these sensitive and emotionally charged issues that may have been severely repressed and distorted.

Art therapy is ideal for this task. It is both art and therapy and represents a powerful healing process. It encompasses many dimensions to help patients get in touch with different levels of consciousness. Art is a tool used in the service of discharging, uncovering, defending, and communicating. While it is more difficult to hide unconscious feelings and conflicts in artwork, it also enables the patient to feel control over the confusion. The creator can manipulate the media to feel a sense of mastery over the unspeakable (Wadeson 1980; Naitove 1982).

A further, unrecognized use for art therapy is in the treatment of perpetrators. A frequent therapeutic component to perpetrator treatment is the monitoring of deviant fantasies. Perpetrators are usually required to report sexual fantasies in individual or group therapy sessions by reading from their logs, journals, and diaries. These methods can be highly unreliable and threatening. The use of art as an accessing and monitoring tool for fantasy work in perpetrator treatment deserves further systematic exploration. (For more discussion of the use of arts therapy in the treatment of adult sexual offenders, see Connie Naitove's chapter in volume 1 of *Vulnerable Populations.*)

Family Treatment

The patient's family is expected to attend evaluation and counseling sessions with the social worker and psychiatrist. During these sessions, the family system is evaluated, and therapeutic interventions are initiated. The interventions vary depending on the strengths and weaknesses of individual family systems and the presenting problems.

During the family evaluation, social workers elicit family histories, routinely screening parents regarding discipline styles and possible concerns of sexual abuse of their children. Occasionally parents report a suspicion or incidence of sexual abuse that the unit screening procedures failed to uncover. A typical example is a parent reporting a prior history of sexual molestation at the hands of a babysitter. This confirms the value of including routine victimization screening in procedures for obtaining family histories on adolescent inpatients.

Some of the most sensitve and difficult issues arise around the process of reporting suspected sexual abuse. Parents, relatives, siblings, or close family friends might be implicated directly or indirectly as potential perpetrators. It is our policy to work closely with local protective service agencies in dealing with these questions. We always inform the custodial parent or legal guardian of our intention and reasons for reporting. We emphasize the importance of informing the family since the physician and staff are attempting to model and foster an honest and trusting relationship with the patient and family. The patient's physical safety and protection from extreme personal or family reactions are maximized due to the structure imposed by the inpatient setting. Families frequently react negatively to the reporting process; however, with firm support and explanations of reporting requirements, they are usually able to move past their initial disbelief and anxiety. The family treatment focus then becomes one of evaluating, planning and coordinating posthospital treatment in conjunction with local protective service agencies. The foundation for long-term treatment can be laid by the expeditious and proficient handling of patient and family reactions to these painful disclosures. Due to the victimization component of our unit, our hospital is used by community professionals for conducting in-depth assessments of potentially difficult and confusing abusive family situations. This assessment process is an underutilized and valid function for adolescent psychiatric inpatient units to provide for their local communities and protective service personnel.

Staff Development

Ongoing staff supervision and training are an important and dynamic part of the adolescent program. The victimization component has its own well-attended staff development program, which takes place in the form of a lunchtime weekly journal club. A journal club is a regular inservice meeting in which the professional staff take responsibility in rotation for presenting a current journal article that deals with a relevant issue within the victimization field. This process enables the staff to become familiar with the major literature in the field and encourages a high degree of quality and professionalism in relation to patient care. It also serves as a support mechanism for the staff members who are providing victim treatment. After the journal article is presented and discussed, the patients involved in the victimization component of the program are reviewed. Frequently the previous week's artwork from individual or group therapy is presented by the art therapists. The week's treatment goals and strategies are evaluated prior to the conclusion of the meeting. This review occurs in addition to the weekly treatment planning team meetings and is an important factor in facilitating staff skill development and enthusiasm in this subspecialty area.

In this chapter we have presented our approach to the assessment and treatment of sexually abused adolescents. This approach emphasizes the use of multiple measures for assessment and interdisciplinary participation in developing treatment strategies for such abuse. Based on our experience, we believe that inpatient settings can make a significant contribution toward identifying and treating victimized adolescents and their families.

Appendix 2–1
Adolescent Sexual Concern Questionnaire

Many teenagers have concerns or questions about health, relationships, and sexuality. The purpose of this form is to identify which areas you may have questions or concerns about so we can help you with them.

I. The first is about your *health*. Please circle how often you have had *concerns* or *questions* about:

   1. Trouble sleeping
   never   almost never   sometimes   often   very often

   2. Sleeping too much
   never   almost never   sometimes   often   very often

   3. Wetting the bed
   never   almost never   sometimes   often   very often

   4. Having dreams or nightmares
   never   almost never   sometimes   often   very often

   5. Headaches or stomach aches
   never   almost never   sometimes   often   very often

II. The following is a list about *relationships* and *sex*. Please circle how often you have had *questions* or *concerns* about:

   1. Being liked by the opposite sex
   never   almost never   sometimes   often   very often

   2. How far to go with sex
   never   almost never   sometimes   often   very often

3. Someone in your family wanting to have sex with you

never   almost never   sometimes   often   very often

4. Using birth control

never   almost never   sometimes   often   very often

5. Being raped or sexually abused

never   almost never   sometimes   often   very often

6. How you look

never   almost never   sometimes   often   very often

Please circle how often you have had *questions* or *concerns* about:

7. Caring for people of your same sex

never   almost never   sometimes   often   very often

8. Getting VD or AIDS

never   almost never   sometimes   often   very often

9. Being talked into doing sexual things you didn't want to do

never   almost never   sometimes   often   very often

10. Having sexual feelings that others think aren't right

never   almost never   sometimes   often   very often

11. Getting an abortion

never   almost never   sometimes   often   very often

12. Showing affection to people of your same sex

never   almost never   sometimes   often   very often

III. The following is a list of *thoughts* and *feelings*. Please circle how often you have had *questions* or *concerns* about the following:

1. Being scared of getting hurt or killed

never   almost never   sometimes   often   very often

2. Getting hurt or beaten up by someone in your family

never   almost never   sometimes   often   very often

3. Feeling upset about sexual things you have done

never   almost never   sometimes   often   very often

4. Feeling upset about sexual things that have happened to you

never   almost never   sometimes   often   very often

5. Running away

never   almost never   sometimes   often   very often

6. Being afraid of the opposite sex

never   almost never   sometimes   often   very often

Please circle how often you have had *questions* or *concerns* about:

7. Having a terrible secret

| never | almost never | sometimes | often | very often |

8. Being different

| never | almost never | sometimes | often | very often |

9. Feeling unloved or uncared about

| never | almost never | sometimes | often | very often |

10. Having difficulty controlling sexual feelings

| never | almost never | sometimes | often | very often |

11. Being touched in a private part of your body against your wishes

| never | almost never | sometimes | often | very often |

12. Using sex to gain affection

| never | almost never | sometimes | often | very often |

References

Alter-Reid, K.; Gibbs, M.S.; Lachenmeyer, J.R.; Siegal, J.; and Massoth, N.A. 1986. "Sexual Abuse of Children: A Review of the Empirical Findings." *Clinical Psychology Review* 6:249–266.

Emslie, G.J., and Rosenfeld, A. 1983. "Incest Reported by Children and Adolescents Hospitalized for Severe Psychiatric Problems." *American Journal of Psychiatry* 140:708–711.

Husain, A., and Chapel, J.L. 1983. "History of Incest in Girls Admitted to a Psychiatric Hospital." *American Journal of Psychiatry* 140:591–593.

Jacobson, A., and Richardson, B. 1987. "Assault Experiences of 100 Psychiatric Inpatients: Evidence of the Need for Routine Inquiry." *American Journal of Psychiatry* 144:908–913.

Jessor, R.; Chase, J.A.; and Donovan, J.E. 1980. "Psychosocial Correlates of Marijuana Use and Problem Drinking in a National Sample of Adolescents." *American Journal of Public Health* 70:604–661.

Los Angeles Times. 1985. "Children's Abuse Report" August 26.

Naitove, C. 1982. "Arts Therapy with Sexually Abused Children." In S. Sgroi, ed., *Handbook of Clinical Intervention in Child Sexual Abuse.* Lexington Mass.: Lexington Books.

Newcomb, M.D., and Bentler, P.M. 1986. "Cocaine Use among Adolescents: Longitudinal Associations with Social Context, Psychopathology, and Use of Other Substances." *Addictive Behaviors* 11:263–273.

Rieker, P.P., and Carmen, E. Hiberman 1986. "The Victim-to-Patient Process: The Disconfirmation and Transformation of Abuse." *American Journal of Orthopsychiatry* 56:360–370.

Schaefer, C. 1988. *Innovative Interventions in Child and Adolescent Therapy.* New York: John Wiley and Sons.

Singer, M.; Petchers, M.; and Hussey, D.L. In press. "Drug and Alcohol Use Patterns among Sexually Abused Adolescent Psychiatric In-Patients." *International Journal of Child Abuse and Neglect.*

Steinhauer, P.D., and Grant, Q. Rae. 1983. *Psychological Problems of the Child in the Family.* 2d ed. New York: Basic Books.

Wadeson, H. 1980. *Art Psychotherapy.* New York: John Wiley and Sons.

Walker, C.E.; Bonner, B.L.; and Kaufman, K.L. 1988. *The Physically and Sexually Abused Child: Evaluation and Treatment.* New York: Pergamon Press.

3
Time-limited Group Therapy for Female Adolescent Victims of Child Sexual Abuse

Kerry Christensen Homstead
Lynn Werthamer

Involving sexually abused adolescent girls in group therapy is often a difficult task, demanding sensitivity to the particular developmental and psychological needs and abilities of adolescent victims. One approach to this form of treatment, the Adolescent Sexual Abuse Treatment (ASAT) program described here, has been successfully utilized in Northampton, Massachusetts, for several years by two community-based agencies serving this population.

The group therapy approach examined in this chapter, as well as the treatment context for this approach, have not been highlighted previously in the literature. While supportive of group treatment for adolescent victims, the literature has presented little in the way of models to inform practitioners working on sexual abuse treatment, particularly those working in a group context. Often these practitioners work in less than ideal circumstances without any team or coordinated system of treatment for support.

Among the advantages of group therapy cited in the literature are those outlined by Knittle and Tauna (1980). These advantages include the "special response of group therapy" to adolescent victims that enables individual members to make "therapeutic gains at a tolerable pace" (pp. 237, 239). In group therapy, "physical contact and emotional support are not threatening" as compared to the pressures of individual therapy (p. 239). Similarly, for adolescent victims who feel isolated and alienated from peers, group therapy is "reassuring and diminishes these feelings of isolation" (p. 237). Being in a group with other victims "facilitates the building of trust and self-disclosure, which leads to the exploration and expression of feelings" (p. 238). Further, group therapy provides adolescents with an opportunity to "express feelings for others that they cannot express regarding their own situations" (p. 238).

Recognizing these advantages of group therapy, we implemented the ASAT group to serve adolescent clients who presented for treatment with disparate histories of disclosure, investigation, and treatment. Unlike many well-established programs that funnel clients into treatment immediately or soon after disclosure, few of the clients referred to the ASAT group had received any services following disclosure and/or had little or no experience with any form of sexual abuse treatment. The ASAT group was developed in isolation from other treatment programs because of the lack of coordinated sexual abuse treatment services in the community.

We continue to implement an approach that involves a twenty-week group cycle time frame, followed by an "intersession" of four to six weeks. Group therapy takes place on a 90-minute session per week basis for twenty consecutive weeks. Group membership is usually closed after the third meeting, and the average group size has been seven members ranging in age from 13 to 18 years old. After the twenty-week cycle is completed, the intersession offers an opportunity for recruiting and screening new group referrals, while the previous group members take a break. Following the break, another twenty-week cycle begins, and both new and old clients form another treatment group. An important feature of this approach is that group members are encouraged and usually choose to participate in more than one treatment cycle.

The format used is developed for each group of adolescent girls and is based on several principles and guidelines integral to our approach to sexual abuse treatment. We believe that safety must be enforced and maintained, if not highlighted, by the group facilitators. Since lack of safety has been, and in some cases continues to be, such a strong issue for most victims, safety in the therapeutic setting becomes paramount. We enforce safety at the beginning of the group cycle by presenting a contract that stresses four points: confidentiality, respect and support of others, freedom regarding participation ("You don't have to talk if you don't want to") and promptness ("Come on time!"). During the early weeks of the group, we post the contract and spend time referring to and talking about safety both within the context and process of the group and in reference to outside events raised by the girls. For example, a discussion about the early darkness in the fall season brought up in the beginning stages of a cycle might present an opportunity to acknowledge group members' fears as expressed metaphorically in issues of light and dark and day and night.

Our approach to therapy incorporates a variety of ways to make talking "safe." In very defended groups, we have found that maintaining a sense of safety requires creative and flexible therapeutic approaches. One approach is through the use of journal sheets to introduce topics and allow clients to reflect on them. Having a journal sheet to look at reduces the threat of intimacy and frees clients to respond to issues related to abuse without feeling overly pressured. One client may crumple up her journal sheet and toss it in the wastebasket at the end of group time; others may leave the journal blank, color over questions, or write one- or two-word replies to questions. This approach permits each girl to address the topic at her own pace within the group setting.

Providing a consistent weekly group format also strengthens a sense of safety for clients, who are easily overwhelmed by the unpredictable. We usually begin sessions with business agendas (announcements and news items), proceed to the weekly journal sheet, and follow with a discussion. As the girls become more secure, group discussions take more of the time, and the group format becomes more relaxed and substantive.

Another emphasis in our groups is education. Outside of their own experience, adolescent victims have little factual information about sexual abuse. Education helps to break down myths and misinformation and also increases awareness of the healing and therapeutic process in a way that will help them anticipate and cope with their experience in therapy, as well as counter some of their ideas about group process. It may surprise clients to learn, for example, that it is natural to have some ambivalent feelings about the sexual abuse experience and/or the abuser. Such insight may allow clients to address feelings they might otherwise hide and increasingly feel guilty about. Similarly, education within the group helps adolescents to develop a vocabulary for talking about their emotions and history.

Our therapeutic approach also emphasizes modeling. We think that by cofacilitating the group, we give adolescents an opportunity to see two adults interacting positively, discussing material appropriately, and maintaining boundaries. In addition, cofacilitating establishes a mutual support system for the therapists, which is helpful as they respond to and process material that can be overwhelming. Cofacilitating is particularly helpful in treatment settings where sexual abuse work is conducted in relative isolation from other programs. In addition, since our format involves using therapists from two separate agencies, we have found that a broader sense of mutual collaboration and networking has been promoted on the level of interagency adolescent services.

A final guiding principle that dominates our approach is a willingness to allow clients to control their own treatment process. This does not imply that we give up our role as group leaders in any way; rather, it underscores that our responsibility is to respect each client's need to approach difficult material appropriately. Premature disclosure, for example, can exacerbate a client's sense of isolation and dissociative tendencies and thereby thwart the therapeutic goal of the client's cognitive and emotional integration of the traumatic experience. Thus, we encourage clients to talk in the group while we provide adequate safety and monitor the disclosure of difficult material. This ensures that clients are not simply trying to please facilitators but are truly able to handle disclosure. We recognize the need to encourage clients to pace themselves carefully and thus decrease opportunities for them to reengage or replay aspects of their victimization through such behaviors as pleasing others and dissociating from their trauma. We also provide means through which clients can express themselves when verbal expression is clearly overwhelming. For example, shifting gears into an art project (figure 3–1) often allows clients to feel in control while processing difficult material and externalizing feelings that they cannot yet articulate.

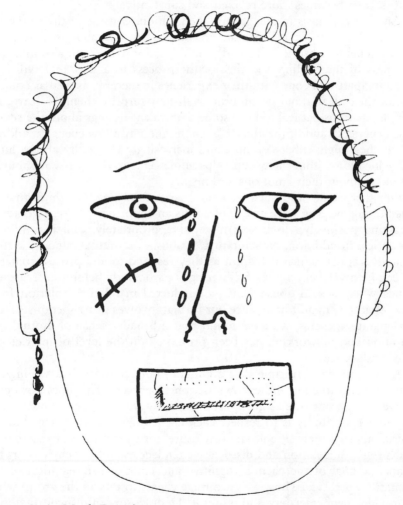

Figure 3–1. Mask Drawing
Reconstruction of a group art project in which group members worked together to create a mask. The mouth was made with a wooden toy block covered with heavy tape.

Client Background

This model of group therapy has worked well for our adolescent population. The sample of these clients is documented in table 3–1, which reflects client involvement in six group cycles and provides the data base for this chapter. The majority of clients participated in more than one ASAT group cycle. These clients reflect the varied abuse-disclosure-treatment histories typical of the adolescent victim populations that emerge in settings where few appropriate or coordinated treatment options exist. This population presents a diversity of psychodynamic issues based on their varied histories and current life realities. Two particular group members illustrate this diversity well and describe the client extremes served by the ASAT group.

> Carla was referred for group therapy at the same time she was referred into a foster care program. The initial intake with her for the group was conducted in an inpatient setting where for the second time, Carla disclosed sexual abuse and, finally, was believed.
>
> During her subsequent involvement in group therapy, Carla's life was in an almost constant state of flux. While she was able to stabilize temporarily in a foster home with constant intervention, a series of "anniversary dates" sparked a suicide attempt. This attempt resulted in another inpatient placement, a DWI (driving while intoxicated) spree, and subsequent referral to the state hospital. The hospitalization dragged on because the social service system to which Carla had been remanded for custody could neither find nor fund appropriate services for her. Carla finally left the state hospital and at age 18 chose to live on her own in the community. Throughout this sequence of events, she remained in the ASAT group.
>
> Carla's turmoil, a hallmark of many adolescent victims of sexual abuse, indicated that she was not only at risk but also desperately in need of treatment that would help to reduce her isolation, self-destructiveness, and burden of guilt. These traumas were amplified by Carla's abandonment and blame by her family and also by Carla's further victimization by the legal and social services systems.
>
> Carla's initial relationship with the group was one of painful participation. She was typically fidgety and often played with her cigarette lighter. She said little, but chose to relate to others by passing out chewing gum, thereby taking care of others, a role at which she was adept. Carla was quite bright and had easily attained her graduate equivalency degree, but her self-esteem was very low and her ability to care for herself was minimal.
>
> Sandy presented different needs and abilities. She had a relatively stable current living situation with her natural father and sister and

Table 3–1
Summary of Client Involvement in Six ASAT Group Cycles

Client	Age(s) Abuse Took Place	Perpetrator	Reported to Police	Substantiated	Prosecuted	Prosecuted While in Group
				Legal Status of Perpetrator		
Holly	9–12	stepfather	yes	yes	yes	
Darlene	12–14	stepfather	yes	yes	yes	
Betty	12 (other incidents when younger)	uncle, stepfather	no			
Valerie	12–14	brother	yes	yes	no	
Tara	10–13	stepfather	yes	yes	yes	
Jamie	7–15	father	no			
Carla	3–15	adoptive brother	yes	yes		yes
Denise	10–13	brother	yes	no	no	
Sandy	11–13	stepfather	yes	yes	yes	
Lynn	4–12	father	yes	yes	no	
Sarah	8–11	uncle	yes	yes	no	
Mary	12	father	yes	yes	no	
Robin	4–6	stepfather	no			
Paula	9–10	stepfather	yes	yes		yes
Ann	12–14	stepfather	yes	no	no	
Alison	16–17	brother	no	no	no	

thus did not suffer from a sense of total family rejection. She also had a comparatively good treatment history, which involved parental support and a timely and sensitive prosecution of her stepfather-abuser.

From the beginning of her relationship with the ASAT group, Sandy was able to articulate more than most other clients regarding her experience with sexual abuse. She took advantage of the group therapy and resolved many of the conflicts she faced with relative ease. Because survival was not a major issue for her, she was freer to explore the impact of sexual abuse in her life. Being younger than Carla, still in school, and involved with activities such as church group, Sandy had a structure to her life that minimized her daily stress and provided her with guidelines to follow on a regular basis that reinforced different aspects of her identity and emphasized, positively, different aspects of her life.

Other Therapy: I (Individual), F (Family)	Age Entered Group	Age Left Group	Group Cycles Attended
I	15	16	1,2,3
I	16	17	1,2
I	13	16	1,2,3,4,5
I, F	15	18	1,2,3,4,5,6
I, F	15	16	1,2,3
I	18	20	4,5
I	16	18	4,5,6
I	18	18	6
I	13	14	4,5
I	18	18	6
I	14	14	6
F	14	14	6
I	14	16	4,5,6
I	13	15	5,6
I	13	13	3
I	19	19	3

Carla and Sandy are typical of the range of adolescent victims who have participated in the ASAT groups and represent many of the challenges that adolescent victims of sexual abuse present in a treatment setting. The success with which the ASAT group structure enables clinicians to respond to and manage these different traumas can be examined from several points of view based on our experiences over the course of seven group cycles.

Benefits of the Model

The approach used has the important advantage of being practical. This is an asset in a small community-based agency where sexual abuse treatment funds and services are limited. The twenty-week treatment cycle followed by a break offers an effective mechanism for cycling in new group members without disrupting an ongoing group. Similarly, members who choose to discontinue group therapy have a clear and natural exit time provided by the time-limited format. The group cycle approach also gives clients regular opportunities to recommit themselves by opting to continue in new ASAT cycles. This seems to strengthen clients' buying into their treatment plans and personal development.

The twenty-week cycle is a good mechanism for presenting sexual abuse content to adolescents. The time-limited cycle offers enough time to conduct intensive group work and has built-in opportunities to reintroduce concepts and allow clients to progress in a variety of ways. For example, a client participating in her first treatment cycle may begin to hear new ideas about guilt and self-blame relating to sexual abuse. Having been introduced to this basic step, she can continue to develop her ability to integrate and explore these new ideas. And as she participates in successive cycles, she is able to expand her understanding of treatment content that was initially new and threatening.

For adolescent victims of sexual abuse, making therapeutic gains regarding sexual abuse trauma such as guilt, involves many steps. Although the group setting is the most appropriate setting for such clients, it must be structured carefully to accommodate both the process of treatment and the needs of individual clients. Our experience has indicated that introducing adolescents to basic concepts such as "It's not your fault" is a long-term process and cannot be accomplished in one treatment cycle. Many clients need to start by learning that they can survive the treatment process and that they will not be overwhelmed. Then they can begin to engage, listen, and gradually realize that their right to be guilt free does not equate with betraying their families. A client may begin to allow herself to think, "It's not my fault!" at which time she can begin internalizing this idea. Our treatment format helps to modulate the therapeutic material that clients are exposed to and is most beneficial.

Another advantage to the twenty-week cycle is that it limits the exposure for each participant to the stress related to the lives of other members. In groups where the flux in clients' lives is particularly great and outside support systems are often inadequate or unpredictable, members could be overwhelmed or paralyzed by events such as suicide attempts, rapes, and endless court proceedings. Time-frame boundaries for group therapy help to prevent this and makes survival more realistic for the members. Each participant's self-esteem is enhanced by the group's ability to assist other members in dealing with their crises. Members feel important to each other. Understanding someone else's issues helps each girl to clarify her own problems and aids individual growth and progress.

Another practical benefit of the time-limited cycle is that it offers the group leaders time to take a break and evaluate the clients' progress. This can be especially important in treatment settings where there is no built-in support or adequate supervision system for staff members working on sexual abuse cases.

A final advantage of time-limited sequential group cycles is that this modality effectively addresses the particular treatment needs of adolescent victims. As noted in the literature, adolescent victims may find it "impossible to maintain a sense of self-esteem," and it appears that "the impact of abuse is most serious during the girls' adolescence" (Lubell and Soong 1982, 311). Many clients feel guilty and responsible for having had sexual contact with family members and have learned to protect their families by keeping details obscured or secret. Concurrently many have learned to hate themselves, fear intimate relationships, and please others at their own expense or to their own detriment. Adolescent victims are often masters at repressing feelings that can be deeply threatening and overwhelming for them to recognize, and related events such as repeated somatic complaints can seem like a mystery to them. Given these and other potential treatment needs, Carozza and Hiersteiner have noted that

> the challenge in working with incest victims is to provide treatment which paradoxically offers protection while encouraging expression and insight. Patterns of resistance, isolation, secrecy, denial and repression are to be expected among children growing up in incestuous families. When these children are offered treatment . . . which respects their need for protection, they are likely to respond positively. (1983, 172)

We have found that the time-limited aspect of the ASAT group cycle effectively creates a sense of safety for clients without compromising their ability to discuss relationships and significant treatment issues that would be more difficult to address in a shorter group therapy cycle.

Because the ending of the group cycle is defined, clients can develop relationships with each other and safely explore intimacy without feeling pressured by the potentially threatening and undefined relationships that a more open-ended treatment format could foster. Twenty weeks seems to provide adolescent group members with important practice in establishing appropriate relationships with peers within the safety of the carefully defined beginning and ending of the cycle. Given a foreseeable end to the group cycle, clients who cannot tolerate or negotiate positive, appropriate relationships are given a boundary. This helps them feel safe enough to risk developing new social skills as they establish and test relationships with group members and group leaders. Similarly, the twenty-week cycle provides clients with an important sharing limit, which helps them to pace the sharing of difficult material without overly exposing themselves. Adolescent victims need to have opportunities to learn how to talk about their sexual abuse experiences without devastating the well-developed internal defenses they have come to rely upon for survival. In the time-limited cycle, clients can safely moderate how much material they share as they make progress in discussing painful and previously unverbalized material. Also, the cycle seems to maintain an effective balance between encouraging clients to gain control over their lives and to participate in treatment. Because of the regular breaks, clients cannot become overly dependent on the group. Instead, they are encouraged to exercise what they have learned by trying out new skills in their lives outside the group.

For adolescents who have experienced betrayal by trusted adults, the enforcement of clear boundaries and safety in the treatment setting is vital. The series of controls and safety valves or boundaries offered in the ASAT group cycle seems to enable adolescents to develop trust and regain their sense of control and pride, thus reversing some of their confusion and fear.

Our observations in the course of conducting multiple cycles of time-limited groups have indicated that most adolescent clients need a great deal of time to make progress, particularly in changing aspects of their negative self-image. A deep-seated sense of guilt, for example, is often intricately tied up with the adolescent victim's self-image. Current realities in their lives, such as abandonment by their families and failure to stabilize or succeed in school, fuel guilt and aggravate the unresolved feelings clients have toward their families and abusers. The result is that they feel a sense of familiarity and stability about their negative self-images that they are not eager to abandon for healthier alternatives. The process of developing a new, positive identity is charged and threatening and should not be rushed by helping professionals who are eager to convince victims that "it is not their fault."

As demonstrated by many of the clients we have worked with in group therapy, an adolescent victim's negative self-concept is often the strongest and best-established aspect of her identity; similarly, it is often the only lifeline to her family. Until she has established a firm new foundation on which to establish a new identity and new lifelines, she must rely on the old and familiar. We have found that the pace of therapeutic growth that is possible in the ASAT group cycles has accommodated many individual adolescent clients during conflicted events in their lives without jeopardizing treatment goals. In sum, the ASAT group cycle seems to have provided the kind of therapeutic intervention appropriate for many adolescent victims of sexual abuse.

Stages of Group Development

The stages of group development in different cycles inevitably vary in accordance with the individual clients. In the course of conducting several cycles, however, we have observed general trends in group development associated with this form of therapy and have constructed a framework for understanding the development of an ASAT group.

A major trend in the evolution of the ASAT group is the prominence of the early stages of group development, indicative of the impact of presenting sexual abuse trauma. This trend is most notable and clearly presented in a beginning group composed of new clients who, as is typical in our caseload, have had little, if any, experience in therapy.

Prior to the ASAT group therapy, these adolescents are significantly handicapped by sexual abuse trauma and related developmental characteristics, including a lack of trust in self and others, social isolation, low self-esteem, a lack of vocabulary necessary to express their history or emotions, and a tremendous ambivalence associated with discussion of their abuse and participation in therapy. These factors handicap individual clients and group evolution and also restrict initial therapeutic goals. Previously used adaptive behaviors and attitudes, such as lack of trust, interfere with early stages of group development by impeding the rate at which basic trust and group information occur; consequently, the time in which a group remains in a beginning state of development is prolonged.

We have seen that this early stage pattern continues until group members have made sufficient progress on basic therapeutic goals to enable group evolution. It is not unusual for a new group of clients to spend a full twenty-week cycle in a beginning stage of development during which they constantly struggle with fundamental aspects of their trauma, unable to evolve into a middle stage of group development. While facilitating this less evolved group is highly frustrating at times, it is clear that clients are taking part in necessary therapeutic work that will serve as a foundation for future progress in therapy.

Recognizing the need for a frame of reference with which to understand group development in work with adolescent victims, we have found it helpful to plot the beginning stage of these groups as indicated in table 3–2. This framework applies to both less and more evolved groups with the less evolved groups devoting most, if not all, of their attention to beginning concerns. In groups that can tolerate greater change, we have identified a transition phase into a middle, more intimate, stage of group development. This occurs when a sufficient number of clients have gained the skills and perspective necessary to refocus their involvement in the group beyond elementary survival issues. When group composition consists of clients who have had experience in previous groups and new clients, we have found that group movement is much more fluid as experienced members help to accelerate the pace of group development. We view the transition phase as indicated in table 3–3.

Following the transition phase, more evolved groups enter into a middle stage that is often relatively short and emotionally charged. This phase re-

Table 3–2
Beginning Stage Framework

Therapy Goals	Client Agendas	Typical Remarks	Group Characteristics	Characteristics of Stage
To address present trauma	To survive the group	"Nothing bothers me"	Minimal ability to process material	Tends to dominate, if not monopolize, new groups, is fundamental to further progress, can be very frustrating to facilitate
To provide a safe therapeutic experience	To test others for acceptance	"I just want to go on with my life and forget about it"	Denial	
	To begin to trust (tentatively)		Defensiveness	
To provide an appropriate Peer setting		"I almost didn't come today"	Little self-reflection	
	To begin to engage in the group: superficial bonding		Reliance on old coping skills	
To support "retooling," softening negative adaptive skills	To defend		Resistant to change	
	To learn		Frequent regressed behavior	
To introduce vocabulary and information about sexual abuse and the healing process			Blaming the victim	

Table 3–3
Transitional Stage Framework

Therapy Goals	Client Agendas	Typical Remarks	Group Characteristics	Characteristics of Stage
To prepare clients for talking about aspects of sexual abuse histories	To attain sufficient trust in others	"I suppose you want us to talk"	Sense of group emerges	Usually short, change oriented
	To be convinced to talk	"It's depressing in here"	Feeling tone emerges, first as depression	
To achieve sufficient cohesion	To get ready to take a risk	"Men are jerks"		
	To prepare for intimacy		Surfacing of group anger toward perpetrators, often disguised and misplaced	

flects the intensity generated when clients concentrate on their abuse experiences and share painful material. The group intimacy that is a hallmark of middle stages in groups particularly affects adolescent victims, who are greatly confused regarding intimacy.

Boundaries of the middle stage are striking in their clarity, especially given the boundary confusion typical among sexual abuse victims. Adolescents are well able to state their limits regarding the amount and extent to which they can focus on their abuse histories in any one group. When talking has gone far enough, group members end the middle stage rather abruptly, often by behavioral changes signaling that they have generated sufficient material and need to modulate their sharing. The process of talking about their abuse experiences is difficult for adolescents. The degree of sharing is relative to each member's individual developmental abilities and the group experience. It is complicated by family dynamics of secret keeping, denial, and punishment. This difficulty is well illustrated by the mask presented in figure 3–1 and deserves respect and attention during the middle stage, as summarized in table 3–4.

The ending stage in more evolved groups evinces a retreat from talking and preparation for termination. Often we have noted that the intense atmosphere of the middle stage evaporates, and early behaviors such as laughing and acting out reappear. Activities promoting reflection on accomplishments made in the group help to solidify gains clients have made and help to define future needs, including whether clients will participate in future group cycles and/or leave open the option of further involvement. This stage is outlined in table 3–5.

In addition to having a framework for stages of group development, we have found it helpful to compare and contrast less and more evolved groups. This has given us a sense of the influence that different mixes of clients have on the group development framework. It also allows us to track each groups' evolution. Figure 3–2 charts less and more evolved group patterns and points out themes that tend to emerge. It is important to note here that we do not usually see the issue of control dominating group stages as mentioned in the

Table 3–4
Middle Stage Framework

Therapy Goals	Client Agendas	Typical Remarks	Group Characteristics	Characteristics of Stage
To gain some control over traumatic material through disclosure To respect clients' limits	To share some history To survive "talking" To listen to each other To connect feelings with events	"I can't believe you said that—I felt that way too" "That must have been so hard for you" "I never had a childhood" "I hate my mother"	Emotionally charged, serious Bonding around similar experiences Appreciation for sharing Expressing vulnerability and emotions More integrated Empathic responses	Relatively short, clear ending; clients are in greatest control of therapeutic process

Table 3–5
Ending Stage

Therapy Goals	Client Agendas	Typical Remarks	Group Characteristics	Characteristics of Stage
To gain closure on group experience	To retreat from talking	"I wish I had said more"	Some regression in behavior	Somewhat businesslike
To promote evaluation of group experience	To verify that "I survived the group intimacy"	"When does the next group start?"	Less confusion, greater clarity	
To affirm mastery of difficult material	To say goodbye	"I never thought I could say that"	Sense of relief and accomplishment	
	To give up control of the group	"I'm ready for a break"	Sense of loss of ending	
To fashion a positive ending	To state my regrets			
To focus on present issues and "survivorship"	To focus on the present			

literature on traditional group development. We believe this to be true because of the overriding tendency of these clients to be caretakers. Thus, their ways of storming group leaders, for example, will not typically present in overt or disruptive fashions.

The mix of clients in any one group affects how a group ultimately evolves in treatment. As clients repeat the group therapy experience, they are successively able to master new and deeper material, and thus a pattern of individual evolution affecting the degree of group evolution is clear. Nevertheless, this is a long-term process for adolescents, particularly victims who have received less than ideal treatment following disclosure.

Following clients through a series of group cycles will illustrate the treatment impact this model provides. The cases below represent different responses to group participation in an ASAT group.

Valerie had been involved with the group from its inception. When we met her, she had recently been removed from her home and placed in foster care with one of the ASAT group sponsoring agencies. Both Valerie's foster care worker and individual therapist encouraged her ASAT group membership. Although fearful, Valerie expressed an interest in joining the group. A long-standing history of secrecy surrounded her abuse, and she was reluctant to abandon her well-constructed survival and coping skills. The full extent of her sexual abuse history was suspected but unclear.

Valerie agreed to try the group and attended the initial meeting, demonstrating closed body language; she spoke only to give her

Stages	Less Evolved	More Evolved
Beginning	• Superficial, fragmented bonding, making connections • Establishing position in the group • Insecure, regressed, acting out to relieve stress • Highly defended posture, resistant to change • "Can I tolerate the group?" • "Will I be safe here?"	• Preliminary acting out, often humorous • Joining, development of group feeling • Anticipating intimacy, talking • Group depression, tuning into real feelings • "This is going to be a heavy group"
Middle	• No specific intimate stage • Sporadic disclosure of details, low affect • General avoidance of painful feelings • Fear of talking, lack of vocabulary, immature coping skills • Feeling of friendship among members • Parentified behavior, defense of mothers	• Lowering of defenses, entry into intimate stage • Mourning, accessing anger, especially toward mothers • Disclosure of details • Group takes control • Support among group members • Affect more integrated
End	• Projected regrets: "You didn't let us talk about it" • "I didn't get anything out of this group, except friends forever" • Shallow "going through" motions	• Retreat from intimacy, return to humor, giving up control • Internalized regrets; "I wish I had done more" • "I'll miss the group"

(Twenty-Week Cycle)

Figure 3–2. Comparative Group Evolution in ASAT Groups

name. She did not return to any subsequent meetings, although she often visited other staff in the agency during the time the group met. She exhibited extreme ambivalence, and her approach-avoidance behavior indicated both her wish to be part of the group and her inability to engage in it. During this time, her individual therapist and her foster care worker spent time with Valerie helping her to get ready for a group experience.

Valerie sporadically attended the second group cycle. When the emotional content became difficult, she left the room. Although her attendance gradually improved, Valerie continued to engage in this avoidance behavior until the fifth cycle. She said very little in group sessions during the second cycle; however, she began to develop relationships with other group members that enabled her to feel more comfortable with them.

During the third group cycle, Valerie's attendance improved greatly. She began to display a heightened sense of self. Her body language was more open, and she carried herself with greater confidence. In addition, she maintained a job and was able to make the transition from a foster placement into an apartment with friends. Her growth in individual treatment paralleled these changes as well. Clearly Valerie no longer thought of herself as a new member and was able to use her status as an old member to help new members assimilate and feel comfortable in the group. She began to refer to "our" group and showed other signs of her increasing sense of belonging to and ownership of the group.

During the fourth, fifth, and sixth group cycles, Valerie began to share intimate feelings and slowly relaxed her well-constructed and formerly necessary defenses. The emphasis on the group as a safe place was certainly important to Valerie's progress in group therapy. Valerie became a strong role model to other members by expressing fears and sharing feelings in the group. She openly talked about her developing participation in the group and gave hope to new members who were in earlier stages of the healing and group approach process. She told them how difficult it was initially for her to express her feelings and that it became easier with time. She was able to participate in the group process and struggled with staying in the group when interactions with other members became difficult for her.

In later cycles, Valerie was a significant force behind the increased speed at which group trust and intimacy evolved. In individual therapy, Valerie's growth was reflected in her decision to enter an alcohol treatment program as she admitted her drinking problem and decided to work on it.

Valerie's experience illustrates the need for the availability of long-term treatment for sexually abused adolescents whose impaired trust and self-esteem can often paralyze the therapeutic process. What might have occurred for other group members in the working, or intimacy stage, of one group cycle's development took eighteen months and two completed group cycles to emerge for Valerie. Her first group cycle was virtually monopolized by the process of getting ready for a group experience. This can be seen as an extended engagement process and underscores the need for adolescents with a sexual abuse history to have control over the pace at which they choose to trust and to engage in the treatment process.

Our observations have indicated that once a client engages in a group, there is usually a rapid growth period in terms of her own developmental process. This growth often is mirrored in the other forms of therapy in which the client may participate.

Betty was referred to the ASAT group after she disclosed childhood sexual abuse, a disclosure that occurred in a short-term emergency shelter placement following an incident of running away from home. Like Valerie, Betty was involved with the group from its first cycle. Her relationship with the group through five cycles provides further perspective on the treatment approach we have employed, as well as further emphasis on the need for long-term treatment for victims of sexual abuse during their adolescent years.

Betty's history of sexual abuse was cloudy, and she had not received any therapy except some recent individual counseling and advocacy. While extremely likable, Betty was very well defended and unpredictable, and it was difficult to engage her in individual therapy.

In her first ASAT group cycle, Betty's behavior was annoying and disruptive, and her appropriateness for the group was often questioned in consultation sessions. However, her dedication to the group and her bond with other members convinced us to give her the option of entering a second cycle. Gradually Betty's behavior became less disruptive as she softened some of her defenses and tentatively engaged in the work of the group. In the second cycle, she revealed material about her history that she had never previously talked about. Betty also began to share some of her perceptions regarding other group members' behaviors and comments.

By her third cycle, Betty was able to articulate the purpose of the group to others and helped to pave the way for discussions concerning loss of childhood and abandonment by parents. Her awareness demonstrated that she had internalized many of the concepts and ideas presented in the previous cycles. In the fourth and fifth cycles, Betty was clearly a leader, and the group was central to her individual growth and development.

Events in Betty's life outside the group continued to reflect her inability to trust or to develop long-standing intimate relationships. She had multiple foster home placements and crises and was adept at finding caring individuals who would rescue her, only to abandon her later. Betty was able to maintain a long-term relationship with her individual therapist, but events in her life never provided the stability necessary for her to advance beyond basic issues of trust and consistency in her therapy, as well as in her life.

In contrast, the ASAT group was a safe place for Betty. With her peers, she was free from the stigmas that adult relationships necessarily involved for her. The group was Betty's substitute family and the one consistent aspect of her life. She regularly shared her problems with the group, telling members of her frustration with foster homes and her wish to live on her own. These problems represented her struggle with the adolescent tasks of separation from family and the development of an independent identity. During her fifth and final group cycle, Betty showed some sense of resolution regarding these issues. She had become pregnant—"My first nonabusive relationship"—and was preparing to live on her own in an apartment.

While these resolutions may not have been ideal, they represent invaluable developmental gains for a client like Betty who, was able to piece together many aspects of her fragmented life and address some maturational conflicts. Given Betty's lack of previous treatment and her unstable life, the ASAT group seems to have been the ideal forum for her growth, combining opportunities for her to progress at her own pace, practice new skills and knowledge, and maintain relationships within the negotiable boundaries of the twenty-week cycle.

Betty and Valerie still have many unresolved traumas associated with their sexual abuse histories, but they have been able to graduate from the ASAT group and tackle other aspects of their lives with heightened sense of self-esteem, They developed a set of skills that helped them negotiate problems in their lives and continue their transition from victim to survivor. Once able to engage in and commit to the ASAT group, these clients allowed an important therapeutic intervention to occur in their lives and began to address some of the ongoing sexual victimization issues affecting them. For clients such as Betty and Valerie, whose experience with sexual abuse treatment was minimal and whose negative defenses were well established, the ASAT group offered an apparently effective treatment model.

For clients who represent other segments of the adolescent sexual abuse victim population, the ASAT group also appears to have worked effectively.

Sandy enjoyed a greater support system at home and thus could engage in the group without many of the internal and external stressors experienced by others in the group. The ASAT group gave Sandy a place to talk freely about her stepfather-abuser and mourn how much she missed her mother. Other group members often commended her for her ability to talk about difficult material "at such an early age" (13 years old).

As early as her first group cycle, Sandy expressed some raw emotion concerning her mother and stepfather and presented some of the details concerning her sexual abuse history, the prosecution of her stepfather, and subsequent events in her family. Sandy used her second group cycle to resolve her feelings toward her mother and stepfather and presented a more complete picture of her experience with sexual abuse. She gained a greater understanding of her stepfather and also gained confirmation from the group for her present safety in living with her father. Having gained these perspectives and having shared family secrets that burdened her, Sandy was ready to end her involvement with the ASAT group. In two cycles, she was comfortably able to accomplish what other group members took several cycles to accomplish only partially.

These client experiences describe a varied pattern of involvement in sexual abuse treatment typical of the adolescent population. Many factors influence this pattern, such as the support for being in the group that Valerie had from her individual therapist. For other clients such as Mary or Lynn, the ability to stay in treatment may be complicated by parental interference. For clients such as Carla, group treatment will be affected by events in their lives outside the group. And participation by still other clients will be dominated by the confusion of adolescent developmental tasks or the pressure of events such as testifying in court. Given this portrait of adolescent victims, treatment modalities must be available to accommodate their needs without compromising treatment goals. This is critical in settings where the population that presents for sexual abuse treatment tends to be particularly diverse.

The treatment approach offered in the ASAT group seems to be especially well suited for such a diverse population. It offers the important option of long-term treatment, so critical for many adolescents, combined with a structure that emphasizes safety, boundaries, and completion while leaving ample room for a client to progress at her own pace. The break between group cycles gives adolescents an opportunity to exercise and internalize what they have learned. In addition, clients must regularly recommit themselves to each new group, where they can continue to reverse many of the negative effects of sexual abuse in their lives. For adolescent victims of sexual abuse, whose lives are often very stressful, the ASAT group seems to have enabled them to approach what might have otherwise been overwhelming.

References

Carozza, Phylis M., and Heirsteiner, Catherine L. 1983. "Young Female Incest Victims in Treatment: Stages of Growth Seen with a Group Art Therapy Model." *Clinical Social Work Journal* 10:165–175.

Knittle, Beverly J., and Tuana, Susan J. 1980. "Group Therapy as Primary Treatment for Adolescent Victims of Intrafamilial Sexual Abuse." *Clinical Social Work Journal* 8:234–242.

Lubell, Derryl, and Soong, Mei-tsueu 1982. "Group Therapy with Sexually Abused Adolescents." *Canadian Journal of Psychiatry* 27:311–315.

4
Sexual Abuse of Boys by Males: Theoretical and Treatment Implications

Francis J. Pescosolido

C urrent epidemiological studies indicate that boys are at greater risk
for sexual molestation than previously considered (Finkelhor 1979,
1984; Ellerstein and Canavan 1980; DeJong, Emmet, and Hervada
1982; Spencer and Dunklee 1986; Reinhart 1987) and reveal that molestation against male children is most often perpetrated by adult male offenders.
Abel et al. (1987), in a study of 561 self-reported nonincarcerated male
sexual offenders, found an unexpectedly high proportion of sexual abuse
perpetrated against boys away from home. In their sample, sexual exploitation acts against male children comprised the "greatest number of child
victims compared to those who molested girls or those who molested boys
in the same home" (Abel et al. 1987, 22). This finding is clearly noteworthy
and in sharp contrast with prevalence studies of reported male and female
sexual abuse victims whereby the sample proportion of male to female victims is quite low (Jaffe, Dynneson, and TenBensel 1975; Finklehor 1979;
Orr and Prietto 1979; Ellerstein and Canavan 1980; Tilelli, Turek, and Jaffe
1980; DeJong, Emmet, and Hervada 1982; Pierce and Pierce 1985; Spencer
and Dunklee 1986). Nasjeleti (1980), as well as many of the investigators
already cited, however, repeatedly point to a number of variables that are
believed to confound this finding: societal bias, homophobia, familial reluctance to report molestation of male children, societal reaction to males
being the victims of physical and particularly sexual aggression, and unsup-
portive and negative peer reactions.

Continuing descriptive epidemiological exploration of the patterns, dynamics, and relative risk factors of sexually abused male children has begun
to provide a wealth of information specific to a variety of variables of sexual

I wish to express and acknowledge my appreciation to Diane M. Petrella, MSW, administrative
director, the East Side Center, Inc., Providence, Rhode Island; and to Linda Tschirhart-Sanford,
MSW, director, Forensic Interventions, Quincy, Massachusetts, for their editorial assistance
with various drafts of the manuscript for this chapter. Their insightful comments were especially
helpful.

offenses toward males. Ellerstein and Canavan (1980) conducted a study of sexually abused boys seen at an emergency room of a children's hospital during a two-year period and presented findings related to age range of victims, site of molestation, and resulting physical trauma relative to female victims. DeJong, Emmet, and Hervada (1982) studied records of 142 boy victims seen at a university hospital sexual assault center and presented findings of the relationship of ethnicity to victimization, victim age distributions, relationship between victim and perpetrator, site of molestation, frequency of assault, aspects of physical trauma, nature of molestation, pattern of male sexual abuse associated with relationship of the perpetrator to victim, and the age of the victim. Finklehor (1984) reviewed existing studies and research regarding male sexual victimization and summarized that male children are commonly victimized by males and explored the relationship of the perpetrator to the victim, socioeconomic status of the victims, family composition, and reporting phenomenon of abused boys. Pierce and Pierce (1985) compared 25 substantiated cases of male child sexual assaults with 180 cases of female child sexual assaults and provided findings in relation to age, family composition, psychological health of caretaker(s), treatment differences, perpetrators, sexual acts committed, role of alcohol relative to sexual assault, and employment status of caretaker(s). Reinhart (1987) conducted a retrospective study of 189 boys referred to a medical center during a two-year period. Patterns of disclosure, perpetrator characteristics, age range of perpetrators, abusive acts committed relative to the age of the victim, and age match comparison to female victims were explored. Spencer and Dunklee (1986) reviewed 140 male child sexual abuse cases referred to a children's hospital sexual abuse team with respect to victim age and race, marital status of victim's parent(s), relationship to offender, physical findings relative to the sexual assault, and nature of the sexual assault.

As these studies demonstrate, research of sexual victimology is burgeoning; however, as David Finklehor (1984), a pioneering researcher on childhood sexual abuse notes, a critical void remains in the field in relationship to victimized male children and is "in crying need of research on . . . the sexual abuse of boys. Probably, the most serious question in regard to boys is how their response to victimization differs from that of girls and how clinicians can take this difference into account" (p. 230). He believes this gap is so significant that he recommends and almost implores that "even purely descriptive accounts of work with sexually abused boys would be an important resource given the current state of ignorance on the subject" (p. 230). Finklehor is not alone in his concerns. DeYoung (1982) noted that the molestation of boys by their fathers is a "tragically understudied type of sexual victimization. The literature boasts a large number of cases studied but virtually no theory construction and little consideration of the effects of this type of incest on the victims" (p.73).

Clearly the concern raised by DeYoung relative to the impact issues of victimization on boys who experienced molestation by their fathers remained status quo two years later when Finklehor reviewed the issue of molestation of boys at large. Pierce and Pierce (1985) studied characteristic differences between male and female sexual abuse victims relative to victim variables—family factors, perpetrator's relationship to victim, and treatment services—and found that "significant differences" exist relative to these issues. They concluded that it is critical to be aware of the difference and to "focus research more closely on the abused males themselves, particularly those factors, psychological and sociological . . . and on the male's psychological reactions to the abusive situation" (pp. 198–199). With this clinical clarification, they believe that professional understanding will be more "sensitive to the situational differences found when males are sexually abused, and develop treatment programs accordingly."

The term *same-sex victimization* means that the sexual abuse perpetrator and the victim are of the same sex. Same-sex molestation of boys has not been well understood, particularly in relation to father-son incest, with "only two dozen cases reported in the literature," (Mrazek 1981). Early writers about father-son incest reported classic psychoanalytic yet inappropriate interpretations to explain the behavior (Medlicott 1967; Raybin 1969; Awad 1976) as compared with the growing psychological understanding of sexual victimization. Other studies present brief and generic themes relative to the son's emotional functioning: homicidal or suicidal ideation, history of self-destructive behavior (self-mutilation), "reckless" drug abuse with no psychotic features (Dixon, Arnold, and Calestro 1978), chronic neurotic homophobia, and suicide (Medlicott 1967). DeYoung (1982) considers four generic categories of potential emotional impact for boys who have experienced "paternal incest": self-destructive acting out, homicidal ideation, mental illness, and sexual problems. Justice and Justice (1979) consider the probability that young male prostitutes were victims of paternal sexual abuse. Except for these few and brief reports, there has been very little attention focused on the psychological impact of same-sex victimization for male children. The critical need for the study of psychological impact on sexually victimized male children is well recognized and articulated. (DeJong, Emmet, and Hervada, 1982; DeYoung 1982; Mrazek 1982; Finklehor 1984; Pierce and Pierce 1985). Finklehor (1984) noted that "theories about child sexual abuse have been slow to emerge and the slowness has, in turn, hampered research as well as practice" (p. 221). He reflects that it is important to attract professionals with theoretical orientations to foster new child sexual abuse theory; however, "such people are often from academic backgrounds and have been in short supply of the field, partly because sexual abuse treatment and research have grown up outside academic institutions, i.e., social service agencies, prosecutor's offices and rape crisis centers." He concludes that "theoretically oriented people" will enter the field of child sexual abuse and "apply new theoretical approaches" in time.

This chapter is an effort to begin to respond to the existing lack of theoretical understanding of the psychological impact issues experienced by males who have been sexually abused by male offenders. It is based on my clinical experience over a seven-year period in the evaluation, treatment, and consultation on several hundred cases of male same-sex victimization. Repetitive themes of victim's psychological conflict emerged and have been categorized into ten issues: gender identity confusion, body imagery, intimacy impairment with males, intimacy impairment with females, depression, self-destructive manifestations, traumatic rage, aggression, hypervigilance toward males, and guilt. The psychological process involved in each of these issues for the male victim is explored. Table 4–1 presents various behaviors that clinicians might observe in same-sex male abuse victims. This table is designed to bridge an understanding between the internal psychological conflict connected to specific behavioral signs and/or acting out.

The concept of grounded theory (Glaser and Strauss 1967) provides the theoretical basis for this chapter. As Glaser and Strauss describe, through consistent observation, behavior can be categorized according to repetitive patterns, themes, and manifestations. Based on that theoretical model, this chapter illustrates the connections between clinical observations and theoretical conceptualization of the emotional impact of male same-sex molestation upon the victim.

I refer to male children who have experienced molestation by male perpetrators as victims of same-sex molestation and/or victims. I use this term purposefully in lieu of the term *homosexual molestation* or *homosexual incest,* which are misleading and erroneous. Homosexual molestation implies that the primary motivation for the abuse is sexual, and the victim is exploited as a homosexual object choice. As well, this label falsely assumes that there is an equality of age and psychological maturation between victim and perpetrator. The term *homosexual molestation* reinforces the concept of homosexual drive as the cause for the offense, a gross misconception given well-established clinical knowledge of sexual offense dynamics: psychosexual arrest in personality formation, abuse of power, and relationship between earlier sexual victimization and subsequent victimizing behavior (Groth 1979, 1982). (This issue is also discussed in chapter 13.)

Clinical Sample and Setting

Male victims were drawn from two practice sources: referral for specialized sexual abuse assessment and treatment and/or clinical consultation. Victims designated as appropriate for inclusion in the sample met two primary criteria. First, they were males who had been sexually abused by a male perpetrator. The victim's perpetrator could be a close relative, a distant relative, a male known to the child (such as a babysitter) or a stranger. Second, in cases of perpetrators who were also minors (under 18 years of age), a minimum five-year age difference between victim and perpetrator must have existed at the time of the victimization for the case to be included in the sample.

Adolescent male perpetrators who had acknowledged personal sexual victimization were included in the sample if the two previous criteria were met; however, those who denied a sexual victimization history even when strong clinical suspicion existed were excluded from this sample. Male children referred for sexual abuse evaluation who denied victimization, even with strong clinical suspicion given their behavioral manifestations, were also excluded from this sample.

Impact Issues

Gender Identity Confusion

While same-sex molestation of boys may mask as homosexually driven, increasing study and research of sexually deviant, criminal, and abusive behavior notes that, paradoxically, sexual desire has very little to do with the motivation of these behaviors (Groth 1979, 1982). It is well accepted that rape is not motivated by sexual desire but rather by the abuse of power and/or aggression (Burgess and Holstrom 1979; Groth 1979). It is well accepted that pedophilia is the result of psychosexual developmental arrest, largely prevalent in men, in which the adult's psychosexual identification and excitation is to a prepubertal child and not an adult (Groth 1982). Therefore, the pedophile is identifying as a psychological peer to his victim, not as an adult, although the child victim's experience is that of a child who is relating to an adult. It is also understandable that the victim's perception is that of being involved in homosexual behavior. As a result, the victim is left with emotional confusion regarding his developing psychosexual identity. Essentially the victim may believe that something within himself almost magically communicated a homosexual invitation prompting the molestation. He can be left with a distorted sense of sexual identity, even though homosexual desire was not a motivating factor in the perpetrator's choice of a victim or decision to commit the offense.

The male child victim's anatomy and physiology provide further complicating responses, which add to his confusion. Penile erection and ejaculation are normal physiological responses when the male genitals are orally and/or digitally manipulated and stimulated. These reactions provide seem-

Table 4–1
Impact Issues for Male Victims

Gender Identity Confusion	Body Imagery	Intimacy Impairment with Males	Intimacy Impairment with Females	Depression
Preoccupation with teasing effeminate and/or gay peers	Self-destructive behaviors/gestures emphasizing mutilation, disfiguring	Overall apprehension in engaging with peers	In adolescence, physically aggressive to female peers	Clinging to nonoffending parent
Younger boys express wish to cross-dress	Excessive preoccupation with physique, overly concerned with masculine physical presentation to world	Physical education distance—refusal to participate; insidious yet too frequent excuses to participate (forgetting gym sneakers; fear of showering)	Outright disregard for girls (repeated obscene language)	Isolation from peers
Need to be perceived as hypermasculine				Social withdrawal from male peers
Physically aggressive behavior focused on overpowering peers	Overt/covert exhibitionism of genitals and/or body[a]	Withdrawal/distance from participation in developmental peer activities (cub scouts, boy scouts, boys' club)	Fear of engaging with girls, social isolation	Mood variations: depressed, irritable, agitated, flat or blunt affect
	Excessive tattooing		Creating fantasy of girl to be with	Self-destructive gesturing
In mid- to late adolescence, need to be perceived as hyperheterosexual, i.e., "stud"	Efforts to desexualize self through large-fitting clothing; covering up	Hypermasculine behavior/bravado	Immature behavior toward girls (in adolescence)	Regression to behavior reminiscent of younger age
Heightened/extreme homophobia	Eating disorders (obesity, bulimia, anorexia)[a]	Consistent "ringleader-bully" behavior to vulnerable peers and younger children		Developmental delays to age at which abuse began
Sexual phobia		Homophobia		
		Overinvolvement with younger boys		
		Avoidance of significantly older male children and/or adult males		

Note: Behaviors are listed under their associated impact issue. A constellation of these behaviors indicates potential same-sex molestation.

[a]Primary indicators of same-sex abuse.

[b]The therapist should rule out organic etiology.

ingly irrefutable evidence to the victim that he was sexually aroused by another male during the molestation. It becomes difficult and almost emotionally impossible for the victim to deny the physical reactions usually associated with sexual pleasure and arousal. Accordingly, the victim is left to

Self-Destructive Manifestations	Traumatic Rage	Aggression	Hypervigilance toward Males	Guilt
Refer to behaviors listed under "Guilt"	Firesetting or playing with matches[a] Sexually abusive to vulnerable peers and/or younger children[a] Sadistic, cruel, tormenting behavior directed at: younger children, animals, vulnerable peers, male and/or female Encopresis[a,b] Violent, impulsive, assaultive, and/or homicidal behavior[b] Consistent disregard for law, authority and rights of others Sexually perverse behavior (e.g., bestiality, sadism, masochism)[a]	Hypermasculine bravado Consistent aggressive "ringleader-bully" behavior to vulnerable peers and younger children Sexually abusive to vulnerable peers and/or younger children[a] Identification as sexually abusive[a]	Refer to behaviors listed under "Intimacy Impairment with Males"	Superficial self-destructive behavior (e.g., self-scratching, hair pulling) Alcohol or drug abuse Daredevil, reckless behavior Self-mutilating behavior (e.g., nail and/or skin biting, picking at scalp, hair pulling, self-scratching, excessive tattooing, general disregard for physical care or well-being) Obsessive cleanliness Disassociation and disregard for body[a] Body distortion/body image Repeated "accidents" (falls with broken bones, car accidents) Self-destructive ideation

question his sexual orientation, asking himself, "Why else do these physical responses occur?"

Mark, age 20 was sexually molested at age 12 for one year by his brother who performed anal penetration on him. When questioned what he was thinking of during the abuse, he responded, "Why can't he find someone his own age? Why can't he find a girl?" He also reflected concerns that "sometimes" he thinks he "might be gay" as a result of the abuse. He reflected and reported experiencing sadness, anxiety, and fear that he "doesn't want it to happen" (being gay), almost like magic, "all of a sudden." He also acknowledged sometimes, but not recently, he "could have had" homosexual fantasies.

John, age 11, was molested by his stepfather. The sexual abuse included mutual masturbation, simulated intercourse, and anal penetration. Through the treatment process, he acknowledged penile erection when sexually fantasizing about men but not women, which "scared" and frightened him.

The more closely the victim is psychologically identified with the perpetrator, the more intense and exacerbated are his own identity issues. The identification process for boys is largely formulated by significant psychological males (Anthony and Benedek 1970; Biller 1971)—father figures and/or psychological male caretakers. When the sexual abuse is perpetrated by a male who occupies a close psychological relationship, the victim is left with significant emotional confusion regarding his psychosexual sense of self as related to identity struggles with the offender, that is, "Like father like son," "I am my father's son." These struggles can range from the unconscious level to full awareness. The conflicts can evolve into characterological phenomena that may continue to cause the victim subjective distress or become integrated, without emotional strife, as a personality characteristic in an unconscious process, described by Anna Freud (1946), known as identification with the aggressor.

Regardless of the perpetrator's emotional relationship to the victim, the same-sex nature of the molestation exacerbates the boy's identity issues. Essentially it may become more difficult for the victim to differentiate himself psychologically from the perpetrator. Victims of same-sex molestation are therefore likely to experience intense identity struggles.

Body Imagery

It is well established that the victims of sexual abuse experience psychological assault to their sense of body integrity (Sgroi 1982; Pescosolido and Petrella 1986). Sgroi's (pp. 112–115) term, *damaged goods syndrome,* is the classic description of this impact. Some of the male victims' reactions, however, are not necessarily gender specific. Essentially themes related to body strangeness (perceiving their bodies as different from peers') and fears of body mutilation related to penetration of oral and anal cavities are clinically considered to be usual sequelae.

Larry, age 12, was sexually abused by his biological father for approximately one year. The abuse included fellatio, mutual masturbation, and anal penetration. A significant theme in his treatment
was the state of his physical health. He often reflected upon his long-
standing fear that he "was dying" because rectal bleeding had epi-
sodically occurred subsequent to the anal penetration. Larry reflected acute anxiety that "inside [his body] things weren't quite
right" as a result of his sexual abuse.

For the male victim, penile erection is a specific physiological response
that during the molestation is often simultaneously experienced with psychological confusion, anger, and disdain. Within the context of the molestation, the victim is frequently confused that he would experience sexual
arousal as evidenced by an erection. The experience was likely to have been
frightening, guilt and anxiety inducing, and also sexually arousing. In some
ways, this physiological reaction can be perceived by the victim as concrete
evidence that he liked and/or enjoyed the molestation. Moreover, this physical response can be psychologically distorted by the victim to validate a
homosexual identity: "I must be homosexual because why else would I have
an erection?" Similarly, most male victims that I have treated have acknowledged anger directed at their bodies, particularly the genitals, for experiencing an erection during the molestation. As well, many victims acknowledge
a deep psychological sense of betrayal by their bodies for having experienced
the erection. This sense of body betrayal is very real despite the involuntary
nature of penile erections under conditions of fear or stress. Male victims
are left with anger, confusion, and conflict regarding their bodies. Some
victims are ashamed of and frightened by normative genital functioning that
occurs after the abuse.

Louis, age 13, was molested by his stepfather. The abuse included
mutual masturbation and anal penetration. He denied any masturbatory behavior, perceiving that "it would be molesting myself."
Also he periodically voiced concerns regarding his physical well-
being, having predisclosure fantasies that he "had cancer of the knee
[and] that he would need acid treatments for a long time to get rid
of it."

Because of the genital arousal response to the abuse, the victim is at risk
to act out against his body. This self-directed anger can manifest itself on a
continuum from insidious to overt self-destructive behaviors. Hypochon-
driacal features and/or somatic complaints are also common.

Intimacy Impairment with Males

The male victim has experienced his gender as sexually, physically, and emotionally exploitative and assaultive. At the same time, however, the sexual abuse also carried with it some isolated elements of sexual excitation and arousal. The latter are common sequelae for sexual abuse victims and need to be understood as such. The equating of involuntary sexual arousal or erections with the victim's "liking" and/or "enjoying" the molestation represents an insidious yet powerful effort by the perpetrator (and society) to blame the victim, as well as to rationalize the often continued pattern of the abuse. While the victim may not generally view all males as abusive, psychological confusion is nevertheless very real. Conflict is particularly intense when the abuse is perpetrated by a male involved in a caretaking role, such as biological fathers, stepfathers, older brothers, family friends, or coaches.

> Paul, age 8, was molested by his stepfather for approximately one year. The abuse included fellatio. In treatment, Paul stated. "I hate all big men . . . I hate them all."

The impact of the abuse regarding closeness with other males can vary depending on the victim's anxiety level and the nature of his emotional defenses. In my clinical experience, the victim's defenses often function on a preconscious level and are readily available for insight, understanding, and relief from conflict.

The victim may also experience psychological uneasiness when he must be in close proximity to male peers. Vulnerability, real or on a fantasy level, seems to predominate.

> Sam, age 12, was sexually abused by his biological father for approximately two years. The abuse included fondling, as well as mutual oral sex. Six months postdisclosure, Sam would not participate at a local Boy's Club for fear that "the boys will pull my pants down" while taking communal showers.

Sam feared further sexual abuse. His anxiety ranged from fearing an aggressive and forceful assault to fearing that another male would try to seduce him. Regardless, normal development of intimacy with same-sex peers by participating in activities is often retarded by the effects of the molestation. For male victims, such activities as competitive sports, organizations, and clubs are experienced within a framework in which they fear and guard against exploitation.

Closeness with peers can be connected with a potentially eroticized element. Through his abuse, the victim has experienced another male as sexually stimulating, since males do not have the ability to respond selectively when the genitals are being fondled or orally manipulated. Thus, sexual arousal, which the victim misunderstood during the abuse, is subsequently experienced as confusing and shameful yet stimulating. The victim fears in an omnipotent fashion that he can easily sexually stimulate his peers or adults. Conversely, he fears that he will be easily stimulated and aroused in return. This seems exacerbated by normal male activities. Participating in sports, physical education classes, and showering are activities that normally involve physical closeness and exposure and can be especially problematic. The male victim may fear that others can read through his abuse and thus seek him out for sexual gratification and/or exploitation.

To defend against this conflict, the male victim's behavior may fall anywhere along a continuum. He may present with a hypermacho facade—aggressively "rough and tough"—bullying to peers, or very distant and guarded. The victim is struggling with issues of vulnerability. To be distant physically and emotionally is to be safe from potential repeated molestation, regardless of the behavioral facade and defense the world observes.

Intimacy Impairment with Females

A usual victim impact issue has been to experience other males as sexually stimulating. Adolescent boys are particularly at risk to displace confusion about their sexuality onto their female peers.

On different psychological levels, the boy questions the nature of his masculinity. Due to the pseudohomosexual aspects of the abuse, the victim is left with a distorted sense of his masculine self. He may experience gender identity confusion, as well as a fear and hatred of homosexual men. These reactions can range from acute episodic emotional responses to low-level lingering distress. On a continuum, victims experience some level of emotional assault to their masculine integrity.

When adolescent male victims have an injured sense of masculinity, they are at risk to act out against male peers. Essentially they may use counterphobic reaction as a defense to counteract a faulty and insecure internal sense of masculine self. The victim in adolescence may need to portray a hypermasculine and/or sophisticated exterior when dealing with female peers to counteract his sexual insecurity and homophobic struggles resulting from the molestation. Paradoxically the victim may fear that others may view him as not truly masculine or that the secret of his victimization will be found out. To guard against realization of these fears, the victim may adopt an exaggerated sexualized style of relating to others. The frequency and pervasity with which he seeks out female peers for sexual conquest is an indication of the depth of injury to his masculine self-image.

Simultaneously the victim may be looking to his relationships with potential female sexual partners, and associated heterosexual arousal, as a concrete mechanism to erase, disprove, or cure his sexualized confusion resulting from the molestation. However, the victim is in a bind regarding future experiences of sexual interaction. It is not unusual to discover that for many victims, the sexual abuse was often their first interactive sexual experience. Therefore, in a manner similar to imprinting (Lorenz 1974), the male victim's psychological associations of sexual arousal may be closely linked to the abuse perpetrated by a male. Some victims need frequently to assure themselves that they can be aroused by females. Their sexual behavior with females is thus likely to become compulsive and ritualistic.

> James, age 16, was molested for two years by a priest. The abuse included masturbation, fondling, and simulated intercourse. He reflected that since the disclosure, "It's been girls, girls, girls. In the middle of having sex I'll get soft." He reflected that the molestation continues to "haunt" him because he loses his erection during intercourse and experiences a flashback to the molestation. "I'll see him on top of me [and] smell his cologne and house." James also acknowledged that he gets angry at most of his female partners because they are not able to "keep him from thinking" about his molestation when sexually aroused. He described compulsive sexual behavior with girls in an attempt to confirm a heterosexual identity.

In adolescence, the victim is at risk to externalize the problems he experiences with sexual arousal, or lack of it, onto the female peer he is with rather than looking within himself. If he is not able to be aroused sexually by interacting with his female partner, his fears that he is not "masculine enough" or that he is homosexually inclined are likely to be confirmed. In response, he may displace his anger on his female partner for not being able to arouse him sexually as a defense against the memory of the sexually arousing elements of the previous abuse experiences.

Depression

On several levels, the victim experiences deep sadness regarding the abuse. This sadness may in intensity, but it is likely to be present. When the molestation is of long-standing duration, the victim also experiences a sense of helplessness to stop the abuse, particularly when perpetrated by a caretaker or relative (Herman 1981). In many instances over time and without psychological intervention, sadness evolves into depression.

As the molestation continues, the sense of helplessness evolves into despair and hopelessness. The duration of the abuse, coupled with the relationship of the perpetrator to victim, can be used as a gauge to assess the depth and intensity of the victim's depression. If the molestation occurred over a long period of time, the depression may insidiously manifest itself in subtle characterological personality features as the boy experiences sadness regarding what has happened to his emotional and physical self.

The victim is at risk to act out the depression with self destructive behaviors against his body in an effort to punish his body-self for the molestation. Victims who abuse drugs or alcohol are able to combine a self-destructive behavior with an anesthetizing or pain-dulling experience.

> Bob, age 14, was molested by his stepfather for approximately one year. Coerced into performing oral sex, Bob stated, "I keep it in [and] don't think about it. I get so sad."

> Richard, age 14, was molested by two of his mother's boyfriends. The abuse involved mutual masturbation and oral sex. Richard reflected that when he begins to talk about it, he gets mad, which "keeps me from being real sad."

When the molestation has occurred for months or years, the victim carries a deep sense of uncertainty. He may question his basic sense of self-worth, often feeling that he was not worthy of experiencing protection from the abuse.

Self-Destructive Manifestations

Psychological struggles and themes related to self-destructiveness are part of the impact on the victim. These conflicts may range along a continuum from unconscious to fully conscious, or they may take the form of ideation as opposed to overt gestures. The manifestations may range from insidiously self-destructive to overtly self-destructive behaviors. Several dynamics complicate and exacerbate this impact. The victim has a sense of himself as "bad" because of the molestation (Pescosolido and Petrella 1986). There exists, therefore, the potential to punish the self for the molestation. The capacity for self-destructiveness is usually influenced by the psychological relationship of the perpetrator to the victim and the duration and frequency of the molestation. The extent to which the victim sees himself as bad and is unable to differentiate a self apart from the exploitation is a clinical gauge of the potential for self-destructive tendencies. The body is a concrete representation and tangible host of the sexual abuse (Pescosolido and Petrella 1986). What impresses as initially confusing, emotionally painful, embarrassing, and conflictual are the myriad of physiological responses the victim experiences during the act of molestation. Also, the victim is confused regarding the sexual excitation and arousal experienced, regardless of the fear, confusion, and upset he simultaneously experienced during the abuse. Male victims perceive their sexual arousal, coupled with the penile erection, as concrete evidence that they have both "liked" yet have been betrayed by their body.

My clinical practice with male victims has revealed that many would silently admonish their genitals "not to get hard" during the molestation—obviously physiologically difficult, if not impossible, particularly when the genitals had been manually or orally stimulated. To the victim, the production and maintenance of an erection during the molestation is cognitively and emotionally distorted to be clear and convincing evidence that he enjoyed the molestation. A psychoeducational approach in treatment is essential to help the victim integrate these aspects as normative sequelae of the sexual abuse.

Within the context of the confusion, the male victim is burdened, carrying anger and resentment directed at his physical self; self-punishment is therefore unconsciously justified. Frequent car accidents, substance abuse, and daredevil and hypermacho behaviors can be a camouflage for a male victim who carries anger and resentment for the betrayal experienced by his physical self. Overt examples of self-destructive behaviors such as self-mutilation and wrist slashing may also be manifested. Violent self-destructive behavior may also be a way for the victim "to create a more familiar external pain to distract from the less familiar and more threatening internal intrapsychic pain resulting from the abuse."(Sanford 1988)

> Bob, age 7, was molested by his stepfather for approximately one year. The abuse included oral sex. Early in treatment, Bob often stated, "I could kill myself if I think about it—I can't think about it." When he did think about the molestation, he stated he would be "so mad and sad" that he would "hold his breath" until his "face got red."

> John, age 11, was molested by his stepfather. The abuse involved mutual masturbation, simulated intercourse, and anal penetration. He stated that he often thought of "throwing myself out of a window or eating poison dog berries . . . so the molesting would stop."

Traumatic Rage

Childhood sexual abuse is well recognized as a trauma (Sgroi 1982; Herman 1981; Van der Kolk 1987). Rage clinically captures the level of deep and intense anger and indignation as a result of the molestation. The victim is reacting with rage to the psychological and physical invasion that he experienced during the molestation. He has also undergone intense affective experiences of shame, humiliation, confusion, and powerlessness.

The male victim directs his rage at three distinct yet interrelated persons: himself, the offender, and his caretaker(s) who failed to protect him from the abuse. It has been my clinical experience that male victims also often project their rage onto world at large.

> Jason, age 13, was molested by his stepfather for approximately one year. The abuse involved fondling, mutual masturbation, and mutual oral sex. In treatment, he periodically stated that he was "mad at everyone for having it happen to me. . . . I would be so mad and wouldn't talk to anybody—I'd want to be alone in the world." Jason also reflected that he would "get so mad [that he] would want to blow up all the molesters in the world. . . . No more molesters would live!"

> Keith, age 12, was abused by his stepfather and stepuncle. The abuse lasted approximately two years and included mutual oral sex, anal penetration, and exposure to pornography. He stated, "I want to blow up the whole world—that's how mad I get [when thinking about the abuse]!"

Simultaneously the victim is at risk to direct rage against himself. He is likely to experience intense self-hatred for having been the object of sexual aggression.

> Patrick, age 9, was molested by his father for several years. The abuse included fondling and mutual oral sex. Early in treatment, he stated he was "afraid to think about it . . . because I'm so mad I'll kill myself—I can't think about it."

In our society, it is particularly humiliating for a male child or adolescent to be sexually abused. Male victimization carries two stigmatizing dynamics: being a male victim and being sexually victimized (Groth 1979; Nasjleti 1980). The victim's emotional experience of rage is both cognitively and affectively associated with a diffuse sense of powerlessness reminiscent of his helplessness while he was being abused. He is raging at the world for allowing the abuse to occur, particularly when the exploitation had continued over a period of time; he believed that others were aware of the abuse and chose to ignore and deny it. This type of magical thinking intensifies the victim's rage, yet it also diffuses the responsibility for the abuse. Paradoxically, by making the world at large responsible for the sexual abuse perpetrated against him, the male victim is at risk to act out his traumatic rage against innocent bystanders.

Aggression

The male victim often perceives himself as emotionally and physically inadequate because he was the object of sexual assault. Vulnerability, retribution, and identification with the aggressor thus become core issues. Psychologically the victim internalizes a sense of vulnerability and weakness. To defend against this, he is at risk to develop a hypermasculine bravado. He attempts not to present as passive and/or weak, which on some emotional level is synonymous with exploitation and assault. A hypermasculine style serves as an emotional defense against the fear of future assault.

Identification with the aggressor is a well-established principle (Freud 1946) useful in understanding the victim's identification with his sexual aggressor. When the victim and aggressor are of the same sex, the male victim is at risk for acquiring a distorted sense of masculinity. Masculinity becomes equated with aggression but also with victimization. The victim is left with the struggle to differentiate who he is from who he is not regarding the abuse: victim versus victimizer. Within this context, he may identify with the aggressor on either end of the continuum depending on several factors: treatment intervention (or lack thereof), nature of caretaking milieu, history of familial violence, presence of alternative male role models, and the like. Although many boys who are sexually abused by males do identify with their aggressors, many others do not. Boys who have been sexually abused by their fathers and other psychologically significant males are particularly at risk for conflict regarding an aggressive male identity, especially when they have observed that these men utilize violence as a means to deal with conflicts, relationships, and stress. Essentially the more the victim attempts unconsciously to disengage from an aggressive masculine identification, the more he may feel that he is identifying as passive and nonmasculine. Potential homophobic issues can be amplified and become entangled within these struggles.

Retribution for having experienced sexual assault is also a predictable victim impact issue. My clinical experience has been that male victims often fantasize wishes to maim, disfigure, or annihilate their abusers.

> Bob, age 7, was sexually molested by his stepfather for approximately one year. The molestation included mutual oral sex. Bob episodically voiced in therapy that "when you're a kid you can't get even [with the perpetrator]; but when you're big you can get even."

> Mark, age 12, was sexually molested by his stepfather for approximately two years. The abuse included mutual oral sex, fondling and

anal penetration. Mark learned that his stepfather was also sexually abused as a child and commented, "I'm glad he was—he deserved it."

Male victims may act out aggressively toward others, particularly toward those who are more vulnerable, in an unconscious attempt to experience control over their own victimization.

John, age 11, was molested by his stepfather. The abuse included mutual masturbation, simulated intercourse, and anal penetration. He stated that he was afraid he too would "molest kids." He reflected that while at a local Boys' Club, he developed an erection while looking at a younger boy who was showering. He stated, "I thought about molesting him 'cause he was like younger than me like my father who is older and molested me."

Jimmy, age 7, was forcefully sexually abused by his adolescent babysitter for approximately one year. The abuse included genital fondling, mutual oral sex, and attempts at anal penetration. Jimmy reflected, "Doug is sick. . . . he did it to me. . . . I'm sick. . . . It's contagious. . . . Someone did it to him; he did it to me. . . . I'll do it."

Hypervigilance toward Males

Child sexual abuse victims often magically believe that the world is aware of their victimization. A psychological sense of being transparent and exposed, specifically in regard to the sexual exploitation, appears best to describe this internal perception. The male victim therefore may project apprehension into subsequent interpersonal relationships with males.

An exaggerated suspiciousness of males, sometimes bordering on clinical paranoia, can become integrated within the male victim's personality. If physiological reactions such as erection and ejaculation occurred during the abuse, the victim may have a sense that he is transparent to other males. Therefore he may believe that the world knows of his sexual exploitation. He further fears that other males, magically knowing about his abuse, may seek him out for sexual arousal.

The degree to which the victim experiences difficulty in male interpersonal relationships or presents with counterphobic behavior styles, such as hypermachismo, homophobia, extreme withdrawal from male peers, and bully-like behavior, can serve as a clinical gauge of the level of hypervigilance.

Kenny, age 15, was sexually molested by a neighborhood man for a year and a half. The abuse involved fondling and mutual oral sex. During an overnight visit at his father's home, he awoke to his father's removing his underwear and performing fellatio on him; he pretended to be asleep but disclosed several months later. He repeatedly failed to take physical education classes, fearing that other boys "could tell" he was molested and that they would want to molest him. Kenny also stated that he feared developing an erection while showering with peers. In time and with active exploration, Kenny was able to acknowledge a psychological perception of a parallel between his molestation and his treatment. He acknowledged being given money by the neighbor who molested him. He reflected that one reason he would return to be molested was that the neighborhood man would "pay" him. He stated that he felt like a "prostitute." He felt that the therapy, also "in a way, was using" him so that the therapist "could get money." He thought this clinician "got paid anyway," even if he did not show for a treatment session. He was able to articulate his feelings that men, in an effort to "get close, want something from me." Thus, he often "felt like a prostitute with men."

Guilt

Female victims report a misplaced sense of responsibility for the occurrence of the abuse (Herman 1981). So too with male victims of sexual abuse. In our culture, males are expected to protect themselves. The "invulnerable" male is almost magically capable of protecting himself against any assault at any time (Groth 1979). Consequently, while our society on some levels may empathize with female victims of sexual abuse, it is intolerant of male sexual abuse victims, particularly boys in mid-childhood and adolescence. This societal response reinforces the male victim's distorted sense of responsibility for his own molestation and amplifies his guilt for his inability to protect himself. This greatly lessens the victim's tendency to report his molestation (Groth 1979; Nasjleti 1980; Finklehor 1984).

In addition, physiological responses such as erection and ejaculation are concrete evidence to the victim that he was aroused by the molestation, serving to exacerbate his profound sense of self-betrayal and guilt. These physiological responses are often misperceived by our culture as indications that the male victim liked or enjoyed the molestation.

Jimmy, age 7, was forcefully sexually abused by his adolescent babysitter for approximately one year. Abuse included genital fondling, mutual oral sex, and attempted anal penetration. When reviewing various aspects of the molestation, he recounted the following: "He told me to get under the covers and lay on his wic. . . . He tried to put his wic in my bum but it didn't fit in, even when he told me to bend over; but I told him to rub my bum because it felt good. Honest, that wasn't his fault, it was mine." Jimmy was embarrassed when reflecting this and continued to believe that "a lot" of the molestation was his fault, and he would "ask" the perpetrator to "rub his bum."

Treatment Implications

Treatment of psychological trauma appears to be both indicated and appropriate for male victims of child sexual abuse (Van der Kolk 1987). To date, an overwhelming percentage of the literature on child sexual abuse focuses on female children sexually abused by males. Almost nothing in the professional literature exists regarding the dynamics, the structure, and the process of treatment of male children who are sexually abused by males.

The clinical knowledge that exists regarding the treatment of sexually victimized female children, adolescents and adults certainly could be adjusted and utilized in the treatment of male victims. Certain aspects of sexual victimology transcend gender, and thus some treatment implications remain constant. A clear psychoeducational approach could serve as a therapeutic foundation for young male victims. This approach encourages therapists to share information didactically about the general dynamics, process, and impact of traumata on the individual while simultaneously encouraging them to recognize the unique meaning the sexual abuse has for individual clients. The focus is on understanding the sequelae of child sexual abuse on the victim, not on a psychopathological response. This is not to suggest that such responses are impossible or that emotional dysfunction linked to the abuse is dismissed. On the contrary, emotional dysfunction is actively explored, as are the connections between maladaptive behavioral and emotional patterns and their possible link to the original trauma. Drawing emotional and behavioral links between post-traumatic stress and the original trauma is a critical clinical tool, as are education and cognitive reframing. Transference, countertransference, and the concept of therapeutic alliance initially are given less priority. The essence of this treatment is to help the victim make cognitive and psychological sense of the trauma particularly as it relates to post-traumatic stress dysfunction and to secondary emotional and behavioral symptomatology. It is not requisite to the treatment that the victim articulate the variety and complexity of the impact of the sexual abuse to him. Such an expectation would be both unnecessary and unrealistic. This treatment provides the victim with a general knowledge of trauma response as it affects all aspects of human functioning (Van der Kolk 1987) and assists the victim to understand and alter his response. This occurs within a treatment atmosphere of emotional safety and therapeutic partnership.

The treatment process recommended for male victims of same-sex molestation has two phases: individual and group psychotherapy.

Individual Treatment

The primary emphasis of individual therapy for the male victim is to facilitate cognitive and psychological meaning of the victimization. This is largely based on such variables as the child's developmental phase, the child's cognitive maturation, the family's capacity to support the victim, the perpetrator's emotional relationship to the victim and the victim's family, the child's prior history of sexual abuse, and the pertinent ethnic and cultural reactions to male child sexual victimization.

Within the relative safety of the individual treatment, the victim can begin to test the emotional impact of the victimization. Too frequently, however, the child victim may not be able to translate into words what the victimization meant to him. Within this context, the psychoeducational component of therapy is integrated into the treatment. It is important to note that the victim's apparent verbal reluctance to discuss the emotional impact of the sexual abuse does not necessarily imply therapeutic resistance. In fact, clinical practice with traumatized individuals increasingly advocates assisting the victim to verbalize the abuse experience as a crucial step toward the victim's achieving a sense of mastery over the abuse (Van der Kolk 1987).

The victim impact issues could serve as guidelines for the individual treatment. Essentially it is anticipated that the victim would experience a safe, effective, and empathic therapeutic milieu that would simultaneously allow for and encourage individual expression and reflection. The ultimate goal of therapy is the client's emotional mastery and integration of the sexual victimization. The impact issues would be introduced by the therapist as normative results of the emotional conflict and confusion regarding same-sex victimization. These issues reviewed early in the treatment would be explored as possibly connected to the victim's unique psychological sequelae.

Transference and countertransference dynamics are important, but they are less important in the initial treatment phase, when the psychoeducational efforts are given priority. As treatment continues, however, these issues become quite significant. Transference reactions clearly may be amplified when the treatment is provided by a male therapist. Countertransference may be particularly useful to understand the meaning that the victim places on the sexual offense based on his experience of prior male authority figures in his psychological development. The therapist's clear and concrete interpretation of countertransference in a psychoeducational manner can clarify and support both cognitively and emotionally the victim's differentiation of the offender from other significant males. This therapeutic work is built upon and connected to the client's prior experience of males who were critical of him. It calls for the therapist appropriately to interpret the client's transference reactions regarding male authority figures—reactions that are probably apparent in other aspects of his life as well.

The nature of the involvement of the victim's parents and family in the treatment is contingent on several dynamics: the relationship of the perpetrator to the victim, the relationship of the perpetrator to the victim's caretakers, the history of the family's prior traumatization with emphasis on post-traumatic adjustment, the victim and family's prior experiences with mental health services, and the methods by which the family copes with shame, humiliation, guilt, and responsibility—dynamics normally associated with trauma (Van der Kolk 1987). Essentially the closer is the offender's relationship to the victim (biological caretaking, psychological, and/or any combination), the more convoluted the treatment process can become. Individual therapy for members of the family other than the victim and family therapy as adjunct treatments need to be considered as priorities. The duration of the victim's individual treatment is clearly dependent on his progress in post-traumatic adjustment as related to secondary trauma symptomatology, such as acting out, and a decrease in his perceived emotional conflict. As yet, no specific time frame for individual child sexual assault victims is documented; however, a one- to two-year therapeutic period is generally suggested in an informal poll of my colleagues who specialize in child sexual abuse treatment.

A clinical agenda inherent in individual treatment is to help the victim to become "group ready"—that is, ready to participate in group therapy with other boys similarly victimized. This second treatment phase, and the boy's interaction with other victims of child sexual abuse, is particularly crucial to treatment because of the interpersonal stresses and personal conflicts associated with the trauma of sexual victimization.

Group Therapy

The importance of group therapy for individuals who have experienced similar life trauma is clinically well established (Fogelman and Savran 1979; Hawley and Brown 1981; Rounsaville, Lifton, and Bieber 1979; Walker 1981; Parson 1984; Yassen and Glass 1984).

Chapter 3, in this book discusses this modality as related to female adolescent victims. Group treatment for female adult incest survivors has received particular attention as one facet of the therapeutic process as it specifically relates to issues of emotional isolation, reality testing, guilt, secondary trauma, and interpersonal dynamics. It is increasingly reported as a critical psychotherapeutic component inherent to adaptive post-traumatic adjustment (Gordy 1983; Faria and Beloklavek 1984; Herman and Schatzow 1984; Blake-White and Kline 1985; Goodman and Nowak-Scibelli 1985; Cole and Barney 1987). Very little in the professional literature exists regarding group treatment of child, adolescent, or adult male sexual abuse victims. Since clinical experience based on theoretical knowledge and understanding of the issues of same-sex victimized male children is in its early stages (DeJong, Emmet, and Hervada 1982; DeYoung 1982; Mrazek 1981; Finklehor 1984; Pierce and Pierce 1985), it is not surprising that little about group psychotherapy with male victims has been reported (Johanek 1988; Yalom 1975).

The victim impact issues discussed may serve as content for the internal structure of a group similar to groups described by Pescosolido and Petrella (1986) in their evaluation of group psychotherapy with sexually abused preschool girls. In recognition of the levels of child development, a twelve-week period of group therapy is recommended for preschool as well as latency-age boys, and a twenty-four-week period is recommended for adolescents. This time frame is consonant with the predictable resistances of males entering therapy with other males who have been sexually abused. The suggested time frame also reflects my prior clinical experience with an open-ended group for male adolescent same-sex victims. The absence of a specific time frame and a specific agenda allowed the therapeutic experience to become less effective than it might have been if it had been given a tighter structure. The twenty-four-week time period allows for the working through of resistance dynamics, as well as for the development of group process and group formation tasks specifically effective in dealing with same-sex abuse issues. Group admission criteria, process, and structure as articulated by Cole and Barney (1987) seem to be as relevant to the screening of male adolescent victims for group members as it is with female adult incest survivors. Of particular importance are the victim's suicidal history, the victim's experience of individual therapy, and the timing of the victim's entrance into the group. Cole and Barney also make significant suggestions regarding internal group tasks and termination of the group.

It is anticipated that group psychotherapy for male victims can provide the environment of safety in which each victim can test his experience of victimization against that of other male victims. Therapy could specifically focus on cognitive and psychological processes within the group context. Through this group treatment effort, potentially destructive sequelae could be actively worked through; the therapeutic process could be focused on peer support, empathy, and the opportunity for reality testing. This model of group therapy enables victims to have a constructive experience of same-sex closeness independent of exploitation or sexual stimulation. As the group process evolves, there may be a decrease in the members' perceptions of themselves solely as victims. It is hoped that this combination of individual and peer group therapy for male same-sex victims will greatly lessen the potential for these issues to become characterological. With the courage and support of other males similarly abused, the victim can continue to grow toward emotional mastery of the trauma and, finally, toward integration.

References

Abel, G.; Becker, J.V.; Mittleman, M.; Cunningham-Rathner, J.; Rouleau, J.L. and Murphy, W.D. 1987. "Self-reported Sex Crimes of Non-incarcerated Paraphiliacs." *Journal of Interpersonal Violence* 2:3–25.

Anthony, E.J., and Benedek, T. eds. 1970. *Parenthood: Its Psychology and Psychopathology*. Boston: Little, Brown.

Awad, G.A. 1976. "Father-son Incest: A Case Report." *Journal of Nervous and Mental Disease* 162:135–139.

Biller, H.B. 1971. *Father, Child and Sex Role: Paternal Determinants of Personality Development*. Lexington, Mass.: Lexington Books.

Blake-White, J., and Kline, C. 1985. "Treating the Disassociation Process in Adult Victims of Childhood Incest." *Social Casework* 66:399–402.

Burgess, A.W., and Holstrom, L.L. 1979. *Rape: Crisis and Recovery*. Bowie, Md.: Robert J. Brady Co.

Cole, C., and Barney, E. 1987. "Safeguards and the Therapeutic Window—A Group Treatment Strategy for Adult Incest Survivors." *American Journal of Orthopsychiatry* 57:601–609.

DeJong, A.R.; Emmet, G.A.; and Hervada, A.A. 1982. "Epidemiologic Factors in Sexual Abuse of Boys." *American Journal of Diseases of Children* 136:990–993.

DeYoung, M. 1982. *The Sexual Victimization of Children*. Jefferson, N.C.: McFarland & Company.

Dixon, K.A.; Arnold, L.E.; and Calestro, K. 1978. "Father-Son Incest: Underreported Psychiatric Problem?" *American Journal of Psychiatry* 135:835–838.

Donaldson, M.A., and Gardner, R. 1985. "Diagnosis and Treatment of Traumatic Stress among Women after Childhood Incest." In Charles Figley, ed. *Trauma and Its Wake*. New York: Brunner Mazel.

Ellerstein, N.S., and Canavan, M.D. 1980. "Sexual Abuse of Boys." *American Journal of Diseases of Children* 134:255–257.

Faria, G., and Beloklavek, N. 1984. "Treating Female Adult Survivors of Childhood Incest." *Social Casework* 65:465–471.

Ferenczi, S. 1955. "Confusion of Tongues between Adults and the Child: The Language of Tenderness and Passion." In S. Ferenczi, ed., *Problems and Methods of Psychoanalysis*. London: Hogarth Press.

Finklehor, D. 1979. *Sexually Victimized Children*. New York: Free Press.

Finklehor, D. 1984. *Child Sexual Abuse: New Theory and Research*. New York: Free Press.

Fogelman, E., and Savran, B. 1979. "Therapeutic Groups for Children of Holocaust Survivors." *International Journal of Group Psychotherapy* 29:211–236.

108 • *Vulnerable Populations*

Freud, A. 1946. *The Ego and Mechanisms of Defense*. New York: International University Press.

Gelinas, D.J. 1983. "The Persistent Negative Effects of Incest." *Psychiatry* 46:312–332.

Glaser, B.G., and Strauss, A.L. 1967. *The Discovery of Grounded Theory*. Chicago: Adline Publishers.

Goodman, B., and Nowak-Scibelli, D. 1985. "Group Treatment for Women Incestuously Abused as Children." *International Journal of Group Psychotherapy* 35:531–544.

Gordy, 1982. "Group Work That Supports Adult Victims of Childhood Incest." *Social Casework* 64:300–307.

Groth, A.N. 1979. *Men Who Rape*. New York: Plenum Press.

Groth, A.N. 1982. "The Incest Offender." In S.M. Sgroi, ed., *Handbook of Clinical Intervention in Child Sexual Abuse*. Lexington, Mass.: Lexington Books.

Hawley, N.P., and Brown, E.L. 1981. "The Use of Group Treatment with Children of Alcoholics." *Social Casework* 62:40–46.

Herman, J.L. 1981. *Father-Daughter Incest*. Cambridge: Harvard University Press.

Herman, J., and Schatzow, E. 1984. "Time-limited Group Therapy for Women with a History of Incest." *International Journal of Group Psychotherapy* 34:605–616.

Jaffe, A.C.; Dynneson, L.; and TenBensel, R.W. 1975. "Sexual Abuse of Children: An Epidemiologic Study." *American Journal of Diseases of Children* 129:689–692.

Johanek, M.F. 1988. "Treatment of Male Victims of Child Sexual Abuse in Military Service." In S. Sgroi, ed., *Vulnerable Populations: Evaluation and Treatment of Sexually Abused Children and Adult Survivors,* vol. 1. Lexington, Mass.: Lexington Books.

Justice B., and Justice, R. 1979. *The Broken Taboo*. New York: Human Science Press.

Lorenz, C. 1974. *On Aggression*. New York: Harcourt Brace Jovanovich.

Medlicott, R.W. 1967. "Parent-Child Incest." *Australian and New Zealand Journal of Psychiatry* 1:180–187.

Mrazek, P.B. 1981. "The Nature of Incest: A Review of Contributing Factors." In P.B. Mrazek and C.H. Kempe, eds., *Sexually Abused Children and Their Families*. Oxford, England: Pergamon.

Nasjleti, M. 1980. "Suffering in Silence: The Male Incest Victim." *Child Welfare* 59:269–275.

Orr, D.P., and Prietto, S.V. 1979. "Emergency Management of Sexually Abused Children." *American Journal of Diseases of Children* 133:628–631.

Parson, E.R. 1984. "The Role of Psychodynamic Group Psychotherapy in the Treatment of the Combat Veteran." In H.J. Schwartz, ed., *Psychotherapy of the Combat Veteran*. New York: Spectrum Publications.

Pierce, R., and Pierce, L.H. 1985. "The Sexually Abused Child: A Comparison of Male and Female Victims." *Child Abuse and Neglect* 9:191–199.

Pescosolido, F.J., and Petrella, D.M. 1986. "The Development Process and Evaluation of Group Psychotherapy with Sexually Abused Preschool Girls." *International Journal of Group Psychotherapy* 36:447–469.

Raybin, J.B. 1969. "Homosexual Incest." *Journal of Nervous and Mental Disease* 148:105–110.

Reinhart, M.A. 1987. "Sexually Abused Boys." *Child Abuse and Neglect* 11:229–235.

Rounsaville, B.; Lifton, N.; and Bieber, M. 1979. "The Natural History of a Psychotherapy Group for Battered Women." *Psychiatry* 42:63–78.

Sanford, L.T. 1988. Personal communication.

Sgroi, S.M. 1982. *Handbook of Clinical Intervention in Child Sexual Abuse.* Lexington, Mass.: Lexington Books.

Spencer, M.J., and Dunklee, P. 1986. "Sexual Abuse of Boys." *Pediatrics* 78:133–138.

Tilelli, J.A.; Turek, D; and Jaffe, A.C. 1980. "Sexual Abuse of Children: Clinical Findings and Implications for Management." *New England Journal of Medicine* 302:319–323.

Van der Kolk, B.A. 1987. *Psychological Trauma.* Washington, D.C.: American Psychiatric Press.

Walker, J.I. 1981. "Group Psychotherapy with Vietnam Veterans." *International Journal of Group Psychotherapy* 31:379–389.

Yalom, I. 1975. *The Theory and Practice of Group Psychotherapy.* New York: Basic Books.

Yassen, J., and Glass, L. 1984. "Sexual Assault Survivor Groups." *Social Work* 27:252–257.

5
Stages of Recovery for Adult Survivors of Child Sexual Abuse

Suzanne M. Sgroi

Much has been written in recent years about the traumatic impact of child sexual abuse. Less is known about the recovery process for adult survivors. By what means do adults who were sexually abused when they were children recover from the emotional trauma sustained by many? Is it possible to put childhood sexual victimization experiences entirely behind oneself—not burying them by repression or compensating by using dysfunctional coping mechanisms but rather by processing and integrating them and moving beyond? Are paths to recovery unpredictable and totally idiosyncratic? Or can adult survivors realistically hope to find healing in an incremental and, to some degree, predictable fashion? Will therapeutic intervention aid in the recovery process?

The answer to the last two questions is a qualified "yes." My colleagues and I at New England Clinical Associates now believe that it is possible to identify predictable stages of recovery for adult survivors whose capacity for healthy emotional functioning is impaired in some way associated with the traumatic impact of their childhood sexual abuse experiences. We also believe that peer group therapy is the most effective type of clinical intervention to assist adult survivors to move through the stages of recovery in a timely fashion. To justify and explain these beliefs, it is necessary first to describe the stages of recovery and a recovery process. Within this framework, it will then be possible in the next chapter to describe an approach for conducting peer group therapy for adult survivors in a manner that enables the participants to facilitate their own healing and recovery.

There are five stages of recovery:

1. Acknowledging the reality of the abuse.
2. Overcoming secondary responses to the abuse.
3. Forgiving oneself (ending self-punishment).
4. Adopting positive coping behaviors.
5. Relinquishing survivor identity.

Both the stages of recovery listed above, and the recovery process associated with each were conceptualized as a result of working with numerous women and men who requested treatment over the years. This means that our impressions are derived from a population of adult survivors who were actively seeking help for a condition they perceived as problematic. Therefore, it is important to remember that the recovery process described in this chapter may not be pertinent for all adults who were sexually abused in childhood, since not all persons who experience childhood sexual abuse are necessarily or inevitably traumatized by that experience. Others may recover from their victimization in different ways by seeking therapeutic help. However, the following observations are offered in the hope that they may assist clinicians who are working with those adult survivors who do request treatment for emotional trauma associated with their victimization experience.

Acknowledging the Reality of the Abuse

In this critical first stage of recovery, the survivor must overcome the *protective denial* that she or he used to tolerate the abuse during childhood and thereafter. This denial often takes the form of repressing some or all of the memories of the actual abuse experiences. Some adults who were emotionally traumatized by sexual abuse in childhood have significant memory gaps for months or years, not just for infancy and early childhood (which is normal) but for primary school ages and older. We speculate that these gaps in memory not only protect them from recalling the details of their abusive experiences but also from remembering that any type of abuse occurred at all. This was true for a woman survivor who successfully repressed until age 40 all of her memories of early physical abuse by her mother, later sexual molestation by her father, and a sexual assault by three strangers that occurred when she was 4 years old. Although her memory block was protective in many ways, it also cut her off from a significant part of her past history and left her without a plausible explanation for her very negative self-image and her low self-esteem. This woman's memory block also enabled her to function well by using numerous protective coping mechanisms that required an enormous energy investment from her and for which she had literally forgotten the original cause.

These coping mechanisms have been described in detail (Sgroi and Bunk 1988). Dissociative coping mechanisms allow the child victim to distance herself or himself from the powerful emotions of fear, shame, or anger or from a sense of being totally overwhelmed by physiologic responses to the sexual stimulation component of the abuse. Distancing or dissociation at times of psychological stress may have become lifelong coping mechanisms for the survivor that are invoked repeatedly when triggered by minimal cues

(Sgroi and Bunk 1988, 181). Another coping mechanism involves maintaining multiple relationships in which the survivor as a caretaker gives but does not expect (and is not expected) to receive nurturance from others. Practicing nonreciprocal caretaking also may be associated with "busyness"; the survivor fills her or his life with multiple commitments that distract her or him from experiencing emotional pain and emptiness. Other distracting behaviors include a variety of self-abusive behaviors, among them substance abuse, self-mutilation, and eating disorders.

Another group of survivors did not repress the content of the memories of the abuse but instead coped by shielding themselves from the disturbing affect that would otherwise be associated with those memories. These survivors may remember some or all of the details of the abuse experiences but in a detached and unemotional way. One woman said, "It's as if I'm watching the whole thing through a telescope—it's happening, I mean, I can see my father having sex with me, but I'm so far away that it doesn't really matter." When these clients come to treatment, it is not unusual for them to be matter-of-fact about the lack of affect associated with their memories. Sometimes they have concluded that the sexual abuse was not serious or traumatic for them since they can recall or describe the content of the abusive experiences without apparent distress. It is also likely, however, that they are putting a great deal of psychic energy into continued repression or supression of the powerful emotions associated with the abuse.

Still other survivors have protected themselves from the affect associated with their memories of childhood sexual abuse experiences by denying that the episodes were abusive in nature. Some have recall for the episodes but have relabeled them as "sex education" or have "rewritten the script" (a process described in *Vulnerable Populations,* volume 1) so that they perceive themselves as being responsible for initiating the abuse (Sgroi and Bunk 1988, 162). This group of survivors usually must invest heavily in their denial. Persistence in relabeling the abuse requires the victim to ignore repeated challenges from television programs and magazine articles that frequently bring accurate information about the real dynamics of child sexual abuse before the public. The person who has "rewritten the script" so that she or he is to blame must do so in the milieu of increased publicity and a far more enlightened public attitude about sexual victimization of children.

It is likely that most child victims used a combination of forms of denial from the time that their sexual abuse experiences became emotionally traumatic for them. The adult survivors we have treated are persons who had continued to utilize coping mechanisms of denial, distancing, and dissociation on a lifelong basis. We describe this form of denial as protective denial because the combination of coping mechanisms that they use to deal with stress was originally devised to protect them from the intense emotional pain they would otherwise have experienced when the abuse was taking place.

Protective denial serves a dual function: it prevents adult survivors from remembering the content of their abusive experiences or serves as a barrier to experiencing the affect associated with conscious memories; at the same time, it is a response to current stresses that serves as a barrier to experiencing present-day emotional pain.

We believe that the first stage of recovery for adults who experienced emotional trauma as a consequence of sexual abuse in childhood is to overcome protective denial to an extent that they are able to accomplish the tasks of memory retrieval and coupling associated affect with memory content.

Memory Retrieval

If memories of the abusive experiences were wholly or partially repressed or blocked, it appears to be important for the adult survivor to bring these memories into consciousness. This will certainly involve verbalizing them to others, first with an individual therapist and then in peer group therapy. Often it is helpful to sketch a floor plan of the scene where the abuse took place; verbalizing and visualizing details of the context of the abuse is frequently a bridge to remembering the content of the experience itself (Sgroi and Bunk 1988, 155). Many survivors find that it is helpful to confirm their memories with sympathetic others who knew the survivor in childhood such as family members, friends, or teachers. Others find that it helps to visit the scene where the abuse took place or perhaps the school the victim attended during the time when the abuse was occurring.

It should be emphasized that the retrieval of blocked or repressed memories should be, for the most part, a self-initiated process by the survivor. Therapists can guide the process to some extent; peers (other adult survivors), family members, or friends can be supportive and help to validate the memories when they reemerge into consciousness. But the impetus to recapture memories should be at the behest of the survivor and proceed at a pace congruent with the individual's own internal timetable rather than according to a schedule imposed by someone else. "Memory chasing" is unlikely to be productive (Agosta and Loring 1988, 124). A woman survivor put it this way: "The harder I try to remember, the more blocked I feel. Sometimes I can do something to push myself a little, like talk to a friend I knew in high school. But I'm more likely to remember something important when I'm not trying to remember at all!"

Repression of traumatic memories serves a useful purpose for the survivor: it protects her or him from experiencing the intense emotions that threatened to overwhelm the child victim at the time that the abuse was occurring. Far from pressuring adult survivors to remember episodes of abuse, we are more likely to advise a person who reports a disquieting sense that a repressed memory is there and frustration that she or he is unable to retrieve it by saying, "When you are ready to remember, you will. When you are ready to deal with them, the memories come." This is a reassuring and useful way to reframe an otherwise frustrating situation for the client. Both clinician and client thus agree that the client is in control of the recovery process and that her or his own pace of healing will determine the time when traumatic memories (and their associated affect) will reemerge.

Most adult survivors of child sexual abuse are highly invested in being in control of themselves and their lives. For this reason we try to shape all therapeutic interventions within the context of the patients' or clients' *choosing* to participate, *choosing* to listen, *choosing* to talk, *choosing* to interact with others, *choosing* to remember past traumas, and the like. Accordingly, it seems important to avoid utilizing techniques to assist in memory retrieval that the survivor may perceive as experiences of being out of control. Participating in age-regression hypnosis may assist some survivors to retrieve memories of their abuse; however, if this is the person's first formal experience with heterohypnosis, even when the therapist-hypnotist utilizes Ericksonian techniques emphasizing cooperation, the adult survivor is at risk for becoming terrified (during the trance or, more likely, after) by a perception that control was taken away from her or him. If a memory was retrieved during the trance, there is the additional risk that the client may believe that the memory was too frightening or dangerous to bring to consciousness without personal control being transferred to the hypnotist. In turn, this may be a serious obstacle to processing further the memory of the abuse and its associated affect. As a result, the client may repress the memory again entirely or try to suppress its meaning by employing coping mechanisms such as distancing or dissociation to avoid experiencing the associated emotions. In summary, clinicians are well advised to be cautious about employing the technique of age-regression hypnosis for the purpose of helping adult survivors to retrieve memories. If used at all, it should be used in a timely fashion— not as the survivor's first experience of formal therapeutic heterohypnosis. It should be used only when the client repeatedly has had opportunities to experience therapeutic trance and has perceived the trance experience as safe, gradually having learned that subjects themselves choose the degree to which they cooperate with the therapist-hypnotizer and the trance experience itself.

Let us remember that memory retrieval of repressed abusive experiences in childhood should not be viewed as an end in itself. It is useful only insofar as it helps clients to acknowledge the reality of the abuse and to overcome denial processes that, although originally protective and expedient in childhood, are by now cumbersome and dysfunctional for the adult survivor.

Coupling Associated Affect with Memory Content

Paradoxically, adult survivors tend to fear "reliving" as adults and abusive experiences they did in fact survive in childhood. We believe that what they really fear is that they will be unable to tolerate experiencing the intense emotions of fear, anger, and the sense of being overwhelmed that accompanied the abuse. Some survivors successfully repressed these emotions throughout their childhood and well into adulthood. Many adults who were victims of child sexual abuse request treatment when they begin to experience flashbacks of the abusive experiences. We define flashbacks in this context as sudden vivid memories of the abuse in which content *is* coupled with affect. Some have the quality of waking dreams or nightmares except that the individual is not asleep prior to the flashback's occurrence. Understandably, clients are usually terrified by the flashbacks, especially because they occur unpredictably and not by conscious volition.

It is not unusual for adult survivors who have suddenly begun to experience flashbacks to expect and demand symptom relief from clinicians; they request therapeutic interventions aimed at suppressing the flashbacks. They are not pleased to learn that the therapeutic goal is not to suppress flashbacks or disturbing memories but rather to experience and process them as a necessary step in coming to terms with and moving beyond the entire victimization experience. Clinicians can help adult survivors by reframing the flashbacks as harbingers of recovery: "This is a sign that you are ready to recover or to move ahead in the recovery process." It is important to remember, however, that persons who have not already had positive experiences of recovery are unlikely to be convinced that feeling worse is a sign of getting better!

Beginning peer group therapy may be associated with the onset of flashbacks for some adult survivors or with increased frequency of the occurrence of flashbacks for others. Since many adult survivors are already afraid to participate in peer group therapy for other reasons, the dysphoria associated with flashbacks may be cited as a convenient reason to stop participating in this therapy modality or as a reason not to begin at all. Clinicians can use anticipatory guidance with clients by predicting that the flashbacks may occur or increase while simultaneously assuring survivors that they can tolerate the memories along with the associated affect. The advantage to clients of participating in peer group therapy for adult survivors of child sexual abuse is that they will be able to meet and identify with others who are also "surviving" this stage of recovery; often these others can report success in coupling memories of their abuse with the associated affect because they are at a later stage in their own recovery process. We believe that it has been far more beneficial for our clients to receive support and encouragement about experiencing flashbacks from their peers than from their clinicians.

On the other hand, an important prerequisite to participating in peer group therapy for adult survivors is the individual's capacity to talk about the victimization experience. Although it is not necessary to remember or to verbalize every episode of child sexual abuse that may have occurred (a highly unrealistic expectation), we find that it is necessary for a person to be able to share some of the content of at least one episode of abuse in an individual session with a clinician prior to beginning peer group therapy. That is not to say that it is easy to talk about one's victimization—quite the contrary. Nevertheless, our experience is that a useful screening device is to ask a new client who is a candidate for peer group therapy to tell the clinician, in the first session some of the details of her or his sexual abuse. A person who is unable to do so, for whatever combination of reasons, is usually not ready for peer group therapy. Some clients hope that it will be easier to talk about their victimization in a group setting. These persons usually also have an unrealistic and inaccurate view of peer group therapy. Either they hope that they will be so enfolded and buoyed up by group support that heretofore impossible tasks will magically be facilitated for them, or they fantasize that the atmosphere during the group therapy session will be so authoritative and confronting that they will be forced to do that which until now they were unable to do.

Peer group therapy for adult survivors, will not fulfill either magical expectation even when it is led by competent clinicians. Instead such clients are likely to feel intimidated and threatened by group pressure to perform self-disclosure. A predictable result under these circumstances is for the client to withdraw and fail to participate in the group process or else to "dance around" the issue while engaging in various defensive or distracting maneuvers. If the reaction is one of withdrawal or silence, other group members are likely to channel their energies into trying to help the silent group member to disclose or participate. If these efforts fail, all members are at risk for becoming angry and frustrated. If they succeed, the previously silent or withdrawn client may react with a perception of feeling overcome or out of control, and other group members may be left with an uneasy perception that they wrested control away from or overpowered one of their peers. On the other hand, if the client who is not ready to perform self-disclosure to the group has a defensive style that involves "dancing around" the issue and engaging in distracting maneuvers, much energy may be expended by all as they respond to the distractions. As a result, the other group members may become angry and frustrated, believing that their time and energies are being wasted. In her or his turn, the evasive and distracting client is at risk for feeling abandoned and scapegoated by her or his peers in conjunction with having "won" a power struggle by successfully avoiding self-disclosure. In chapter 6, the point is made that the clinician's responsibility is to ensure that power struggles between two or more group members or between therapists and clients are avoided.

We recommend that adult survivors who are unable to describe any details of their childhood sexual abuse in an individual screening session wait to participate in peer group therapy until they develop the capacity for self-disclosure in a one-on-one milieu. This may seem to be a contradiction of the recommendation in volume 1 of *Vulnerable Populations* that individual therapy for sexual abuse be limited to six to ten session (Sgroi and Bunk 1988, 157). It is not; some clients may benefit from a planned and mutually agreed-upon postponement of working upon their victimization issues, choosing instead to address other matters in longer-term therapy. Still others may benefit from a group therapy or self-help group experience for another problem, such as substance abuse or being an adult child of an alcoholic. Some of the adult survivors we have seen gained the confidence to disclose their childhood sexual abuse to others by first participating in Alcoholics Anonymous or in A1-Anon or in a group for Adult Children of Alcoholics. We do not, however, recommend that clients who are advised against participating in peer group therapy for adult survivors join a support for adult survivors instead. This is because a self-help or support group may lack the structure and competent clinical leadership that should characterize well-conducted peer group therapy. Yet a person unable to disclose her or his abuse in a one-on-one milieu is likely to encounter the same difficulties in a self-help or support group setting.

What about the person who believes that she or he may be an adult survivor of child sexual abuse but has no memories of abuse experiences? Clinicians may encounter such persons who nevertheless believe that they may be adult survivors, perhaps because they have siblings who do remember being abused by a parent or a caretaker. Some adults have no memory of sexual victimization but believe that their current dysfunctional coping mechanisms coupled with memory blocks for significant portions of their childhood are an indication that they were sexually abused. Clinicians may be tempted to accede to requests that persons who do not remember childhood sexual abuse be permitted to participate in peer group therapy for adult survivors. These are often persons who feel alienated from others and want desperately to belong somewhere. At the same time, they are eagerly pursuing an answer or a theory that explains their problems. They are willing to embrace an identity as an adult survivor of child sexual abuse in order to feel less alienated and because they hope that finding an explanation for their psychological distress will help them feel better.

We have not found that participating in peer group therapy for adult survivors has been helpful to persons who have no memory of childhood sexual abuse. First, in their eagerness to belong and to identify with other group members, these clients tend to place enormous pressure on themselves to remember an abuse experience once they begin a cycle of group therapy. As stated earlier, pressuring oneself to remember a repressed victimization experience is nearly always counterproductive. Our experience has been that receiving support and/or pressure to remember from other group members has not been helpful for those who have no memory of sexual abuse. On the contrary, these persons in a group setting of identified adult survivors are now at risk for experiencing two negative sequelae: (1) viewing an inability to remember an abusive experience during or after group therapy as yet another failure, or (2) feeling an even greater sense of isolation or alienation from others. (One woman said, "Now I've learned that I don't belong here, either!")

These clients may benefit from longer-term individual therapy that addresses their complaints or symptoms from a different perspective. All of the caveats about using age-regression hypnosis to assist identified child sexual abuse victims are applicable to persons who believe they might have been sexually abused but have no memories of abusive experiences. An intriguing approach (not yet attempted at New England Clinical Associates) might be to invite a number of these clients to participate in a time-limited cycle of group therapy with peers who have a similar history. If all of the members are persons who believe that they might be victims of childhood sexual abuse but none of them have memories of victimization, the potential benefits of peer group therapy may possibly be derived (whether or not they eventually do remember an abuse experience).

Overcoming Secondary Responses to the Abuse

In the second stage of recovery, adult survivors must now cope with their secondary responses to the reality of their child sexual abuse experiences. Along with fear, anger, and a sense of being overwhelmed and out of control while the abusive sexual interactions were occurring, many child victims also experienced guilt and shame and a pervasive sense of damage as secondary responses to their victimization. Most of them shielded themselves from fully experiencing these disturbing reactions by some type of early protective denial. As they recover their repressed memories of the abuse, many adult survivors are initially preoccupied by learning, as adults, that they can tolerate the primary responses of fear, anger, and a perception of loss of control. As they begin to reexperience the secondary responses of guilt, shame, and sense of damage, now within the context of their adult perceptions, survivors often respond with a *contemporary denial phase*. As one woman put it, "I can live with the fear and the anger; I can't live with the shame and the guilt." Another client said in a group therapy session, "I kept saying to myself, 'This didn't happen to me—not me!' " It is important to remember that both of these women had been through the process of recapturing memories of the abuse and the affect associated with those memories. Their contemporary denial was on a different level—a level of minimizing, even to the extent of trivializing, the importance of their childhood sexual victimization.

Our impression has been that survivors utilize the same coping mechanisms to shield themselves from experiencing current responses to child sexual abuse as they used to block memories of the abuse or the disturbing affect associated with those memories. Yet contemporary denial appears to be less effective than early protective denial because adult survivors report that they *do* feel guilty, they *do* feel ashamed, they *do* feel damaged as a result of the abuse. Paradoxically the second stage of recovery involves coping with all of these responses while denying the importance of the victimization that produced the responses. Having acknowledged the reality of the abuse in the first stage of recovery, the survivor now attempts to minimize the significance of the abuse in order to shield herself or himself from experiencing the emotional pain associated with the secondary responses.

It is possible that some adult survivors remain stuck and do not progress beyond the second stage of recovery for the rest of their lives. We have certainly seen numerous clients who are in a contemporary denial phase and have been unable to overcome their secondary responses of guilt, shame, and a pervasive sense of damage associated with the abuse. At New England Clinical Associates, our experience is that peer group therapy is the modality that best helps adult survivors to overcome secondary responses to their abuse. (In chapter 6, in this volume, "Healing Together: Peer Group Therapy for Adult Survivors," the benefits of this treatment modality are described in greater detail.) In peer group therapy, an adult survivor can identify with other women and men who were sexually abused in childhood in a way that affirms the reality of her or his own abuse as a consequence of accepting the validity of childhood sexual abuse for one's peers. At the same time, the survivor can challenge the distortions of reality described by other members, when they make statements such as "I'm sure it was all my fault!" and "I know it sounds silly, but I've always believed that other people would find out I'm a bad person if they really got to know me!" In turn, the survivor who participates in peer group therapy can experience acceptance of the validity of her or his abuse experiences by other members at the same time that they are challenging her or his distortions of reality. Overcoming personal guilt, shame, and sense of damage is thus closely linked to communicating to one's peers that they are not viewed as guilty, shameful, or damaged while simultaneously receiving analogous affirming messages about oneself: "We do not believe that you are guilty, shameful, or damaged."

The amount of time and effort required to overcome contemporary denial varies markedly for each individual. In general, it seems necessary for survivors to prove to themselves that they can repeatedly experience intense feelings of guilt and shame and perceptions of personal damage without being overwhelmed. Group support is of incalculable value in this part of the recovery process. One woman said, "I used to be sure that I would die if I let myself feel how bad I am. Now I look around the room and I see that there are a lot of other people who feel the same way about themselves, and they are living through it. If they can live through it, then maybe I won't die either!" What was also occurring for this woman was the experience of having others challenge her distorted self-perceptions of being bad, evil, contaminated, and blameworthy. A peer group therapy setting enables survivors gradually to acquire more positive self-perceptions because the intensive support from others and the challenges of distortions of reality are occurring simultaneously. These processes are reciprocal as well as mutual. In a well-run peer group therapy setting, each member has the opportunity to give and receive the support, to challenge others' distortions of reality, and to receive reciprocal challenges from peers.

Our experience has been that participating in time-limited cycles of peer group therapy for adult survivors over a period of time ranging from one to three years has been most helpful. Overcoming contemporary denial does not appear to be a static, one-time-only occurrence. Instead, it seems to be helpful for clients to be reminded at intervals by their peers that they are engaging in familiar self-blaming and self-deriding practices. Many clients describe this process as "playing old tapes." One survivor described it in this way: "I've got all these old tapes in my head—tapes of me telling myself that I'm no good. I'm so used to pushing the button inside my head that plays those tapes that I usually don't even notice that 'I'm doing it." One way for our clients to change this pattern has been to participate in time-limited cycles of peer group therapy at intervals.

Readers may have noticed that there is significant overlap among the stages of recovery described in this chapter. As well, it is impossible to talk about any single stage of recovery without also mentioning the processes that preceded that stage and/or those that will soon be succeeding it. None of the stages of recovery is static or immutable. Until now, the two-dimensional format of the printed page may have unintentionally conveyed a vertical hierarchical or straight-line representation of the recovery process. Nothing could be further from the observations based on our work with adult survivors at New England Clinical Associates. Instead, we view the recovery process in a three-dimensional spiral format.

As figure 5–1 shows, recovery is not a straight-line one-dimensional process. Survivors do not "finish" one stage before they move to the next; the recovery process is more accurately described as flowing from one stage to another in a spiral fashion. When the client expresses dismay at what appears to be a step backwards ("I've been here before! I thought I was finished with this"), it will be helpful for the clinician to reply. "Yes, but

Acknowledging Reality
of the Abuse

Overcoming Secondary
Responses to the Abuse

Forgiving Oneself

Relinquishing Survivor
Identity

Moving Beyond

Acknowledging Reality

Overcoming Secondary Responses
to the Abuse

Forgiving Oneself

Relinquishing
Survivor
Identity

Moving Beyond

Acknowledging Reality

Overcoming Secondary Responses

Forgiving Oneself

Relinquishing
Survivor Identity

Moving Beyond

Figure 5–1. The Recovery Spiral

you are in a different place now. It may seem like a step backward but it is not!" Upon reflection, a dynamic, developmental, eclectic, and ecological perspective for the process of recovering from emotional trauma resulting from child sexual abuse is highly congruent with much of contemporary psychological theory and current practices in psychotherapy.

Forgiving Oneself (Ending Self-Punishment)

Discussion of the third stage of recovery illustrates the observation that appreciation of what was occurring in the preceding stage is necessary to understand what is transpiring in the next. Adult survivors have perceived themselves as having engaged in shameful behaviors for which they are deserving of blame. The third stage of recovery is crucial in that it represents a turning point: to forgive oneself is an immensely freeing process through which a person also tacitly gives permission to herself or himself to end self-punishment for whatever she or he deemed was blameworthy The importance of forgiving oneself for being victimized can be mystifying to anyone who lacks first-hand experience with the recovery process. It is true, nonetheless, that victims of all types of abuse tend to blame themselves for a variety of things, including being selected as victims, cooperating with the abuser, and for (magically) causing the abuse to occur in the first place. A detailed discussion of this concept can be found in volume 1 of *Vulnerable Populations* (Sgroi and Bunk 1988, 162), where we speculated that feeling guilty because the abuse occurred can serve as a coping mechanism to help child victims feel less anxious and more in control of themselves. Adults who were emotionally traumatized by sexual abuse in childhood tend to continue a pattern of self-blame and self-punishment on a lifelong basis. Feeling guilty and blaming oneself in a patterned and repetitive fashion for a variety of present-day situations is a way for many adult survivors to utilize a familiar and now dysfunctional coping mechanism that used to help them feel less anxious and more in control but now is less likely to do so.

For most adult survivors, it does not seem to be enough to have distortions of reality ("I am bad! I do deserve to be punished") challenged successfully by their clinicians or even by their peers. It also seems necessary for adult survivors to feel acceptance and forgiveness from their peers as a necessary step toward accepting and forgiving themselves. The process can be described sequentially:

1. Accepting that one's peers were victims and that they feel guilty about their sexual victimization in childhood.

2. Caring about one's peers and perceiving them as intrinsically good and decent human beings who are not blameworthy and deserving of punishment.

3. Recognizing self-blaming and self-punishing behaviors in one's peers and identifying them at appropriate times.

4. Communicating a sincere wish to one's peers that they choose to end their self-punishing behaviors (coupled with observations and concrete suggestions regarding fewer self-blaming and more self-affirming behaviors).

5. Conveying to one's peers that you forgive them both for their previous victimization and their present-day responses to it.

It must be remembered that each of these steps has a mirror image. At the same time that the survivor is practicing the steps as applied to her or his peers, a reciprocal flow of acceptance, caring, recognition, and forgiveness aimed toward oneself is taking place. Thus the following reciprocal sequence should also be occurring:

1. The individual receives acceptance of the validity of her or his childhood victimization and present-day responses to it.

2. Caring from others is also received coupled with a message that the individual is viewed by her or his peers as good and not blameworthy or deserving of punishment.

3. The survivor also receives feedback regarding her or his self-blaming and self-punishing behaviors that have been recognized and identified by other group members.

4. Observations and concrete suggestions for ending self-blaming behaviors and substituting self-affirming behaviors are also received by the individual in the context of other members' wishes that she or he will choose to stop practicing self-punishment.

5. The survivor additionally experiences forgiveness from her or his peers for the childhood sexual victimization and current secondary responses to it.

In essence, the third stage of recovery entails the survivor's recognition *that she or he has become a self-abuser,* the she or he is now inflicting the emotional pain that results from continuing to use dysfunctional coping mechanisms developed in response to the sexual abuse in childhood, and that she or he is in control of (and responsible for) ending self-punishment. A significant component of the emotional trauma that many child victims experience is a perception that the sexual abuse magically set them apart and made them different from others—blameworthy, evil, contaminated, damaged, and damned. Cognitive restructuring of the intellectual part of this perception does not appear to be sufficient. It seems to be necessary to feel forgiven by one's peers—other human beings—in order to forgive oneself. Ironically, adult survivors who practice self-blame and self-punishment for their present-day errors and shortcomings (real or imagined) are actually punishing themselves for being fallible human beings. Adult survivors of child sexual abuse (and many, many other people who never experienced childhood sexual victimization but also practice self-blame and self-punishment for a variety of other reasons) need to forgive themselves for being human. Oddly, since they set themselves apart as a response to their victimization, they must choose formally to rejoin the human race—which means accepting one's fallibility, imperfections, and capacity to make mistakes coupled with affirming one's worthiness, achievements, and capacity to be successful and do good.

Adopting Positive Coping Behaviors

This stage of recovery requires substituting more functional coping mechanisms for everyday living as dysfunctional coping mechanisms are used less often and eventually discarded. The latter range from the various forms of intrapsychic distancing and dissociation to distracting behaviors (such as substance abuse and self-mutilating behaviors), to the various forms of interpersonal distancing such as secret keeping and pathologic caretaking of others (to the exclusion of taking care of oneself or receiving caretaking from others). In other words, in this fourth stage of recovery, adult survivors learn to practice more positive behaviors that enable them to live in the world and interact with others in a way that is nurturing and satisfying.

Although effort is required to carry out positive coping behaviors, they require less energy investment in the long run and often result in energy replenishment. Tolerating the anxiety of living through a stressful situation (a court appearance, for example) without dissociating oneself requires less psychic energy than disconnecting or numbing oneself. An advantage of staying connected and not dissociating is that the individual is able to process what is happening while it is actually going on. Dissociation prevents contemporary processing of a stressful event and delays rather than erases the associated anxiety. Later processing usually involves coping with amplified anxiety, which requires a greater total expenditure of psychic energy. Meanwhile the person who copes with a stressful situation in a state of dissociation is likely also to be cut off from neutral or positive aspects of that experience.

Secret keeping is a familiar activity for most adults who were sexually abused in childhood. Creating a secret to combat the anxiety generated by a close relationship is a coping mechanism some survivors use (Sgroi and Bunk 1988, 184). Some adult survivors create secrets to serve as a barrier between themselves and their friends, spouses, or therapists, for example. Prolonged secret keeping demands increasing amounts of energy exerted by the secret holders because secrets about anything that is important are inherently unstable; more and more energy is required to overcome the tension that builds as the content of the secret is held back from the unaware (Karpel 1980).

Secret keeping and pathologic caretaking are but two examples of coping mechanisms adult survivors use to avoid the exposure and the self-disclosure they fear will result if other human beings get too close to them or come to know them too well. Fear of exposure is thus the reason that it is extremely difficult for adult survivors to have their intimacy needs met while they are erecting and maintaining barriers against intimate relationships. The tragic results are loneliness, isolation, and emotional depletion; being cut off from others to protect against exposure also cuts off genuine caring and nurturance.

Accordingly, we believe that the fourth stage of recovery for adult survivors encompasses practicing the communications and interactional skills that are the building blocks of successful intimate relationships. Participating in peer group therapy permits adult survivors to do this in a safe and guided setting. The basic building blocks of intimacy are the capacity to share with another person the following information: this is who I am; this is how I feel; this is what I want from you; this is what I will give to you; this is what I will let you give to me; this is what I will not do or give to you; this is what I will not take or receive from you (Scarf 1986, 49). All require expressive and receptive communications skills. It obviously requires a capacity for self-disclosure; it also necessitates an ability to identify one's own emotions and wishes accurately, as well as to perceive accurately the information communicated by another person regarding her or his emotions and wishes. Intimacy requires that each person not only be able to give caring and affection to the other and to receive caring and affection from the other; it also requires that each party have the capacity for maintaining personal boundaries and performing limit setting. Chapter 6 in this volume, describes the structure and techniques that enable clients to practice these skills within the peer group therapy milieu.

The experience at New England Clinical Associates has been that it is unrealistic to expect that adult survivors will suddenly discard all of their dysfunctional coping mechanisms and acquire and utilize positive coping behaviors exclusively thereafter. No other important human coping behaviors change dramatically in this magical fashion. *Practice* is the operative word in the fourth stage of recovery. Adult survivors need to practice checking themselves inwardly ("What is going on for me right now?" "What *do*

I want?"); they need to practice direct and honest communication with others ("I'm not sure what you were meaning to say just now, but this is what I think happened"); they need to practice asking for help ("Could you let me know if you see me doing things to distract myself while we are here together?"); they need to practice self-affirming behaviors; they need to practice setting limits for themselves and others; and so forth. The spiral nature of the recovery process also means that they will again find themselves lapsing into the old and familiar dysfunctional behaviors and will need both reminders and encouragement to adopt positive alternates.

Group support is extremely important for adult survivors who are struggling to adopt positive coping behaviors. This is especially true in regard to the phenomenon experienced by many clients of "feeling worse while they are getting better." The anxiety experienced when a person reveals herself or himself is painfully real, and the individual does not always receive an immediate reward for being honest. Choosing not to distance or dissociate in a stressful situation often results in the client's hearing or perceiving the things that were new and threatening but failing to attend to that which was supportive or affirmative. Discarding dysfunctional coping mechanisms that served the functions of helping the person to feel safe and in control is probably happening during a time when she or he is fumbling while practicing the communications skills that enable intimacy and satisfaction to be derived from interpersonal relationships. When a person chooses to set limits and stop fulfilling many requests (and demands) received from others, it is not unusual to encounter howls of protest and anger from the recipients of all that pathologic caretaking. Group support and affirmation can be invaluable during the plateaus in the recovery process.

Relinquishing Survivor Identity

The fifth stage of recovery can be elusive for adult survivors. Relinquishing a survivor identity means that the individual has accomplished all of the foregoing tasks of recovery and no longer finds it necessary (or helpful) to view herself or himself as a victim *or* as a survivor. She or he has acknowledged the reality of the abuse and discarded all of the distancing or dissociative coping mechanisms, that first, helped the child victim and, later, the adult to block out or tolerate the pain of the affect associated with abuse. The person has also identified her or his current responses of guilt and shame and the pervasive sense of damage that influenced a contemporary denial phase during which the importance of the abuse was minimized. The person has forgiven herself or himself for the victimization and the secondary responses and realized that she or he had become a contemporary self-abuser.

She or he has chosen to end self-punishment and to discard self-blaming and destructive behaviors and to adopt positive coping behaviors instead.

What remains in the recovery process is to move beyond: to see oneself in a multidimensional perspective. Now the person can say, "I am a human being, a person with strengths and weaknesses, good qualities and faults; a person who makes mistakes but also has useful and positive accomplishments. I was sexually abused when I was a child and that is an important part of my history. But that was then; this is now, and I no longer need to identify myself as a survivor. Instead it is accurate for me simply to identify myself as a person and a self—no more and no less."

Relinquishing a survivor identity also means the person is ready to take responsibility for her or his own present and future happiness in totality. That is, the person believes that she or he is no longer a helpless child victim at the mercy of a powerful abuser nor a wounded adult whose current destiny is influenced by hidden or poorly understood emotional sequelae of child sexual abuse experiences. It seems unlikely that a person will be ready to relinquish a survivor identity until she or he has experienced some successes in adopting and utilizing positive coping behaviors. Experiencing success is a wonderful way for people to build self-confidence and to convince themselves that future success is possible and attainable.

It is likewise necessary to achieve multidimensional views of one's abuser(s) and, frequently, the caretakers who failed to protect the individual from the abuse in childhood. Many adult survivors never come to terms with their relationships with the abuser(s) or nonoffending parents or caretakers. If a survivor tenaciously clings to the perception that the abuser was or is an all-powerful monster with no redeeming human qualities, then she or he is at risk to retain some measure of a victim identity as well. Some clients choose to work directly with their abusers; others work through their relationships with their abusers by role plays, psychodrama, and the like. Direct interaction with the abuser or with nonoffending parents as individuals is less important than working through and coming to terms with one's relationships with these people.

A significant number of adult survivors become heavily invested in improving or normalizing their relationships with their parents. If the client is a survivor of intrafamily child sexual abuse, she or he may yearn to have the abuse validated by the abuser (if that person is still alive) or by other family members. In other words, the client wants the abuser to admit that she or he committed the abusive acts and apologize for doing so; wants the nonoffending parents(s) to admit that the abuse occurred and take responsibility for failure to protect the child victim; wants siblings or other close family members also to admit that the abuse occurred and convey their sympathy or regrets about its occurrence. These wishes, although understandable, are highly unrealistic and reflect a magical expectation that, as an adult, one can experience the benevolent caretaking by parents and family members that is, alas, infrequently experienced by young children, even when they grow up in nonabusive families. To expect now-middle-aged or elderly parents or one's grown-up siblings to validate the childhood sexual abuse and now "make up for" past inattention is risky at best.

In keeping with the latter observations, we consistently advise adult survivors to engage in a recovery process that involves things that *they* learn, that *they* practice, that *they* can accomplish for themselves. It is perilous to measure the success (or failure) of one's own recovery process by the actions (or inactions) of others. To set as a goal that another person will behave or respond in a wished-for fashion is counterproductive because it is not possible to control the behaviors or responses of another person; it is possible to be in control only of oneself. By the same token, to be dependent for one's own happiness or someone else's behavior is to relinquish control inappropriately to that person. This is a hard lesson for adult survivors to learn; many missed entirely the benevolent caretaking in childhood to which they were entitled. To be told by one's clinicians and one's peers, "You and you alone are responsible for your own happiness!" is perceived by some as a harsh and uncaring message.

We caution clinicians who work with adult survivors to be aware that the final stage of recovery is to relinquish a survivor identity and, with it, the pursuit of benevolent caretaking by one's family of origin, one's spouse, one's children, one's peers, or one's clinicians. All adult survivors wish for benevolent caretaking, as do all other human beings; some adult survivors pursue it untiringly for years. We believe that the most effective way to help adult survivors to avoid getting sidetracked in this fashion is to encourage them to practice the skills that will enable them to have successful intimate relationships with spouses, partners, and friends, they will be able to have their needs for affection, affiliation, and nurturance met in a milieu of mutuality and reciprocity (not benevolent caretaking).

Summary

This chapter has described a recovery process for adult survivors within a conceptual framework of stages of recovery. The recovery process is viewed as dynamic rather than static and is best described as occurring in a three-dimensional spiral rather in a vertical linear fashion. The next, companion, chapter offers approaches and techniques for conducting the peer group therapy interventions that were so frequently mentioned in this chapter.

130 • *Vulnerable Populations*

References

Agosta, Carol, and Loring, Mary. 1988. "Understanding and Treating the Adult Retrospective Victim of Child Sexual Abuse." In S.M. Sgroi, ed. *Vulnerable Populations,* 1:115–135. Lexington, Mass.: Lexington Books.

Karpel, Mark A. 1980. "Family Secrets: I. Conceptual and Ethical Issues in the Relational Context: II. Ethical and Practical Considerations in Therapeutic Management." *Family Process* 19:295–306.

Scarf, Maggie. November, 1986. "Intimate Partners: Patterns in Love and Marriage." *Atlantic* 258:45–93.

Sgroi, Suzanne M., and Bunk, Barbara S. 1988. "A Clinical Approach to Adult Survivors of Child Sexual Abuse." In S.M. Sgroi, ed. *Vulnerable Populations,* 1:137–186. Lexington, Massachusetts: Lexington Books.

6
Healing Together: Peer Group Therapy for Adult Survivors of Child Sexual Abuse

Suzanne M. Sgroi

Peer group therapy affords a milieu in which adult survivors can work together to heal the emotional trauma they experienced when they were victims of sexual abuse in childhood. The use of this therapy modality with adult survivors has been described in numerous reports and articles (Bergart 1986, Blake-White and Kline 1985; Goodman and Nowak-Scibelli 1985; Herman and Schatzow 1984; Tsai and Wagner 1978). This chapter presents a methodology for conducting time-limited peer group therapy that was evolved at New England Clinical Associates, a private office specializing in the treatment of child sexual abuse.

There appear to be three types of benefits afforded by peer group therapy that cannot be derived in any other therapeutic milieu:

1. Group members can identify with and receive support from their peers.
2. Clients can both issue and receive challenges (in a reciprocal fashion with their peers) to the distortions of reality perceived by many victims of child sexual abuse.
3. Participants can practice the social and communications interactions that are the building blocks for successful intimate relationships, such as identifying and communicating emotions, wishes, and requests, giving and receiving help, affection and caring, engaging in limit setting for self and others, and, defining and maintaining personal boundaries.

Chapter 5 in this volume describes these foregoing benefits in the context of attempting to explain the recovery process. This chapter focuses on the methodology of creating a therapeutic milieu that provides a safe, guided setting in which clients can experience these benefits. Unlike a support or self-help group for which clinical leadership is not required, peer group therapy should always be conducted by clinically competent therapists who have the responsibility for providing both structure and therapeutic interventions. Group therapists are responsible for carrying out these tasks:

1. Identifying the individual therapy needs of each member.
2. Planning and facilitating clinical interventions to meet those therapy needs that can best be addressed in a group setting.
3. Guarding against emotional injury to any client that might otherwise be incurred.

The last task needs further clarification. It is up to the therapists to see to it that clients are not encouraged to become enmeshed and overidentify with each other or to challenge each other in a hostile or punitive fashion. Likewise the goal is for members to identify and express their own reactions and feelings (which often include disappointed and angry feelings); however, the therapists must guard against anger and blame being displaced on anyone in the group. In well-conducted peer group therapy sessions, adult survivors can safely be guided to practice self-disclosure, to identify wishes and needs, request help from others, and so forth. Meanwhile, they receive help from the therapists, whenever necessary, to set limits for themselves and others and to define and maintain their personal boundaries.

Format

At the New England Clinical Associates office, we have utilized a format of time-limited cycles of peer group therapy for female adult survivors. The cycles have varied in length from ten to fourteen weeks. It has proved feasible to conduct three cycles each year: a twelve to fourteen-week cycle from the end of January to mid-April; a ten-week cycle from June to mid-August; and a twelve to fourteen-week cycle from late September to mid-December. This planned format for each year allows a four- or five-week interval between each cycle, which is invaluable for planning and allowing both the staff and clients to have time to process what occurred in the last cycle. It also allows time for staff vacations, a necessary consideration! At the same time, there are both consistency and continuity to this format, which are very helpful to clients. Some of the women have chosen to participate in just one cycle. Others have chosen to participate in each cycle of peer group therapy that has been offered after their initial experience in the program. Still others have participated intermittently, perhaps choosing to participate in one cycle each year while sitting out the other cycles. Each pattern of participation has its own advantages. Some adult survivors decide they wish to work continuously on unresolved trauma secondary to sexual victimization experiences in childhood, especially when they believe they have experienced immediate benefits from peer group therapy. Others find that intermittent participation (joining in every other cycle or perhaps in every third or fourth cycle) is more appropriate for them. The latter clients are sometimes limited by financial constraints and cannot afford to participate more often. Or they may be able to make a commitment to attend an entire cycle at odd times, depending on work or personal obligations. Lastly, participating in only one cycle can also be beneficial and help meet those therapy needs that can best be addressed in peer group therapy for some clients.

In general, it has been easier to convince clients, especially those new to treatment, to participate in a time-limited cycle of peer group therapy. An open-ended format with no projected stopping point or identified date for ending the therapy tends to be threatening and difficult to "sell". People are afraid to make open-ended commitments to a process that is unfamiliar and often downright threatening. It is normal to ask, "When will I be finished? When can I stop?" The response, "We'll let you know when you are ready to stop," is not very reassuring! Worse, it may be perceived by clients as surrendering or giving up control to a threatening authority figure. By contrast, agreeing to attend every session of a time-limited cycle of peer group therapy scheduled to extend over ten to fourteen weeks tends to perceived as less threatening. It seems to be helpful to know in advance when the therapy modality is scheduled to stop and be able to plan around the stopping date. As well, it enables some of the clients to feel more secure in the light of the financial commitment. Before they begin, they know exactly how much their participation will cost.

Yet another advantage to the time-limited format is that it parallels the experience of participating in most public education programs in the United States. Nearly all of the adult survivors will have had the life experience of attending grammar school and high school with attendance periods divided into quarters, semesters, or trimesters. Thus the experience of attending a class or participating in a program for a projected number of weeks or months and then stopping is already a familiar life experience for the clients. Many group members will also have taken time-limited courses in which they worked on a topic for a limited period of time and then experienced both closure and a sense of accomplishment when the course ended.

The size of our groups has ranged from six to ten women, always with two female cotherapists. A group size of eight to ten is ideal; then when absences occur (inevitable even when members are sincerely committed to attend all of the sessions in a cycle), there are enough members present to permit group process to take place. Our experience has been that a minimum of five or six members must be present in each session for the interactions that enable the support, challenge, and practice benefits to occur. With the exception of one member in one cycle, the groups have been limited to women who remember distinctly at least one episode of childhood sexual abuse. Membership has not been limited to women who were sexually abused in childhood by family members as opposed to women who were victimized by extrafamily abusers; however, the majority of the clients were abused by their fathers, stepfathers, older brothers, or grandfathers.

Ten cycles of peer group therapy for adult survivors of child sexual abuse were conducted at the New England Clinical Associates office between September 1985 and December 1988. The last eight cycles had a theme selected by the cotherapists and announced to the members at the initial session of each cycle. The theme provides a focus for clients and therapists and helps the members to set goals for their work in that cycle. In addition to addressing a topic area pertinent to the members' common experience of childhood sexual abuse, the theme must also be one that the clients can relate to the coping mechanisms that they utilized to function in their everyday lives as adults.

For example, the theme for a cycle of time-limited group therapy for adult survivors of child sexual abuse might be "Dealing with Fear." The group cotherapists would announce the the theme at the first session and encourage the clients to think about how they were "dealing with fear" during childhood when the sexual abuse was taking place. In subsequent sessions, the therapists will urge clients to examine how they are "dealing with fear" now. There will be opportunities for clients to reflect for themselves and each other on any similarities that may exist between their past and current methods of "dealing with fear." Soon the therapists will encourage the clients to set goals for working on "dealing with fear" for the rest of the cycle. Each member will be asked to identify some way in which she is willing to let the others help her in working on a goal related to the theme. One woman remembered that, as a child, her way of dealing with the fear that other children might learn of her sexual abuse by her brother had been to distance herself physically from others. In the adult survivor group, the other women noticed that she pushed her chair back from the circle whenever she was anxious. They pointed out to her that moving her chair back was a way of putting physical distance between herself and others, as well as between herself and a threatening situation. This woman asked the others to help her to remain present in the group in a psychological sense by telling her whenever they observed that she was pushing her chair back or otherwise distancing from her peers and the present situation on a psychological level.

Other examples of themes that have worked well in cycles of time-limited group therapy for adult survivors are "Coping with Pain," "Exercising Control," and "Taking Care of Myself," and "Relating to Time." Chapter 7 in this volume contains a description of effectively using "Exploring My Spirituality " as a theme for a cycle of peer group therapy for adult survivors. By contrast "Accepting Myself" did not prove to be a very workable theme for a cycle of group therapy for this client population. The clients found it very difficult to address the theme at all and had a hard time in setting tasks or goals for themselves in the group. Similarly the therapists found it difficult to help the clients identify material related to the theme that they were willing to let their peers assist them with during the group sessions.

It is important for the therapists to take responsibility for maintaining both the format and the structure. If they abandon talking about the theme during the middle sessions in the cycle, it is highly unlikely that the clients will find that it was relevant to their recovery process or afforded them useful opportunities to work effectively in a group setting. If the therapists are not diligent in helping clients to set tasks or goals, if they do not facilitate a process in which clients can request and receive help from their peers, it is unlikely that these desirable goals will be reached during the group therapy. Format and structure do not ensure that time-limited peer group therapy will be successful; the therapists must believe in the feasibility of the methodology and be committed to practicing within it and making it work. It is preferable not to have an announced theme than to announce a theme and then ignore it. The latter actions constitute, in effect, a broken promise by the therapists, highly undesirable in any type of therapy.

The methodology described in this chapter was evolved over time and is still being used because it has seemed to assist adult survivors to practice more functional coping mechanisms as a step to discarding patterns of coping that were dysfunctional or destructive or both. Readers are asked to remember that no format is perfect and that the structure and methodology described in this chapter are meant to be enabling rather than confining and to be viewed as starting points rather than as end points.

Requirements for Participation

At New England Clinical Associates we have accepted adult survivors who are self-referred and those referred by other clinicians. Since it is the philosophy of the program that healing together in peer group therapy is the treatment of choice for adult survivors, we do not see, even for an initial visit, adult survivors who refuse at the outset to consider participation in peer group therapy. Clients who fit the description are told on the telephone that the policy of the office is to avoid becoming involved in a long-term individual therapy relationship with adult survivors who do not wish to participate in peer group therapy.

Most of the adult survivors we have seen are women; a few (fewer than ten) have been men. Although the male adult survivors were all considered to be candidates for peer group therapy, it has not been possible to date (January, 1989) to sponsor a cycle of peer group therapy for them because there have been too few of them at any one time for a core group to be formed. We hope in the future to sponsor a cycle of peer group therapy for male adult survivors at the New England Clinical Associates office, and plan to sponsor a cycle of coeducational group therapy for adult survivors whenever it is feasible in the future.

The screening process was evolved primarily in working with female adult survivors. We have found it useful to explore general areas with potential candidates for peer group therapy in one to three screening interviews. (Some persons who call to inquire about participation in peer group therapy can be screened out on the telephone and will not need to expend the cost for even a single screening interview.) From our experience, we have formulated these requirements for participation.

Stabilization of Acting-out or Severe System Behavior

Although the majority of the clients who have participated in peer group therapy for adult survivors have had a late presentation pattern, we have also accepted clients with an early presentation pattern (Sgroi and Bunk 1988, 149) into groups. The type of presentation pattern (early versus late) is less important than is the stabilization of the acting-out or severe symptom behaviors that appear in mid-adolescence or young adulthood and characterize the early presentation pattern. In general, it seems to be necessary for adult survivors who have an early presentation pattern to have been stabilized with regard to their acting out or severe symptom behaviors for at least one year. To date, none of the early presenters who had not been stabilized for at least one year have been able to finish a ten-to fourteen-week cycle. They dropped out, usually because they began to drink or to abuse drugs or to have psychotic symptomatology or else because they began to experience intense desires to engage in the symptom or acting-out behavior soon after starting to participate in peer group therapy. We speculate that these women had had insufficient experience in negotiating the demands of day-to-day living in the world without practicing the acting-out or severe symptom behaviors. Accordingly, all of their energy was consumed by their battle to abstain from drinking alcohol, abusing drugs, eating normally, and the like. It appeared that for these women, participating in peer group therapy for adult survivors required them to divert energy away from avoiding the severe symptom or acting-out behaviors. We theorized that they could not sustain a commitment to finishing a relatively short cycle of peer group therapy; the stresses generated by peer pressure to examine the meaning of their cooperation with the abuser and participation in the sexually abusive acts were too much for them to handle.

In practical terms, we obtain a careful past and present history in regard to the presence or absence of severe symptoms of acting-out behaviors. If present in the previous history, we try to find out for how long the survivor has been able to live in the world without practicing one of these behaviors.

In general, it has seemed to be necessary for a survivor to have abstained from any severe symptom or acting-out behavior for a minimum of one year prior to participating in peer group therapy for the purpose of working on emotional sequelae of childhood sexual abuse. If it is discovered that the client who wishes to participate in peer group therapy for adult survivors has recently required a psychiatric hospitalization or has had a recent reactivation of one of the severe symptom or acting-out behaviors, we now require that the person wait and contact us later, to be reconsidered after she has been able to stabilize the behavior for at least one year.

Ability to Discuss the Sexual Victimization Experience

It seems to be necessary for the survivor to demonstrate the capacity in an individual session to tell a clinician at least some details of at least one episode of her abuse (refer to chapter 5 in this volume and to Sgroi and Bunk 1988). Survivors who are unable to do so in an individual session have been unable to work effectively in a group setting in our office. Sometimes we contract for a limited number of individual sessions with such clients; for some, this has proved to be helpful in enabling them to disclose their abuse, and we have then accepted them for participation in peer group therapy.

Willingness to Participate in Group Therapy (Versus a Support Group)

We find that it is important to explain the differences between support groups or self-help groups and peer group therapy as part of the screening process. The following definitions have been useful. Support groups or self-help groups are consumer directed, often with a requirement that the leader(s) (if any) also be consumers (for example a self-help group for adult survivors might have as a requirement that the leader(s) be professed adult survivors). Self-help or support groups tend to have democratic structures; members decide among themselves, sometimes by voting, the issues they will address, the positions they will take, who will be responsible for leadership, and so forth. Often such groups will be governed like clubs with elected leadership, an agenda, dues, projects, and the like. Participation is voluntary, but it may be necessary for new members to be voted in by the current members. Attendance may be sporadic, although a certain attendance record may also be required in order to sustain membership.

By contrast, group therapy is clinician directed or therapist directed at all levels. Clients pay fees for participation, in return for which they can expect competent clinical leadership. Injury to group members is thus avoided because the therapists are clinically competent and are able to ensure that the structure and format of the group therapy afford the safety and consistency that are needed for effective group *therapy* to take place. In peer group therapy, democratic process is not utilized. For example, the therapists decide who will participate, what the theme will be, how long and under what circumstances a topic will be discussed, and so forth. Also attendance and membership will be consistent. (One advantage of time-limited group therapy, by the way, is that membership is closed after the first or second session of a cycle.) Although members occasionally have unavoidable absences (usually due to illness), it is the responsibility of the therapists to see that a pattern of inconsistent attendance by any member is not permitted to continue.

A careful explanation of these differences is very helpful for survivors considering participation in peer group therapy. Some are not interested in clinician-directed recovery process and choose not to participate for that reason. Others may examine their personal calendars and discover that they have enough other commitments during the time slot scheduled for an upcoming cycle of peer group therapy that it will not be feasible for them to participate. Still others may have difficulty with the fee-for-service aspect of privately conducted nonsubsidized group therapy. Interestingly, the last difficulty for some survivors does not always represent an economic barrier to participation but rather a psychological barrier. Although some survivors can afford to pay for therapy to help them address emotional sequelae of sexual victimization in childhood, they may be unwilling to do so because they view the requirement that they pay for their therapy as a victimization. These women seem to feel more in control of their own recovery process in a consumer-directed setting. A careful explanation of the advantages and disadvantages of consumer-directed group versus a clinician-directed groups is clarifying at the outset and can help potential clients to decide which approach they wish to try.

Relationship to Individual Therapy

Participating in a cycle of time-limited peer group therapy is not intended to address all of the therapy needs for group members, nor is it possible for this to occur. It is advisable for adult survivors who are already participating in individual therapy to continue to see their therapist while participating in a cycle of peer group therapy. For logistical or financial reasons, some may wish to see their individual therapist less frequently (perhaps every two weeks or even once month) while they are also attending weekly sessions of peer group therapy. Others may wish to continue individual therapy on a weekly basis. Whatever the arrangement, it is essential for the clinician who has conducted individual therapy with the adult survivor to approve of the plan for the client now to participate in peer group therapy. Many of our clients were directly referred to the New England Clinical Associates office by therapists who are familiar with our program and believe it will help their clients.

If the potential candidate is self-referred but is seeing another clinician for individual therapy, we have found it best to be in contact with that clinician before a final decision is made. We ask the adult survivor on the telephone or at the first screening session to sign a release permitting two-way communication with the other clinician. Then one of the group co-therapists can call the other clinician and verify her or his approval of the plan for the adult survivor to participate in a cycle of peer group therapy at the New England Clinical Associates office. Part of the joint planning will include a clarification of the arrangements for therapy at each office, as well as an agreement about ongoing communication between the clinicians before, during, and immediately after the adult survivor participates in the cycle. Interestingly, when the clarification and communication between clinicians occurs in advance, we often find that there is little or no need for communication between the clinicians while the adult survivor is actually participating in a cycle of peer group therapy.

It is counterproductive for all concerned to permit an adult survivor to participate in peer group therapy if the individual therapist is unaware or disapproves of the plan. We insist that the person being screened for participation sign a release giving us permission for communication between the clinicians. If this is refused, for whatever reason, we do not see her or him even for an initial screening session. In other words, the individual therapist's disapproval or a refusal by the adult survivor to permit communication between the clinicians precludes participation in a cycle of peer group therapy.

Maintaining a firm stance on this issue is important. It is never appropriate for a clinician to participate in secret keeping with a client with regard to concealing important information from another clinician who also sees the client. A refusal to do so is a significant clinical intervention that role models open and honest communication and an unwillingness to become involved in a triangulation process between the client and another clinician. An adult survivor who wishes to participate in peer group therapy aimed at recovering from unresolved emotional trauma that resulted from childhood sexual abuse has a right to express this wish to her or his clinician. If the clinician disapproves, the client then has the right to engage in open and direct discussion and negotiation with the clinician about this issue within the larger context of their psychotherapeutic relationship. Adult survivors sometimes tell us that they are afraid to verbalize wishes or to express disagreement with their clinicians within the context of an individual psychotherapeutic relationship. Our response is to affirm their right to do so nevertheless. Sometimes their fears of rejection or even retaliation by a powerful authority figure are totally unrealistic; sometimes, alas, the fears are reality based. Either way, New England Clinical Associates will not join in secret keeping with a client who is unwilling to inform her or his clinician of an intention to seek therapy at our office. Nor will we knowingly permit an adult survivor to participate in peer group therapy at our office if the individual therapist disapproves of this action; to do so would be tantamount to joining the client in an act of rebellion against an ongoing treatment provider. Finally, we will not accept an adult survivor as a new client "on the rebound" from a power struggle with her or his clinician over an issue such as the client's participation in peer group therapy at our office. If an adult survivor wishes to terminate an ongoing psychotherapeutic relationship over this issue, we would recommend that she or he choose either of the following courses:

- Wait at least one year after ending the previous relationship before requesting services at New England Clinical Associates
- Work for at least three months with yet a different clinician who does support a plan to participate also in peer group therapy before requesting admission to the New England Clinical Associates program.

When adult survivors who are not receiving psychotherapy from another office request admission to a cycle of time-limited peer group therapy at New England Clinical Associates, we advise them that they should plan to be seen individually at least as often as once each month during the cycle. Our experience has been that participating in well-conducted peer group therapy tends to raise many issues and conflicts for group members, especially with respect to a resurgence of memories about the sexual abuse experiences, which are often accompanied by powerful affective responses. A weekly ninety minute peer group therapy format does not afford enough time to process and work through all of the individual issues likely to be raised. Hence the suggestion that new clients who are not participating in individual therapy elsewhere plan to be seen individually at least once a month.

Permission to Videotape Sessions

All group therapy sessions at the New England Clinical Associates office are videotaped for the purpose of study and review so that clinicians can monitor the progress of the group and its individual members and modify the treatment plan in a timely fashion. Since it would be unethical to videotape clients without their permission, each group member must sign a video tape agreement that sets out these purposes and affirms that the videotape will be held in strict confidentiality.

The videotaping is done from an adjoining room through a view mirror;

the camera is not visible during the session, although the microphone can be easily seen. New clients are shown the meeting room, the view mirror, and the camera. Although some are initially uncomfortable about it, nearly all of them later comment that they forgot about the recording process soon after the cycle began. Refusal to sign the videotape agreement precludes participation in peer group therapy. To date, we know of only one woman who chose not to pursue inquiries further after she learned in a screening telephone conversation that the sessions would be videotaped. Nor are we aware of any adult survivor who was interviewed at least once at the New England Clinical Associates office and was accepted into the program but then refused to participate because of the videotaping policy.

The videotaped record of each session has been helpful in monitoring the progress of group members and the performance of the group cotherapists. It has been an invaluable asset for planning future therapy interventions, as well as an effective learning tool. The videotaping has been directly helpful to clients as well. In return for agreeing to be videotaped, each group member is permitted to review the videotape of any session in which she has participated, at no charge and at a mutually convenient time. Sometimes the therapists make a specific request or assignment to a group member to review a specific segment of the videotape of a session. Clients have reported again and again that they used the intrapsychic coping mechanisms of distancing or dissociation when they felt stressed during particular sessions. As a result, they may then have misinterpreted or even missed entirely what they or others said or did during a particular segment of a session or series of interactions. Reviewing the videotape and then discussing it in an individual session can be enormously helpful in many other areas. For example, the survivor who does not know exactly when she invokes one of these coping mechanisms can see herself do so and be helped to understand the process on a conscious level by reviewing the videotape and discussing what took place. Using the videotape to review one's interpersonal interactions with others, including body language, tone of voice and voice level, and timing of responses (to name a few), can also be very helpful. In other words, we have found that videotaping peer group therapy sessions helps us to deliver the reeducation component of treatment for child sexual abuse (See also chapter 1 in this volume.)

Therapy Interventions

As previously discussed a ratio of two cotherapists for six to ten clients has been found to be workable for time-limited cycles of peer group therapy for adult survivors at the New England Clinical Associates office. Having two cotherapists lead the group affords a lower client-to-therapist ratio and allows the clinicians to provide a wider variety of services to clients. It also allows them to role model appropriate adult-to-adult interactions with each other for the clients.

The two cotherapists can divide the labor. One can take primary responsibility for ensuring that the individual therapy needs for each member are being met, and the other can take primary responsibility for attending to and facilitating the group process. When one of the cotherapists has less experience than the other, a good initial approach is for the more experienced person to attend to group process, while the less experienced therapist takes responsibility for monitoring the individual therapy needs of the members. As the two become accustomed to working together and to working in this therapy milieu with adult survivors, they can trade responsibilities for the balance of the cycle or perhaps in alternate sessions. Experienced cotherapists who are accustomed to working together and to coleading peer group therapy with adult survivors can be flexible in their approach and share responsibility for both tasks.

A rigidly unyielding division of labor with regard to these two tasks would never be appropriate and might even be counterproductive if it was a source of tension between the cotherapists. Tension and conflict or lack of respect and trust between cotherapists in a peer group setting will immediately be perceived by the clients and will inevitably interfere with their treatment. The cotherapists must have a good working relationship and work out any disagreements between them in supervisory meetings or in a collegial fashion as they review the progress of the group members and plan the therapy on a week-by-week basis. We have found it very helpful at the New England Clinical Associates office to review part or all of the videotape of the last session as we plan for the next. This affords a good opportunity also for the cotherapists and other staff members to review how they are working together and address any problems that may have arisen between them in a fashion that will avoid future difficulties.

Addressing Individual Therapy Needs for Group Members

This task requires the therapists to be familiar with each group member's personal history of sexual victimization in childhood and to learn, by direct questioning and by inference, the coping mechanisms the survivor used when the abuse was taking place. The therapists must discover how the survivor is currently functioning and identify the coping mechanisms she is using. These can be identified by direct questioning and by observing the survivor's interactions with the therapists and with her peers in the group setting. The therapists must see to it that each woman shares some information about her childhood sexual victimization in the first session. The following questions can be asked of each member:

- How often do you think about the sexual abuse now?
- How do these memories affect you?
- Do you have dreams or nightmares about the abuse or your abuser?
- Do you have sudden flashes of memories during the day (flashbacks)? If so, what happens after that? How do you handle it?

If there are several clients in the group who have participated in previous cycles of peer group therapy, they may ask such questions of each other and of the newer members without much need for guidance by the therapists. If not, it may be necessary for the therapists to see to it that the questions are asked as each member is invited to practice self-disclosure by sharing some details of victimization experience(s). As will be discussed later, it is preferable for the therapists to invite or encourage group members to ask each other these questions rather than to ask the questions themselves.

The introduction of the theme for the cycle affords an opportunity for the therapists to begin to learn about each member's early coping mechanisms during the time when she was being abused in childhood. Careful listening is usually all that is required to discover what each woman believes is the meaning of her cooperation with the engagement strategies used by her abuser as well as the significance of her participation in the sexual behaviors initiated by her abuser. If the theme is "Coping with Pain" the question, "How were you coping with pain while you were being abused?" will begin to elicit both the coping mechanisms and the affect associated with each woman's victimization experience. In subsequent sessions, each client will be asked, "How are you coping with pain now, as an adult?" This question will begin to elicit the survivor's present-day coping mechanisms and also leads into identifying her secondary responses to the abuse (guilt, shame, and the like).

Some adult survivors are already good at identifying their emotional reactions to specific situations or interactions with others; some are not. It is the responsibility of the therapists to find out to what degree each client can identify her own emotions and see to it that women who need to practice looking inward and identifying emotions, especially in response to interpersonal interactions with peers, are encouraged to do so during the sessions. By the same token, some clients will already be skilled at identifying their own wants and needs and verbalizing them; other will not. Still other group members will be skilled at giving feedback to their peers but some will not be accustomed to telling other people that a communication was received or expressing agreement or disagreement with someone else or giving praise or encouragement to another person. For some clients, differentiating between their own emotional reaction and that of another person will be a major treatment issue; other clients will have much less difficulty in identifying and maintaining personal boundaries. Some adult survivors will be adept at offering help and caretaking to their peers but will need more practice in asking for and receiving help from others. Lastly, some of the women will already be very skilled at limit setting (sometimes to the point of erecting barriers and shutting others out altogether) but will need practice in becoming more open to receiving help from and giving help to their peers.

Although it is suggested that one of the group cotherapists take primary responsibility for ensuring that each member's individual therapy needs are addressed, it is obvious that it will be necessary for both therapists to contribute to this task. They can pool their observations and insights about each group member and plan jointly regarding future therapy interventions before each session. Although it is unrealistic to expect that all of the therapy needs for each member will be met by the end of the cycle, it is not unrealistic to expect that the therapist will remember each person's individual needs and be mindful of taking advantage of or creating opportunities for addressing at least one important area for each member during every session of the cycle. Despite the impossibility of mathematically allocating equal amounts of attention to each member during every session, the therapists are responsible for ensuring an equitable division of the group's time and energy over the course of the cycle. At the least, it is the clinicians' responsibility to see to it that each member has an opportunity to work in the group setting toward addressing her personal therapy needs. Some members will seize opportunities to practice and to accomplish therapeutic tasks, others require coaxing, and still others need gentle prodding. Inevitably a few clients will refuse to work at all during a cycle; it is nonetheless important for them to be given the chance to refuse to work rather than to have the experience of being ignored as they withdraw and fall behind their peers with respect to participation in the group process.

Addressing Group Process

The cotherapist who takes primary responsibility for monitoring and facilitating the group process must be committed to the idea that the clients will receive more direct help from each other than they will from the therapist. Otherwise that therapist will find the task very difficult to carry out. Without exception, the most important intervention to facilitate group process is to create a time space for the members to interact with each other. In practical terms, this means that the therapists must remain silent most of the time in order to allow the clients an opportunity to speak. This can be harder to accomplish than may immediately be apparent. Most clinicians are genuinely concerned about their clients and are eager to interact with them directly. But they must avoid temptations to protect or to rescue clients during group therapy sessions. The temptation to make a clinical interpretation every time a client speaks must be avoided at all costs. When a clinician desires to make an interpretation or a comment, she or he must learn to remain silent in order to create a space for the members of the group to ask a question, make a comment, agree, disagree, or the like. If no client speaks, the therapist can eventually encourage or ask another client to respond to the situation: "Molly, give Joanne some feedback on that!" or "Felicia, please tell Judy what you think might be happening right now."

Initially group members tend to be reticent in their interactions, especially if they have little experience in peer group therapy. As they gain experience, most come to realize that the peer group milieu is a laboratory in which they can practice interpersonal interactions in a safe and guided setting. At the same time, they can try out new or unfamiliar methods to cope with stress, to identify their own emotional reactions to various situations, and to connect with others by direct communication. In addition to needing the time, space, and opportunities to practice these skills, they usually also need to observe demonstrations of interactional skills and to receive encouragement and stimulation to participate actively.

Special Techniques

Many special techniques can be used in a group therapy setting to facilitate group process and address individual therapy needs as well. This section will describe several techniques used at the New England Clinical Associates office.

Role Playing. This technique involves at least two members. They can be selected by the therapists, or group members can be asked to volunteer to role play interactions. For example, in response to hearing one client describe an interaction between herself and her mother, a therapist might suggest that the client role play an alternative scenario with another group member cast in the mother's role. A second option is to invite the first client to select two other group members or ask for volunteers to play the mother and daughter roles. After the scenario is enacted, the therapists can encourage discussion about the content of what occurred, members' emotional reactions to observing or participating in the role play, and the like. A third option is to ask two other group members to role play mother and daughter, while a fourth group member comments on what is occurring or shares her thoughts about the role players' personal reactions to participating in a psychodrama and so forth. Many variations of these interventions are possible. The second and third options are generally viewed as less threatening by clients than the first option.

Body Sculpting. This is a kinesthetic technique that clients tend to enjoy. The therapist might invite a group member to enlist the aid of the other members in the group in the following way: "Jane, I want you to select four other people in the group to be stand-ins for members of your family. You can ask them to stand up or move around the room so that their positions reflect how you and the members of your family interact with each other." When Jane has selected whom she wants to represent members of her family and assigned them to various positions in relation to each other (ahead, behind, standing, sitting, kneeling, facing or not facing each other), the therapist can then invite the stand-ins to share their personal reactions to the process and speculate on how the family members they are representing might be feeling with regard to their relationships. Or the therapist can ask one of the group members who is an observer to comment on what the family sculpting has revealed with respect to the client whose family was portrayed.

This technique has many variations. The therapist might direct one group member to ask all of her peers to assume different positions in the room in a manner that reflects the first client's opinion of the progress they are all making in their recovery processes as compared to each other. However it is used, it is important for the therapist to monitor the sculpting process closely to ensure that no one's personal space is violated, no one is humiliated, and so on. Occasionally a group member will refuse to participate in a body sculpting process. Her right to refuse should be respected; pressuring her to participate is likely to be perceived as threatening and exploitative.

In this context it may useful to recount three rules that were formulated in an impromptu fashion at a session of peer group therapy for adult survivors conducted at the New England Clinical Associates office. One of the women said, "You've never told us what the rules are here. What are they?" The clinician responded:

"(1) Respect yourself; (2) respect others; (3) no physical violence." To the surprise of the therapists, the rules were taken very seriously by the clients and frequently quoted during the rest of the cycle. Thereafter, these rules were adopted as office policy and announced at the beginning of each cycle of peer group therapy. Possibly these simple requirements have enabled adult survivors to feel more secure in the peer group therapy setting.

Utilizing Consultants or Resource Persons. This technique may be used for several reasons. First it enables the therapists to bring in another service provider who has something special to share with the clients. We utilized a sexual therapist as a resource person during the cycle for which the theme was "Exercising Control." It can be appropriate to invite someone who is visiting the program to attend a session for similar reasons. Obviously, a consultant or resource person must agree to observe client confidentiality in a scrupulous manner, and the clients must be assured that their confidentiality will be respected.

Another reason for using a consultant or resource person is the absence of one of the cotherapists. This will be most effective if the decision to utilize a consultant or a resource person as an alternative to one of the group cotherapists is planned and announced to group members well in advance. Since the consultant or resource person will usually be someone who was not previously known to the clients, the presence of a stranger in the group may cause some adult survivors to feel unsafe, especially if there was no prior announcement or warning prior to the visit. On the other hand, we have also noticed that one of the principal advantages in the occasional use of a consultant or resource person is actually a side effect of the visit in that the visitor inevitably is an outsider. Accordingly, establishing a connection with the consultant or resource person and interacting with him or her can be a symbolic linking process between group members and a representative of the "outside world." Thus it is useful for group members to have the opportunity to tell the consultant something about themselves and about their recovery process, especially with respect to their work on a goal that is in some way associated with the theme for the current cycle. This affords another opportunity for them to practice self-disclosure and to identify their own wishes and express them in the form of questions to the consultant. They can use the opportunity to practice receiving help and nurturance from a stranger, perhaps in the form of listening to her or his responses to their questions or perhaps by receiving the consultant's impressions or comments about the recovery work that members have described. For some, the experience of interacting with the consultant may be an initial opportunity to practice open and direct communication involving wishes and requests with a new person who knows that they are adult survivors of child sexual abuse. Although it will be perceived by some as a threatening experience, it will probably be a useful experience for all of them.

The consultant or resource person should be prepared for the visit. She or he should be knowledgeable about adult survivors, as well as about the treatment program and its philosophy and format. As well, it will be helpful for the consultant to receive some information about the theme of the cycle and how the members have worked with it to date. If the group cotherapists hope that the consultant or resource person will address (from her or his own experiences) specific questions or issues already raised by group members, these should be reviewed in advance with her or him.

Arts Therapy Approaches. Much has already been written about using the arts therapies to facilitate recovery for child sexual abuse clients (Naitove

1982, 1988). Chapter 7 in this volume, describes one type or arts therapy intervention: during one of the sessions group members do free drawings that are in some way related to the theme of the cycle. The arts therapies are evocative, and adult victims of child sexual abuse can learn much about themselves and their past and current coping mechanisms by using some type of media in a representative and creative fashion. (For further discussion of this modality as it relates to treatment of adolescent victims, refer to chapters 2 and 3 in this volume.)

Hypnotic Storytelling and Use of Metaphor. There has been an outpouring of professional literature recounting the clinical uses of metaphor with nearly every type of psychotherapy client. At the New England Clinical Associates office, we have frequently used hypnotic storytelling employing the utilization techniques described by Milton Erickson (Gilligan 1987) in cycles of peer group therapy for adults survivors. Briefly, for readers who are unfamiliar with this approach, it involves telling a story using hypnotic technique so that the process of recounting the story becomes itself a form of trance induction. The group members relax as they listen to the story, and most will go into a light trance. The therapist who is telling the story uses pacing, tone of voice, cadence, and repetition to emphasize certain points or embedded commands (Gordon 1978). Although there may not be much group discussion of the metaphoric implications of the story immediately after it is told, it is likely that the clients will continue to process it consciously and unconsciously for weeks or months. We generally find that at least one of the group members will bring up the story in a subsequent session; sometimes it will be brought up recurrently by several members as they continue to process it over a period of time. (The last section of this chapter contains an extensive case example of a fictitious adult survivor's initial experience with a cycle of time-limited peer group therapy. An illustration of hypnotic storytelling is included in the case example and discussed.)

There are many ways to utilize metaphor as a therapeutic intervention. The appropriate use of hypnotic storytelling requires specialized training; clinicians would be well advised to receive this training before they attempt to use the technique in peer group therapy for adult survivors. Narrative or social storytelling, on the other hand, does not require specialized training and may constitute a timely and useful therapeutic intervention. Therapists may tell stories to the group, read stories or poems, or encourage mutual storytelling by clients. Selecting stories or topics for storytelling that are related to the theme of the cycle or to a treatment issue that is being addressed by one or more group members can be helpful in addressing individual therapy needs for clients and in facilitating group process.

The following case describes how an adult survivor who is participating in peer group therapy for the first time might experience the benefits afforded by this treatment modality. (The narrative is about a fictitious adult survivor; it is a composite drawn from experience with many clients.)

Anita Grant, a 38-year-old woman, expressed great eagerness to begin peer group therapy for adult survivors when she was seen for a screening interview. Anita had been sexually abused by her father in childhood, with frequent episodes occurring from ages 5 to 13. The abuse had begun with sexual exposure and fondling and progressed to oral sex and simulated intercourse. Anita told her mother about the abuse when she was 13 years old and her father attempted vaginal penetration for the first time. Anita's mother confronted her husband, who denied the abuse but stayed away from Anita thereafter. Later they learned that the father had continued to molest a younger sister for years after the abuse of Anita had stopped. The case was never reported to Child Welfare authorities or to the police. Neither sister received any treatment for the sexual abuse.

Anita had been a good student and received excellent grades in high school and college; she subsequently earned a master's degree in business administration. Thereafter, she went to work for a large company and steadily advanced up the ranks to a respected middle management position. She dated frequently while she was in college and married a fellow student just before they entered graduate school. Their marriage was a stable one for ten years; they deferred having children, at first for financial reasons. Anita said that by the time she was 30, her husband was pressing her to have children, but she said, "I lost my nerve." By the twelfth year of their marriage, each discovered the other was having an affair. They decided to separate and divorce. Anita had had several boyfriends since her divorce; she described her current relationship as "serious" saying, "He's really pushing to get married, but I want to hold off for a while."

Although Anita had sought personal therapy several times during her adulthood and had seen psychotherapists intermittently for short periods, she had never worked in therapy on the impact of her sexual victimization by her father. When a former therapist suggested that she talk about the sexual abuse, Anita declined, saying, "It doesn't seem important now. It was so many years ago."

In the month prior to Anita's screening interview, she suddenly began to have dreams at night and daytime flashbacks about the sexual abuse. She was surprised and terrified by the flashbacks but initially took no action because she "hoped it would stop by itself." When she finally called a previous therapist and asked for help, she was referred to an office that specialized in treating sexual abuse and conducted cycles of peer group therapy for adult survivors on a regular basis.

Anita was seen individually for several sessions before she began a cycle of peer group therapy. Initially she asked many questions about how the group would be conducted and was impatient for the cycle to begin. In the week prior to the first group session, she expressed some reluctance to start the cycle but was unable to explain why she was concerned. She also balked at scheduling regular individual sessions during the cycle but agreed (after some negotiation) to be seen one time after the cycle began.

During the first group session, Anita was silent for most of the meeting. There were ten women in the group and two women co-therapists. The therapists welcomed the women and spent a few minutes talking about policies of the program. The clients were told that there were no rules prohibiting them from having social interactions outside the group and that the office neither encouraged or discouraged them from doing so. "However," one therapist remarked, "we ask you to respect each other's confidentiality and privacy at all times. If you do meet socially, please do not discuss anything that was brought up during a group session, even if it concerns only yourselves. If, by accident, you do talk about anything that took place here, please bring that back to the group in the very next session."

The second therapist added, "Actually we have only three rules for these sessions. Respect yourself; respect others; and no physical violence!" Anita noticed that several of the women smiled or nodded, as if they had heard it before. For her own part, Anita was not sure what she thought about the rules but certainly did not find them to be amusing.

Lost in thought, Anita suddenly realized that she had not been paying attention for several minutes. One of the therapists had introduced the topic of the theme for the cycle and the plan for each member to identify a goal to work on during group sessions that would be related to the theme. "For the rest of tonight's session, however, we'll talk about the reasons that you are here." Then the therapists asked each woman to share some details about her child sexual abuse experience. Members were also asked to speak about their experiences in therapy to date and to tell the group why they had decided to participate in this cycle of therapy and what they were hoping to accomplish. Anita listened carefully to the others. All but one of the women besides Anita had participated in at least one previous cycle of group therapy.

Anita was the last to speak. She told the others that she had been sexually abused by her father and then stopped speaking. After a moment of silence, one of the women asked gently, "How old were you when it started?" Anita replied, "I'm not sure. I think I might have been 5 or 6." Another women asked, "When did it stop?" After Anita's reply, still another group member asked, "Did anybody else find out about the abuse when you were still a child?" Although she had been terrified to begin to tell her story, Anita found that she was able to respond to their questions. When someone asked, "What did you think would happen if people found out about what was going on?" Anita began to cry. "I thought I would die," she said between sobs. "Even after I told my mother and he stayed away from me, I thought that other people would think I was bad if they ever found out the terrible things that I did with my father when I was little!"

Someone picked up a box of tissues and passed them to Anita. The woman sitting next to her handed the box to her and patted her on the shoulder. Somebody else remarked, "I'm sorry to hear that you thought you were bad, but I'm not surprised. I convinced myself that I was bad because I didn't . . . couldn't . . . stop my brother from having sex with me when I was little. I really did a good job of blaming myself for being abused." Then another woman chimed in, "What helped me a lot was to look at some pictures of myself when I was three. That's when my dad started to abuse me. I kept saying to myself over and over again, 'Look at yourself in that picture! You were only a baby! There wasn't anything you could have done to make him stop!'," The focus then shifted from Anita to a more general discussion about a child's inability to control the behavior of the abuser.

As it was then time for the session to end, the therapists praised everyone for coming, for deciding to work in group therapy, and for working hard that evening by sharing information that was difficult to relate. The members were reminded that sometimes adult survivors find that the experience of talking about their own victimization in a group and hearing about others' abuse seems to trigger intense memories or flashbacks for some. Others may discover that they become sad and depressed; still others may experience intermittent waves of anger. The therapists urged the women to call their own clinicians or the group therapists if these or other related problems arose and they wanted some individual time and help.

Anita left the office in a daze. Later she said, "I couldn't believe I said so much!" (She had actually spoken for only five minutes.) In the subsequent week, she did not experience an increase in flashbacks or intrusive memories about the abuse but, rather, felt less troubled about her past difficulties than she had in weeks. It was surprising, therefore, that it was even harder for her to make herself come to the second session than it had been to attend the first. She arrived five minutes late (she had not allowed an adequate amount of time for the trip) and crept into her chair without looking directly at anyone else in the room or acknowledging their waves and nods. The session had already begun, and one of the therapists was reminding everyone that the theme for this fourteen-week cycle of group therapy was exercising control. The theme had already been announced in the first session, and the members had been encouraged to think during the intervening week about how they had been exercising control when they were children and their sexual abuse had been going on. At the beginning of this session, the therapist defined exercising control as the process of sometimes exerting and sometimes relinquishing (or giving up) being in control of events or situations in which one is involved. Then the other therapist asked, "Can anyone talk about exerting control? How important is that for you? What about giving up control? What is it like when you do that?

A general discussion followed in which most of the women participated. The consensus they expressed was that most of them believed that they had to exert control all of the time to protect themselves and that giving up control was hard to do, often terrifying, and likely to be perceived by others as an invitation to become abusive. "What do you have to protect yourselves against?" asked one of the therapists. "Being exploited!" was one reply. "Letting down my guard so that I get sloppy and make mistakes," said another. "Falling apart," said someone else. "Letting anyone get close enough to see through all the stuff I do to hide how bad I really am," was another response.

After some more discussion, a therapist remarked, "What we are talking about now relates to why you exercise control now. How about looking at how you were exercising control when the sexual abuse was happening to you?" There was a pause. Then a woman named Carol said, "I exercised control then by hiding." For a long time, no one said anything. After the silence had lengthened beyond two minutes, one of the therapists leaned to her right and said, "Bonnie, please ask Carol what 'hiding' means." Carol immediately began to reply, and the therapist said, "Wait, please." After an uncomfortable pause, Bonnie, now red-faced, said, "I think she means that she tried to be invisible, so no one would notice her. That's what I tried to do. Another thing I tried to do was . . . " "Wait," said the therapist again, this time to Bonnie. "Tell us about what you did in another minute. You can be next." Bonnie emitted a deep sigh, and several others laughed nervously. Turning to Carol, the therapist asked, "Was she right, or was she wrong? Was that what you meant by hiding? Please tell her—and the rest of us."

Anita hunched forward and stared at the floor during this interchange, which she found terrifying. She was fervently hoping that no one would notice her discomfort and comment on it or invite her to participate in the dialogue. When she finally did look up, she noticed that the woman sitting across from her had been watching her with concern. She smiled reassuringly, but Anita could not maintain eye contact with her for more than a few seconds. Instead Anita's eyes strayed to a bookshelf in the corner; she stared at it fixedly for a moment and then began to count the volumes on the shelves. It took all of her concentration to keep track of the total as her eyes moved methodically from shelf to shelf. Later, after the session was over, she discovered that she could not remember anything that had taken place after she walked into the group room at the beginning of the session. She also could not remember leaving the office, getting into her car, driving home, or going to bed that night.

It is not unusual for an adult survivor to wish she had not committed herself to participate in a cycle of peer group therapy as the time draws closer to the first session, even if she fought hard to join the program in the first place. Anita's experience of discovering that she could open up about herself at that first session, unexpectedly finding that she could feel supported by her peers, is also not unusual. Paradoxically, her experience of symptom relief (a temporary cessation of the nightmares and flashbacks about the abuse) did not have the effect of making her more comfortable about attending the second session. Instead, her anxiety mounted as the next session approached. When the therapists directed the members toward thinking about and discussing the coping mechanisms they had used as children while the sexual abuse was actually occurring, Anita's anxiety became so intense that she believed she could not tolerate attending to the discussion (much less contributing to it) any longer. Accordingly, she used the same coping mechanism that had served her so well in childhood, now in the service of extricating herself from a stressful situation in peer group therapy. First, she distracted herself by counting the books on the bookshelf, and then she dissociated herself entirely from the surrounding environment. As she later discovered, her intrapsychic control measure of self-distraction followed by dissociation (some clinicians would describe this process as autohypnosis) remained in effect for the rest of the evening. Once triggered, the coping mechanism that helped her to tolerate the intense anxiety that she herself generated in response to the suggestion that she look into her past also cut her off from everything else—the content of the rest of the session, the opportunity to receive support from others, even the data recorded by her senses during the drive home.

Anita is one of many adult survivors whose history fit a late presentation pattern. For many years after her sexual victimization, she retained the content of her memories of the abuse by her father while repressing the associated affect. She used an intrapsychic coping mechanism that protected her from an intense emotional response while the abuse was taking place (dissociation) and soon after began a lifelong pattern of using that same intrapsychic coping mechanism to deal with ordinary types of stress. Meanwhile, she used an interpersonal coping mechanism to protect others from discovering how bad and blameworthy she was; she became a high-performing person who formed a relational pattern of keeping others from discovering her "faults" (some might substitute "sins" for "faults") by preventing anyone from getting too close to her. Anita accomplished the latter by repeatedly performing caretaking tasks for others without ever communicating that she expected (and deserved) some reciprocal attention to her wishes and needs.

We speculate that adult survivors such as Anita become emotionally depleted and exhausted by midlife and that their intrapsychic and interpersonal coping mechanisms increasingly fail to protect them at times of stress. In Anita's case, we would speculate that her current relationship with a man who is pursuing ever greater intimacy with her is sufficiently stressful in an extremely vulnerable area associated with her childhood sexual abuse that she begins to experience the flashbacks that finally drive her into treatment. Predictably, however, she employs the same defenses against the treatment process that she customarily uses to protect herself against other stressful situations. Meanwhile, as she periodically experiences symptom relief with respect to the flashbacks, her fear of self-exposure moves to the fore and amplifies her anxiety about participating in any type of therapy that focuses on her sexual victimization and its consequences.

In addition to noticing Anita's distress, a knowledgeable observer would also have realized that the therapists had made three important interventions shortly before Anita disconnected herself from the group. First, they encouraged group process when both therapists remained silent after Carol's initial comment, thereby creating both a space and an opportunity for a dialogue. Second, when no member said anything, the therapist who finally did speak promoted group process and direct interaction by requesting (actually directing) another member to respond to Carol. When Carol immediately started to respond to the therapist (unintentionally cutting off Bonnie), she (Carol) was asked to wait. Thus prodded, Bonnie finally answered the question but directed her answer back to the therapist. She also moved quickly from responding to Carol to talking about herself. Her initial reluctance to become involved at all was an indication of her anxiety about participating.

Once launched into responding, Bonnie found it easier to talk to an authority figure (the therapist) than to interact with a peer. She then shifted to talking about herself, not only to justify her response but because it was less threatening by then to talk about herself than to undertake the unfamiliar and therefore frightening step of engaging in a dialogue with Carol.

In this fictitious case example, at least one or both of the therapists undoubtedly would have noticed Anita's distress while the interactions discussed above were taking place (as did one of the other group members). It would not be surprising if they made a clinical judgment simply to observe how a new client chose to react to stress during a session of peer group therapy that was close to the beginning of a cycle, especially if she was not evidencing overt distress. It is timely to return to the case example to see what might happen next to Anita.

Two days later, Anita received a telephone call at work from the therapist who had conducted her screening sessions prior to beginning a cycle of peer group therapy. The therapist explained that it would be necessary for her to change her appointment to see Anita for an individual session on the following day. She apologized for the inconvenience and suggested that they reschedule the appointment. Anita was dumbfounded to receive the call because she had forgotten the appointment entirely. She stared at her engagement book, in which the appointment had been clearly recorded, and tried to think of a reason not to reschedule. Failing to do so, she accepted another hour for the appointment.

When she entered the therapist's office, Anita tried to appear nonchalant. "There's something I need to tell you," she began. The therapist waited. After several false starts, Anita gave up and sat miserably in her chair, mutely shaking her head. "Have you been having a hard time since Monday night?" the therapist asked. Anita nodded. "That's not surprising," the therapist continued. "Lots of people are having a rough time by the second session. In fact, it's pretty usual for someone who is new to working in a group. It can be a sign that you're making progress." She smiled at Anita's grimace. "Suppose you tell me a little bit about what's been going on."

Haltingly, Anita told her about waking up on Tuesday morning and discovering that she had totally blocked out all of the events of the previous evening, beginning with the therapy session. The therapist listened patiently and made supportive responses at intervals. Anita used the phrase "I checked out" to describe her dissociative process. The therapist then asked if she could remember other times when she had "checked out" and asked if she knew why it occurred. Anita related two other incidents in the recent past. She then told the therapist that she was afraid to continue to participate in the cycle of group therapy. "I can't keep this up!" she blurted. "I'm really afraid this means I'm beginning to lose it!"

The therapist leaned forward and said to Anita, "I'm not at all surprised to hear you say that. You are *not* going to lose it. It doesn't sound to me like you're getting worse. I can't promise you that you are going to feel better soon. I can tell you this: the best advice I can give you is, don't stop now."

By the end of the session, Anita had agreed to come to at least one more session of group therapy. She also agreed to come back to the office the following day and view at least part of the videotape of the session. The therapist promised to be in her office while Anita was watching the videotape in an adjoining room. When Anita arrived the next day as planned, she learned that the therapist had cued the videotape to a point approximately ten minutes prior to the time that Anita had "checked out" of the session. Anita watched the videotape in disbelief. It was necessary for her to stop it several times because she was crying hard enough that she had difficulty following the action of the screen. In about thirty minutes, her therapist tapped on the door, entered the room, and remarked, "I just thought I'd look in on you while I have a few minutes between appointments. How's it going?"

Anita shook her head. "I can't believe it," she said, starting to cry. "I don't even know why I'm crying right now!"

"That's okay," said the therapist, laying her hand on Anita's shoulder. "When you're ready to figure it out, you will."

"This is crazy!" Anita wailed. "I can't handle this—and I can't keep crying all of the time for no reason!"

"Wait," said the therapist. "Stay with what you're feeling right now for a minute. No, I really mean that," she said as Anita made a gesture of dissent. "You *can* handle this. You *can* tolerate whatever you are reacting to right now. It isn't necessary to *do* anything. Just allow yourself to *be* for a while."

Several minutes passed. Then Anita said in a small voice, "What should I do now?"

"How about watching the rest of the tape?" asked the therapist.

"Okay," said Anita grimly. "If you say so."

"I said it because I think it would be better for you to see and hear what you missed last time," said the therapist. "What you decide to do is up to *you!*"

"At least this time, I *know* that I am deciding about something," was Anita's rejoinder.

"That's right," said the therapist. "That's right . . . you're doing a good job." She drew out the last two words, waited a moment, and then left the room.

Anita watched the rest of the videotape. When she was finished, her therapist's door was closed because she was seeing another client. Anita scribbled a note ("Thanks. See you Monday night. A.G.") and left it with the videotape. At home that night and for the rest of the week, the words "good job" kept echoing in her mind.

Early in the next group session, the therapist who had spent time with Anita remarked, "I think Anita may have something to tell us." Turning to Anita, she asked directly, "How about sharing some of what has been happening to you?"

Anita, who looked considerably calmer than she had appeared last week, smiled and said, "I was expecting to be asked."

One of the other women said, "You could have counted on it!" The others laughed, and Anita plunged in bravely telling them about her "checking-out" experience at the last group meeting. She also talked about watching the videotape of the session.

"I couldn't have told you anything last Tuesday about what happened on Monday night," she concluded. "Now I at least know what everybody said."

"Maybe you know some more things about yourself," said one of the others. Anita nodded.

"I thought you were "spacing out" or something like that," said the group member who had viewed Anita with concern at the preceding session.

"I think it was the expression on your face that pushed me over the edge," Anita responded. "Don't get me wrong," she added quickly.

The other woman laughed. "That didn't hurt my feelings," she replied. "Would it be okay if we let you know that you are looking like you are about to disconnect from the rest of us? I mean, if it happens again and somebody sees it? Would it be all right just to ask you?"

"Sure," said Anita through her teeth. There was general laughter, in which Anita joined after a while.

"Just watch out for flying objects, Kathy!" someone joked.

"Remember no physical violence!" someone else exclaimed. More laughter followed.

"This seems like a good time for everyone to identify a goal for the rest of this cycle," said one of the therapists. "Remember, our theme this time is 'Exercising Control.' "

"Not to mention that you can also be telling us how you are willing to let others help you work on the goal," said the other therapist. She turned to Anita and asked, "Would it be fair to say that you would like to work on being present all of the time, during every session?" Anita nodded assent. "Would it also be fair to say that you are agreeing to let people here in the group let you know that they are wondering if you might be getting ready to 'check out,' as you call it?"

There was a pause. Then, with an air of sudden decisiveness, Anita said, "Yes!" very firmly. "And there's something else I've found out," she continued. She turned to the therapist who had seen her individually. "You told me I could live through this. I think you said that you thought I could *stay* with it, while I was watching the videotape. Well, I found out that I could. I didn't have to push it all away. I didn't need to push myself away!"

"That was an important learning about exercising control," was the therapist's quiet response. "Good job . . ." she said, drawing out the words again. After a pause, she looked around the room and asked, "Who else is ready to identify a goal?"

Most of the next three sessions of the cycle was spent with each woman identifying goals that related to the theme of "Exercising Control." The women were encouraged by the therapists to tell the group their recollections about exercising control at the time when their sexual victimization was taking place in childhood. Each client was also asked to tell the group how she was exercising control in the present, as an adult. Some women found it much harder to find some aspect of exercising control that they *wanted* to work on in the group setting for the rest of the cycle. Sometimes the problem was that the goals were too general: for example, "I just want to stop feeling like a victim and have more control over my life!" Others initially proposed goals that involved their relationships with people outside the group: for example, "I'd like to learn not to get terrified when my husband gets mad at me." The therapists and group members worked together to try to help each person find something she could work on *in the group setting* so that she could ask for and receive some direct assistance from her peers. "How can we help you with that?" was asked more and more frequently. Sometimes the response was a shrug and a negative headshake.

Often suggestions were offered, either for an individual's goal or for a way in which the others could help her work on that goal during the cycle. Some of the suggestions were gratefully, even eagerly accepted. Others were rejected by the individual member to whom they had been addressed. The therapists never pressured the women to agree to the suggestions, but they always required the clients to verbalize agreement or disagreement, acceptance or rejection of a suggestion.

Anita noticed that the therapists related stories to the group from time to time usually at least once in each session. Sometimes two or three stories were told. One evening, there was a great deal of discussion about the need to be in control all of the time so that other people would have no opportunity to penetrate one's defenses and do something hurtful. One of the therapists remarked, "It sounds like you're saying that it's necessary to be on guard all of the time, so you won't be attacked by someone else."

"You've got it," said Carol.

Anita heard herself saying, "I feel like that, too. I'm afraid that people will find out how bad I really am if I give them a chance. So I can't let them get too close. And I don't!"

Several of the others nodded or murmured assent. One of the women who had more experience with treatment did not join in the general agreement, however. "I used to do that too—keep people away, I mean," she remarked. The others turned to her as she continued, "But I found that there were two problems with that way of staying in control. One, it got so terribly lonely to be by myself all the time."

There was a long pause, and Anita started to feel very small. She thought that no one else was noticing her, and then she looked up and met the eyes of the woman who had been speaking. The other woman, said, "You can 'check out' if you want to, Anita. But you told us that we could tell you when you look like you are going far away from the rest of us. Right?"

Anita clenched her teeth, gripped the arms of her chair, and sat there rigidly for a moment. No one moved or spoke. Then she emitted a long sigh and relaxed. "Welcome back," someone remarked.

Sandy, the woman who had been speaking, resumed her comment. "The second problem was a lot harder for me to figure out than the first one," she said. "But then it finally came to me. It wasn't enough for me to keep busy by keeping everybody else at a distance. I found out I had just fooled myself into thinking I always had to be worried about the other guy, whoever the other guy happened to be—it could be my husband or my girlfriend or my sister or my boss—whoever was handy. Then one day, I woke up to the fact that somebody was always beating on me anyway. Even though I wasn't letting anybody get near me." She paused. "It took me a long time, but I finally got the message. I was beating myself up! I was really doing a number on myself. Nobody else could get close enough to hurt me, so I was hurting myself!"

"How?" someone asked.

"By being down on myself or feeling sad all the time or working harder than I have to work or setting myself up to fail at something!" She threw up her hands, exclaiming, "And it's usually about little things, silly things, not big stuff at all!"

"How did you stop?" asked Anita.

"Well I haven't stopped altogether," Sandy replied. "But I'm trying to be gentler with myself. It takes me a while to get on the right track. But I don't beat myself up so much now." She paused again and then continued, "It's a funny thing, because I've noticed that now that I don't do a number on myself so often, I'm not as afraid as I used to be that other people are going to turn on me or try to hurt me."

"That reminds me of a story," one of the therapists said dreamily.

"Good!" said Sandy and settled down in her chair.

The therapist pivoted her head from side to side, slowly, looking at each person in turn. Then, in the same dreamy voice, she continued.

"Once I knew a woman who had a terrible accident while she was driving her car. It was a dark, rainy day, and the roads were very slippery. A little child darted into the street in front of the car, and the woman could not stop in time. Accidents can't always be prevented. The child was run over and killed.

"The woman was arrested for failure to control her vehicle. The dead child's parents and other people in the small town where they lived were very bitter. They all blamed her for the child's death. She and her family endured great stress. Three months later at a hearing, a judge dismissed all of the charges against her. He had reviewed the evidence and decided that there was no proof of wrongdoing. After the hearing, the child's parents apologized for blaming her right after the accident. They said that they had come to realize that sometimes no one is to blame when something bad has happened.

"Shortly thereafter the woman became very very sad and depressed. She lost weight, had difficulty sleeping, and stopped going out of her house. This lasted for nearly a year. During this time, she was helped a little by medication for depression. Then one day I saw her, and she looked much better. She said to me, "I'm going to be feeling a lot better now." I asked her, "How do you know that?" She replied, 'I've decided to stop punishing myself.' "

"I saw her in a month, and she had continued to do well. She said to me again, 'I'm not punishing myself anymore. I've decided that I punished myself enough.' For the next year I saw her at intervals. Each time she said, 'I don't deserve to be punished now. I'm not hurting myself anymore.' And she was doing very well."

"It's not necessary to keep punishing ourselves all the time. Forgiveness is possible. When we are ready to stop punishing ourselves, we will. It's okay for people to be gentle with themselves."

The therapist stopped speaking for a long moment and then looked slowly at each person in the room again. No one spoke for another three or four moments. Then Sandy said, "I like that story. I feel very close to that woman. It fits for me."

The other therapist remarked, "It fits for all of us, I think. It fits for anybody who thinks she deserved to be punished."

There was no further discussion of the story or, for that matter, the topics of self-blame or self-punishment that night. The meeting ended shortly after, and the women were unusually subdued as they left the office. For the rest of the cycle, however, the therapists (and sometimes the group members) would remark, "It's not necessary to keep punishing yourself." Or someone might say, "I'm trying to be gentler, with myself." Anita found that although she forgot most of the content of the story, these phrases popped into her mind from time to time.

Although the timing of the therapist's call to Anita after the second session of peer group therapy appeared to be accidental, there is a high probability that one of the therapists would have called her even if it had not been necessary to make contact with her to reschedule an appointment. The appointment time itself is noteworthy. It is desirable to plan to make an individual appointment to see a client who is just beginning treatment for the emotional sequelae of childhood sexual abuse soon after the beginning of a cycle of peer group therapy. Anita had been unwilling to make a commitment for regular individual sessions during the cycle; hence the therapist's plan (to which Anita had agreed) to schedule one individual session to explore her reactions to being in peer group therapy before many sessions had taken place.

Having already observed Anita's apparent intense preoccupation with the bookcase during the Monday night session, the therapist would certainly not be surprised to discover that Anita had forgotten that she had an appointment for an individual session later that week. Not all adult survivors would necessarily be as surprised and confused as Anita was by the dissociation she experienced during the group meeting or by the amnesia for what had occurred during the entire meeting or by the experience of learning that she had totally blocked out the previously scheduled appointment for an individual session. Some might not have been aware of any of these reactions and therefore have not been distressed; others might have been aware of some or all of the reactions but still might have had little emotional response. However, Anita's fear that her experiences were an indication that she was losing control of her mental processes is both usual and predictable. Ironically, her experiences of dissociation and amnesia during the group session and "forgetting" the scheduled appointment afterward did not occur because she exerted too little control but rather because she exerted too much control over her thoughts and emotions. Survivors such as Anita are understandably terrified by the consequences that are in fact artifacts of their intrapsychic coping mechanisms (experiencing amnesia not only for the group interactions that triggered her dissociative processes but also for the events of the entire evening).

In the case example, the therapist anticipated that Anita might conclude that she was not strong enough or sufficiently well integrated to attend another session of the group. The therapist then made an intervention to try to help Anita to learn that she could tolerate the emotions triggered by the interactions that had taken place during the session; she encouraged her to watch and listen to the videotape of the meeting. The arrangements for viewing the videotape were important. The client was not left alone in the office without a clinician nearby, and the therapist made a strategic visit during the time Anita was viewing the videotape. Used in this way, a videotape of a group therapy session became a powerful clinical tool. The client has total control over the viewing process; she could turn it off, freeze the action, turn off the sound, rewind a section of the videotape and play it again. Or she could skip entire sections in order to focus on others. At the same time, there was the safety afforded by the therapist's presence nearby and the opportunity to share reactions with her, as well as to hear her comments. Although adult survivors frequently have had powerful emotional reactions to viewing themselves in a group setting on videotape, we have found that viewing videotapes of sessions when recommended by the therapist (or requested by the client) has been consistently beneficial and empowering. For Anita, it provided a dramatic opportunity for her to demonstrate to herself, with the help of a machine, that she could solve her problem of intense fear of self-exposure under stress in a different way. The videorecorder allowed her temporarily to be in control of time in a limited but extremely useful fashion: she could stop the action as often as necessary, thereby enabling her to integrate and absorb a frightening experience that she had previously believed she could not tolerate.

Obviously there is a more than one way to help an adult survivor to accomplish these tasks. Later in the cycle, in fact, Anita agreed to permit her peers in the group to let her know when they suspected that she might be distancing herself from a stressful situation as well as from them. This can also be a powerful therapeutic intervention, of the interpersonal variety rather than an interaction between a person and a machine.

It is necessary to comment on another obvious aspect of the case example: the point when Anita's therapist decided that her client, who was expressing fears that she would "lose it" (a common slang expression for losing control or becoming crazy), was not in fact a danger to herself or to others or (seriously) decompensating in any way. This of course, is always a matter of clinical judgment, to be addressed on a case-by-case basis. In an actual clinical situation (as opposed to a narrative case example), it would be the therapist's responsibility to explore carefully with the client what "losing it" means and to ascertain that it is safe and appropriate to encourage the client to face directly a stressful issue or situation in an outpatient context.

Although necessarily abbreviated, the group interactions described in the case example are intended to illustrate that the support, challenge, and practice benefits afforded by peer group therapy are most likely to occur if an atmosphere of gentleness and caring prevails. It is also up to the therapists to foster a climate in which group members can joke and laugh about painful issues without belittling either the experiences or the person undergoing them. Likewise, the therapists must demonstrate by their own interactions with clients and with each other that direct, open communication and challenge can be performed gently and in a caring fashion. By contrast, a crucible-type atmosphere and a punitive style of confrontation and challenge have no place in peer group therapy for adult survivors of child sexual abuse.

Anita's peers were, by turns, serious and jocular but always affirming in their approaches to her as she disclosed that she had "checked out" in an effort to cope with stress during the preceding group session. They helped her to set a goal on which she could work during the rest of the cycle (recognizing and letting others know that she was frightened and beginning to distance herself), as well as to give permission to others to help her accomplish that goal. It was important for her to verbalize agreement or disagreement during this process. Anita's peers helped her to formulate a request for help; however, she needed to agree verbally to accept their help as it was proposed to her. It would also have been a therapeutic experience if she had verbalized disagreement with the goal or refusal to accept the help as it was suggested to her. What was occurring for Anita was an experience of self-disclosure, followed by identifying wants and needs; in turn, she also experienced receiving an offer of help and then agreeing to accept the help that was offered. All of this practice was performed in a safe setting with her peers. In time, she might have taken a more advanced step by asking for help in a more direct fashion or refusing to accept a suggestion.

The therapists in the case example were monitoring the group's interactions while trying to see to it that as many members as possible had opportunities to practice within the context of identifying goals, asking for help, receiving and giving feedback and assistance, and the like. Between them, the therapists first clarified what had taken place with regard to Anita's goal for the cycle and then saw that everyone stayed on task while the focus shifted to the other members. Whenever possible, they tried to create opportunities for the women to interact with each other instead of responding only to the therapists. Although this model for peer group therapy is therapist directed, it should always be remembered that it is the client-to-client interactions that are likely to be most effective in empowering the group members to advance in their own recovery.

In addition to illustrating praise, encouragement, and positive reinforcement throughout, the case example concludes with an illustration of a different type of nurturing by the therapists. Hypnotic storytelling, when used by an experienced clinician in a group setting, enables both a relaxing and a joining process for the members. It can also accomplish a different type of nurturing: by communicating that there are different ways to cope or to solve problems and by giving permission to the clients to nurture and care for themselves. The story of the woman who accidentally ran over a child and then punished herself by becoming extremely depressed is one with which clients can easily identify. The story's inherent messages are that people are in control of their own happiness (or their own sadness) and that they have both the capacity and the right to punish themselves or to be gentle with themselves. In large measure, the choice to punish or to be gentle is available to every human being. By telling the story with the use of hypnotic technique, the therapist was tapping into unconscious and conscious processes. Each person could use the story and its embedded messages for her own healing at her own pace, depending on her readiness and willingness to advance in her recovery process. Although the case example did not follow Anita (and the other clients) through every session of the rest of the cycle of peer group therapy, it would be highly likely that these women would work on self-forgiveness both during and between the group sessions and after.

Needless to say, no single clinical intervention or therapeutic experience can, by itself, accomplish or facilitate all of the elements of recovery for adults who were emotionally traumatized by sexual abuse in childhood. This chapter has attempted to describe how participating in cycles of peer group therapy can help adult survivors to bring away more than insights from a therapy experience. Healing together, in the company of peers, affords the support, challenge, and practice that are essential to the recovery process.

References

Bergart, Ann M. 1986. "Isolation to Intimacy: Incest to Intimacy: Incest Survivors in Group Therapy." *Social Casework* 67:266–275.
Blake-White, Jill, and Kline, Christine M. 1985. "Treating the Dissociative Process in Adult Victims of Childhood Incest." *Social Casework* 66:394–402.

Gilligan, Stephen G. 1987. *Therapeutic Traces: The Cooperation Principle in Ericksonian Hypnotherapy.* New York: Brunner/Mazel.

Goodman, Barbara, and Nowak-Scibelli, Donna. 1985. "Group Treatment for Women Incestuously Abused as Children." *International Journal of Group Psychotherapy.* 35:531–544.

Gordon, David. 1978. *Therapeutic Metaphors.* Cupertino, Calif.: META Publications.

Herman, Judith, and Schatzow, Emily, 1984. "Time-limited Group Therapy for Women with a History of Incest." *International Journal of Group Psychotherapy* 34:605–616.

Naitove, Connie E. 1982. "Arts Therapy with Sexually Abused Children." In S.M. Sgroi, ed., *Handbook of Clinical Intervention in Child Sexual Abuse,* 269–308. Lexington, Mass.: Lexington Books.

Naitove, Connie E. 1988. "Arts Therapies in Treatment of Sexual Offenders." In S.M. Sgroi, ed. *Vulnerable Populations,* 1:265–298 Lexington, Mass.: Lexington Books.

Sgroi, Suzanne M., and Bunk, Barbara S. 1988. "A Clinical Approach to Adult Survivors of Child Sexual Abuse." In S.M. Sgroi, ed., *Vulnerable Populations,* 1:137–186. Lexington, Mass.: Lexington Books.

Tsai, Mavis, and Wagner, Nathaniel N. 1978. "Therapy Groups for Women Sexually Molested as Children." *Archives of Sexual Behavior* 7:417–427.

Yassen, J., and Glass, Lois. 1984. "Sexual Assault Survivors Groups: A Feminist Practice Perspective." *Social Work* 29:252–257.

7

Spirituality and Adult Survivors of Child Sexual Abuse: Some Treatment Issues

Norah M. Sargent

T here is an area of the adult survivor's life about which there has been a deafening silence: her or his spirituality. The question of spirituality, or religious ideation, and its influence on psychological development has been raised by such early theorists as Jung (1933) in his discussion of the transcendant function, Allport (1950) in his work on religious sentiment, and Maslow (1962) in his treatment of peak experiences. Whether clinicians view religion as an integral and redeeming part of human existence or as a manifestation of a full-blown neurosis, recent research indicates that religious issues are significant in the clinical setting (Brown 1987; Hillowe 1985; Landis 1987; Quakenbos, Privette, and Klentz 1985; Shafranske and Maloney 1985). Might they not be of particular significance in therapy with adult survivors of child sexual abuse? If the degree of impact of the sexual abuse depends on the meaning that the victim ascribes to it (Sgroi and Bunk 1988), how might that interpretation be influenced further by the victim's belief system or existential interpretation of a world order?

Let the reader reflect on a few of the teachings that children traditionally hear about God. Consistently God is called "Father," "Brother," and "Son of God" or "Son of Man" in the New Testament (Matthew 4:3; 6:8–9, 18; 10:20; 11:25–27; 12:46–50, and so forth through the other evangelists), while He is King, Lord, Master, and Lover in the Old Testament (Deuteronomy 32; Psalms 24, 35; Song of Solomon in its entirety, and so forth). Some clinicians would posit that such an exclusively male rendering of God is sexist at best and thus detrimental to one's feminine identity. Exclusive language aside, the point here is the effect these male images have on the child who in a crucial developmental period of her or his life is sexually abused by an older or more powerful male family member or trusted caretaker.

"Adult men and women are amazingly complex and diverse beings who are capable of a staggering array of responses, experiences and behaviors" (Sgroi and Bunk 1988, 139). Adult survivors develop a staggering array of responses to being sexually abused in childhood. This chapter will focus on the effects of sexual abuse on the spiritual development of female children since my experience is limited to working with female victims and adult survivors. Before continuing with a discussion of the effects of sexual abuse on the spirituality and the attendant recovery of the adult survivor, it will be helpful to review the possible coping mechanisms employed by the victim/survivor and to survey proposed spiritual milestones of normal human development described by others.

A Review of Clinical Theories of the Impact of Child Sexual Victimization

Gelinas (1983) notes that intrafamilial sexual abuse "is relationally-based sexual abuse; for its victims, the traumatic event occurs within the family and by the parent's agency" (p. 319) The child may attempt to control the reality that her parent is sexually abusing her by denying the adult's culpability and assuming the blame for the sexual abuse. It is more comforting for Sara to believe that she is bad and seductive than it is for her to conclude that her abuser and primary caretaker, her father, cares little about her well-being and her feelings. It is also less threatening for Sara to believe herself to be evil than to understand that her mother will not or cannot protect her from the sexual abuse. Believing that she is the source of the trauma is, for the time being, less traumatic to her than feeling powerless and out of control. In her childhood feeling of omnipotence, Annie may think that she is causing her older brother to abuse her sexually or Suzie to believe that she is somehow luring her "helpless" grandfather into her bedroom at night. The reality is that Annie and Suzie are children and that an older or more powerful person has coerced or threatened them into cooperating in the sexual behaviors; the reality is that Annie and Suzie are being sexually abused.

Frequently a child learns to repress or deny her feelings in order to cope with the intrafamilial sexual abuse. As an adult, this denial of feelings may carry over into somatic complaints or phobias (Blick and Porter 1982; Forward and Buck 1979; Josephson and Fong-Beyette 1987; Kempe and Kempe 1984), or passivity, hopelessness, and depression (Gelinas 1983; Gil 1988; Herman 1981; Josephson and Fong-Beyette 1987; Leehan and Wilson 1985; Porter, Blick, and Sgroi 1982; Tsai and Wagner 1978). She may feel unable to express anger at her parents (and the abuser if this is not a parent); in fact, she may be afraid that her rage is so great that releasing it will inflict harm on someone else or, at best, completely and irrevocably overwhelm her (Blick and Porter 1982, Herman 1981; Joy 1987; Leehan and Wilson 1985; Owens 1984; Porter, Blick, and Sgroi 1982; Tsai and Wagner 1978; Wheeler 1981). Internalized, this anger may become self-hatred and lead her to such self-destructive behaviors as substance addiction, eating disorders, prostitution, and/or suicide (Blick and Porter 1982; Forward and Buck 1979; Gelinas 1983; James 1977; Josephson and Fong-Beyette 1987; Joy 1987; Katlan 1973; Kempe and Kempe 1984; Shapiro 1987). What was an effective coping mechanism for the child may be destructive or, debilitating to the adult.

McCann et. al.(1988), posit that a sexually abused child may cope with the abuse by minimizing its significance to herself. She may deny its importance; "This isn't really so bad. Anyhow, it won't last much longer," "I'm not here. I'm in a field of grass," or "I can't feel what he's doing. I don't feel my body." The child may attempt to integrate what is happening to her with what she understands about right and wrong, family roles, and her own reality in general. "Uncle Billy said to keep 'our game' a secret from Mommy because she'd get mad at me. If Mommy would get mad, it must be because I'm doing something bad." She may utilize her accommodation processes by stretching the reality to produce more positive beliefs and expectations. "Franky's only doing the same things to me that Charley did when he was Franky's age. This must be something brothers need to do. Little sisters are just supposed to put up with it. It'll stop when he's older." Or she can reframe the event by limiting her expectations of others: "Dad shouldn't have done what he did to me. He's like all men; they can't be trusted. And Mom didn't stop him. I can only trust myself!"

Manifestations of injury such an inability to establish or to maintain intimate relationships, sexual dysfunction, role confusion, and feelings of shame and unworthiness will be considered later in this chapter in the specific discussion of the adult survivor's spiritually. They are mentioned here merely to allow readers to be mindful of them during the later discussion. The following brief review of theories of spiritual development is included for the same purpose.

A Review of Theories of Spiritual Development

Haims (1944 in Brown 1987, 189) noted a progression, or perhaps it is regression, in children's beliefs about God by studying children's drawings. Children 8 to 10 years old identified attributes of God yet indicated that God was remote; children 11 to 14 years old portrayed God in personal terms; those 14 to 16 years old revealed internalized perceptions of God, but many also began to indicate doubt and fear.

Fowler (1976), a developmental psychologist, formulated a structural-developmental approach to the stages of faith development parallel to Piaget's stages of cognitive development and to Kohlberg's stages of moral development. Very briefly stated, the childhood stages of faith development move from the 4 year old's fantasy-filled and adult-influenced beliefs through the 8 year old's literal adaptation of adult rituals, symbols, and stories in which God is a benevolent but just monarch, and broaden in adolescence with the influence of peers, social groups, and adults. At this point and for years to come, the young person's beliefs are decentralized as she or he becomes aware of herself or himself in relation to all of creation. Fowler posits that the human experience forms a "triadic relationship" among the person, society, and God (Fowler in Groome 1989, 68). What might the triad be like if the 4 year old is raped? How would this influence the formation of her belief system? What is the triad like for the molested 8 old or the adolescent?

Allport's discussion of religion and religious responses (1950) suggests a broader categorization but a similar spiritual developmental task for each stage. The child's belief system is governed by "egocentrism, magical thought and anthropomorphism" (Allport 1950, 35). With characteristic egocentricity the sexually abused child blames herself for her abuse: "I stole that candy, and so God is punishing me by making my uncle do these things to me." Or she turns to God for a magical solution: "Tomorrow when we all wake up, this will be a dream and our family will be just like the Cosbys [or the Waltons or the Nelsons]." Often the child blends what she hears about God with what she experiences on a daily basis: "God is big and powerful and knows what I do, just like my dad, only more so." What if her dad is her abuser? Significant to this discussion is Allport's emphasis on the child's inability to integrate contrary messages: "If God is good and God is my father, yet my father in reality is terrifying, threatening, or hurtful, then . . ." Allport suggests that the child can conclude either that "God is not my father" or "I am not good."

Allport suggests that during adolescence, a stage typified by rebellion against parental authority, by sexual conflicts, and often by harsh moral judgments, the youth may experience a religious crisis. In rejecting the parental belief system, the child may reject religiosity altogether while suffering guilt and doubt about the appropriateness of this action. Or in an effort to resolve the religious question, the adolescent may become a moral absolutist and reason that God must exist if only to bring order to the struggle of good and evil (Allport 1950, 38). In either case, the overtones of a God of retribution all clear. This crisis of existence may be amelioriated only partially during young adulthood with the imaging of a humanitarian Godfigure or with an "ethical meliorism" that replaces religious faith (Allport 1950, 55). Allport recommends that clergy be trained in clinical skills to assist church members through stages of growth and further states that both psychology and religion are intimately tied to the future destiny of the human race.

Josselson (1987, 191) describes religion as particularly significant in the lives and the development of women for whom "ideology . . . is fundamentally interpersonal." Josselson recounts, "Communion, connection, relational embeddedness, spiritually, affiliations—with these women construct an identity" (p. 191). For most child victims, the sexual abuse influenced the "relational embeddedness, spirituality and affiliation" with which they constructed their identity.

Impact of Child Sexual Abuse on the Spiritual Development of Female Victims

What might these theories reveal to us if used as a template over the adult survivor's life? The personal history of the adult survivor of child sexual abuse includes the betrayal of trust by an older, more powerful, and parental figure in the child's life, along with a perceived absence of control over what happens to oneself. Some insights into this are found in the comments made by adult survivors of child sexual abuse.

Images of God

> "I was taught that God was my father in heaven," related Kathy, "and that my own father was like God on earth. Well, I wanted no part of God the Father, then. Later, I heard about Jesus as loving and so forth, but the problem with that was, if I was a good girl and did what he wanted, I'd be happy and everything would be fine. Well, that didn't work either."

> "I used to cringe when they'd talk about Jesus as our brother," said Nadine. "It was especially awful because he always seemed to be presented as sort of soft and persuasive, yet he also had this temper or an ability to verbally put down people like the pharisees. My own brother alternated between belittling me in front of others and talking to me in a syrupy, persuasive voice when he'd want to touch me. I stayed as far away from Jesus as I could!"

> Sally, a member of women's religious community, recalled "the time I was on a retreat and my retreat director told me to spend the day reading the Song of Songs. I thought I'd never live through that day, and the rest of my retreat I did on remote control—no feelings. I mean, there's all of that very specific language about the beloved's body, and it sounded so much like things my stepfather said to me as he molested me—about how beautiful I was. And here I was, all alone on a retreat, and God was supposed to be saying that to me!

How do you get away from someone you can't see?! So I stopped feeling, just like I did as a child."

For Kathy, the image of God as her own violent and sexually abusive father was unimaginable, but Jesus as "loving and so forth" was problematic also. If Jesus took care of "good girls," then what were the horns of Kathy's childhood dilemma? On the one hand, if she was good, then Jesus would take care of her; the sexual abuse would stop. In reality, the abuse continued despite Kathy's most unselfish responses to other people. Kathy's conclusion: "Jesus is nice but a fraud just like Santa Claus." On the other hand, if the abuse did not stop, it could be because Jesus knew she was a bad girl, somehow responsible for the abuse. Her conclusion: "Jesus is not intervening because I deserve to be punished. I am bad." Neither conclusion is untenable for the sexually abused child's schemata. Courtois (1988, 45) suggests that two of the messages delivered to sexually abused children by their family members are: "Don't trust yourself or anyone else. No one is trustworthy" and "Be ashamed of yourself. You are to blame for everything."

For Nadine and Sally, religious personages or God-figures were confusing and intrusive but very familiar. What might have been the cognitive assonance between this divine being or spirit, an unseen being, and the reality one survivor related: "Think of it: every time you relaxed, someone came up behind you and 'got you' one way or the other." The sexually abused child or adolescent's heightened sense of vulnerability may render her unable, in her adult life, to trust in general, causing her to keep interactions on a superficial level, to disconnect from others, distance herself when a relationship threatens to become intimate, or drive others away with her hostile behaviors (Berliner and Ernst 1983; Josephson and Fong-Beyette 1987). For some adults abused as children, a relationship with God as a personified being is as frightening and potentially abusive as the relationship with their abusers had been in childhood and as any intimate human relationship might be in their present lives.

Frequently the child who was sexually abused by a trusted male member of her family also is wary of maternal images of God. She may have felt abandoned by her mother prior to or during the time of the abuse or in fact may have been emotionally abandoned or rejected by her mother after disclosure. How might she reconcile a maternal image of God as comforting and nurturing if her reality defines "mother" as distant, cold, needy, or uncaring? One survivor achieved this reconciliation by creating a comforting but impersonal maternal God image.

Carla, a member of a therapy group for adult survivors, participated in a group exercise in which each woman was asked to draw God as God existed during the time of the sexual abuse. As Carla explained her drawing, she told the group that her memories of her father's raping her were sketchy. She did remember "awakening" in a bathtub of water colored by her own blood. Indicating her drawing, she went on, "I used to turn to the moon for comfort." "The man in the moon?" another group member asked. "Oh no!" Carla replied, "I couldn't buy into all that male stuff. This was more like the woman in the moon and it was somehow comforting."

It is reassuring to note that some sexually abused children were able to find solace in a father image of God despite the abusiveness of their earthly fathers. And so do some adult survivors find the personal and maternal images of God to be desirable. Certainly there are such comforting images offered throughout the Scriptures. Exegetes and scholars like Boff (1987), Mollenkott (1987), and Trible (1978) have done excellent work in identifying and explaining such passages. However, these works were unwritten fifteen to twenty years ago when many of today's adult survivors were experiencing sexual abuse. Even now, the general public is only just becoming aware of a maternal face as a legitimate image of God. Even if the concept of an intimate relationship with a maternal God was not anathema, the sexually abused child often was unable to find a comforting or positive feminine image. In turning, unaided, to the Bible for comfort, she sometimes discovered representations of women that all too readily added to her own low self-esteem. On the Old Testament side of the Bible, women were the source of temptation (Genesis 3), were sometimes the downfall of men (Genesis 38), and always were man's possession (Genesis 24). On the New Testament side of the biblical pasture, women were either reformed prostitutes (John 8:3–11), cured lunatics or newly unpossessed (Luke 8:1–3), healed outcasts (Luke 8:42–48), or silent, serving and, apparently, asexual (John 12:1–8).

It is not surprising that many adult survivors turned from traditional religious teachings and related to God solely on a nonpersonified basis, as illustrated in one adult survivor's musing during a therapy session: "I have no remembrance of God from my childhood. I'm just comfortable with nature as my God." Certainly a spiritual relating to nature is not unique to adults who were sexually abused as children, but frequently the survivor reports pointedly leaving a personified image of God and seeking out a nonpersonified one. In the case of Paula who was abused as a child by her stepfather, this pattern is clearly intentional.

I was raised in the Bible Belt, and sex was a taboo subject. Hell was always being talked about, however, and the way I heard it, anyone's chances of escaping hell were pretty slim. I knew I was doomed. When I was about 12, my mother and I moved to the West Coast.

There, things eased up a little, but the seeds of guilt were deep, and God, the very male judge, knew I was bad.

Then in my early twenties and in the midst of a bad battering marriage, I found a real community in the neighborhood Episcopal church. But after a while, even the nice sense of community couldn't make up for the oppressive feeling I had of God as male, male and powerful, judging and controlling my life. I struck out on my own to look for other women who felt like me. We formed a group and started exploring the female image of God—you know, there are some! And at first that was a wonderful relief, but after a while, I realized that I was furious with Mother for never having seen what was happening, and I couldn't live with that either. Now I relate to God as energy, as the life force in us. I don't know if that's the image I'll keep—I'm just starting to work on the incest—but at least, it feels comfortable in this, my sixth decade!

Internalizing Contradictory Messages

For some victims of sexual abuse it might be truly "good news" to learn that the outcast could be healed or the crazy woman cured; both personas are familiar to them. Because of the secrecy of the abuse (Sgroi and Bunk 1988, 171–173; Karpel 1980, 297) and the family messages that contradicted their own perceptions of reality, the victim eventually may have come to doubt her own sanity. How does the sexually abused child translate the dissonant messages of "always tell the truth," and "don't tell anyone about this or I'll tell them you're lying"?

> Edie recalled, "I could be shivering and blue, and my father would look at me with this odd smile and tell me that I wasn't cold. And if he said it, no matter what else you knew or felt, what he said was the way it was!" Sherri added, "I was always thinking, 'Well, maybe it's my imagination.' I mean I was brainwashed. You believe what you're brought up to believe, what's drilled into your head; then you tend to believe it. I mean you have nothing else . . . Mostly everything I experienced in my life, I thought was my imagination. I had no reality except for [my family]."
>
> Although Sherri was not the only one in her family to be sexually abused by her stepfather, she was the only one who confronted her abuser and was soundly told by other family members that the sexual abuse had done her no harm.

Because the messages she received from family or significant others were so consistently contradictory to her own experience of reality, the victim may become hypervigilant in her interactions with everyone else. As an adult, she continues to watch the responses of those around her in order to see how she should react to the situation at hand. "I don't know how I should feel" is a familiar statement for the adult survivor. Assuming someone else's affect is a means of dealing with that confusion. As Sherri explained to the group, the child victim learns to accept someone else's interpretation of reality instead of her own. It matters little whether the interpretation is positive or negative; she only understands that her own judgments are not to be trusted. It becomes easy for her to accept another's judgment that she is responsible for her abuse.

Isolation and Blame

It also becomes easy for the child victim and, later, the adult survivor to believe that she is indelibly marked and deserves to be isolated—outcast—from society (Blick and Porter 1982; Burgess 1984; Herman 1981). In a group therapy session Colleen remarked, "I can't remember how old I was before I realized that all fathers weren't doing this to their little girls, but I remember feeling very alone." Her peers all nodded. "I still do," Lisa sighed. "I'm always afraid someone is going to find out who I am and walk away from me, so I act like I'm supercompetent. What I really feel like is a little kid who says, 'Hi, I'm Lisa, Oh, won't you *please* come out and play with me?' "

Some survivors unconsciously sense that relieving oneself of the blame for the abuse and placing it on the abuser's shoulders is too disruptive to their established belief system. Others consciously believe themselves to be deserving of punishment because, later, as adolescents or as adults, they used their sexuality as a means of controlling their reality. Maria commented, "The only time I knew connectedness in my family was during the abuse. Now I'm not sure I can have an intimate relationship without sexualizing it." Frequently the survivor's sense of shame at having participated in sexual behaviors—having been sexually abused—manifests itself in some sort of sexual dysfunction, frigidity, conversion hysteria, promiscuity, an aversion to sex, or, as Maria suggested, the compulsive sexualization of all relationships (Berliner and Ernst 1983; Gelinas 1983; Joy 1987; Meiselman 1978; Tsai and Wagner 1978).

What might the adult survivor or the sexually abused child take from the many sermons and homilies that focus exclusively on the God-sinner relationship, presenting humanity as fallen and, too often, presenting God as a record keeper of sin who holds "damnation" in his hand like some hair-triggered weapon? She doubtless has heard that Eve was responsible for bringing sin into the world, for tempting feckless Adam, and for luring him away from his friendship with God. There is far too much in the traditional teaching that easily reinforces the sexually abused girl's worst fears; she, like a modern-day Eve, is evil because of her "sexual sin." And she believes herself to be judged and found guilty by a very male and very powerful God.

Messages from Ministers

Sometimes the child victim fought these feelings of responsibility and sought the help of the clergy. And although as "long ago" as 1950, Gordon Allport recommended that clergy be trained to deal with psychological matters, little was effectively offered on a widescale basis prior to the early 1970s. Even as programs in pastoral counseling and in spiritual direction have burgeoned on college campuses, the cleric or religious counselor was rarely prepared to deal with the possible impact of child sexual abuse upon the victim. Thus, contemporary adult survivors report a wide range of responses by clergy. On some occasions, the victim approached the pastor and was relieved of her guilt either because of the cleric's direct intervention on the child's behalf or because of his or her compassionate response when protective intervention was no longer a necessary intervention for the adult survivor.

> Marty had been molested over a period of years by an uncle eight years her senior. At the age of 18, she decided to enter a Roman Catholic religious community of women. She remembered many years later: "Nuns were supposed to be pure and virginal, and just before I entered, I had this terrible fear that, somehow, someone would find out that I wasn't a virgin, or they'd ask me and I'd have to tell. I imagined that once they knew the truth, they wouldn't let me be a nun. I finally went to confession, and at the end, I told the priest my fear. He got red in the face and very angry. At first I thought he was angry at me because I wanted to be a nun and wasn't a virgin. But it turned out he was angry at the idea that anyone would *ask* whether I was a virgin! 'They have no right to ask you that!' I remember him saying indignantly. I felt better. I hadn't told him why I wasn't a virgin—telling him that my uncle had sex with me would have been too much! But the priest's response, knowing as much as he knew, was comforting."

But for every story like Marty's, there are dozens more suggesting that the more common experience for child victims or adult survivors was far from comforting. In some instances, the pastor's only intervention was to pray with the adolescent and ask God to heal her abusing parent. No earthly intervention or assistance was given. At other times, the child was cautioned to stay away from her abusing brother because he was an adolescent boy experiencing the throes of pubescent sexuality. This subtly reinforced her faulty premise that she was in control of the situation. Sometimes her responsibility and control were not so subtly suggested; the guilt for the abuse was laid squarely on the victims shoulders (Pellauer 1987, 90).

> Jessi was sexually abused by both her older sister, and brother. With an 8 year old's moral sensibility, she reasoned that she must have been doing something wrong for "this" to have happened twice. She recalled: "Over and over I went to confession, and each time I confessed that my sister and brother were touching me, the priest got angry and gave me a penance. I used to sit in church and feel like the worst little girl in the world. . . . Now I feel angry because for years, those priests were the only people I told about the sexual abuse and instead of asking me more about what I was telling them and helping me, they blamed me."

Sadly, her interpretation of theology changes little as the child victim becomes the adult survivor. The classical and Eastern mystical writers often are heard by the adult survivor only in ways that overemphasize the unworthiness and sinfulness of the "pray-er." The language of spirituality itself seems passive and threatening: give over control, "Let go and let God." Remember, this is said to a woman who as a child relinquished control to a trusted adult; as a result of that experience, she likely has spent a number of years building defenses that ensured her control in the future.

Control and Forgiveness

With normal egocentric efforts to control her dissonant reality, the child victim often developed the belief system that she was in fact responsible for and in control of her abuser and her abuse. One adult survivor's comments about this bring up the issue of forgiveness.

> Phyllis told the group that in order for her to feel whole, she needed to forgive herself. "For what?" demanded Gina. "You didn't do anything wrong!" Phyllis said in a tearful and childlike voice, "Maybe if I was a better child, my parents would have loved me."

That she deserves to be punished for not being a "better child" is a frequent conclusion drawn by the adult survivor.

> Another woman remembered, "What's hardest for me is the feeling of guilt that I still carry around with me. When I was little, I was afraid of God because he kept tabs on things and was terribly punishing. He would know what was happening, and it would be my

fault. That's stayed with me for years and years. Now I realize that I need to forgive myself. If someone else told me I was forgiven, it was just words. It never touched my heart. There has never really been a way to work off the punishment. The 'judging God' is still the more powerful."

The need for self-forgiveness is a theme common to many adult survivors. The woman just quoted sought forgiveness for not being a better child and thus causing her own abuse. Another believed that she needed to be forgiven because she accepted money for the sexual favors Grandpa "bought" from her as a 10-year-old child. Another could not forgive herself for being "beautiful," a remark frequently crooned by her abusive stepfather. Still another asked the members of her therapy group to forgive her for having lived through her sexual abuse.

All of these examples are cited to assist clinicians in understanding the impact of child sexual abuse on the spirituality of the adult survivor. Adult survivors seeking clinical help often present with multiple areas of confusion and conflict. It is important for clinicians to recognize these areas of distress—be they interpersonal, sexual, or spiritual.

Implications for Clinical Practice

How can clinicians help the adult survivor identify the areas of her spirituality that are enmeshed in self-blame or poor self-images? One approach is to pose a series of questions during the therapy. For example, the question, "Where was God when the child was abused?" now raised by the clinician probably was posed repeatedly by the adult survivor during her childhood. Cautious exploration of this question during therapy will help the clinician to address the adult survivor's contemporary relationship to God. The latter is important because it is likely that the client's current difficulties with self-image are intertwined with her current explanation, or "story," about God's relationship to her abuse. In this section, questions will be addressed with case examples and suggestions for clinical intervention. These questions are not posed as intellectual queries about moral and/or spiritual development. Rather, they are raised as a means of unearthing some of the artifacts of the sexual abuse experience that the adult survivor carries with her. This section closes with a discussion of clinical limitations in addressing the adult survivor's spirituality.

Where Was God When the Child Was Abused?

Frequently the adult survivor muses, "I prayed but nothing happened." Some survivors as children invoked God for a miraculous intervention that in fairy-tale fashion would stop the abuse and create an idyllic family life. Others pleaded for deliverance by asking God to inspire the abuser voluntarily and peacefully to go away. And some children begged for a more direct solution: they prayed that they or their abusers would die. All of these prayers seemingly met with the same silence—not precisely a refusal on God's part but a nonresponse. The clinician can appropriately ask the survivor about the conclusions she drew from that silence. Her response may reveal more about the manner in which she coped with the abuse as a child, for example:

> Pseudomaturity: "I guessed that I should have been able to handle it. So I took care of myself and kept my little brothers and sisters away from my father."

> Minimization: "I figured that God was too busy with wars and starving people. I had a roof over my head and food. It was just 'this problem' with my brother."

> Passivity: "God just wasn't interested. He wasn't mean or anything. He just created me and then went away."

> Self-blame: "God was punishing me because somehow I must have caused my mother to act that way. This didn't happen to *good* kids."

There is no therapeutic recipe or formula to be applied here; obviously the therapist must use clinical judgment to assess the needs of each client, but some possible responses are offered.

The underlying theme for the rationalizations listed can be summarized in one general statement: "I am unimportant; in fact, I am worthless, and I didn't deserve help." Before addressing the God issue, then, it is useful for some clients to look at childhood pictures of themselves at the ages they were before the abuse began or at the age of their earliest memories of the sexual abuse. Many adult survivors look back at themselves during the early stages of the abuse and anachronistically attribute adult insights and powers to the children they were. Bringing a childhood picture to a therapy session is particularly helpful because it gives the therapist the opportunity to draw attention to observable facts about the child in the picture: she is a child's size, a child's weight, a child's age. For the first time, the adult survivor may see herself as the child that she was and not as the miniature adult postulated by her self-blame and pseudomaturity.

> Tracy brought a picture of herself and her four brothers as children to the therapy session. She had looked through her family album at her therapist's request for a picture of herself at 3 years of age—the age when the oldest of the four brothers, twelve years her senior,

began to abuse her. Tracy seemed bemused when the therapy session began, and slowly, as she and the therapist talked about the picture, her affect shifted. In an astonished voice, she said, "I was a baby! I did what very little kids do when they're scared. When my parents fought, I went to find someone to make it all right—safe." For the first time in therapy, she began to cry, "I wasn't bad! I wasn't bad!" "No," said her therapist gently, "You weren't bad. Yes, you were just a very little girl who was scared. You were a little girl who did what little girls do when they're scared. And you're not bad now either."

That session and the one that immediately followed, focused on the positive things Tracy could remember about herself as a child, utilizing other old photographs. Tracy and her therapist then began to address the "Where was God?" issue. When Tracy tried to return to her rationalization that she must have been a worthless or bad child, the therapist reminded her of the reality they had newly discovered: she had been a little girl, no better *and no worse* than other children. When Tracy began to minimize—"One kid's problems aren't important compared to the big stuff going on in the world"—the therapist challenged her. "Gee," said her therapist thoughtfully, "I've worked with a lot of children, Tracy, of all ages, and I can't imagine thinking they're unimportant. They seem very important to me. I'm not God, but do you think this God of yours feels differently?" They then spent time identifying Tracy's present-day expectations of God and comparing and contrasting them with what she had wished and prayed for as a child.

Three interventions can be observed in the case example. Through the use of childhood pictures, Tracy could begin to see herself at the time her abuse began as a young child and, thus, not the person responsible for causing or controlling the abuse. Years of self-blame cannot be definitively reversed in a few sessions, but the faulty perception of self can be challenged. Because Tracy looked at these pictures with her therapist, the clinician could consistently and persistently challenge her when she slipped into old rationalizations. The therapist also was able to model acceptance of and fondness for the child Tracy discovered herself to have been years ago. The therapist did not see a miniature and culpable adult in those pictures, nor did she see a wayward or evil child. She suggested to Tracy that perhaps Tracy's God might also have viewed her with acceptance and fondness. This suggestion of transference could allow Tracy to check out on a human, tangible level what acceptance and understanding might feel like from her God figure. Finally, Tracy and her therapist together began to look at Tracy's past and present expectations of her God. Sgroi and Bunk (1988, 143–144) suggest that the age of onset and the duration of the sexual abuse may influence the child's successful passage through developmental stages. Anna Freud (1982, 34) ranked incest higher than any other form of abuse "where the chances of harming a child's normal developmental growth are concerned." Johanek (1988, 106) noted that there may be "an arrest of emotional and social development, which began around the time of the original assault."

A premise of this chapter is that the child's spiritual development also may have been hindered, if not arrested, when the sexual abuse took place. Identifying the adult survivor's present-day and former childhood expectations of God can help her to confront her own possible fantasy-ridden beliefs and magical expectations. If the adult survivor still anticipates a miraculous intervention that will cause her abuser to announce his wrongdoing and seek forgiveness and also cause her previously distant family to rally around her, then the clinician is wise to anticipate the client's frustration. If these magical expectations are persisting, it is likely that her self-defeating behaviors will continue in all close relationships.

What Is the Survivor's Contemporary Relationship to God?

Often there is a parallel that can be drawn between the ways by which the adult survivor as a child was engaged in the sexual behaviors and the way in which she as an adult relates to her God. In turn, her relationship to God may reflect her capacity for intimacy on any level (Jakubiak and Murphy 1987: Stoudt 1987). It is useful to remember that a relationship to God is a relationship with the same potential for healthy or dysfunctional characteristics as would be true for relationships between human beings. This is not a suggestion that all psychologically healthy people relate to God in a similar fashion (or that they relate to God at all). The emphasis here is on dysfunction. If the adult survivor has a relationship with a God figure and that relationship is dysfunctional, then it is likely that the dysfunctional aspects of her relationship with God will shed light on her less divine relationships.

An adult who was coerced or enticed into participation in sexual behaviors as a child may believe that she must continue to "make deals" with God in order to gain favor—happiness, peace, health—or in order to avert tragedy. There is always an element of cost and payment in her relationships. Nothing comes to her gratuitously; there is a price, and she pays it. She became the overachieving, overresponsible child who matured into the too-good-to-be-true adult, appearing to the outside world to have endless reserves of energy. This is the adult survivor who tells her therapist that she probably should discontinue therapy because she finds that fifty minutes a week is taking too much time from a schedule that includes full-time employment, volunteer work at the hospital, chairing the PTA, singing in her church choir, running the local boy scout troop and, incidentally, taking care of her husband and children. Or this is an adult survivor like Sally who stated earnestly, "I think it's time for me to take on more penance. I'm being soft on myself, and look at all God's done for me. I'm going to talk with my minister." This was said after her recent hospitalization for alcoholism and two weeks after her only child's suicide.

The therapist can and should address the client's motivation. What underlies her need to "do" for others to the degree that an hour's therapy for herself is out of the question? What underlies the need for penance? Does her God always demand repayment? Does her God permit taking care of oneself? grieving? being angry? How does this adult behavior resemble the pattern of responsibility or guilt that developed in childhood during the time of her abuse? Is she relating to God as she did to her abuser?

The adult who as a child was threatened or violently forced into cooperation with abuser may fear displeasing her God. She fears that any perceived transgression, anything less than perfection, will result in a just punishment. One woman asked her therapist, "Do you understand that having anything less than a logical answer meant my father could punish me? I could never have said, 'I don't know.' I'm not sure I can say it now!" Another said, "Meeting my own needs meant death! But there was this constant battle because I did have needs." The latter came to therapy because she was worn out and was terrified by what her fatigue could mean. Did admitting that she had needs for rest and replenishment mean that God would take her life?

If the client is sufficiently engaged in her therapy to understand that the therapeutic setting is a safe place where she may challenge old fears or experiment with new behaviors, the clinician may find it useful to teach this client relaxation techniques. Beginning with simple deep-breathing exercises may be beneficial; some adult survivors have lived with such hypervigilance that they literally do not dare to breathe deeply lest they draw attention to themselves or somehow cause themselves to miss cues and respond inappropriately. Breathing in rhythm with the therapist's direction may help the client to relax and may also become a metaphor for changing negative beliefs about herself: "As you breathe in, you feel FRESH air enter your body and REPLACE the old air; as you breathe out, you SEND AWAY the old air you NO LONGER NEED." A breathing exercise also may focus on refreshing particular parts of the body. One adult survivor noted that as she talked about her abuse and began to lose her fear of telling she no longer felt the tightness in her throat and chest. Breathing exercises can help to relax such areas. Familiarity with the client's current God image is helpful here. Breath may be used as a symbol for the life force within the woman. She invites the life force that is the source of healing (inspiration), and she releases what is used (expiration). The life force may be the "Energy," the "Breath of Jahweh first given to Adam," or the "Spirit of Life," whatever image corresponds to the woman's contemporary image of God.

Guided meditation, or imagery, is useful in helping adult survivors to feel safe in letting go. There is a plethora of audiotapes with such guided imagery on the market today, and those that simply suggest rest and peaceful relaxation may be quite helpful to this client population. Introducing them in the therapeutic situation allows the client to learn to relax in relative safety and permits the clinician to observe the client's reaction. Some adult survivors become frightened by what they perceive as vulnerability when they relax. Responding quietly and calmly to a client's fear of vulnerability can reassure her of the safety of the setting; hearing the clinician's voice may remind her that she is in the present, not the past, and that she is with the therapist, not her abuser.

Another protective device may be given by suggesting that the client draw a "light" around herself, a light that is impermeable to destructive forces and will surround her for those few minutes of relaxation during the guided imagery. Some clinicians suggest a white light (Allison in Kluft 1988, 92; Mariechild 1981, 4); however, allowing the client the freedom of choosing the color and shape of her "light space" not only gives her another means of control but gives the therapist another piece of information. What color is the protective light? What does the client associate with that color? When did she previously experience the feelings she associates with that color? Where might be God be in those feelings? that color? that protection? How does this differ from her ideation of God as threatening and vindictive? These questions are raised after the guided meditation and imagery exercise, and they also are pertinent to the imagery exercise itself. What was it like to feel quiet and safe? Has there ever been an experience or a dream in the client's life that she can associate with those experiences?

The goal here is to loosen the grip of fear in which the woman lives. How might helping her to reframe her image of God and her contemporary relationship with God assist in this? Is the God whom she identifies in the guided imagery as the "Breath of Life" or the "Giver of Peace" compatible with the vindictive God of her hypervigilance or the insatiable God of her overachievement? The therapist's presence can help the client to ground in reality her current experience of peace and relaxation and question her need to relate dysfunctionally with God and with others. The phrase "need to relate dysfunctionally" is used advisedly and leads to the next question.

How Does the Adult Survivor's God Image Support the "Story" She Tells Herself?

It is not unusual for a woman who was abused physically, sexually, or emotionally in childhood to "discover" in adulthood that she was an abused, battered, or neglected child. What series of rationalizations did she employ in order to deny that reality until as an adult she could integrate the truth? What story did she tell herself about her life? What was the family mythology? How did God function in that myth? What needs does it serve for her to have a God who is highly moralistic or punishing? A look at the adult survivor's pattern of presentation will give some information about this.

In volume 1 of *Vulnerable Populations,* Sgroi and Bunk outline two typical presentation patterns for adult survivors: early and late (1988, 149–153). The late presenter generally resembles the case examples already used: the super achiever, the woman who "has it all together," so "together" that one wonders how her family, office, church, school, and town could ever get along without her. This adult survivor often believes that her identity is synonymous with productivity. She may believe further that the secret of her abuse is so reprehensible that, once discovered, it will drive others from her. If repression is insufficient to keep the memory of this secret from consciousness, then she tells herself what one adult survivor reported "I believed that if anyone saw beneath my 'perfect exterior' I'd be abandoned because I was disgusting. In fact, people wouldn't just leave me; they'd run me out or town." She believed that she could keep the secret of her "responsibility" for her abuse, the secret of her "badness," by denying her own human needs and living for others. She may have believed that her God would abandon or revile her if she failed to hide her sexual victimization. She particularly may have feared the anger that she suspected might reside within her.

In her study of shame, Lewis (1987) makes two points salient to this discussion. Overt shame may appear as an acute state of self-hatred, leading to incessant ideation about one's role in the shaming event (pp. 22–23). In the late presenter, this self-hatred may be the impetus behind her constant activity; she may believe that she must somehow work off her sin and hide her secret at all costs. Therefore when in the midst of her "together life" the late presenter finds herself face to face with unresolved emotional sequelae of her childhood sexual abuse, she truly may experience terror. One means of controlling her terror is to focus on guilt, and here the second of Lewis's points is pertinent: "Guilt clearly rests on the bypassed humiliated fury or shame-rage that the patient has been harbouring and simultaneously recognizing as unjust"(p. 24). Immersing herself in guilt may seem preferable to the adult survivor to uncapping a rage that she fears is overwhelming and destructive, and her apocryphal God supports this control-by-guilt. She relates to a God who is at once gullible and omnipotent, rather like the giants of fairy tales. She can and must keep the secret of her abuse from this God who would cast her to Gehenna or otherwise righteously punish her if her culpability were discovered. She must be active continually and must not feel or allow herself to risk the mutual knowing that intimacy implies.

The adult survivor who was an early presenter may need to relate dysfunctionally to her God figure because that allows her to maintain her story that she is unworthy of healing. She may need to believe that God refused to help her during the time of her abuse because there was—and is—something about her that is intrinsically bad, something repugnant even to God. And so she establishes an internal consistency, then and now, by creating and maintaining a God of retribution: she was bad; she caused the abuse; she is a bad person, and God is punishing her. In adolescence she may have run away, abused drugs and/or alcohol, attempted suicide, or enacted some combination of self-injurious behaviors for which she believes she is now beyond forgiveness; after all, those were all "sins against the self"!

And what is the reported God relationship of the woman, early or late presenter, who was impregnated by her abuser and had an abortion-often at the behest of the abuser? This was the teen-aged daughter whose sexual abuse began prior to menarche and whose abuser ignored the need to protect against pregnancy after its onset. This was the child who was taken to a clinic, a hospital, or a back room, depending on the era of the abuse, and to whom nothing was explained about the abortion procedure. What is the story she has told herself to rationalize these events over the years? What does she believe would be her God's reaction and response to the abortion? Very rarely has this adult survivor told herself anything about a compassionate God. Too often she has subscribed to an image of God that supports her self-hatred.

Obviously the transference in the therapeutic relationship can be useful here also. The therapist's empathic response challenges the adult survivor's self hatred and guilt and, perhaps, challenges the need for punishing relationships, human or divine. She deserves healthy relationships. She deserves to be cared about even when her secret is known. Issues of self-esteem and intimacy are addressed appropriately in therapy at this juncture. Challenging the dysfunctional God relationship surely is within the clinician's range of capability; assisting the client to reevaluate and reform her beliefs may be beyond it. This leads to the fourth and last question.

What Are the Clinical Limitations in Addressing the Adult Survivor's Spirituality?

In his writing on psychological crisis as an opportunity for spiritual growth, Nicolosi (1987) posits that psychotherapists "not only assume the task of resolution and psychological growth but . . . hope for spiritual maturity" (p. 12). Despite that ideal, it is unrealistic for any therapist who is without dual training in psychotherapy and spiritual direction to do more than hope for her or his client's spiritual maturity. Although this chapter focuses on the spirituality of the adult survivor, it does so from the perspective that the woman's spirituality helps or hinders her psychological healing. Clinical in-

186 · *Vulnerable Populations*

terventions are directed at the client's greater acceptance of self; becoming more comfortable with her relationship with God is a by-product of this therapy. It is unlikely that psychotherapy will otherwise help the adult survivor's spiritual growth and development. This is likely to be a reflection of the limitations of the clinical milieu and, possibly, the developmental needs of the client. In chapter 5 of this volume Sgroi describes a spiral of recovery in which the adult survivor confronts different issues as she passes through stages of recovery. The women described in the case examples in this chapter needed to deal with their sexual victimization in a clinical milieu first. After they worked on and resolved some of their clinical issues, they might have needed to shift from the clinical milieu to the spiritual forum in their movement toward wholeness. It is unrealistic to expect clinicians to be more knowledgeable about spirituality than the well-read layperson. It is unrealistic likewise to expect clergy or spiritual guides to be clinicians. Both groups of professionals must be sensitive to the need to work cooperatively and to recognize when they are out of their depth with a particular client. Fortune and Hertze (1987) make the point that such cooperation and self-knowledge enable the professionals to utilize their skills efficiently while serving clients' needs (70–71).

A trained member of the spiritual ministry, upon reading this chapter, might emerge with greater insight into some of the clinical or psychological issues of the adult survivor and the indications for psychotherapy as opposed to her spiritual or religious issues and need for spiritual direction. As a result of this insight, the minister might reexamine some of the spiritual blocks that he or she has encountered with adult survivors. One spiritual director found that her new knowledge about adult survivors opened long-barred doors with a directee, which enabled the client to move toward greater spiritual development. Another minister remarked with astonishment that before she had attended a workshop on the spirituality of the adult survivor, she was unaware of ever working with a person who had been sexually abused in childhood. After the workshop, the minister discovered that half of the women she counseled were adult survivors. What had happened? She had learned to ask her spiritual directees about sexual victimization. She had begun to listen differently to their struggles with trust and their perceptions of sinfulness. She had begun to ask questions about the genesis of their God images. She reported that she now felt better equipped to work spiritually with directees who were adult survivors and also had a better sense of when her directees needed clinical help as well.

Some adult survivors who are interested in their spiritual development or are involved in religious organizations will be able to maintain a commitment to spiritual direction simultaneously with their clinical work on issues of sexual victimization. In fact, their religious affiliation may generate support for their therapeutic work. Others will feel the need to put their spiritual growth on hold while they focus on therapeutic issues because they find it emotionally draining to work with their therapists and their ministers at the same time. It may be necessary for the minister to suggest that an adult survivor take a temporary rest from spiritual direction while she works through a particularly difficult stage of clinical recovery. Because it is easy for this client population to assume that self-initiated respites are indicative of spiritual indolence and so to become mired further in guilt and self-loathing, the permission to rest—indeed a spiritual prescription for rest—may be warranted. It is also important for the spiritual director to communicate an openness to the adult survivor's return to spiritual direction. Issues of separation and abandonment are particularly significant for adult survivors. The spiritual director who keeps in touch at intervals and supports a return to spiritual direction "when you are ready" can be an invaluable asset.

On the therapeutic side of the coin, it is important for the clinician to develop some familiarity with the client's religious and spiritual support system. If her network of support includes a minister, rabbi, spiritual director, or pastoral assistant, the clinician is well advised to establish (with the client's permission) contact with the support person. Opening this channel of communication can enable the cleric to contact the therapist, again with the client's permission, when necessary. Establishing contact with this support person also brings new information to the clinician: what kind of person does the minister seem to be? How aware is she or he of the issues of adult survivors? How supportive is she or he of psychotherapy? From what spiritual viewpoint does she or he operate? In the section on the adult survivor's contemporary relationship to God, the example was used of Sally who believed she should do more penance and was going to seek out her minister's advice. Would the minister and the therapist be working in tandem or at cross-purposes? Knowing whether the minister would encourage or discourage Sally's penitential approach to healing could influence the clinician's response.

Addressing the spirituality of adult survivors may strike personal chords in the clinician. Jakubiak and Murphy (1987, 162) recommend that clinicians examine their own beliefs but warn that "this may require painful excursions through religious belief systems and may threaten long-held notions about the social and divine order." It is of paramount importance that the clinician have a clear understanding of her or his own spirituality and have addressed existential questions of suffering and meaning. Issues of countertransference are no less real in the therapeutic area of spirituality than they are in other clinical areas.

How important is it for the clinician's belief systems to be congruent with the client's? It is likely that there will be problems if their belief systems are antagonistic. The clinician who discovers that her or his own belief system is so dichotomous to the client's as to be a therapeutic barrier will do best to refer the client to a colleague with whom she is more likely to work successfully. Consulting or seeking supervision from respected professionals, particularly those with a background in spirituality, is highly desirable.

Peer Group Therapy with a Theme of Spirituality

Peer group therapy can afford a safe milieu for adult survivors to explore together how sexual abuse in childhood affected their spiritual development and present-day spirituality. (Chapter 6 in this volume describes the benefits of peer group therapy for adult survivors.) "Exploring My Spirituality" is one of many possible themes for a cycle of time-limited peer group therapy. Apart from the general goals of peer group therapy for adult survivors as enumerated in chapter 6, a group designed to focus specifically on the spirituality of the adult survivor has special goals. These goals might include:

1. Identifying attributions of God as each woman perceived God during the time of the sexual abuse.

2. Identifying ways in which one's self-image might be influenced by one's image of God.

3 Identifying ways in which a childhood image of God reflected significant people, that is, adults, in a child's life.

4. Providing a safe atmosphere in which a client might confront a dysfunctional image of God.

5. Providing disparate God images that would include female, male, and nonpersonified images of God that are compassionate and healing.

6. Stimulating the client's powers of creativity so that they may expand, enhance, and/or solidify healthy images of God reflective of each woman's personal identity, values, and hopes.

7. Decreasing a sense of isolation by identifying other women in the group and in history who have experienced injustice, alienation, and confusion and have wrongly been identified as "sinners."

8. Identifying positive attributes of each woman that reflect her spirituality and perhaps suggest a God image.

No one cycle of peer group therapy will or should effectively address all of these goals. Nor is the preceding an exhaustive list of goals related to the adult survivor's spirituality and overall recovery. These goals and the model that follows for a twelve-week cycle of peer group therapy are merely suggestions, drawn from experiences that have been beneficial for some clients. They are presented here as rough guidelines for other clinicians to use as they develop their own approaches to addressing the spirituality of the adult survivor from a clinical perspective.

Members

There is a vast difference between women who have participated in one or more other cycles of peer group therapy and those who are experiencing it for the first time. Women who have been in previous cycles understand the basics of participating in a therapy group, have talked with other survivors about being sexually abused, and have learned, at least peripherally, that group therapy is always hard work and sometimes disruptive to their daily functioning but frequently of tremendous benefit. When focusing specifically on the issue of one's spirituality as it relates to one's present self-esteem, it becomes a matter of how many threads each woman is able to weave at one time into the tapestry of her life. Focusing on the genesis of one's God image and one's own spirituality may be frightening and threatening. If the adult survivor is already familiar with the group therapy milieu, she may feel safer in confronting often painful but basic beliefs. This is not to say that a new group member might not benefit from a cycle of group therapy that focuses on spirituality, nor would every experienced group member be a candidate for such a group. Clinical knowledge about the woman's needs, emotional stability, and stage of recovery are the best indicators of the appropriateness of working on a theme of spirituality. However, I have observed that in one group that focused on spirituality and was comprised mostly of experienced members, only the new members opted to skip the next cycle of therapy. By contrast, in another group composed of predominantly new members, the focus consistently was drawn to issues of personal victimization and safety and away from spirituality. Adult survivors who had experienced at least one cycle of peer group therapy prior to the spirituality-themed group seemed to identify their exploration of spirituality as one more way to confront victimization issues and move toward recovery. Whatever the client's prior group experience, it is recommended that she continue her individual work and participate in the group with her therapist's support.

NiCarthy, Merriam, and Coffman (1984, 123) advise limiting participation in "groups for women of faith" to broad categories of orthodoxy, for examples, Christian, Jewish, or Muslim members. They reason that the group leaders should have a working familiarity with the basic tenets of the faiths of their group members in order better to understand, anticipate, and work with faith issues as they arise. They also surmise that the group leader is rare who has this facility in a variety of orthodoxies.

Horton and Williamson (1988, 133–143) underline the importance of the therapeutic implications of culture and ethnicity (and incidentally religion) in dealing with any client population and offer useful suggestions in this regard. However, even if the group is intentionally opened only to women from one broad base of religious persuasions, the members are likely to have tremendous variations of beliefs, misbeliefs, personal investment, and understanding.

Sally comes to the group a practicing Baptist; Allie was raised Catholic but her lesbianism is in conflict with her feelings about her faith; Lisa, raised a Mormon, believes that God is male—only and absolutely male—while Hannah, not raised in any particular faith, believes with equal verve that God is female—only female; Betty, raised in the Episcopal faith, now dabbles with Zen philosophy; Trudy is "into" crystals and energy; while Gracie, a former Lutheran, is exploring the beliefs and rituals of Native Americans. A caricature? Perhaps, but the reality often is only slightly less diverse. The point is that these are all women who were sexually abused as children, who are seeking therapy for issues related to that abuse, and who are coming to a treatment group with a spirituality theme. It is not a forum for proselytizing one's beliefs; rather it is an opportunity to test one's beliefs about God against reality in the company of others and to move toward recovery. It would be enormously helpful to the therapist's understanding of religious dynamics if the group was homogeneous with regard to both beliefs and misconceptions, but such homogeneity seems beyond the scope of this era. Limiting the group to eight to ten women of vaguely similar religious backgrounds may be the most that can and, for reasons of richness and diversity perhaps, should be done regarding membership.

Sessions

The model proposed here is for a ten to twelve-week cycle of peer group therapy. The opening session begins with introductory remarks, group guidelines and rules, and introductions. The therapists (and it is highly desirable for the group to be led by two cotherapists) open the introductions by commenting briefly on the theme for the cycle, "Exploring My Spirituality." It is helpful if, in their introduction, the therapists broadly define spirituality, for example, "Spirituality may be thought of as moving toward personal holiness, or whole-ness, or as becoming most fully one's self." Then the group members are asked to introduce themselves, telling briefly about their experience of sexual abuse (When do they remember its beginning? Who abused them?) and sharing why they chose to participate in a cycle of group therapy with a spirituality theme.

This latter explanation will give the cotherapists some indication of the group's homogeneity and heterogeneity and will help them to tailor the following sessions to the needs of this unique grouping of women. Shearer and Herbert (1987, 170) composed a table of characteristics of adult survivors of child sexual abuse and note as one characteristic the "defection from family's religion." Some of the women may have been motivated to join the group as part of their search for a new definition of God. Others may have come in order to address ambivalent feelings about God, particularly in relation to their child sexual abuse. Still others may have come because spirituality is the one area of their lives with which they feel comfortable, and so they decided to broach the frightening aspect of their sexual victimization in this more comfortable milieu. And finally, others have come out of curiosity: "I can't imagine what God could have had to do with my being sexually abused." Knowing the members' initial understanding of their own motivations for participation in this group gives the cotherapists a direction as to how they will approach the theme in future sessions. It should be noted here that any planned session may be subject to partial or total alterations depending on the needs of the group members.

The second session of this cycle focuses on the question, "Where was God when I was being abused?" As she answers the question in the presence of her peers, each woman tells more about her personal experience and identifies some of her questions and/or her explanations about being sexually abused as a child. The cotherapists might ask, "What was God thinking about the abuse? about the child? What was God feeling about the abuse? about the child? How was God present or absent at that time?" For some, answers to these questions are familiar and comforting: "God kept me from killing myself or going crazy." For others, answers are familiar but painful: "I prayed, but the abuse didn't stop." Women who are experienced in the group process often suggest other perspectives or offer reflections about another group member's response to the question. For example, when Tara told the group about "escaping into" the wallpaper of her bedroom during her abuse, another group member, Melody, commented reflectively, "Maybe God was in that wallpaper. . . . That's why you could live through the abuse." Tara tentatively explored this possibility with the group after which Melody wondered aloud, "I wonder what *my* wallpaper was," and went on to tell about her experiences of abuse and the presence of God at that time.

Hypnotic storytelling (see also chapter 6) and readings are effective techniques during this cycle, and both can be employed for a variety of reasons throughout the sessions. Sometimes a reading is used as an introduction to a group discussion or activity. At other times, a story is told as an indirect suggestion for change or healing or as a means of nurturance. Women who were sexually abused as children are women from whom something was taken without permission. In the case of rape, this was done by force or threat of force. In the case of molestation, it was done by coercion or entrapment. In either case, the abuser took advantage of the child's size, lack of power, innocence, trust, or fear. It is my contention that it is important for group members to experience some sort of "giving to," as one woman put it, "without a hook." Storytelling can be one way in which to do this. It is useful also in some groups to introduce a topic or an activity with relaxation exercises:

> Only let go of that tension which is unnecessary—that tension which you do not need—
>
> Maintain all the boundaries, all the privacy, all the protections that really help you to feel safe; you will know when you are ready to let down unnecessary barriers—
>
> You have an ability to center and focus and find a place that is safe and peaceful and positive; you can experience that place, that peaceful, restful symbol whenever you wish. Your unconscious mind will give you all the protection you need. You all have enough strength and enough resources to be here and to work productively and to learn.

The last line often is repeated by group members as a mantra of self-comfort and self-reassurance: "I have enough strength and enough resources to be here." It also implies that the cotherapists are responsibly monitoring members' progress, as well as the interactions within the group and the group's overall tenor.

The third session focuses directly on the images of God that people develop. There are a variety of resources, including the creativity of the therapists, that could set the focus for this session. One is an excerpt from Alice Walker's *The Color Purple* (1982, 175–176). The section may be pre-taped and, after a brief introduction, played at the beginning of the group or one of the co-therapists may read it. It is a short section during which two of the characters discuss their childhood images of God. Celie says that because she felt ignored by the God she imaged, she now has chosen to ignore God. Shug challenges the image.

In the previous session, the group members began to identify their childhood images of God during the abuse. Now they are asked to draw or otherwise illustrate "the God of my childhood." (For those uncomfortable with art therapy, see Rubin 1987 or Landgarten 1981.) This is not necessarily the image of God they had during the abuse; it is simply identified as the God of their childhood. A reasonable amount of time should be allowed for the women to draw this childhood God image. Each woman chooses not only the colors she wishes but the period of her life upon which she wishes to focus. Some consciously portray the image of God they perceived during their abuse. Others draw the image of God they cherish from some happier period of their childhood. The choosing, the drawing, and the sharing that follows combine to make this a powerful experience for most group members. Some wish to keep their drawings, others wish to throw them away, and sometimes, others ask the cotherapists to keep their drawings. One woman said, "I don't want this image anymore, but still, it was part of me. Will you keep it for me so I can look at it again later when I'm ready to?"

It is an easy progression for the fourth session to focus on "What do I think God looks like now?" Again, Walker's Celie and Shug provide a wonderful example of how one might go about changing a dysfunctional image (177–179). It is a simple task for the cotherapists to suggest how a healthy childhood image might be brought into adulthood. Art therapy may be employed as a means of making visual the often vague images people have. It is startling to some adult survivors to discover that they have maintained a frightening and childish image of God well into their adult lives simply because it has gone unexamined. Others realize that they have claimed power by making God a distant entity. And some find that their God as imaged is much more compassionate than they are to themselves. How does their image of God or their formulation about themselves need to change?

At this point in the cycle, the cotherapists might introduce a plan for each group member to identify a personal goal to work on for the rest of the cycle. What does each woman hope to accomplish in this spirituality-themed cycle of therapy for adult survivors of child sexual abuse? How does she envision moving toward her goal, and what does she see as the group's role in her movement? Other group members might be encouraged to ask her questions about their role in this if she is open to questions. It is unlikely that the goals of each member will be articulated in this fourth session, particularly if art therapy is the medium by which the women have examined their current images of God. In fact, it is probable that the cotherapists will have time only to introduce the concept of goals and suggest that the group members think about what they would describe as goals during the intervening week. If the therapists choose to limit this cycle to ten weeks, then introducing the goals by week 4 and limiting the art experience to one session for the sake of time is preferable. If this is a twelve-week cycle, the therapists have greater leeway.

In addition to timing, the uniqueness of each group influences the format. It may be an easy progression to move from the third session's "God of my childhood" to the fourth's "God of my present"; however, depending on the size of the group and the impact of the third session, it may be more desirable to take another course. If the group is large—eight to ten members—there may not be sufficient time for all members to share the fruits of their artistic or symbolic labors during the third session, and the fourth session would be a continuation of that sharing. And possibly the art experience may be so strong for a particular group that the therapists choose to create a storytelling session for the fourth session while also encouraging group members to talk about their experience of the previous week.

The fifth session uses a storytelling base as its format. Since the group will focus on goals—their initial articulation or their continuation from the previous week's session—the choice of story might have a creation-recreation theme. Particularly suited are Higgins' (1988) "Dream's Renascence" and/

or the narrative poem "God's Birthdance" (Wilson in Clark, Ronan, and Walker 1981). In the former, Dream finds herself released from the box on the shelf where she had been so carefully placed years before and ventures out to explore new territory. The venture is sometimes painful, but as she weeps, Dream discovers the sound of her own heartbeat and is eventually faced with the decision of embracing more of life. The creation poem is retelling of God's discovering the orderliness of marching mountains and seas and then becoming somewhat bemused but pleased by the waltzing of green and growing things. Finally God is delighted to discover the need and the glory of their both residing in the one Godhead. Whether one of these stories or another of the cotherapists' choosing is used, the response to the story will be another unique aspect of that group. In some groups, members easily see the links between the story and the formulation of their own goals. They focus readily on their own ventures into new territory or are able to address the conflicting feelings they may have within themselves. "It's okay to be angry and sad. It's okay to feel as though I'm not ready to forgive while also feeling that I'm a good person. It's okay to feel good about growing while also feeling scared about this process of therapy. It's okay to be angry with God while also feeling safe with God. It's okay to have paradoxical feelings in my life now." Other groups or other members within the group do not move readily into goals; they find the experience threatening. Members may need help in discovering goals during the coming sessions. Again, depending on the character and composition of the group, this fifth session may become two sessions.

The theme of creation-recreation is continued in the sixth session. Otto Freidrich (1988) wrote an essay about the mystery of life springing from seeds and the wonder of growing things. This or any other work that focuses on the slow process of growth and the promise held within unpretentious seeds is useful. Six weeks into a cycle, the women usually are very committed to group work and, not infrequently, impatient for results. "Why doesn't God *do* something?" "Why can't I be over 'this' yet?" "Will I ever feel good about myself? Will I ever trust?" Seeds and plants are useful metaphors. Generally by this time the group members have become accustomed to the soothing sounds of storytelling and settle back restfully at the cotherapist's words, "That reminds me of a story . . ." In the midst of a great deal of pain or confusion, the story can be a gentling experience and simultaneously a suggestion for new solutions, further work, and possible reframing. Planting seeds suggests that one contains elements of growth (seeds) and the power to release those seeds (the planting). The group members explore what seeds they might have in their hands at this time and which seeds they wish to plant—which seeds they choose to give life to. As children, they chose to live through their abuse, and they chose not to withdraw forever from reality as they coped with the abuse. How are they choosing life now? Can they now move beyond issues of basic survival and vigilance to choices for fullness? How are the images they now hold of themselves and of their God helpful or detrimental to such choices? Each woman focuses on aspects of these questions as she selects a packet of flower seeds from an earthen bowl. Whether the group members actually plant the seeds they have selected is of little importance. It is important only that they experience in the simplest of rituals that they can choose to grow and to hope. Fox (1987, 9) wrote, "A ritual that works or is effective is one that holds power for transformation. One that effects change."

The seventh and eighth sessions, focusing on forgiveness, follow naturally upon the sixth. In "choosing life," the adult survivor often stumbles on old issues of shame, guilt, and the need for forgiveness. Before anyone, adult survivor or otherwise, can address the issue of forgiveness, four questions need to be answered: Whom am I forgiving and for what? Can I forgive (am I capable)? May I forgive (is it acceptable)? Must I forgive (is it mandatory)? It is important for the cotherapists to keep in mind that forgiveness of the abuser and/or of other significant members of the adult survivor's childhood generally ranks below self-forgiveness in importance. The adult survivor frequently feels a need to forgive herself for what she feels or believes to have been her wrongdoing in relation to the abuse.

At the opening of the seventh session, the therapist might reflect that many people feel guilty for making healthy choices about their lives and about their responses to others, even though the choices they make are necessary to their own growth. Recognizing that one is overcommitted and saying "no" to a colleague, friend, or family member's request for "more" is logically a good choice but often leaves a residual of guilt with the "overcommitted" person. Allowing oneself to put energy into recovery through therapy is a healthy choice, but is it permissible to lessen the energy one formerly put into other avenues? Choosing not to keep the secret of the sexual abuse any longer is likely dysphoric not only to the adult survivor but to her spouse, her family, and her family of origin. "Why are you putting us through this?" or "It happened years ago, and now it's over. Why don't you just forget it?" are responses commonly heard by the adult survivor when she chooses to work in therapy on her history of being sexually abused as a child. Distancing one's self from specific family members in order to move toward personal recovery is a painful exercise of choice, particularly if the adult survivor held the familial role of caretaker, nurturer, or peacemaker. Changing old patterns of dysfunctional behavior also may disturb family members because in making personal changes, albeit for the better, the adult survivor is altering the family system. All of these and countless nuances on a similar theme can cause the adult survivor to fell guilty for her choices. Verbalizing these guilty feelings in a group opens the adult survivor to challenges from her peers. Listening to other group members verbalize their feelings of guilt and recognizing that often they are not blameworthy invites her to reexamine her own reasons for guilt. It is helpful to raise the questions, "How might your guilt about x, y, or z serve you? How does it help you not to forgive yourself?" Defenses develop as responses to perceived threats. Sometimes assuming the blame or the guilt for something helps the survivor to deny a different painful reality. Raising these questions regarding guilt and forgiveness means only that: raising them and not forcing them.

When the adult survivor is ready to let go of past defenses, she will be able to look at them and the underlying realities. Some women will be ready and able to address this issue during this cycle of therapy; others will not and in fact find the issue threatening. Each member of the group must move at her own pace. A group member who is unable to address this issue herself may benefit greatly from hearing how her peers address it.

In the eighth session, the topic shifts from blame and guilt to forgiveness. The session begins with a brief introduction by one of the cotherapists to the theme of forgiveness and moves into a relaxation-visualization format. The group members are led to visualize a beach, forest, glen, meadow—whatever may have been an image of growth or peace in previous sessions. In this quiet, peaceful place, they are guided to discover a gift they are pleased to find. What does this gift look like? What shape is it? Is it easily seen? When the gift is examined, opened, or uncovered, they discover that it is forgiveness. What color is it? What does it feel like? What does forgiveness do? for the forgiver? for the forgivee? After a sufficient period of quiet imaging, the members are directed to put their gift wherever they would like to; it will be easily accessible to them, and it always will be there—as much as each person needs. Then they are slowly brought back to the reality of the room and the group.

The group members are asked to share the shape, color, and feeling of their forgiveness and to describe how the forgiveness they found is peculiarly their own. Other group members will be helpful in pointing out ways in which one woman's image of forgiveness relates to what she shared previously about guilt and shame. They might even suggest ways in which she could use her forgiveness image effectively. Notice that the adult survivors are not directed to use their gift of forgiveness immediately, nor is it suggested for whom or in what manner they should use it. Forgiveness is a uniquely personal experience, and each woman must have the freedom she needs to exercise control, explore her feelings, her memories, and her reality, and forgive herself and others.

It is suitable at the end of the session to give the women some symbolic reminder of their forgiveness imaging. If the opening scene of the guided imagery was a beach, each woman might select one seashell from a collection of shells provided by the cotherapists; if the opening scene was a forest, pieces of bark or small pine cones; if a meadow, dried flowers; if a glen, smooth river rocks. Whatever is a tangible reminder of the image can serve as a symbolic reminder of the closing suggestion: "It is always accessible to you, and it is always there in this safe place, and it is all the forgiveness you need. There will be more than enough as you want it."

The ninth session uses another form of guided imagery to focus on healing and the power to heal. Haughton (1985) has the storyteller's gift for presenting a theme. She uses the biblical story of the woman with hemorrhage to tell of courage, healing and hope, calling it "The Woman Who Came Out of the Shadows" (pp. 1–12). Although it is a beautiful portrayal of a woman cast out for something over which she has no control (hemorrhaging), Haughton also plainly retains its Christian roots. The many parallels to be drawn between the "unclean" woman of the story and the adult survivors of the group may be strengthened if the cotherapists describe the healer in more anonymous terms. In fact, after telling the story, the cotherapists might ask each group member to identify which person or persons in the story she found herself to be. Some group members may have seen themselves as the woman as she first appeared in the story—cursed by God, punished for an unknown and unintended sin, and alienated because of her affliction. Others may have identified themselves as the woman as she became a woman of immense courage who challenged the system that told her to keep silent, reached out for healing through her own power, and gained wholeness. Some group members may have identified with members of the crowd who told the woman not to jostle them or the healer, to keep her place and to be still. And some group members may have found that they were each of these characters and the healer as well. They were also the person who looked lovingly, empathically, and compassionately on the woman who reached out for healing, and told her of her own power.

The tenth session is titled "The Great Mandala." The mandala, an ancient word for circle, has long been used by artists, mystics, and arts therapists as a representation for the cosmos, the spiritual world, and the inner self. Mayer (1983, 191), who works with women sexually abused as children, suggests the use of mandalas in therapy. She writes, "Within an outlined circle, the participant draws marks, forms or shapes in various colors, starting in the center and working outwards to represent her . . . core." Because the concept of the mandala is not easily understood—and frequently misunderstood—the mandala used in this closing session is likely to be one in name only.

The initial portion of this session is devoted to members' reflections from the past weeks. The mandala exercise is offered only as a means of helping each woman to focus on her goals based on the previous nine to eleven weeks of peer group therapy with a spirituality theme. She is quietly guided to focus on the images of God that come to her and flow through her as she is still. She is reminded that she can keep those images that will help her to grow and to heal and that she can release those that are no longer helpful. She is then directed to image the symbol, form, color, or word, which will represent her movement toward recovery and wholeness. A simple sharing of these mandalas will close the group and this cycle.

Although only ten sessions are described here, the reader will find material for twelve and, depending on the group, perhaps more. This section of the chapter is not intended to be a cookbook for therapy sessions; rather, it is the description of some techniques that were found to be effective in working with spirituality-themed cycles of group therapy for adult survivors of child sexual abuse. Numerous other useful techniques were not mentioned: the Gestalt empty chair technique in which the adult survivor addresses her image of God; incorporating healing God images into rituals for energy or healing such as those offered by Mariechild (1981), Pellauer, Chester, and Boyajian (1987), or Satir (1988, 338–339); using guided images in which God is described in inclusive language such as those written by Diltz (1987); adapting Craghan's (1985) description of themes of orientation, disorientation, and reorientation to the preabuse, abuse, and recovery periods of the adult survivors life; or adapting any of Gil's (1988) suggested group therapy formats to focus specifically on the theme of spirituality. Any of these techniques might also be incorporated into the plan for the cycle.

It is hoped that thoughtful reading of this chapter will germinate insights and creative methods by which the adult survivor's spirituality may be addressed in psychotherapy.

In presenting this topic at conferences, I have been helped by other clinicians who have come forward to share their experiences. Clinicians who work with holocaust survivors and with Vietnam veterans have noted similarities in the treatment needs of these clients to those of adult survivors of child sexual abuse. All of these vulnerable populations raise cognitive-humanistic questions (Hilbert 1984, 259–275): How does one make sense out of the insensible? As we learn more from each other and from our clients, creative ways to respond to such questions and the underlying clinical issues may emerge.

References

Allport, Gordon W. 1950. *The Individual and His Religion: A Psychological Interpretation.* New York: Macmillan.
Berliner, Lucy, and Ernst, Elise 1983. "Group Work with Preadolescent Sexual Assault Victims." In I.R. Stuart and J.C. Greer, eds., *Victims of Sexual Aggression: Treatment of Children, Women, and Men.* 105–124. New York: Van Nostrand Reinhold.

Blick, Linda Canfield and Porter, Francis Sarnacki. 1982. "Group Therapy with Female Adolescent Incest Victims." In S.M. Sgroi, *Handbook of Clinical Intervention in Child Sexual Abuse,* 109–145. Lexington, Mass.: Lexington Books.

Boff, Leonardo. 1987. *The Maternal Face of God: The Feminine And Its Religious Experience.* San Francisco: Harper & Row.

Brown, L.B. 1987. *The Psychology of Religious Belief.* New York: Academic Press.

Burgess Ann Wolpert. 1984. "Intrafamilial Sexual Abuse." In J. Campell and J. Humphreys, eds. *Nursing Care of Victims of Family Violence,* 190–215. Reston, Va: Reston Publishing Co.

Clark, Linda; Ronan, Marian; and Walker, Eleanor. 1981. *Image-Breaking/Image-Building: A Handbook for Creative Worship with Women of Christian Tradition.* N.Y.: Pilgrim Press.

Courtois, Christine. 1988. *Healing the Incest Wound: Adult Survivors in Therapy.* New York: W.W. Norton.

Craghan, John. 1985. *Prayers for Ups, Downs and In-Betweens.* Wilmington, Del.: Glazier Pub.

Diltz, Judith. 1987. "An Agrarian Fantasy" and "A Garden Fantasy." In National Sisters Vocation Conference, eds. *Woman Song II,* 97, 107–108. Chicago: NSVC.

Forward, Susan, and Buck, Craig. 1978. *Betrayal of Innocence: Incest and Its Devastation.* New York: Penguin Books, Ltd.

Fortune, M.M. and Hertze, J. 1987. "A Commentary on Religious Issues in Family Violence," In M.D. Pellauer, B. Chester, and J. Boyajian, eds. *Sexual Assault and Abuse: A Handbook for Clergy and Religious Professionals,* 67–83. San Francisco: Harper & Row.

Fowler, James. 1976. "Stages in Faith." In Thos. C. Hennessy, ed., *Values in Moral Development,* 173–185. New York: Paulist Press.

Fox, Matthew. 1987. "Native American Spirituality." *Creation* 2(6):8–9.

Freidrich, Otto. 1988. "Of Apple Trees and Roses." *Time,* June 20, 1988, 70.

Freud, Anna. 1982. "A Psychoanalytic View of Sexual Abuse by Parents." In P.B. Mrazek and C.H. Kempe, eds., *Sexually Abused Children and Their Families,* 33–34. New York: Pergamon.

Gelinas, Denise J. 1983. "The Persisting Negative Effects Of Incest." *Psychiatry* 46:312–332.

Gil, Eliana. 1988. *Treatment of Adult Survivors of Childhood Abuse.* Walnut Creek, Calif.: Launch Press.

Groome, Thomas H. 1980. *Christian Religious Education—Sharing Our Story and Vision.* Philadelphia: Harper & Row.

Haughton, Rosemary. 1985. *The Recreation of Eve.* Springfield, Ill.: Templegate Press.

Herman, Judith Lewis. 1981. *Father-Daughter Incest.* Cambridge: Harvard University Press.

Higgins, Betty Louise. 1985. "Dream's Renascense." *Daughters of Sarah,* Jan–Feb: 4–6.

Hilbert, Harvey C. 1984. "The Viet Nam Veteran: Working with Moral Anguish." In H. Goldstein, H. Hilbert, and J. Hilbert eds., *Creative Change: A Cognitive*

Humanistic Approach to Social Work Practice, 259–275. New York: Tavistock Publications.

Hillowe, Bruce V. 1985. "The Effect of Religiosity of Therapist and Patient on Clinical Judgment." *Dissertation Abstracts,* 1687-B.

Horton, Anne L., and Williamson, Judith A., eds. 1988 *Abuse and Religion: When Praying Isn't Enough.* Lexington, Mass.: Lexington Books.

Jakubiak, Mary, and Murphy, Sheila. 1987. "Incest Survivors in Women's Communities." *Human Development* 8(2):19–25.

James, Kathleen Lehigh. 1977. "Incest: The Teen-ager's Perspective." *Psychotherapy: Theory, Research and Practice* 14(2):146–155.

Johanek, Michael. 1988. "Treatment of Male Victims of Child Sexual Abuse in Military Service." In S.M. Sgroi, ed., *Vulnerable Populations: Evaluation and Treatment of Sexually Abused Children and Adult Survivors,* 1:103–114. Lexington, Mass.: Lexington Books.

Josephson, Gilda S., and Fong-Beyette, Margaret L. 1987. "Factors Assisting Female Clients' Disclosure of Incest during Counseling." *Journal of Counseling and Development* 65(9):475–478.

Josselson, Ruthellen. 1987. *Finding Herself: Pathways to Identity Development in Women.* San Francisco: Jossey-Bass.

Joy, Stephany. 1987. "Retrospective Presentations of Incest: Treatment Strategies for use with Adult Women." *Journal of Counseling and Development* 65(6):317–319.

Jung, Carl G. 1933. *Modern Man in Search of a Soul.* New York: Harcourt Brace Jovanovich.

Karpel, Mark. 1980. "Family Secrets: I. Conceptual and Ethical Issues in the Relational Context; II. Ethical and Practical Consideration in Therapeutic Management." *Family Process.* 19:295–306.

Katlan, Anny. 1973. "Children Who Were Raped." *Psychoanalytic Studies of Children* 28:208–224.

Kempe, R., and Kempe, C.H. 1984. *The Common Secret: Sexual Abuse of Children and Adolescents.* New York: W.H. Freeman.

Kluft, Richard P. 1988. "Autohypnotic Resolution of the Incipient Relapse in an Integrated Multiple Personality Disorder Patient: A Clinical Note." *American Journal of Clinical Hypnosis.* 31 (2):91–96.

Landgarten, Helen B. 1981. *Clinical Art Therapy: A Comprehensive Guide.* New York: Brunner/Mazel.

Landis, Laurie. 1987. "Counselors Address Spiritual Needs of Clients." *Guidepost: American Association of Counseling and Development* 30 (2):1, 6, 13.

Leehan, James, and Wilson, Laura P. 1985. *Grown-up Abused Children.* Springfield, Ill.: Charles C. Thomas Publisher.

Lewis, Helen Block. 1987. *The Role of Shame in Symptom Formation.* Totowas N.J.: Earlbaum Associates.

McCann, Lisa; Pearlman, L.A.; Sakheim, D.K.; and Abrahamson, D.J. 1988. "Assessment and Treatment of the Adult Survivor of Childhood Sexual Abuse within a Schema Framework." In S.M. Sgroi, ed., *Vulnerable Populations: Evaluation* and Treatment of Sexually Abused Children and Adult Survivors, 1:77–101. Lexington, Mass.: Lexington Books.

Mariechild, Diane, 1981. *Mother Wit: a Feminist Guide to Psychic Development.* New York: Crossing Road.

Maslow, Abraham H. 1962. *Religions, Values and Peak-Experiences.* Columbus: Ohio State University Press.

Mayer,Adele. 1983. *Incest:A Treatment Manual for Therapy With Victims, Spouses and Offenders.* Holmes Beach, Fla.: Learning Publications.

Meiselman, Karin. 1978. *Incest: A Psychological Study of Cause and Effect with Treatment Recommendations.* San Francisco: Jossey-Bass.

Mollenkott, Virginia Ramey. 1987. *The Divine-Feminine: The Biblical Imagery of God as Female.* New York: Crossroad Press.

NiCarthy, Ginny; Merriam, Karen; and Coffman, Sandra. 1984. *Talking It Out: A Guide to Groups for Abused Women.* Seattle, Wash.: Seal Press.

Nicolosi, Joseph J. 1987. "Psychological Crisis: An Opportunity for Spiritual Growth." *Human Development* 8 (3):12–13.

Owens, Travis H. 1984. "Personality Traits of Female Psychotherapy Patients with a History of Incest: A Research Note." *Journal of Personality Assessment* 48(6):606–609.

Pellauer, Mary D.; 1987. "Violence Against Women: The Theological Dimension." In M.D. Pellauer, B. Chester and J. Boyajian, eds. *Sexual Assault and Abuse: A Handbook for Clergy and Religious Professionals.* 51–61. San Francisco: Harper & Row.

Pellauer, Mary D.; Chester, Barbara; and Boyajian, Jane. 1987. *Sexual Assault and Abuse: A Handbook for Clergy and Religious Professionals.* San Francisco: Harper & Row.

Porter, F.S.; Blick, L.C.; and Sgroi, S.M. 1982. "Treatment of Sexually Abused Children." In S.M. Sgroi, ed. *Handbook of Clinical Intervention in Child Sexual Abuse,* 109–145. Lexington, Mass.: Lexington Books.

Quackenbos, Stephen; Privette, Gayle; and Klentz, Bonnel. 1985. "Psychotherapy: Sacred of Secular?" *Journal of Counseling and Development* 63(5):290–293.

Rubin, Judith Aron, ed. 1987. *Approaches to Art Therapy.* New York: Brunner/ Mazel.

Satir, Virginia. 1988. "Spirituality." In V. Satir. The New Peoplemaking, 334-341. Mountain View, Calif.: Science and Behavior Books, Inc.

Sgroi, S.M., and Bunk, B.B. 1988. "A Clinical Approach to Adult Survivors of Child Sexual Abuse." In S.M. Sgroi, ed., *Vulnerable Populations: Evaluation and Treatment of Sexually Abused Children and Adult Survivors,* 1:137–186. Lexington, Mass.: Lexington Books.

Shafranske, Edward P., and Maloney, H. Newton. 1985. "Psychologists' Religious and Spiritual Orientations and Their Practice of Psychotherapy—A Report of the California State Psychological Association Committee on Spirituality and Psychotherapy." Paper presented at the meeting of the American Psychological Association, Los Angeles, August.

Shapiro, Shanti. 1987. "Self-Mutilation and Self-Blame in Incest Victims." *American Journal of Psychotherapy* 41(1):46–54.

Shearer, Steven L., and Herbert, Carol A. 1987. "Long-term Effects of Unresolved Sexual Trauma." *American Family Practice* 36(4):169–175.

Stoudt, Robert S. 1987. "Religion as Passion." *Living Prayer* 20(6):6–12.

Trible, Phyllis. 1978. *God and the Rhetoric of Sexuality*. Philadelphia: Fortress Press.

Tsai, Mavis, and Wagner, Nathaniel N. 1978. "Therapy Groups for Women Sexually Molested as Children." *Archives of Sexual Behavior* 7(5):417–427.

Vander May, Brenda J., and Neff, Roland L. 1982. "Adult-Child Incest: A Review of Research and Treatment." *Adolescence* 17(68):717–733.

Walker, Alice. 1982. *The Color Purple*. New York: Washington Square Press.

Wheeler, Hollis. 1981. "Silent Victims of Incest—Peer-Group Support Project." In A.W. Burgess and B.A. Baldwin, *Crisis Intervention Theory and Practice—A Clinical Handbook*, 258–272. Englewood Cliffs, N.J.: Prentice-Hall.

Wilson, David. 1981. "God's Birthdance." In L. Clark, M. Ronan, and Eleanor Walker, *Image-Breaking/Image-Building: A Handbook for Creative Worship with Women of Christian Tradition*. New York: Pilgrim Press.

8

Sexual Abuse Avoidance Training for Adults with Mental Retardation

Suzanne M. Sgroi
Judith A. Carey
Amy B. Wheaton

S ociety has been making radical changes in the way it views persons with mental retardation. For hundreds of years they were seen as an embarrassment, segregated from the community, and kept away in institutions. Beginning in the 1950s, society was challenged to change these views and see each person as a valuable human being capable of being part of the community, regardless of the level of disability or retardation.

From the 1970s to the present, there have been significant advancements in the integration, education, and training of children and adults who are mentally retarded within the community at large. Persons with mental retardation have begun to move back into local community settings in group homes, apartments, and other neighborhood residences. This process has had many labels—the *principle of normalization* and *deinstitutionalization,* to name two. Persons with retardation ranging from mild or moderate to severe retardation have begun to be educated and trained with their normally functioning peers.

The enactment in 1975 of Public Law 94-142, the Education for All Handicapped Children's Act. expanded appropriate educational opportunities for children with retardation. Parental participation in the decision making about their children's special educational and vocational needs increased collaboration efforts between home and school. Fewer children were being institutionalized, and those already in institutions were being placed in the community.

Vocational training programs have multiplied to prepare adults with retardation for sheltered and competitive community employment. Persons with mental retardation have begun to be recognized as stable and productive members of the community work force. This integration has enabled society to become more fully aware of the developmental potential of persons with retardation.

Today persons with mental retardation are viewed as individuals who have more in common with other human beings than they have differences.

Their opportunities to live in and be a part of communities and to work, entertain themselves, and live their lives to the fullest have improved substantially. This is a credit to the advocates, parents, professionals, and legislators who have labored diligently to ensure that persons with mental retardation are afforded their constitutional rights and equal opportunity.

While much remains to be done, the lives of many of these person have changed qualitatively. This change has prompted policymakers to reflect on a range of issues from housing to employment, transportation, accessibility, and community resources, including theaters, recreation centers, and medical and dental care. These issues are not new; rather they are being raised from a fresh perspective.

Concurrently the reality of persons with retardation within the community has raised other philosophical issues: for example, the right to love others, to develop healthy emotional relationships, and to receive the necessary training and assistance to live appropriately and successfully in a complex society. All professionals, parents, and concerned persons are being challenged to enable the person with mental retardation not only to be in the community but to participate in life experiences to the fullest. Within the many facets of this challenge is the need for appropriate sex education, a daily lifelong learning program.

Sex Education

When institutionalization was the only option, its sexually segregated nature fostered behaviors that were less acceptable in community settings (Money 1973). Segregation of each group, male from female, facilitated the hiding of the real issues.

Many parents struggle with the issue of sexuality. Some parents of children with mental retardation deny the sexuality of their children (Nigro 1975). Others acknowledge that there is need for instruction but are uncomfortable about discussing sexuality with their children (Hall, Morris, and Barker 1973).

It is a paradox that the individuals about whom we have the most ambivalence regarding sex education are the persons who most need it. They have had less opportunity to acquire a realistic understanding of their sexual selves than their nonretarded peers (Baroff 1986). Without proper sex education, there is the risk of sexual exploitation or sexual rejection (Edmonson 1980). How persons with mental retardation conduct their personal lives may depend on the instruction and training they receive in the diverse forms of sex education.

The access of persons with mental retardation to information and education is of critical importance. Within this context is another issue of grave concern: how to enable them to protect themselves from sexual abuse. Inherent in this issue are a number of other factors. Fundamental is the question of how one ensures the right of adults with mental retardation to privacy. In congregate living facilities, this right is often overlooked, yet it is imperative that it be addressed.

In our efforts to afford citizens with mental retardation community living alternatives like those of other citizens, we create residences for four, six, or eight individuals. These "family" settings accommodate unrelated adults of both sexes. The issue remains, however: are we sufficiently sensitive to the privacy rights of these residents—for example, in the location of the bedrooms and bathrooms?

Another issue of significance is the kind and quality of instruction provided to adults with mental retardation that addresses their right to know how to protect themselves from sexual abuse. Specific attention must be given to the curriculum content and the instructional methodology used in order to enable the participants to incorporate it within the context of their daily lives.

The curriculum and instructional methodology described in this chapter were created to respond to a need for training of persons with retardation to protect themselves from sexual abuse. A pilot program was developed and conducted with adults with mental retardation who were living in state-operated facilities in Connecticut. The facilities ranged from a unit within a large institutional setting to medium-sized and small group homes, to supervised apartments within the community. A distinct effort was made to be aware of the living context of each person and incorporate that information within the sexual abuse avoidance training program curriculum.

An extensive literature search conducted in 1985 found no detailed, comprehensive set of guidelines for conducting sexual abuse avoidance training with adults with retardation. Accordingly, it was decided to design and field-test a curriculum for the purpose of utilizing it within the settings in which clients were living. The designers of the curriculum toured the facilities, reviewed appropriate information on the participants, and met with administrators, clinicians, and direct care staff who worked in these facilities. A distinct effort was made to involve staff in the curriculum development and training since the trainers were aware of the critical importance for the persons working with persons with retardation to understand and agree with the concepts of personal safety in order to reinforce them on a daily basis.

It is the belief of the designers that the material presented in the next chapter is adaptable for use with adults with mild and moderate levels of retardation who live in diverse types of settings. Readers are encouraged to test the curriculum and make adaptations and changes. We hope that persons who have less experience will find that the comprehensiveness of the curriculum is helpful. Trainers who are more experienced may wish to make appropriate modifications. The first author, Dr. Sgroi, welcomes inquiries about the curriculum and could explain further, upon request, the teaching aids cited.

Sexual Abuse Avoidance Training for Adults with Mental Retardation

Overview and Guidelines

Goal. The goal is to train adults who are mentally retarded to avoid sexual victimization by others.

Training Objectives. The following three concepts are the objectives:

1. *You have a right to say no* if someone tries to look at your body or touch your body (and you do not want that person to look at you or to touch you in that way).
2. *You can run away* (or use various other avoidance maneuvers) if someone tries to look at you or to touch you (in an unwanted fashion).
3. *You can tell someone* (to get help) if someone tries to look at you or to touch you (against your wishes).

Procedures. The following procedures are recommended.

Participant Selection. Obtain clearance for a review of participants' profiles. Review profiles and consider the need for conducting a pretest screening to have adequate information for the development of appropriate groups. Select small groups for the training based on the functioning level and sex of participants.

- With lower-functioning participants, training groups should be smaller (two to four participants maximum). Higher-functioning participants can be trained in larger groups (eight to ten participants maximum).
- With higher-functioning participants, it will be important to separate the groups according to sex. If a choice must be made, separating by sex is preferred to grouping by functioning level.
- With lower-functioning participants, training sessions should be shorter (maximum thirty minutes) and may need to be planned in greater numbers and at shorter intervals than for higher-functioning participants.

Training Site. It is preferable to conduct the training in familiar surroundings; there is great advantage to conducting the initial training program in the place where the participant lives. One's home is a logical site in which to discuss matters of personal safety and privacy. Also, conducting the training in the participants' residence makes it easy to include direct care staff in the training format and paves the way for direct care staff to reinforce the concepts of the program on a daily basis. Follow-up sessions should also be conducted in the participants' residence. However, there may also be significant advantage to conducting follow-up and reinforcement sessions in other strategic sites (such as schools, workplaces, public transportation vehicles, parks, or recreational centers). In other words, whenever possible, the training objectives should be reiterated and reinforced outside the residence.

Direct Care Staff Participation. Direct care staff should be involved before, during, and after the training. They should be informed of the goals and objectives and the training curriculum in advance and their advice solicited with respect to grouping of partcipants. Because of the knowledge of the participants, direct care staff input on special issues regarding individual participants should be solicited and considered in planning the program. Selected direct care staff should participate in each training session to be informed of the session content, to maintain order, and to assist participants with special needs. After each training session, direct care staff should be prepared to answer participants' questions and to reinforce the training objectives.

Incentives for Participation. Residents should be encouraged to participate in the training and should be offered short-term and long-term incentives to attend all the training sessions. A short-term incentive might take the form of a special dessert or other treat offered at the end of each training session. A long-term incentive might be an opportunity to attend a special outing offered to participants only or to receive a material reward of some type of recognition of perfect attendance. It will be important and often helpful to display to the participants the items that will follow the session—either the material reward (such as food or gift certificates) to be received at the end of the program or a picture representing the reward (such as a photograph of a movie theater or an amusement park).

Rules for Participation. The rules for participation should be announced to the group at the beginning of each session:

- Giving quiet attention to the trainer and each other.
- Raising one's hand for permission to ask questions or to make comments.
- Not interrupting the trainer or each other.
- Avoiding other types of disruptive behavior.

- Staying until the end of each session (remind participants of the short-term incentive).
- Wearing name tags for each session (unless the trainer already knows each participant by name).

Promise Keeping. The agreement to take part in the program completes an implicit contract among the participants, the trainers, and the residence staff. Accordingly those who conduct the training must take care to fulfill all promises in a scrupulous fashion. Sessions should begin and end on time and take place on the days when they are scheduled. Short-term and long-term incentives should be forthcoming exactly as promised. The rules should be enforced: everyone should be given a chance to comment and ask questions; order must be maintained; disruptive behavior should be stopped and redirected; disruptive participants who refuse or are unable to obey the rules with behavior redirection should be asked to leave and removed from the training room.

Observation of Participant Reactions. Trainers and participating direct care staff should watch carefully for signs that individual participants might be upset, embarrassed, frightened, or noncomprehending in response to the training program. Observations should be exchanged at the close of each training session and at the beginning of the next training session to ensure that the trainers are aware of the participants' behaviors during the sessions and the interim between each session. Every effort should be made to assist the participants who need individual support or help regarding personal issues that may be evoked by the avoidance training. Participants who do not comprehend the objectives of the program in group sessions may require one-on-one instruction to supplement the basic training.

Follow-up. Planned follow-up should be an integral part of the training program. Direct care staff should be taught how to reinforce the training objectives with the participants and with what frequency. Trainers should meet with direct care staff before each session to obtain feedback regarding participants' response to the reinforcement procedures, questions raised by participants, and avoidance and problem behaviors observed by the staff. The curriculum and training plan should be modified, if necessary, to respond to particular concerns shared by participants in one residence and/or individual needs of certain participants.

Evaluation. An evaluation, perhaps of the pretest-posttest type, should be conducted at intervals during the training to determine how well the participants have grasped and retained the training objectives. In addition to the review of the material from the previous session at the beginning of each session, it may be necessary to modify the training if evaluation indicates that the desired concepts are not being conveyed adequately to participants or that, once conveyed, participants are not retaining the concepts or seem unable to utilize them effectively.

Frequency of Training Sessions. The curriculum has a format of three training sessions. Conducting these sessions at one-week intervals seemed to be effective with higher-functioning participants. By contrast, shorter intervals between training sessions (two to five days) seemed to be more effective with lower-functioning participants. It may also be desirable to expand the number of training sessions, especially for lower-functioning participants, from three sessions to six. It would also seem to be highly desirable to conduct follow-up sessions at one-month intervals for lower-functioning participants and three to six-month intervals for higher-functioning participants.

Guidelines for Use

This curriculum must be read in its entirety in order to be used most effectively. Since each level builds on the preceding one, there is much internal repetition. Each teaching session is broken down into exercises. The methodology includes sample sentences to use with participants (sample sentences are set off in quotation marks) and directions regarding the use of teaching aids (aids are set off in parentheses). Persons who will be using the curriculum are not expected to memorize the sample sentences; however, trainers may wish to read the sentences out loud and then practice using their own words, phrases, and sentences to introduce the exercises and to convey the training objectives. Trainers should practice with the teaching aids (dressing and undressing the anatomically correct dolls can be especially tricky) before conducting training with participants.

Teaching Aids. This curriculum utilizes teaching aids that are three-dimensional objects the participants can see and touch, as well as a song composed specifically for the purpose of teaching participants who are mentally retarded to avoid sexual abuse. Since the target population has limited capacity to conceptualize and to remember concepts, visual and auditory teaching aids are essential. It was decided to use three-dimensional teaching aids because participants can see them up close, touch them, and relate to them directly. Slides, filmstrips and videotaped teaching instruments were not incorporated into the curriculum because it is easier for participants to distance themselves from a two-dimensional visual image on a screen. And it is much more difficult for participants to tune out a trainer who is standing or sitting in front of them and using a three-dimensional teaching aid to interact with them (as opposed to ignoring a slide or film presentation).

To be effective, this curriculum must also be dynamic. The anatomically correct dolls were incorporated into the curriculum with the rationale that it would be less threatening for the participants if trainers demonstrated avoidance of various types of sexual victimization with the dolls rather than role play with the participants. Interestingly, men and women participants of all ages have reacted positively to these dolls. This teaching aid appears to be relatively nonthreatening and thus far has not been rejected or viewed by participants as childish or undignified.

The song "It's OK to say NO!" referred to in the curriculum was composed by Jack Hartmann, a composer and singer of safety songs for children. A song was commissioned specifically for use with adults who are mentally retarded because the element of choice regarding sexual touching, which is always missing from songs composed for use with children, had to be addressed. Accordingly, the words of the chorus, "It's OK to say NO, if you don't want someone to touch you," are congruent with the concept that adults with mental retardation have choices about intimacy and touching. It is important to communicate to a child that avoidance maneuvers are nearly always indicated if another person wishes to touch private areas of one's body. (Obvious exceptions include appropriate touching by one's parents, medical care providers, and the like.) However, adults with mental retardation may choose to touch and be touched in a sexual fashion, within the constraints of their living environment, their capacity to behave responsibly, and their capacity to consent. Although the curriculum does not attempt to provide training for adults with mental retardation in the area of initiating and maintaining intimate relationships with others, it does attempt to provide a framework for sexual abuse avoidance training, which acknowledges that adults with mental retardation have the right to have intimate relationships under appropriate circumstances.

Most of the other teaching aids are large-scale doll furniture and toys: a small bed, a large toy car, a toy bus. In order to be used as props to illustrate the teaching concepts, the objects must be sturdy and large enough to be seen easily by persons who may have perceptual difficulties. They must also be large enough for the trainers to use in pantomimes involving the anatomically correct dolls; the doll must fit on the bed or into the car to be most effective. People who use this curriculum in their own facilities may also choose to construct models to use as visual aids in the teaching. For example, we found it useful to construct a model of a bathroom, showing toileting and showering areas, in order to illustrate avoidance of sexual abuse in a location in which participants are especially vulnerable. Again, it is exceedingly helpful if the model is large enough to accommodate the anatomically correct dolls.

Participant Functioning Levels. This multilevel curriculum is designed for participants who are mildly, moderately, or severely retarded. The curriculum levels are keyed to classifications found in table 8–1.

It is interesting to note that training to avoid sexual abuse has been designed for normally functioning children who are as young as nursery school age (3–4 years). The lowest functioning level of participants with mental retardation who were found to benefit from the sexual abuse avoidance curriculum were selected participants who could be classified as severely retarded (mental age 3 years, 9 months–6 years). This congruence with training experience in normally functioning children of nursery school age is striking. The following additional characteristics pertained to participants in each functioning level who were able to benefit from sexual abuse avoidance training.

1. Participants with severe retardation

   Expressive capacity—able to demonstrate minimal expressive language (oral or sign or language board); able to convey "yes" and "no"; able to remember and communicate names of body parts; able to communicate simple responses on cue.

   Receptive capacity—able to understand simple one-step concepts; able to understand "yes" and "no"; able to identify a man and a woman; able to grasp actions such as "run away" or "tell someone." These one-step concepts may be conveyed to the participants verbally, through sign, or by demonstration with dolls and other teaching aids. Hearing impairment need not be an absolute barrier to participation if hearing aids are worn or if someone signs the message to the participants.

   Behavior—able to sit in a group. Constant monitoring by staff will be required so that disruptive behavior can be redirected immediately (or the participant removed from the group if redirection of disruptive behavior is not successful).

Table 8–1
Classification of the Mentally Retarded

	IQ		
	Stanford-Binet	*Wechsler*	*Mental Age Range*
Mild	67–52	69–55	8 yrs., 6 mos.–10 yrs., 10 mos.
Moderate	51–36	54–40	6 yrs., 1 mo.–8 yrs., 5 mos.
Severe	35–20	39–25	3 yrs., 9 mos.–6 yrs.
Profound	19 and below	24 or below	Below 3 yrs., 9 mos.

Expected results of training—participants who fit the above criteria should be able to:

- Recognize sexual abuse (especially if the abuser attempts to touch their private parts) as inappropriate behavior.
- Execute some type of avoidance maneuver (say "no" or run away).
- Tell someone else that they need help or are in distress.

2. Participants with moderate retardation

   Expressive capacity—able to speak or sign in simple sentences (noun plus verb).

   Receptive capacity—able to understand two-step concepts; able to grasp a more complex idea such as "You can say no" or "It's okay to say no." These two-step concepts can be conveyed to participants verbally, through sign, or by demonstration with teaching aids or enacted role plays.

   Behavior—able to sit in a group. Disruptive behavior is easily redirected.

   Expected results of training—participants should be able to:

- Recognize sexually abusive behavior by others, including inappropriate viewing of the participant's body and/or sexual touching of the participant's body.
- Execute some type of avoidance maneuver (say "no" or run away).
- Tell an appropriate person about the abuse and ask for help.

3. Participants with mild retardation

   Expressive capacity—able to express complex thoughts (orally or through sign or complex language board) and to carry on a discussion.

   Receptive capacity—able to understand multi-step concepts that can be conveyed to participants by teaching aids, enacted role plays, or discussion led by the trainer.

   Behavior—able to sit in a group without disruptive behavior and to interact positively with both the trainer and other group members.

   Expected results of training—participants should be able to:

- Recognize and avoid a variety of situations when there is high potential for abuse, such as going out alone at night, accepting a ride in a car with a stranger, going into a place separate from others with a stranger or someone who is not familiar or trustworthy.
- Recognize sexual abuse (looking at or touching the participant's body without permission).
- Execute a variety of avoidance maneuvers, such as say "no," yell "fire," or run away.
- Enlist specific help from a number of sources (bus driver, police officer, employer, staff person, friend).

• Recognize the difference between consenting social and sexual interactions and sexual abuse.

Teaching Approach and Trainer Preparation

This curriculum utilizes a matter-of-fact and direct approach to a subject that is difficult for many people even to contemplate, let alone discuss in a group situation. Participants are probably best served when trainers and staff can convey to them that it is permissible to talk about human sexuality in the context of discussing sexual abuse and that it is permissible and appropriate for participants to be taught strategies to avoid sexual victimization. Some participants may be embarrassed or intimidated because sexual abuse avoidance training involves open discussion of some aspects of human sexuality. Trainers can best counteract embarrassment or reluctance to discuss these topics by desensitizing themselves to embarrassing or intimidating aspects of the topic before embarking on participant training.

Ideally trainers should be trained by persons who can assist in the desensitizing process. A review of what is known about sexual abuse in general and sexual abuse of persons who are mentally retarded in particular is essential. This should be followed by a discussion about these topics in a format that allows each person to identify and explore the feelings (embarrassment, shame, inadequacy, fear, excitement) that are aroused by the topic of sexual abuse. The tone of the discussion should be calm and accepting, with an experienced trainer of trainers taking leadership in establishing an atmosphere of safety and acceptance.

It is also helpful to practice saying the words and conducting training exercises. Trainers would be well advised to role play a training session, with other staff playing the roles of the participants, before conducting a training session with actual participants. Trainers will benefit greatly from first observing an experienced trainer conduct sessions with participants and then acting as an assistant to an experienced trainer who is conducting the sessions. When the trainer first undertakes responsibility for leading a training session, it will be highly desirable for a knowledgeable observer to be present to give the trainer feedback on his or her performance, as well as to assist in observing and interpreting participants' reactions to the training.

The exercises and sample sentences deliberately convey an upbeat approach to the curriculum content and to the participants. Enthusiasm, praise, and other types of positive reinforcement are essential elements to arouse and sustain the participants' interest and participation. Trainers should be aware that their own attitudes toward the curriculum, the content, and the participants strongly influence the effectiveness of the most important teaching instrument: the trainer himself or herself. The trainer is constantly role modeling for the participants by demonstrating appropriate social interactions and by representing and personifying societal standards regarding sexual abuse. To be most effective, the trainer must be able to transmit to the participants an elusive entity that is difficult to define but can readily be felt: confidence. Helping persons who are mentally retarded to avoid sexual abuse involves assisting them to be confident in their own perception that certain types of viewing and touching of their bodies are inappropriate and abusive. Moreover, to be successful, sexual abuse avoidance training must convey to the participants that they have a right to set limits on the behavior of others if those other persons are behaving in an abusive fashion. Many participants who have the receptive capacity to grasp the three training objectives on a cognitive level nevertheless lack the self-confidence to carry them out. Since sexual abuse avoidance training involves identifying and responding to certain social interactions in a fashion that sets limits on oneself and others, it also involves addressing issues of self-mastery, control, and empowerment. Trainers can convey that it is possible for persons with mental retardation to be so empowered with regard to the avoidance of sexual abuse by others.

Adapting the Curriculum for Particular Participant Groups

The curriculum format for training participants who are severely mentally retarded to avoid sexual abuse uses ten exercises plus a closing exercise to convey the three training objectives in the initial session: you have a right to say no; you can run away; you can tell someone else. In some groups, participants who are severely retarded may not be able to grasp all three training objectives in the initial session. The attention and receptivity of each group of participants is key. Trainers must observe the participants carefully during the session and be flexible enough to eliminate one or more exercises if it appears that the participants are unduly restless or unable to sustain the level of attention required. With experience, trainers will learn to distinguish the type of restlessness that may occur if participants are embarrassed or upset by the content of the training session versus the signs of inattention that reflect the limited attention span and receptive capacity of persons with mental retardation.

It might, for example, be appropriate with one group of participants who are severely retarded to conduct the training exactly as outlined in the curriculum, with the participants attending three separate training sessions and each session consisting of the number of exercises suggested. However, it might also be appropriate to omit the ninth exercise from the first training session for participants who are severely retarded. Thus, the third training objective (to convey that a participant can tell someone to get help if he or she is looked at or touched in an unwanted fashion) would not be introduced until the second training session. This would probably entail conducting a greater number of training sessions for that group. The curriculum content for participants who are severely retarded could easily be spread over four or six training sessions (instead of the three sessions outlined in the curriculum).

It will be important for trainers to make decisions during each session regarding the amount of time to spend with each participant. Some of the exercises call for approaching participants directly and personalizing the scenario as the trainer demonstrates with the dolls. Flexibility and careful attention to each participant's level of attention and response are important. The assistant can help the trainer by encouraging him or her to focus on a participant or by quietly directing the attention of participants who are wandering back to the trainer. Some participants will not be able to keep up with the group. It may be necessary to shift attention away from such participants during the training session and perhaps plan one-on-one sessions between group training sessions or instead of group training sessions.

It is important to retain the last exercise outlined for each training session (listening to and then joining in with song, "It's OK to Say NO!"). Singing together is an important participatory and reinforcement process for the group and *should not be eliminated*. Also, using the song as the last exercise for each training session provides continuity for the program.

In planning the number of training sessions for any group of participants, trainers should ask the following questions:

- What is the predicted attention span and anticipated receptivity for these participants?
- How many training objectives and sessions are desirable (and feasible) to convey?
- How many training sessions are feasible to plan for this group of participants in this location and at this time?

The answers to these questions and the actual experiences with participants during the first training session will be important factors in adapting the curriculum to meet the needs of a particular participant group. Trainers should remember that the priorities for each session are to identify sexual abuse (as inappropriate viewing or touching of a participant's body) and then to convey as many of the three training objectives as the participants can grasp.

References

Baroff, G.S. 1986. *Adolescent and Adult Concerns. Mental Retardation: Nature, Cause and Management.* Washington, D.C.: Hemisphere Publishing Corporation.

Edmonson, B. 1980. "Sociosexual Education for the Handicapped." *Exceptional Education Quarterly* 1:67–76.

Hall, J.E.; Morris, H.L.; and Barker, H.R. 1973. "Sexual Knowledge and Attitudes of Mentally Retarded Adolescents." *American Journal of Mental Deficiency* 77:706–709.

Money, J.C. 1973. "Some Thoughts on Sexual Tension and the Rights of Retarded," In G.D. LaVeck ed., *Human Sexuality and the Mentally Retarded*. New York: Brunner-Mazel.

Nigro, G. 1975. "Sexuality in the Handicapped; Some Observation on Human Needs." *Rehabilitation Literature* 36:202–205.

9
A Curriculum for Adults with Mental Retardation

Suzanne M. Sgroi
Judith A. Carey

A Curriculum for Adults with Severe Mental Retardation

First Training Session

> Staffing: One trainer; one assistant for a maximum of four participants.
>
> Seating arrangements: Participants are seated in a semicircle or horseshoe shape in direct view of the trainer, who is sitting or standing at the opening of the semicircle. The assistant is positioned for easy access to all the participants and may need to move multiple times during the training session to maintain order or to assist by signing to participants who communicate through this medium.
>
> Teaching aids and materials: Anatomically correct dolls and a small chair or bench for the dolls to sit on; audiotape of "It's OK to Say NO"; tape player; name tags (if necessary).

Exercise 1: Demonstration of appropriate social interactions. The trainer introduces himself or herself and the assistant and then greets each participant by name, shaking hands with each one:

> "Hi Joe, it's nice to meet you. Will you shake hands with me? I like to shake hands when I meet people."

Exercise 2: Reminder of rules and reward(s) for participation. The trainer reviews the rules for participation and reminds the participants of the reward(s) for participation (showing them the reward or something that represents the reward).

Note: Readers are referred to the preceding chapter, which presents an overview of these curricula and guidelines for their use.

Exercise 3: Introduction of the topic of the session. The trainer tells the participants,

> "We're here to talk about what you do if someone tries to look at your body [under your clothes] or to touch your body [under your clothes] and you don't want him or her to do that."

Exercise 4: Introduction to teaching aids and identification of male-female differences. The trainer shows the anatomically correct dolls to the participants and says,

> We are going to use these dolls to talk about looking at your body or touching your body.
>   This doll is like a man [indicating correct doll].
>   This doll is like a woman [indicating correct doll].
>   This doll has a shirt and pants [open the shirt; pull down trousers and shorts].
>   The man doll doesn't have breasts [indicating doll's chest] but he does have a penis [indicating doll's penis]. That's how we know he is a man.
>   The woman doll is wearing a blouse and skirt [open the blouse; remove the skirt and panties].
>   The woman doll has breasts and a vagina [indicating correct areas on the dolls]. That's how we know she is a woman.

The trainer now holds up both dolls (with clothing removed) and says to the participants,

> "Show me the man doll."

If a participant indicates the correct doll, the trainer gives verbal praise using the participant's name ("That's right, Tom, good work!"). Then the trainer asks,

> "Which is the woman doll?"

Again, a correct response should receive verbal praise. If no participant responds, the trainer goes to each participant and repeats the exercise:

> "Joe, this is a man doll [shows the participant the appropriate doll].
> This doll has a penis; that's how we know he is a man.
>   Joe, point to the man doll."

If the participant points to the right doll, the trainee gives verbal reinforcement. Then the trainer repeats the identification exercise with another participant, using the female doll. The exercise is repeated until each participant can correctly identify which doll is like a man and which doll is like a woman.

Exercise 5: Illustrate first training objective: You can say "No!" if someone tries to look at your body and you don't want him to do that. The trainer holds up both dolls (which have been redressed by the assistant) and says to the group,

> "No one has the right to look at your body if you don't want him to look at you like that."

Then the trainer demonstrates having the male doll open the female doll's blouse.

> "He shouldn't do that! He's looking at her breasts. He's looking at her body, and she doesn't want him to!"

The trainer then brings the dolls closer to one of the participants and speaks directly to the participant.

> "Jane, this man [indicating the male doll] is trying to look at this woman's breast and she doesn't want to him to! What could she do? She could say 'No'!"

If the participant responds appropriately, the trainer gives verbal praise and then repeats the exercise with each participant until all have responded appropriately.

Exercise 6: Illustrate first training objective with reversed male-female roles. The trainer again holds up both dolls and this time demonstrates that the female doll is putting her hands inside the pants of the male doll and touching his penis.

> "Look at this! She's trying to put her hands inside his pants! She's trying to touch his penis! He could say 'No'! He could say, 'No, don't do that'!"

Now the trainer brings dolls to each participant in turn and demonstrates with the dolls directly to each participant.

"Susie, this woman is trying to touch this man inside his pants! She is trying to touch his penis, and he doesn't want her to!" [demonstrate with dolls].

> [to the group] "What could he do? He could say 'No'!"

The trainer now goes to each participant in turn and asks,

"Tom what could this man do if she is trying to touch his penis?" [demonstrating with dolls].

If the participant responds correctly, the trainer reinforces with verbal praise. If no response or an incorrect response is made, the trainer repeats,

"He could say 'No'! What would you say, Frank?"

This exercise is repeated with each participant until all have responded appropriately.

Exercise 7: Introduction to teaching aids (dolls and chair). The trainer brings forward the small chair and places both dolls in the chair. Then the trainer points to the dolls and says to the participants,

"This man and this woman are sitting next to each other. Is that okay?"

Each participant is asked in turn,

"Joe, is it okay for them to sit together?"

If the participant says "Yes," the trainer reinforces the participant's response:

"Yes, Joe, it's okay for them to sit next to each other if they want to."

If the participant says "No," the trainer clarifies the dolls' position:

"This man and this woman are just sitting next to each other. They both say it's okay!"

The trainer repeats the statement with another participant:

"Susie, it's okay for them to sit next to each other, right?"

If Susie responds appropriately, the trainer gives verbal praise. If Susie does not respond or responds negatively, the trainer clarifies again:

> "It's okay for a man and a woman to sit next to each other if they both say it's okay."

Then each participant is asked in turn until each has given the correct response. The trainer gives sample verbal praise for each correct response.

Exercise 8: Illustrate second training objective: You can run away or use avoidance maneuvers if someone tries to look at your body or to touch your body and you don't want him to do that. The trainer uses the dolls to demonstrate unwanted looking or touching:

> "Look. The man is trying to look at the woman inside her blouse! He's trying to look at her breasts! He shouldn't do that! She doesn't want him to do that! She could say 'No!' She could get up out of that chair and run away!"

The trainer now moves the chair and the dolls directly in front of one of the participants.

> "Stephen, look at this! This man is trying to look at this woman [demonstrate with dolls] inside her blouse!
> She doesn't want him to! She could say 'No!' She could get up and run away! [demonstrating with dolls].
> Can she run away, Stephen? Is it okay for her to run away from him? [direct question to participant]."

If the participant gives the correct response, the trainer gives verbal praise, repeating the training objectives:

> "That's right Stephen! It's okay for her to run away! She could say 'No!' and she could run away!"

If the participant gives no response or gives a negative response, the trainer rephrases and repeats the training objectives:

> "Stephen, it *is* okay for her to run away. It's okay for her to say 'No.'! He was looking at her and she didn't want him to! [demonstrate with the dolls]."

Then the trainer moves to the other participants and repeats the exercise until each participant gives the correct response.

Exercise 9: Illustrate the third training objective: You can tell someone if a man or a woman tries to touch you inside your clothes and you don't want him or her to touch you. The trainer brings forward the small chair, and puts the female doll in the chair, and says,

> "This woman is sitting in the chair by herself. Look, he wants to sit next to her. Is that okay? [asking the group]."

The trainer reinforces appropriate responses:

> "It *is* okay if she wants him to sit next to her."

Now the trainer demonstrates the male doll touching the female doll inside her clothing. While demonstrating, the trainer can say,

> "Look what he is doing now! The man is trying to touch the woman inside her blouse! Now look. He's trying to touch her breasts, and she doesn't want him to. Is that okay for him to touch her breasts?"

Negative responses from the group should be reinforced by the trainer. If no one responds, the trainer should ask each participant in turn.

> "Susie, is it okay for this man to touch the woman's breasts?"

If there is no response, the trainer then says,

> "No, its's not okay! He shouldn't touch her breasts if she doesn't want him to!"

When the participant responds appropriately, the trainer gives verbal praise and repeats the process until all participants have responded appropriately.
Moving back to the center, the trainer can ask,

> "What can this woman do if the man tries to touch her and she doesn't want him to put his hands on her breasts?"

If no participant responds, the trainer answers the question:

> "She could say 'No!' couldn't she? She could get up and run away! [demonstrating with dolls]."

Each participant is approached individually with the dolls and the exercise is repeated until the appropriate responses are obtained.

Now the trainer can return to the center with the teaching aids and say to the participants,

> "There is something else she could do! She could go tell someone! Who could she tell?"

The trainer then attempts to elicit the names of resource persons for participants, such as staff members, mother, father, friend, or teacher. Then the trainer can bring the dolls and chair up to one of the participants and say,

> "Susie, what if this was you? You're sitting in this chair, and a man is trying to put his hands inside your clothes! Is that okay? No! Who could *you* tell if a man [or a woman] did this to you and you didn't want him [her] to?"

Now the trainer can encourage the participant and the group to name a helping person directly.

> "You could tell Bonnie or George [staff members]. You could tell your mother. You could tell your teacher [or your boss]."

This exercise is repeated with each participant (demonstrating with dolls) until all the participants have been able to name a person whom they could tell about sexual victimization.

Exercise 10: Introduction of audiotape of "It's OK to Say NO." The trainer tells the participants,

> "Now I'm going to play a song for you. This song is about touching people and looking at people. Listen to what this man is telling us."

Then the trainer plays the tape and encourages the participants to sing along with it. Repeating the song a few times may be helpful to the participants.

Closing Exercise. The trainer says to the participants,

> "You did a good job tonight. We talked about a lot of new things. We'll talk about this again on [day for the next scheduled session]."

The trainer reminds participants about the immediate award for participation and the promised reward for attending all the sessions. As they get up to leave, the trainer again demonstrates appropriate social interactions by shaking hands with each participant and saying,

"Let's shake hands Joe. It was good to see you! See you again soon."

Second Training Session

Staffing and seating arrangements: Same as the first training session.

Teaching aids and materials: Anatomically correct dolls; small chair; small bed (small furniture may be used but the bed must be large enough to accommodate one of the dolls); audiotape of "It's OK to Say NO"; tape player.

Exercise 1: Demonstration of appropriate social interactions. The trainer introduces himself or herself and the assistant and then greets each participant by name, shaking hands with each one:

"Hi, Ted, it's nice to see you again. I'm glad you could come tonight! Will you shake hands with me? I like to shake hands when I am saying 'Hi' to people."

Exercise 2: Reminder of rules and rewards for participation. The trainer reviews the rules for participation and reminds the participants of the reward(s) for participation (showing them the reward or something that represents the reward).

Exercise 3: Review of the topic. The trainer tells the participants,

"We're going to talk about looking at people and touching people again. We're going to talk about what to do if someone tries to look at your body underneath your clothes or to touch your body underneath your clothes and you don't want him to."

Exercise 4: Review of the first training objective. The trainer stands in front of the participants and asks,

"Do you remember what you can do if someone tries to look at you under your clothes and you don't want him to? You can say 'No'!"

The trainer then asks the participant,

"What do you think, Fred? What if someone tries to look at you under your clothes? Can you say 'No'?"

If the participant responds affirmatively, the trainer praises him:

"That's right, Fred, you could say 'No'!"

If the participant does not respond appropriately, the trainer repeats the training objective:

"It's okay for you to say 'No!' if someone tries to look under your clothes and you don't want him to."

Turning to the other participants, he or she asks,

"Is it okay for Fred to say 'No!' if someone tries to look under his clothes and he doesn't want him to?"

If one of the participants responds appropriately, the trainer reinforces the correct responses:

"He could say 'No!' It's okay to say 'No!' if someone tries to look at you under your clothes and you don't want him to!"

Exercise 5: Reintroduction of anatomically correct dolls. The trainer holds up fully clothed male and female dolls and says to the participants:

"Do you remember these dolls? One is like a man, and one is like a woman."

Then the trainer brings the dolls and the chair directly in front of one of the participants and says,

"Jane, what if this man and this woman were sitting next to each other and he tried to look up her skirt [demonstrating with dolls]? What could she do?"

If the participant makes no response or responds incorrectly, the trainer should say:

"She could say 'No'! If she doesn't want him to look at her underneath her skirt, she could say 'No'!"

Now the trainer brings the dolls in front of another participant:

"Joe, what if this was you [indicating the male doll]? What if this doll was you, and a woman [indicating female doll] tried to touch you inside your pants? What if she tried to touch you in your private parts [indicating with the dolls]? What could you do?"

The trainer waits to see if the participant makes the correct response; if so, the trainer gives verbal praise. If the participant makes no response or responds incorrectly, the trainer says:

"You could say 'No'! If you don't want someone to touch you inside your pants, you could say 'No!' couldn't you?"

The trainer repeats this exercise with each participant until all have responded correctly.

Exercise 6: Reintroduction of teaching aid (chair) and review of first and second training objectives. See exercises 7 and 8 in the previous section and repeat at this time.

Exercise 7: Introduction of new teaching aid (bed) and discussion of its purpose.

Trainer: "Now we are going to talk about something else. What is this [brings forward a small bed and shows it to the participants]?"

If one (or more) of the participants responds correctly, the trainer gives verbal praise:

"That's right; this is a bed."

If none of the participants can identify the bed correctly, the trainer says to the group,

"This is a bed, isn't it?"

The trainer then ascertains that each participant knows that the toy bed is a bed and also is certain that each participant understands the appropriate function of a bed. For example, the trainer can say,

"Susie, this is a bed isn't it?"

If the participant responds affirmatively, the trainer asks,

"What do we do in the bed? What do we use the bed for?"

If the participant responds verbally or signs that a bed is for sleeping, the trainer can again give verbal praise. If the participant does not respond correctly, the trainer can say,

"We sleep in a bed don't we? What do you think, Joe?"

Turning to another participant and demonstrating with a doll lying on the bed, he or she says,

"This man is sleeping on the bed. Right? Beds are for sleeping, aren't they?"

This interaction using the bed and the doll is repeated in a personalized fashion with each participant.

Exercise 8: Review of first training objective using anatomically correct dolls and bed. The trainer now returns to a central position with the dolls and the bed and says to the participants,

"What if this man [holding up the male doll] is lying in his bed [placing the doll in the bed], and he is asleep [using sign for sleep, if indicated], and another man [bringing forward a second male doll] comes into the bedroom and tries to touch this man's private parts [demonstrating with dolls] while he is asleep? [pause] Is that okay?"

If any of the participants responds correctly, the trainer directs immediate praise to that participant:

"Good for you, Joe! It's not okay! He shouldn't have done that! It's not okay for this man [hold up the "intruder" doll] to come into this man's bedroom while he is asleep and touch him inside his pants [demonstrating with both dolls] if he doesn't want him to do that! It's not okay!"

If no participant responds correctly to the question, "Is that okay?" the trainer says,

"No, it's not okay! It's not okay for him to do that, is it?"

The trainer then says to each participant,

"Fred, that's not okay, is it?"

and redescribes the scene, demonstrating with the dolls, until each participant makes a correct response by affirming that it is not appropriate for one person to enter a bedroom and touch another person who is in bed (and presumably asleep) in an unwanted fashion.

Now the trainer brings the dolls and the bed directly in front of each participant in turn and says,

> "Fred, what if this is *your* bed [pointing first to the participant and then to the bed], and what if this is you [pointing between the participant and the appropriate doll]? Here *you* are in *your* bed [demonstrating with the doll and the bed], and now this man [demonstrating with the "intruder" doll] comes into your bedroom and tries to get in bed with you! Is that okay?"

The trainer answers the question:

> "No, it's not okay if you don't want him to get into bed with you."

If the participant responds appropriately, the trainer praises him. If not, the trainer explains,

> "It's not okay for someone to get into your bed and touch your private parts inside your pants if you don't want him to!"

After the participant acknowledges that this behavior would be inappropriate, the trainer can ask,

> "What could you do, Fred? What could *you* do if some man tried to do this to you? What could *you* do if he [demonstrating again with the dolls] tries to get in bed with you and to touch you in your private parts?"

If the participant responds by saying "No!" or "Say 'No'!" or makes some other appropriate response ("Run away!" or "Tell someone!"), the trainer praises him and reinforces the correct response. If the participant responds incorrectly or is silent, the trainer says,

> "You could say 'No'! You could say 'No!' very loudly! [the trainer raises his or her voice while role playing the correct response for the participant.]

Now the trainer can say,

"Let me hear you say it, Fred! Say 'No'!"

This is repeated until the participant shouts or signs the correct response. At this point, the trainer appeals to the other participants by asking,

"What could Fred do? Could he say 'No!'?"

Any correct responses should be reinforced by the trainer with praise for the correct answer:

"That's right, Sally! Fred could say 'No!' couldn't he?"

Exercise 9: Review of second training objective using anatomically correct dolls (with different male and female interactions) and bed. Next, the trainer focuses on another participant, moving in front of him or her with the teaching aids:

"Joe, what if this is *your* bed [pointing to the bed]? What if this is *you* [indicating an appropriate doll], and you are sleeping [demonstrate] in bed?"

The trainer might also ask,

"What do you wear when you sleep at night? Do you wear pajamas? Do you just sleep in your shorts?"

Depending on the participant's response, the trainer can say:

"Suppose you are ready for bed [demonstrating undressing] and you get into bed and pull up the covers [demonstrating with teaching aids], and you go to sleep. [The trainer may wish to use the sign for sleep to reinforce the message.]
    What if this woman [demonstrating with the appropriate doll] comes into the bedroom and tries to get into bed with you and you don't want her to do that? Is that okay?"

If the participant responds appropriately ("It's not okay" or "No!"), the trainer praises him and reinforces the response. If the participant does not respond appropriately, the trainer says,

"Joe, this woman is trying to get into your bed! She is trying to touch you inside your pants! Do you want her to do that? Is that okay? No! It's not okay!"

If the participant is responding appropriately, the trainer reinforces his response. If not, the trainer reviews the situation again with the participant, demonstrating with the dolls, until the appropriate response is elicited. The trainer interposes questions and statements to other group members during this process (to include them and sustain their attention). At this point, the trainer can ask,

"Joe, what could you do about this?"

If the participant responds appropriately, the trainer praises him and includes other members in the process:

"That's right, Joe. You could say 'No'! Susie [to another participant], Joe could say 'No!' couldn't he?"

If the participant does not respond appropriately, the trainer says,

"Joe, you could say 'No'!"

Now the trainer reintroduces the second training objective:

"Joe, there's something else you could do. You could get up out of bed and run away from her [demonstrating with the doll]! You could get out of bed and run away. You don't have to stay there. You could run away!"

The trainer moves to a more central position now and includes the other participants, saying,

"Look at this. If this woman tries to get into Joe's bed and touch his private parts inside his pants, he could say 'No!' and he could get up and run away from her, couldn't he?"

Depending on the group response and Joe's response, the trainer reinforces appropriate responses at this point but then moves back to Joe and asks,

"Joe, could you run away [demonstrating with the doll]?"

If Joe responds appropriately, the trainer praises him. If not, the exercise is repeated until the correct response is elicited. The trainer then moves to the other participants and personalizes the scenario for each using the appropriate dolls and reviewing the training objectives for each participant.

Exercise 10: Review of third training objective using anatomically correct dolls and bed. Returning to a central position, the trainer says,

> "There is something else you can do if someone tries to get into bed with you or comes in and tries to touch you while you are asleep. [demonstrating with the dolls] You could say 'No!' and you could get up and run away! [demonstrating with the dolls] You could go tell someone!"

The trainer now moves to one of the participants and says,

> "Susie, who could you tell? If this is *your* bed, and you are asleep and someone comes in and tries to touch you under the covers or under your clothes, who could you tell?"

If Susie responds appropriately with the name of a helping person, the trainer can praise her and reinforce her response. If not, the trainer tries to elicit names of helping persons in the following manner:

> [to other participants] "Who could Susie tell? She could tell [staff person]. She could tell her mother [if appropriate]. She could tell her boss!"

The trainer says to Susie,

> "You could tell someone! You could get up out of bed and run away and tell someone, couldn't you?"

If the participant responds appropriately, the trainer praises her. If the response is not appropriate, the trainer reiterates the training objective and then focuses on another participant, repeating the same exercise until each participant grasps the concept and can name at least one person whom he or she could tell about sexual abuse.

Exercise 11. Reintroduction of audiotape of "It's OK to say NO!"

> *Trainer:* "Do you remember that song we heard last time? I'm going to play it again and then we can sing too."

The trainer then plays the tape and encourages the participants to join in and sing at the appropriate times.

Closing Exercise: Same as the first training session.

Third Training Session

Staffing and seating arrangements: Same as the first training session.

Teaching aids and materials: Anatomically correct dolls; small bed; model of bathroom (shower stall and toilet area); audiotape of "It's OK To Say NO!"; tape player.

Exercise 1: Demonstration of appropriate social interactions. Same as in the second training session.

Exercise 2: Reminder of rules and rewards for participation. Same as in the second training session.

Exercise 3: Review of the topic. Same as in the second training session.

Exercise 4: Reintroduction of teaching aids (bed and anatomically correct dolls) and review of first, second, and third training objectives. This is an extensive exercise in which the trainer repeats the content of exercises 7–10 in the second training session using similar methods. It involves taking a central position in full view of all the participants and using the anatomically correct dolls and the bed to review the first training objective. Then the trainer goes directly in front of one participant and personalizes the scenario for that participant (for example, "What if this is your bed? What if this is you? What could you do?"). The trainer moves from focusing on one participant to inclusion of the others in the group for feedback and reinforcement ("What do you think, Fred? What could Joe do?"). As the trainer focuses on each participant in turn, personalizing the scenario for each, the second and third training objectives can also be introduced ("What else could Fred do? He could get up and run away, couldn't he? Could *you* do that, Fred?")

The trainer should remember to apply the same methodology that was illustrated in the curriculum for the first two training sessions, summarized as follows:

1. Use teaching aids to illustrate and dramatize a scenario in which participants might encounter sexual abuse by another person (sitting on a couch, sleeping in one's bed).

2. Tell the group what is occurring in a step-by-step fashion, using the teaching aids: "This man [demonstrating with the dolls] is trying to get into this woman's bed! He is trying to put his hands inside her clothes and touch her in her private parts!"

3. Identify for the group which behaviors are appropriate and which are inappropriate: "It's okay for them to sit together if they want to," or

"He shouldn't do that! He shouldn't put his hands inside her clothes and touch her in her private parts if she doesn't want him to do that!"

4. Rephrase the concept of appropriate and in appropriate behaviors as a question, and ask each participant the question in turn (demonstrating with the teaching aids): "What do you think, Frank? Is it okay for this man to put his hands inside this woman's clothes and touch her breast if she doesn't want him to?"

5. Move back and forth from a central position to a position directly in front of each participant in turn, bringing the teaching aids directly to the participants. Personalize the scenario for the individual participant: "What if this is *your* bed, Frank?" Then alternate the focus on individual participants with a more central focus on the group.

6. Reinforce appropriate responses with verbal praise. If the participant does not respond or responds inappropriately, tell him or her the correct response and then rephrase it as a question: "You could say 'No' couldn't you? *Could* you say 'No'?" This process is repeated until the participant is able to give an appropriate response to the question.

7. Introduce and review the training objectives incrementally as the scenario is personalized for each participant: "Susie could say 'No!' Fred could get up and run away! Joe could tell George that this man is trying to touch him inside his clothes!"

8. Modify the training objectives when necessary for participants with special needs; for example, a wheelchair-bound participant may need to call for help or ring a bell instead of running away from an abusive interaction with another person.

Exercise 5: Introduction of new teaching aid (model of a bathroom with shower stall and toilet area) and review of first, second, and third training objective. This model will help participants with severe retardation to recognize and avoid sexual abuse in the context of additional activities of daily living during which they are especially vulnerable, bathing and toileting. The trainer focuses on one area at a time—for example, the shower first. Participants are told what the model represents, and the trainer verifies with each participant in turn that he or she understands the appropriate function of a shower area or a toilet area. Then the trainer uses the anatomically correct dolls to illustrate the function of the area. He or she can undress a doll and demonstrate taking a shower or illustrate how a male doll would pull down pants and shorts to urinate into the toilet or a female doll would pull down panties to sit on the toilet. An assistant will be needed to demonstrate the abusive situation: another person viewing or touching a man or a woman who is taking a shower or using the toilet.

Trainers utilize the methodology described in exercise 4 to illustrate the scenario, identify appropriate and inappropriate behavior, and review all three training objectives. Participants identify readily with the dolls in this scenario and enjoy the dramatic aspects, especially when the dolls are shown to interact with each other.

Exercise 6: Reintroduction of audiotape of "It's OK to say NO!" Same as in the first and second training sessions.

Closing Exercise. If this is the last exercise, the trainer praises each participant for his or her participation and says goodby to each participant in turn.

A Curriculum for Adults with Moderate Mental Retardation

First Training Session

This section depends heavily on the preceding sections. A careful reading of the Guidelines for Use in chapter 8 and "A Curriculum for Adults with Severe Mental Retardation" is essential since many of the exercises for training adults with severe mental retardation are incorporated into this curriculum for adults with moderate mental retardation. The teaching methodology and recommended approach to training are the same for participants who are severely and moderately mentally retarded.

It is strongly recommended that adults with moderate retardation receive sexual abuse avoidance training in groups that are all male or all female. The training group size for participants at this functioning level may range from four to eight participants, with six being the recommended number. Whenever possible, the member of the direct care staff who attends the training session should be of the same sex as the participants in the group.

Additional teaching aids are incorporated into this curriculum. All teaching aids should be concealed in bags or containers until they are needed and should be removed from sight as soon as other teaching aids are introduced. This curriculum for adults with moderate mental retardation includes a structured role play to demonstrate appropriate social interactions, which was not included in the curriculum for adults with severe mental retardation.

The format of the three training sessions represents the minimum number of sessions required to convey the training objectives. Some groups of adults with moderate retardation may well benefit from a larger number of training sessions with fewer exercises presented in each session. These decisions will be influenced by time constraints and the functioning level and the receptivity of the participant groups involved.

Staffing: One trainer; one assistant for four to eight participants.

Seating arrangements: Participants are seated in a semicircle or a horse-shoe shape in direct line of sight of the trainer, who sits or stands at the open end of the semicircle. The assistant is positioned for easy access to all participants and may need to move many times during the training session to maintain order or to assist by signing to certain participants.

Teaching aids and materials: Anatomically correct dolls; a small chair or bench (large enough to seat two dolls); a toy bus or van (large enough to seat two dolls); audiotape of "It's OK to Say NO!"; tape player.

Exercises 1–9. Same as in the first training session for adults with severe mental retardation.

Exercise 10: Introduction of teaching aid (bus) and the review of three training objectives. The trainer should have participants identify the bus, review its function, and find out which participants have had the experience of riding buses. The same methodology as used with the dolls and the chair should now be applied to riding in the bus. Using the dolls, the trainer can demonstrate a scenario involving a doll (same sex as the participants) getting on the bus, paying the fare, sitting down, and then being accosted by another doll who attempts to view or touch the first doll in an appropriate or unwanted fashion. The techniques of first presenting the scenario using the dolls and the bus and then personalizing the scenario ("Suppose this is *you* on the bus?") should be utilized. All three training objectives should then be reviewed if time constraints and the receptivity of the participants so permit.

Exercise 11: Introduction of audiotape "It's OK to Say NO!" Same as in the curriculum for adults with severe mental retardation.

Closing Exercise. Same as in the curriculum for adults with severe mental retardation.

Second Training Session

Staffing: Same as in the first training session.

Seating arrangements: Same as in the first training session.

Teaching aids and materials: Anatomically correct dolls; small chair; toy bus; small bed; audio tape, "It's OK to Say NO!" tape player.

Exercises 1–10. Same as in the first training session. Depending on the receptivity of the participants, the exercises can be compressed. For example, it may not be necessary to undress all of the dolls or to review the names of the body parts. The scenarios of the two dolls sitting in a chair and the dolls in the bus can also be compressed and consolidated.

Exercise 11: Introduction of teaching aid (bed) and review of all three training objectives. Trainers should refer to "A Curriculum for Adults with Severe Mental Retardation," second training session, exercises 7–10, for instructions.

Exercise 12: Reintroduction of audiotape "It's OK to Say NO!" Same as in the first training session.

Closing Exercise. Same as in the first training session.

Third Training Session

Staffing: Same as in the first and second training sessions.

Seating arrangements: Same as in the first and second training sessions.

Teaching aids and materials: Anatomically correct dolls; small bed; bathroom model; audio tape, "It's OK to Say NO!"; tape player.

Exercises 1–3. Same as in the first and second training sessions.

Exercise 4: Review of all three training objectives with anatomically correct dolls and bed. Same as in the second training session.

Exercise 5: Introduction of bathroom model and review of all three objectives (using anatomically correct dolls). Trainers should refer to "A Curriculum for Adults with Severe Mental Retardation," third training session, exercise 5, for instructions.

Exercise 6: Demonstration by role play; identification of facial cues as responses to social interactions. The trainer puts two empty chairs by the center of the semicircle, in line of sight of all the participants, and asks the assistant to be seated there. The trainer then says:

> "Pat is a friend of mine. I like Pat, and we're friends. Hi, Pat. Glad to see you."

The trainer extends an arm to shake hands with the assistant. The trainer then looks directly at one participant and explains the social interaction:

> "Sally, I just met my friend Pat and shook her hand to say hello. Is that okay?"

When the participant responds affirmatively, the trainer should agree:

> "Sure! It's okay to shake hands. And I can tell it's okay because Pat smiled when I reached for her hand." [pause]

Now the trainer says to another participant,

> "Susie, watch Pat's face when I'm saying hello to her. She smiles when she shake hands."

The trainer again initiates the social interaction:

> "There's my friend, Pat. Hi, Pat! It's good to see you."

The trainer extends hand; trainer and assistant shake hands, while the assistant smiles. The trainer asks,

> "Susie, did you see Pat smile when we were shaking hands?"

If the participant responds affirmatively, the trainer asks another participant,

> "Jane, what did Pat do when I was shaking her hand?"

After a correct response, the trainer repeats,

> "Yes, Pat smiled when I shook her hand."

If the participant(s) respond inappropriately, the trainer reports the social interaction while pointing out the assistant's facial expression:

> "Pat, it's good to see you smile while we're shaking hands. [pause] Jane, see Pat's face? She's smiling while we're shaking hands."

When the trainer is certain that all the participants have noticed the assistant's facial expression, he or she says,

> "Sally, there's an empty chair here. Is it okay to sit down next to Pat?"

When the participant responds affirmatively, the trainer sits in the empty chair near the assistant, who responds by smiling, and says to the participants,

> "Does Pat think it's okay for me to sit here? Jane, what do you think?"

If the participant does not respond appropriately, the trainer says,

> "Look, Jane, Pat's still smiling and I'm sitting next to her. It's okay to sit next to someone."

If the participant responds by saying, "She's smiling. It's okay," then the trainer repeats,

> "Sure. Pat's smiling, and it's okay for me to sit next to her."

The trainer establishes that each participant is aware of the assistant's facial expression and the appropriateness of the social interaction (sitting in a seat next to a friend) before proceeding.

Next, the trainer puts a hand on the assistant's knee. The assistant reacts by grimacing or frowning to convey unhappiness, fear and discomfort. The trainer says,

> "Sally is this okay? Is it okay for me to touch Pat this way?"

If the participant responds affirmatively, the trainer says,

> "Sally. Look at Pat's face. She looks unhappy! She looks scared! What do you think Pat's face is telling us?

If the participant indicates that she cannot identify a negative emotion in the assistant's expression, the trainer attempts to clarify by increasing the involvement of the assistant.

> "Pat, show Sally what your face looks like when you feel happy."

The assistant smiles, and the trainer directs the participant's attention to her smile:

> "Sally, do you see Pat's smile? Her face is telling us that she's happy. [pause] Pat, show us what you look like when you're unhappy or scared."

As the assistant frowns, the trainer says,

> "Pat looks unhappy. [pause] Sally, what is Pat's face telling us now?

When Sally gives an appropriate response, the trainer reinforces the response:

"That's right! Pat's face is telling us that she's unhappy. She doesn't want me to touch her like this. It's not okay!"

Then the trainer and assistant repeat the entire sequence with another participant, again identifying appropriate and inappropriate social interactions and alerting the participants to the differing facial expressions of the assistant in response.

The trainer then asks the participant,

"Jane, what could Pat do if I put my hand on her knee, and she didn't want me to? What could she do?"

If the participant indicates that she does not know what could be done, the trainer states an appropriate response and repeats the question.

"Jane, Pat could say 'No! I don't want you to put your hand on my knee! [short pause] What do you think Pat could do, Jane?"

When the participant responds appropriately, the trainer reaffirms by saying,

"That's right. She could say 'No! Please take your hand off my knee!' [pause] or she could move my hand [assistant demonstrates as trainer is talking] [pause] or she could run away" [assistant gets up and moves away from the trainer].

The trainer now involves another participant:

"What do you think, Susie? What could Pat do?"

Thereafter the trainer asks several participants the same question until all three appropriate responses have been identified. The trainer proceeds to the next step only when the participants have indicated that they could take some appropriate action if they were being touched in a discomforting fashion.

The trainer then reviews:

"People can tell us if they are happy or sad by the expression on their faces. Usually we smile when we're happy about something [trainer smiles widely], and we frown when we're unhappy or confused [trainer frowns]. Whenever you touch someone, you should be sure to look at her or his face to see if she or he likes it or not. [pause] And, remember, if somebody touches you and you don't want her to, what can you do? [elicits all three training objectives from participants] That's right. You can say 'No! I don't want you to do that.' You can move the person's hand. You can run away. And you can tell someone."

Exercise 7: Reintroduction of audiotape "It's OK to Say NO!" Same as in the first and second training sessions.

Closing Exercise. Same as in the third training session of "A Curriculum for Adults with Severe Mental Retardation."

A Curriculum for Adults with Mild Mental Retardation

Unlike the two previous sections, this curriculum is not outlined in a detailed exercise-by-exercise fashion. It will be essential to review all of the preceding material before undertaking sexual abuse avoidance training with adults who are mildly mentally retarded.

It is strongly recommended that this group of participants be trained in same-sex groups. Again, it is desirable that the member of the direct care staff who participates in the training be of the same sex as the participants in that group. The training group size can range from four to eight participants.

The principal teaching aids recommended for this group of participants are the anatomically correct dolls and the audiotape, "It's OK to Say NO!" The chair, bed, and bus may be brought out to illustrate each scenario initially, but it will probably not be necessary or appropriate to use these teaching aids directly in front of each participant or to dramatize the scenario in as concrete a fashion as was necessary for lower-functioning participants or to repeat the scenario as frequently. A toy car (to illustrate the scenario of accepting a ride from a stranger or going out with a date who has a car) may be helpful. Also a picture or a model to illustrate a street corner scenario or a park may be helpful. The trainer is encouraged to use whatever object or scene is most appropriate for the experience and environment of the particular participants of the group.

Participants with mild retardation may be much more familiar with the concept of sexual victimization than lower-functioning participants. Many of the adults at this level may know someone who has been sexually assaulted; some may even tell of their own sexual victimization experiences. Many of the participants are familiar with issues of dating, contraception, pregnancy, and marriage. In addition to their increased cognitive ability and familiarity with the issues, many evidence greater anxiety and discomfort with discussion of the topic. Others may have inaccurate information on all or some of the issues, which is likely to contribute to higher anxiety levels in the training sessions. Trainers should be cautious in their presentation and attentive to participants' behaviors throughout the sessions; the anxiety will often be evidenced by acting-out behaviors during the training session.

Sessions for adults with mild mental retardation differ in format from those described for participants with severe and moderate mental retardation. The initial presentation should begin, however, with the same description as was utilized in other first sessions: sexual abuse is defined as being looked at or touched under one's clothes in a way that is displeasing to the participant. All three major training objectives (to say 'No!' to run away, to tell someone) should be presented in the first session, demonstrating with the anatomically correct dolls. Personalizing the scenarios and the concepts for each participant is extremely important. The time remaining in the first and following sessions can be allocated to engaging the participants in dialogue. In this way, the trainer determines the extent and accuracy of the participants' knowledge and their specific needs regarding avoidance of sexual victimization. The trainer can ask,

> "Can anyone give me an example of the time when you might want to say 'No' to someone? [or] Joe, has anything like this ever happened to you?"

The trainer might also tell the participants,

> "I've talked with other people who work at sheltered workshops, and they sometimes tell me that they've had times when someone wanted to touch them or look at them in a way that's not okay. Have any of you ever had that happen?"

The trainer should be aware that, given permission and opportunity, the participants will provide data and circumstances directly pertinent to their daily living situations; the trainer should be prepared to explore the situations and provide specific and concrete guidance as to what action the participant can take and whom they should tell.

The structured role-play exercise to demonstrate appropriate social interactions is especially helpful with adults with mild retardation. The trainer and the assistant can identify the particular issues that would be appropriate to demonstrate for these participants, although the demonstration need not be as repetitive or concrete as for adults with moderate retardation. Some topics useful to consider are facial cues and body movements as indicators of discomfort; smiling because one is happy versus smiling due to anxiety; and appropriate and inappropriate comforting of someone who is upset.

All three sessions with this group will necessitate dialogue between trainers and participants. Consequently it will also be necessary for the trainer to be flexible regarding the specific topics covered in each session. The needs of these adults are strongly influenced by their individual life circumstances (group home or supervised apartment living, work environment, recreational opportunities). Successful sexual abuse avoidance training must address these identified needs and provide the participants with solutions appropriate to their own lives.

Each training session for adults with mild mental retardation should end with playing the audiotape, "It's OK to Say NO!" and encouraging the participants to sing along with the tape. This participatory and joining exercise provide needed continuity between the training sessions. A closing exercise in which the participants are praised for their participation and reminded of the short-term and long-term incentives for participation should end each session.

Summary Observations

Trainers who have used this curriculum with numerous participants have made the following observations about adults who are mentally retarded and have received the training. Higher-functioning adults tend to become embarrassed if teaching groups are coeducational or if staff members of the opposite sex are present during discussions of sexuality. Higher-functioning adults also tend to be more worried about confidentiality, especially with respect to discussing incidents of victimization with others.

Many adults with mental retardation have been sexually victimized. Sometimes the sexual abuse occurred during their childhood; sometimes it did not occur until after they had reached adulthood. It is therefore not unusual when these people receive sexual abuse avoidance training for some of them to decide to tell the trainers or other participants about an incident of sexual victimization during or after the training. Trainers must realize that disclosures of sexual abuse may occur as a result of the training and must be prepared to receive such disclosures and act upon them. This includes reporting to the appropriate authorities and referring the victim of complainant for counseling. Likewise it is important to be sure that the direct care staff who live and work with the adults are prepared to receive and act upon reports of sexual abuse from the participants as well.

We have found that direct care staff are generally supportive of the concept of sexual abuse avoidance training for adults with mental retardation but are concerned about the potential consequences if a person for whom they have responsibility participates in the training. Specifically, they worry that the participants may be less compliant or less willing to obey commands or receive directions after receiving the training. Likewise, they voice fears that participants will make false or unwarranted accusations of sexual abuse following sexual abuse avoidance training. On the one hand, many persons who work with adults with mental retardation have not been trained to recognize sexual elements or the abusive elements of certain interactive behaviors that may occur between participants or between staff members and participants. On the other hand, direct care staff are often unsure about their responsibility to permit, curb, or redirect the sexual behaviors of adults with mental retardation for whom they are care providers.

We believe that it is essential for agencies that provide care for adults with mental retardation to formulate policies that address sexual abuse of these adults. Such policies will help to guide the staff and provide the appropriate context in which to plan and conduct sexual abuse avoidance training for the adults served by the agency.

At the same time, it is also important to note that the physical characterisitics of the place where adults reside may strongly influence their vulnerability to sexual assualt by others, especially in regard to arrangements for sleeping, bathing, and toileting. This occurs on two levels.

The first is lack of privacy in large communal bathrooms and bedrooms. Becoming accustomed to lack of privacy in regard to dressing, bathing, and toileting conveys a message to all (residents, staff, and families) that the residents do not have a right to privacy. This attitude makes it difficult, if not impossible, for adults to set limits on themselves or others with respect to their own sexuality or sexual victimization. Another level of vulnerability inherent in communal bathrooms and sleeping arrangements is that since there are more people walking in and out of a bathroom or a sleeping area, there are also a greater number of potential abusers and potential victims.

The second level is confusion about sleeping arrangements in coeducational group homes. This situation may be problematic of there are no awake staff at night. Small coed group homes are intended to provide a family atmosphere for residents. However, the practice of having male and female residents sleep in adjacent rooms and share or use adjacent bathroom facilities in a small group home exposes them to the vulnerabilities of a family setting without the protections built into healthy families. Male and female residents in small coed group homes are not siblings and therefore lack the internalized parent-mediated familial role boundaries and psychological barriers to incest that are characteristic of siblings in psychologically healthy families. Accordingly, residents in small coed group homes may have a level of vulnerability to sexual victimization by other residents that is higher than would be expected if these small facilities were all male or all female or were designed or adapted to allow sleeping, bathing, toileting, and dressing areas that are separated by sexes.

We consider the designing and field-testing of this curriculum a preliminary step in learning more effective ways for adults with mental retardation to live full and more satisfying lives in the community. Within the context of necessary policymaking and the careful attention given to some of the issues we have presented, we believe that ongoing sexual abuse avoidance training should become part of the care plan for every adult who can benefit from such training: all adults with mild, moderate, and severe mental retardation and those who have the minimum expressive and receptive capacity required to participate.

10
Evaluation and Treatment of Sexual Offense Behavior in Persons with Mental Retardation

Suzanne M. Sgroi

L ittle has been written to date about persons with mental retardation who are sexually abusive toward others. How does one recognize sexual offense behavior that is initiated and performed by a person who functions below the normal limits of measured intelligence? If there is no question that a man or a woman with mental retardation has sexually victimized someone else, what then? The victim might be male or female, an adult or a child, a family member or a nonrelated person, a designated caretaker or a fellow client, a person with normal intelligence or someone with lower than normal cognitive functioning. Once it is recognized that a sexual assault did occur, what responses are necessary besides the obvious steps of caring for the identified victim, protecting her or him from further assaults, and assessing treatment needs for physical or emotional sequelae of the abuse?

There are few guidelines and less agreement about evaluation and treatment of sexual offense behavior in persons with mental retardation. It seems appropriate, then, to use as guidelines the four components of treatment for sexual offense behavior that are described in chapter 14 in this book. If the sexual abuser is a person with mental retardation, what should be the shape of the control, social intervention, therapy, and reeducation components of treatment? How much control is needed and for how long? What social intervention measures are necessary, and what can realistically be expected to result? Is therapy appropriate for a sexual offender who has limited intellectual functioning? If so, how much of what type of therapy may be indicated, and for how long should therapy be continued? What about reeducation for the adult person with mental retardation who sexually abuses others? What can she or he learn that will help to change a pattern of sexual offense behavior? What educational interventions can be expected to have a beneficial impact and assist a person to meet her or his needs for affection, affiliation, and intimacy with others in socially acceptable ways?

This chapter presents a methodology for evaluating sexual offense behavior in persons with mental retardation and describes some guidelines for training caretakers to recognize and report sexual offense behavior accurately. The chapter ends with a discussion of treatment interventions for common patterns of sexual offense behavior seen in persons with mental retardation. It is important to remember that professional knowledge about working with sexual abusers who have limited cognitive functioning is developmentally at a very eary stage. Undoubtedly there will be an evolutionary progression as different approaches are tried and professionals gain more experience with various interventions. It is of paramount importance to share information about experience gained to date so that we can learn from each other as rapidly as possible.

Recognizing Sexual Offense Behavior in Persons with Mental Retardation

One of the problems encountered when evaluating complaints is that caretakers and others sometimes fail to recognize that a person with mental retardation has in fact sexually abused another person. The operative words here are *sexual* and *abuse*. Some people have a very idiosyncratic definition of what constitutes a *sexual* behavior. One staff person consistently declined to describe a moderately retarded man named Joseph as sexually abusive. Joseph had been found on multiple occasions in the bedrooms of other men and women who resided in the same house. The staff would hear screaming and yelling and rush to the scene, where they would find Joseph, always in a state of total undress, grappling with the other person. By the time a staff person arrived, the second person would usually have torn clothing as a result of Joseph's attempt to rip it off. Usually Joseph would be observed to be rubbing the genital area or breasts of the victim. The staff person who was responsible for transmitting the incident reports however, stated that he did not believe that Joseph was sexually assaulting the other residents. When asked why, the staff person replied, "He always has his clothes off when we find him. No one has ever seen him have an erection while the fight is going on!"

Although it is difficult to understand or appreciate, the staff person had a very clear definition of sexual offense behavior: it must be accompanied by penile erection. Since Joseph did not have an erection at the time he was discovered in the act of assaulting another person, his behavior was not defined as sexual offense behavior. Accordingly he repeatedly sexually assaulted the other men and women who lived in the residence for many more months until a review of the facility was performed by an outside agency.

Sometimes the barrier to recognizing the sexual component of sexual offense behavior stems from an unwillingness to believe that a person with mental retardation has sexual feelings or desires. There still exists a strong tendency on the part of many to infantilize the adult person with mental retardation with regard to sexuality. Overtly sexual behaviors may be ignored altogether or misunderstood by family members or caretakers. This tendency is especially problematic when it results in policies that interfere with a person's capacity to protect herself or himself from sexual assault by others, (For a discussion of sexual abuse avoidance training for persons with mental retardation, see chapters 8 and 9.) The wishful expectation that physically normal adults with mental retardation will not have or act upon sexual feelings or desires can be a covert barrier to recognizing sexual offense behavior when it does occur.

Recognizing that sexual offense behavior is abusive may also present a problem. Broadly defined, sexual abuse involves initiating any sexual act (ranging from sexual exposure to sexual fondling to sexual penetration) with another party for whom there exists a barrier to consent. Sometimes the barrier is a legal one; for example, the second person may be below the legal age of consent, as would be true for a child. Many states have sexual assault statutes that identify physical or mental handicaps as legal barriers to consent. In some states, the presence of a custodial or caretaking relationship between two people may preclude consent to a sexual interaction by the person who is in custody or is the recipient of care. Every state in the United States defines the use of force or a weapon or a threat of force or injury to the second party as legal barriers to that person's consent to sexual interaction.

Psychosocial barriers to consent are more difficult to define, and there is less likelihood of agreement concerning them. This is especially problematic when one is attempting to assess a complaint that involves a sexual interaction between two adults with mental retardation. How can one determine the capacity of these two adults to consent to a sexual interaction if both parties are older than the age of majority, if both have a relative mental handicap (perhaps limited cognitive capacity), if no significant physical handicap is present for either, and if no element of intimidation by force or a weapon exists? The following questions might be asked:

1. Did both agree to the sexual interaction? Or did one person protest, physically resist, or otherwise attempt to avoid engaging in interactive sexual behavior? Any element of protest, resistance, or avoidance that can be demonstrated (even when force or threat of injury were absent) precludes consent.

2. Do both persons understand the very basic elements of interactive sexual behaviors? These include exposure or touching of intimate body parts (the breasts or the genital or anal areas); understanding the concept of privacy (sexual behaviors are not performed in public places or in the

presence of others); exercising choice of partner (people may select their sexual partners based on personal preferences); and right of refusal (a prospective sexual partner has the right to refuse the invitations or advances of another person).

It is usually possible to ascertain if even nonverbal persons understand all of the above by observation of past and present behaviors. For example, persons who test at very low levels of measured intelligence can usually be taught that there are intimate parts of one's body that are different from other body parts with regard to exposure or touching. Even very low functioning persons usually understand that their ears or their noses are different from their genitals or breasts and that there will be very different consequences if they rub or attempt to put their fingers inside their ears as opposed to the likely response if they try to expose or rub their genitals in front of someone else.

It is also possible to draw some conclusions by observation about a person's capacity to exercise choice with regard to a prospective sexual partner, as well as her or his capacity to understand that refusal (of another's invitation or demand for sexual interaction) is permissible. Although most persons with lower than normal cognitive functioning have received intensive training aimed at teaching them to be compliant at all times, many still demonstrate that they have preferences and can exercise choice on many levels. Many also demonstrate a capacity to say "No!" and to refuse to cooperate with or to accede to someone else's requests or demands. Thus a person's previous history with regard to exercising choices and the capacity to refuse can and should be considered when an episode of sexual interaction is being scrutinized closely in order to determine if abuse might have occurred. It must be emphasized that the issue of both parties' capacity to understand the basic elements of interactive sexual behavior becomes most important in situations when no other obvious barrier to consent is present. By contrast, if another barrier to consent does exist, this issue may be of interest only with respect to assessing the impact of the episode of sexual interaction on the parties involved.

Sometimes professionals are asked to assess prospectively a person with mental retardation in order to determine if she or he appears to have the capacity to consent to a sexual interaction. Such assessments may be requested when programs for clients are being planned. It is not unusual for these assessments to address the person's capacity to understand all of the possible consequences of interactive sexual behavior, including pregnancy and transmission of venereal diseases. The assessment may include a test of the person's knowledge of methods of contraception and prevention of sexually transmitted diseases. A person who does not "pass" the test may be deemed incapable of consenting to a sexual interaction even when there are no other obvious barriers to consent (for example, use of a weapon or threat of force). Of course, the requirement that a person demonstrate factual knowledge of the consequences of sexual interaction by passing a test may be useful if the intent of the examiner or the persons who requested the assessment is to be exclusionary and to weight the assessment process in the direction of finding the people who are being assessed incapable of consenting to sexual interactions. On the other hand, nowhere in the United States are there sexual assault statutes that define a person's lack of factual knowledge about pregnancy or venereal disease as a barrier to consenting to sexual interaction. The age of consent for sexual interaction is legally defined in most states as age 16. However, many public schools do not teach children facts about contraception or sexually transmitted diseases by age 16. It seems discriminatory to require such knowledge of persons who score in the lower than normal range of measured intelligence if it is not a requirement for others. When such requirements are enforced, it is usually in response to requests or demands that the programming and living facilities for persons with mental retardation include opportunities for intimate relationships with others. By contrast, the participants' level of knowledge about pregnancy or venereal disease has little relevance in regard to evaluating a concern about sexual abuse when it has been discovered that two adult persons with mental retardation have had a sexual interaction with each other.

3. Is there a power imbalance between them that precludes consent?

The obvious answer to the first part of the question is, "Of course!" No two people are identical, not even so-called identical twins. When two people are sexually interacting, one of them will always be bigger than, stronger than, smarter than, more experienced than, or more assertive than the other. Answering the second part of the question is less obvious or easy. A power imbalance between two people precludes consent when one of them demonstrates a willingness to take advantage of the other or when one of them occupies a decidedly subordinate position in relation to the other.

This discussion is meant to focus only on sexual interactions between two adult persons with mental retardation. There is no need to address the obvious power imbalances inherent in a sexual relationship between a person who functions within the normal range of measured intelligence and a person with mental retardation, between an adult and a child, between a parent and a grown-up child, or between a staff person and a client. In looking at two adult persons with mental retardation, it is also obvious that when one of them uses a weapon or physical force or verbal threats of violence or personal injury to elicit compliance with sexual interaction from the other, that the patently aggressive person is demonstrating a willingness to take advantage of the other person. When a very high functioning person sexually interacts with a very low functioning person, observers are likely to conclude that the higher-functioning person is taking advantage of the lower-functioning partner.

> George, a mild-mannered and generally passive 28-year-old man, sought out and befriended Jerry, age 20, soon after the latter was transferred to a group home where George already resided. George consistently had a full performance IQ in the low 60s; Jerry, by contrast, achieved full performance IQ scores in the high 20s. The direct care staff soon became uneasy because George "haunted" Jerry, monopolizing all of the younger's man's free time and spending every possible hour with him. George appeared to be jealous when anyone else spent time with Jerry. By contrast, Jerry was quiet and compliant and appeared generally satisfied. One night, a staff person discovered George and Jerry in bed together in Jerry's bed. George was performing anal intercourse on Jerry; the younger man did not appear distressed or unhappy and was offering no resistance at the time of discovery. When interviewed afterward, Jerry simply repeated, "It's okay," as a response to all questions.

This case example involves two adult men with mental retardation whose cognitive capacities are widely disparate. The direct care staff became uneasy soon after the higher-functioning man befriended the lower-functioning one; the obvious disparity between them led observers to fear that George's motivations in seeking out Jerry included an awareness that he could take advantage of him. When they were discovered in bed together, the staff's conclusion was that George was in fact exploiting Jerry's subordinate position. There was general agreement that George had not threatened Jerry or physically overpowered him and that Jerry was cooperating with the sexual interaction. However, because George's higher level of intelligence gave him a decided power advantage, Jerry was deemed to be unable to consent to a sexual relationship with George. As a result, although George was not labeled a sexual offender, the relationship was judged to be "not good" for Jerry, and the two men were separated more or less completely (Jerry was moved to another residence, no visits between George and Jerry were permitted, and the staff were instructed to prevent them from talking together or spending time together on the rare occasions when they met in the cafeteria or in a recreational setting). Three years later, George was still obsessively mourning the separation from Jerry. Although less obviously affected by the separation, Jerry still smiled and greeted George enthusiastically whenever a chance (and brief) meeting occurred.

This case raises lingering questions. If an obvious power imbalance exists between two adults with mental retardation, is it appropriate to conclude that significantly lower cognitive functioning is an absolute barrier to consent? Was something about the relationship "not good" for Jerry? If so, what? Might it be that George was being so possessive and so jealous and so focused on Jerry all of the time that neither man had time (or opportunity) for other types of social interactions? What if the intervention had been to make and enforce a rule prohibiting sexual interaction between them while also insisting that George be less exclusive in regard to his social relationship with Jerry? What about using the situation as an opportunity to teach assertiveness skills to Jerry, encouraging him to learn to set limits for others who might be intrusive or monopolize him?

It seems cruel and counterproductive to intervene with a rigid separation policy. Unfortunately, this is a hazard for persons with mental retardation; separations and changes in residence are frequent occurrences for many. In the case example, neither man was afforded the opportunity to prepare for the separation and to say goodbye; neither received assistance or support in the grieving process. Three years later, for George, at least, the grieving continued and had become a pathological process for him.

To summarize this discussion, evaluation and treatment of sexual offense behavior hinge upon recognizing that a person with mental retardation is sexually abusing someone else. It is necessary to recognize that the behavior is both sexual and abusive in nature. For the purposes of this chapter, the following definition of sexual offense behavior is offered:

> Sexual offense behavior involves one person's looking at or touching certain parts of a second person's body (breasts, buttocks, inner aspect of the thighs, or genital and anal areas) for the purpose of gratifying or satisfying the needs of the first person and when a barrier to consent is present for the second person. Sexual offense behavior may also include exposing one's genital area to another person and/or compelling that person to look at or touch the above-mentioned parts of the first person's body when a barrier to consent is present for the second person. (Viewing or touching the breasts of a female but not a male is pertinent to this definition.) Barriers to consent include age less than 16 years; the presence of a parental, custodial, or caretaking relationship between the persons involved; the use of a weapon, threat of injury, or use of force by the first person; the presence of a cognitive inability in the second person to understand the basic elements of sexual behaviors (as described earlier) or the presence of a power imbalance between them which precludes consent by the weaker person.

This definition is not intended to be a legal one. Rather, it is offered in an attempt to provide a working definition of sexual offense behavior that can be used by professionals who work with persons with mental retardation. Some definition is needed for this population, especially for the purposes of policy writing, staff training, and evaluating complaints or concerns related to such behavior. The definition is very broad because it attempts to encompass a wide range of behaviors, as well as to address the especially difficult issue of sexual interactions between two adults with mental retardation. Readers who work in this field are encouraged to familiarize themselves with the definitions sections of the sexual assault statutes in the state where they are employed. Administrators of departments or institutions that serve adults with mental retardation should be familiar with civil and criminal statutory definitions of sexual assault as departmental and institutional policies and guidelines are formulated. People who have worked in the field for years are sometimes surprised to discover the legal implications of some of the behaviors that have been discussed. This is not to say that the policies that provide rules for community living and outline procedures to address complaints necessarily must include verbatim repetitions of the state's sexual assault statutes; quite the contrary. However, it is desirable to be aware of the legal implications of sexual offense behaviors as well as the legal reporting requirements when policies are being formulated.

Reporting Sexual Offense Behavior

Adult Victims with Mental Retardation

Whenever anyone has reason to suspect that a person with mental retardation is a victim of sexual abuse, a report should be made to the civil authority in that state that has been designated by the legislature to receive and investigate such reports. A report also should be made to the director of the agency that provides residential or caretaking services for the suspected victim, as well as to the victim's legal guardians. State laws (which are highly variable) should be followed also with regard to reporting to the police. Most civil agencies designated by the legislature to receive these reports have an internal policy regarding their transmission to the police; this should be followed scrupulously.

It is important for agencies that provide residential or caretaking services to persons with mental retardation to have internal policies regarding the reporting process to the civil authority and the police. The policies should address the reporting process in detail, including who should file the report, what information should be included, and who should receive collateral reports. As well, the policy should contain recommended procedures for ensuring care of the suspected victim, including provisions for medical examination and treatment, assessment of the person's psychological state and need for counseling and/or emotional support, and arrangements to ensure the person's continued physical safety after the reports have been made.

Child Abuse Victims

Suspected sexual abuse of any child must be reported to the statutory child protection agency in that state. In general, the agency will be mandated to receive reports of suspected abuse of children who test within the normal range of measured intelligence, as well as reports concerning children with mental retardation. Administrators of agencies that provide residential or caretaking services to persons with mental retardation must be aware that they almost certainly are considered to be mandated reporters of suspected child abuse in their state. They are required by law to report to child protective services if sexual abuse of a child under their care is suspected or if they have reason to believe that an adult client may have sexually abused a child. Depending on state law or departmental requirements, it may also be necessary to report to the police. Again, it is important to have carefully formulated departmental or institutional policies regarding the reporting process. If a child with mental retardation is the suspected victim, there should also be procedures to ensure that the victim receives appropriate treatment.

Elderly Abuse Victims

Many states require that suspected sexual abuse of elderly persons (usually defined as those 60 years old or older) be reported to a civil authority mandated to receive and investigate such reports. This civil authority usually is separate from the child protection agency or the agency that investigates reports of suspected abuse of persons with mental retardation who are between 18 and 59 years of age. It is also usual for the agency that investigates reports of suspected abuse of elderly persons to have this mandate for elderly persons with mental retardation, as well as for those who fall within a normal range of cognitive functioning.

Agencies that provide care for elderly persons with mental retardation also need policies for reporting suspected sexual abuse of their clients to the appropriate civil authority. Depending on state law or departmental policies, it may be necessary also to report to the police. Policies should include procedures for ensuring that the suspected victim receive appropriate treatment on all levels.

Administrators have an additional duty to report to the appropriate authorities whenever they suspect that an adult person with mental retardation who is under their care may have sexually abused an elderly person.

Internal Investigation of Complaints of Sexual Abuse

Whenever there is reason to believe that a person with mental retardation is either a victim of sexual abuse or an abuser, it is incumbent upon the agency that provides residential or caretaking services for the suspected victim or abuser to conduct an internal investigation. (An exception may be made for cases in which the suspected abuse took place during a time period when someone else was temporarily responsible for the client's care and welfare, such as during a home visit or a hospitalization.) The purpose of the internal investigation is to demonstrate that the agency that provides caretaking or residential services is acting responsibly with regard to the safety of its clients, as well as the safety of the community. In some cases, the responsibility for investigating the above may be transferred (by mutual agreement) to the civil authority that has a mandate to investigate suspected sexual abuse of a vulnerable population. However, it will still be necessary for the agency that provides caretaking or residential services to persons with mental retardation who are suspected victims or abusers to demonstrate that it is exercising an appropriate level of concern for the well-being of its clients.

It is not unusual to find that as many as three investigations of a complaint of suspected sexual abuse involving a person with mental retardation are taking place simultaneously: the statutory civil protective investigation, a criminal investigation by the police, and an internal investigation conducted by agency administrators. It is highly desirable for the persons who are conducting the internal investigation to follow the agency's policy for doing so and to try to coordinate the internal investigation with the civil protective and the police investigations as much as possible.

Each investigative process has a different goal. The civil protective authority is mandated to find out if a member of a vulnerable population (children, elderly persons, or adult persons with mental handicaps) has been sexually abused. If the complaint is validated—that is, if it is determined that sexual abuse did take place—the civil authority is usually also mandated to recommend that steps be taken to ensure the future safety of the victim. Thus the civil authority has some jurisdiction over the victim (especially when it is empowered to petition a civil court on the victim's behalf). However, it usually has little or no authority over the person of the abuser.

By contrast, law enforcement officers are looking for facts to help them to decide if probable cause exists to believe that a crime was committed, that a specific person committed the crime, and that there is evidence that would cause a reasonable person to believe that the suspected perpetrator did commit the crime in question. The police investigator may then make an application for a warrant to arrest the suspected abuser. If the arrest takes place, the suspected abuser is entitled to all of the constitutional protections enjoyed by anyone else arrested on suspicion of committing a crime. If a prosecution ensues, the suspected abuser's guilt must be proved beyond a reasonable doubt.

A police investigator has no authority over a suspected victim of sexual abuse and is rarely in a position to take steps to protect that victim from future abuse. If a criminal prosecution does take place, the victim may be subpoenaed to appear as a witness for the trial. The credibility of the victim's complaint (also an issue in civil protective investigations and internal investigations) is usually assessed by the police investigator as well as by the prosecutor's office in the light of the victim's capacity to appear as a witness in court, both in regard to her or his capacity to articulate the complaint and to withstand cross-examination. Many police investigators decide at a very early stage of the investigation that a report of suspected sexual abuse that consists solely of a verbal complaint by a person with mental retardation, that is, without corroboration (by a witness or by physical evidence), will not meet the standard of belief required for probable cause. Such cases are often not pursued further by the investigating officer, and no criminal proceedings are likely to ensue.

The goal of the internal investigation of a complaint of suspected sexual abuse involving a person with mental retardation is to determine if some aspect of the provision of caretaking or residential services contributed in any way to the abuse. For example, did the agency fail to provide an appropriate level of supervision, safety, or limit setting for the client? The person responsible for providing the internal investigation is likely to look for lapses in performance by agency employees and to try to determine whether the staff are properly trained and deployed to prevent future such episodes. An internal investigation may reveal that there was no way that the abuse could have been prevented, that agency employees need a different level of training, that staffing patterns should be changed, or even that disciplinary action against an employee is warranted. None of this is to say that the internal investigation process should be oblivious to the treatment needs of the clients who are concerned or to the criminal implications of the sexual abuse behavior. However, it is highly appropriate for the foregoing issues regarding the agency's contributions (or lack thereof) to the abuse complaint to be addressed also.

Since each of the three investigations will probably be conducted simultaneously and without coordination, it will be easy for the respective investigators to wind up tripping over each other, undermining each other's ability to accomplish the widely disparate goals of each investigation. It makes sense for the agency providing the caretaking or residential services to the suspected victim or suspected abuser to take leadership in coordinating the three investigations. At a minimum, each of the three separate investigators should meet the others, clarify her or his job responsibilities, and try to agree on the timing of their efforts. There should also be clarification of the extent to which information sharing among them is possible and permissible. Whenever it can be arranged, it is highly desirable for the investigators to conduct joint interviews of clients, staff, and others who must be interviewed to reduce the number of interviews required and improve the quality of interviewing practice.

Investigating the Complaint

Interview Sites

All of the persons who were involved in the abuse situation—the victim(s), the suspected abuser(s), and witnesses to any part of the scenario—must be interviewed separately. In general, these investigative interviews should take place as soon as possible after the complaint of suspected sexual abuse is made. The interviews should take place in a neutral setting. This means that if the suspected victim or suspected abuser (or both) is a person with mental retardation, the interviews should be performed in an office, preferably in a building that is other than the site of the suspected abuse. It is also advantageous to avoid interviewing a suspected victim or a suspected abuser in her or his residence. A dormitory, group home, supervised apartment, or a private home are all places where a person with mental retardation should have the right to feel safe and to close the door against intruders. In other words, selecting a person's home as an interviewing site is counterproductive because the site would then be a place that the interviewee has the right to call "home" and a place where she or he is entitled to refuse to conduct business. As well, there are few truly private places in communal living facilities, and the interviewers could easily be interrupted or the interviewee could be distracted by other residents.

When interviewing staff persons, an office setting away from the area where the individual works is a highly desirable site. Corridor interviews are unprofessional and a violation of the privacy of that employee. Conducting an investigative interview on the job site is not only a potential violation of the employee's privacy, it also can be distracting and influence or contaminate information that may be gained from clients or other staff persons. Locker rooms, staff lounges, and the employee's residence are all to be avoided as interview sites for obvious reasons.

Selection of Interviewers

It is preferable to conduct joint interviews when as many as three separate investigations are being conducted. It may be possible for any two of the three investigators (civil protective, police, or agency) to conduct their interviews as a team. In the joint interview situation, it will be important for the interviewers to decide in advance who will take the lead in conducting the interview to avoid the intimidating and confusing practice of having two people firing questions at the same time at the person being interviewed (especially desirable if the interviewee is a person with mental retardation). If the interviewers agree in advance that one will take the lead in conducting the interview, then the second interviewer should remain silent except for making supportive or clarifying interventions until after the first interviewer has finished. Then the second interviewer can take the lead in questioning the person, with the first interviewer remaining silent for the most part, until the interview is completed.

People frequently ask if the sex of the interviewer(s) is important. In general, the two most important considerations are the interviewer's expertise and degree of comfort in working with a vulnerable population, (persons with mental retardation, children, victims of abuse) and the interviewer's level of expertise in performing nonleading investigative interviewing. The sex of the interviewer becomes a secondary issue by comparison. There may be great advantage in using an interviewing team consisting of a male and a female interviewer. In this way, the person interviewed can always identify with at least one interviewer with regard to gender. It is sometimes assumed that members of a vulnerable population will be more comfortable in discussing matters related to sexuality with a person of the same sex. However, so many variables influence this issue that it is not surprising to discover that many interviewees appear to be less concerned about the gender of the interviewer and more influenced by the interviewer's capacity to establish a relationship with them that is supportive, accepting, and nonjudgmental in nature.

Recording Information

It is very useful to videotape or audiotape investigative interviews, especially if the subject is a member of a vulnerable population. If videotaping or audiotaping is done, the subject should be shown the equipment and told that the recording is taking place. The advantages of recording the interview are obvious: it provides a complete record of the information elicited and demonstrates the technique used by the interviewer(s). The videotape or audiotape must then be treated with the same respect and confidentiality afforded to a written record. Readers should be aware, however, that legal barriers may exist to recording interviews of persons with mental retardation in some states.

Nonleading Interviewing Techniques

In previous work, there has been much discussion about using nonleading techniques in performing investigative interviewing to validate complaints of child sexual abuse (Cage 1988; Delipsey and James 1988; Sgroi 1982). It is equally important to use nonleading techniques when doing investigative interviewing of persons with mental retardation. This means that the interviewer tries to encourage the interviewee to describe what happened in her or his own words. An open-ended nonleading interview technique is a process that facilitates the subject's capacity to supply information about an event in a step-by-step process. The interviewer must take care to avoid communicating by tone of voice, facial expressions, or body language that she or he is surprised, shocked, angry, or disgusted (not to mention relieved, amused, pleased, or elated) by the content of any response made or information supplied by the person being interviewed. The following case example illustrates the open-ended, nonleading technique used to interview a young woman with mild mental retardation who was sexually assaulted on a date with her boyfriend.

Interviewer: Judy, I want to hear about your date with Sam.

Judy: Uh, he raped me.

Interviewer: How did the date start? How did you two get together?

Judy: He picked me up at King Street [the group home where Judy resides]. He said we were going to the movies.

Interviewer: What happened after he picked you up?

Judy: We drove in his car for a long time. I knew we were going the wrong way.

Interviewer: What happened then?

Judy: He stopped the car in the woods. He said he had bought stuff from McDonald's, and we could have a picnic first.

Interviewer: What happened next?

Judy: I don't like to talk about it.

Interviewer: Sometimes it is hard to talk about things, but you are doing a good job. What happened next?

Judy: Nothing, really. It was just . . . [her voice trails off]

Interviewer: You said he stopped the car in the woods and told you he had bought food from McDonald's. What happened next?

Judy: I started to get out of the car.

Interviewer: Yes?

Judy: He started to kiss me.

Interviewer: Yes? And what happened then?

Judy: He started to pull on my clothes.

Interviewer: Yes? What happened then?

Judy: I tried to push him away.
Interviewer: You're doing a good job, talking about this. What happened then?
Judy: He started to touch me.
Interviewer: Can you tell me about that?
Judy: [looking away] No.

Presented as in this case example, open-ended nonleading interviewing appears deceptively simple. In the example, it is apparent that the interviewer is encouraging Judy to relate what happened in chronological event-by-event fashion. This is accomplished in three ways: (1) using a simple interrogative after each of Judy's responses such as "Yes?" or "What happened next?"; (2) deferring asking her to clarify or explain her responses at this time; and (3) avoiding an exploration of her emotional responses yet praising her for doing a good job of telling what occurred. All three of these techniques contribute to the steady flow of information about the event.

Asking, "What happened next?" depersonalizes the narrative and helps the subject to put emotional distance between herself and what occurred. Asking, "What did Sam do next?" is a leading question because it implies that in fact Sam was in control of what occurred and that Sam initiated the next interaction (which may or may not be true). Asking, "What did you do?" may communicate blame in a subtle fashion, especially if the subject did not in fact do anything at that time. In the first stage of the investigative interview, it is important to elicit as much information as possible about the events. Later in that interview or in a subsequent interview, the clarifying process can take place.

Asking clarifying questions in the first stage of the interview may halt the flow of information very early. For example, an inexperienced investigator might be tempted to ask, "What do you mean, he raped you? What's rape?" Any subject might experience this question as challenging or threatening, especially if she or he is a member of a vulnerable population (a child or a person with a mental handicap). Judy may be entirely capable of relating what happened to her on a step-by-step basis if that is encouraged. However, the likelihood is high that she will become embarrassed and confused by being asked for a definition of rape at this early stage of the interview. In turn, she may also correctly assume that her failure to give a satisfactory definition of rape may undermine her credibility in the eyes of an examiner who chooses to test her cognitive capacity in this fashion before she has had an opportunity to relate what actually happened. The sad reality is that persons with mental retardation have a lifetime of experiences of failing or of being found deficient when their cognitive capacities are tested. Judy's capacity to give an accurate definition of rape at this time has no relevance to the issue of whether a sexual assault did or did not occur on her date with Sam. However, testing her capacity to define rape accurately at this time may well inhibit her capacity to describe what actually occurred.

It is also of strategic benefit to avoid exploring the subject's emotional reaction to what is being described in the first stage of the interview. Asking, "How did you feel about that?" or "What was that like for you?" are classic probes used by clinicians in psychotherapy interviews to encourage the subject to focus on her or his emotional responses—highly appropriate for a psychotherapy session but entirely inappropriate for the investigative interview process. The subject who belongs to a vulnerable population is very likely to become confused about what is wanted of her or him by the interviewer. At the same time, she or he may easily become uncomfortable or even overwhelmed if the feelings evoked by the original experience are called up at this time. (This is not to say that emotional responses should never be addressed; instead, there should be a clear distinction made between investigative interviewing and psychotherapeutic interventions.) Sometimes investigative interviewing of persons who belong to a vulnerable population is best accomplished by a team comprised of an investigator and a clinician. The investigator can take the lead in fact-finding, and the clinician can note which events should be explored later for their emotional content.

Interviewing Aids

Anatomically Correct Drawings. The dialogue between Judy and the interviewer stopped when Judy balked at describing the touching by Sam. This would be an appropriate time for the interviewer to utilize some type of interviewing aid to facilitate describing sexual touching. One such aid is the anatomically correct drawing, copied from a book of anatomically correct drawings such as the one published by Groth and Stevens (1984). The book depicts nude front and back views of males and females (white and black) in various stages of development: preschool age, primary school age, adolescent, and adult. Professionals who are conducting investigative or clinical interviews may use a copier to reproduce drawings from the book and bring the copies to the interview.

It would be appropriate to bring to the interview with Judy a copy of the drawings representing an adult woman who is the same color as Judy and an adult male who is the same color as Sam. These copies should be kept out of sight until it is time to use them in the interview. For example, after Judy refused for the second time to tell about the way in which Sam touched her, the interviewer could show her the appropriate drawings and say, "Judy, these are pictures of a woman who does not have any clothes on. You said that Sam touched you. Could you show me on the drawings where he touched you?" Often a person who cannot initially verbalize details of sexual touching can point to areas on a drawing or, preferably, use a pen or pencil to mark the drawing in the pertinent areas. The drawing can then be used to clarify the names used by the subject for various body parts. If Judy points to the breast area on the drawing in response to the request to show the interviewer where the touching occurred, the interviewer can then ask her, "What do you call that part of woman's body?" and note Judy's response.

Anatomically Correct Dolls. A second aid to interviewing is anatomically correct dolls—soft cloth dolls originally designed for use in interviewing children about sexual abuse. Although they have the appearance of conventional dolls when fully dressed, anatomically correct dolls also have breasts on the adult female dolls, external genitalia for the male dolls, and vaginal openings for female dolls. The best models of anatomically correct dolls also have mouth and anal openings and fingers on all of the dolls. Anatomically correct dolls are usually sold as a family of four dolls: adult male, adult female, little boy, and little girl dolls.

When used to interview adults with mental retardation, it must be remembered that the dolls are a tool to assist subjects with limited expressive capacities to communicate. As an alternative to using anatomically correct drawings, the interviewer might have given Judy an adult male doll and an adult female doll with the appropriate skin colors and said "Show me with the dolls what happened next." If Judy had used the dolls to demonstrate any interaction, the interviewer would need to ask, "What are you showing me? What does this mean?" It is not sufficient to observe the subject with the dolls and conclude from her or his behavior only (lacking verbal clarification) with the dolls what might have occurred in the actual situation for which the interview is being conducted.

Props to Recreate the Scene. Additional props might be used to recreate the scene for some subjects. For example, the interviewer might have utilized a toy car and two small conventional dolls in interviewing Judy. These props sometimes help people with more limited verbal capacity to demonstrate what happened during an interaction. A doll's bed can be a useful prop in investigative interviewing, since so many sexual offenses involving persons with mental retardation take place in beds or in bedroom.

The value of such props as investigative tools totally depends on the subject's capacity to use the props as aids to communication or verbalization. The interviewee who ignores any interviewing aid or refuses to use it as a means to show what took place is most likely a person with whom investigative interviewing is impossible.

Free Drawing. Some persons with mental retardation will accept an invitation to communicate by drawing what occurred. If Judy had refused to tell directly about the touching by Sam or had refused to use any of the interviewing aids previously mentioned, she might still have been willing to draw "what happened next." Accordingly the interviewer might have supplied her with several blank sheets of paper and some marking pens or crayons and then waited silently while she used them. After Judy had completed her free drawing(s), the interviewer would then look at the drawing(s) with her and ask her to describe them. A good query would be, "Can you tell me what is in your drawing?" The interviewer could then point to various parts of the drawing and ask, "What's this?" or "What's that?"

Applications to Interviewing Suspected Abusers

All of the nonleading techniques described are equally applicable to performing investigative interviewing of persons with mental retardation who are suspected of sexual abuse of another person. Although it can be very helpful when a suspected abuser admits to sexual offense behavior, it is imperative to avoid using leading techniques in this situation also. Again, it must be remembered that many persons with mental retardation have been trained to be compliant with authority figures, especially with respect to responding in a way that they think will please the questioner. In addition, many people respond positively to questions in the hope and expectation that positive responses will shorten the interviewing process.

> David, a 39-year-old man with moderate mental retardation, was found under a stairwell in an elementary school at 4:00 P.M. on a Friday afternoon. The school was located on the same block as the group home in which David resided. An 8-year-old boy who was a third-grade student at the school was standing with his pants down and his genitals exposed, and David was performing oral sex on him when the two were discovered by a janitor. Later on, in an investigative interview, the following dialogue took place.

Interviewer: David, how did you get to the school?
David: I walked over there.
Interviewer: What happened after you got there?
David: I wanted to play ball with the kids.
Interviewer: Yes? And what happened?
David: Nobody there.
Interviewer: So? Then what?
David: I went inside.
Interviewer: Uh-huh. What happened then?
David: Billy came [the 8-year-old boy].
Interviewer: What happened next?

David: I said, "You want to play ball?"

Interviewer: Yes? Did he say anything?

David: He said, "No."

Interviewer: Then what?

David: I showed him some money.

Interviewer: Yes?

David: I said he could have the money. I wanted to suck him off.

Interviewer: Uh-huh. What happened then?

David: He said, "Okay."

Interviewer: Yes?

David: We were doing it, and a man came. He said we had to stop.

Interviewer: Have you done this with any other kids?

David: No.

Interviewer: Are you sure?

David: No.

Interviewer: What about Eddie and Joseph? [David's nephews].

David: Yeah, I done it to them.

Interviewer: Have you ever done it to Marty [David's roommate at the group home]?

David: Yeah.

Interviewer: How about Mr. Gibbons? [the director of the group home]? Have you ever sucked him off?

David: Yeah.

Interviewer: How many times?

David: Lots of times.

In this case example, the interviewer used non-leading techniques in the beginning of the interview, and David supplied units of information in response. After describing how he engaged Billy in sexual activity by offering to give him money, David then used a slang phrase, "suck him off," to describe the sexual behavior. It would have been preferable for the interviewer to fill in the gaps in David's story at this point, asking him to explain "suck him off" or using an interviewing aid such as an anatomically correct drawing of a primary-school-age boy and showing on the drawing where the touching (or sucking) occurred. Instead the interviewer went in a different direction by asking David to identify other possible victims. David's responses when asked if he had ever done this with others were negative. When the interviewer then began naming various other persons as possible sexual partners, David responded affirmatively to every name suggested by the interviewer.

It is, of course, possible that David had also performed oral sex on his young nephews, his roommate, and the director of the group home. All of these persons should now be questioned with regard to sexual interaction with David as part of the investigative process. However, it would have been less leading to ask, "Who else did you 'suck off'?" and to give David an opportunity to supply other names. Although possible, it is unlikely that David's past history included performing oral sex on all of the persons named by the interviewer. Probably David guessed that the interviewer wanted him to identify other sexual partners and acquiesced when each name was successively proposed in an effort to please (and satisfy) the interviewer. This should not undermine the credibility of the information elicited from David using nonleading techniques.

Readers may also wonder why a person like David would voluntarily supply information about his sexual encounter with Billy. The answer is that people often reply candidly about sexual offense behavior when interviewed in a nonleading fashion by an interviewer who is accepting and nonjudgmental in approach. It would have been easy to stop the flow of information from David by exclaiming, "Didn't you know you're not supposed to do that with kids?" Some interviewers simply cannot contain themselves when they hear someone else calmly describing sexual advances toward or sexual behavior with a vulnerable person. However, an expression of challenge or disgust or anger at any point, although perhaps temporarily satisfying for the interviewer, is likely to be counterproductive if it inhibits the interviewee from sharing information which might otherwise be shared.

Approaches to Avoid

In addition to communicating one's own emotional reactions, either verbally or by body language, there are other pitfalls to avoid when interviewing persons with mental retardation (suspected victims or suspected abusers) about sexual offense behavior. One is to avoid asking leading questions, for example, "It was your father who did this to you, right?" or "That must have really hurt, didn't it?" These are obvious examples of leading by the interviewer; however, almost any other question that can be answered "yes" or "no" is to some degree a leading question. For example, it is less leading to ask, "Who was in the house with you?" than to ask, "Were you alone?" The first question creates the opportunity for the interviewee to respond with someone's name or else to say, "Nobody." The second question requires a two-step response process; the subject must ask herself or himself, "Was I alone?" (this requires an interpretation) followed by, "What should I respond?" Whenever one is interviewing a person with mental retardation, it is preferable to ask open-ended questions that elicit one-step responses (for example, "Who was there? What happened next?") than to ask a question that requires a two-step response and is also limiting.

Another pitfall involves the erroneous belief that the credibility of a person's responses to open-ended questions is undermined by her or his responses to leading questions. Instead, if a person with mental retardation is asked, "Who did this to you?" there is a high degree of probability that a person who is named in response was actually an abuser. If, on the other hand, there is no response to the open-ended question, responses to leading questions are less credible (for example, "Was it your father?"). But after an open-ended question (for example, "Who did this to you?"), some interviewers may try to test the first response by asking a series of leading questions (for example, "Did your mother do it too? Did your older brother do it? Did the president of the United States do it to too?"). If the subject responds positively to the latter questions, some interviewers would doubt the credibility of the first response:—that is, "My father did it." Be that as it may, there is no more reason to believe that a person with mental retardation will misinform or give an inaccurate response to an open-ended question than would be likely for a person with normal cognitive functioning. By contrast, the combination of cognitive impairment coupled with lifelong training toward compliance with authority figures probably increases the likelihood that persons with mental retardation will give an inaccurate response to a leading question.

Record Review

Investigators should review all of the written records available that concern the complaint, paying careful attention to any behavioral incident reports. It is desirable to review the incident reports before interviewing staff persons who may have contributed to the report or perhaps even witnessed the incident that provided the basis for the complaint. It may be useful to remember that the staff who provide direct care for persons with mental retardation are the most likely people to be present when a sexual abuse incident is discovered. Sometimes the staff member witnesses a sexual interaction between two persons with mental retardation; sometimes what is observed is a sexual encounter between a person with mental retardation and a person with normal cognitive functioning. On the other hand, sometimes a staff member is told about a sexual abuse incident involving a person with mental retardation by one of the participants. Alternatively, the staff member may simply discover something that points to the probability (or certainty) that sexual abuse took place. In one case, a staff member discovered a number of photographs of nude children in provocative sexual poses hidden under the mattress of a male client. The children in the photographs were later identified as the client's nieces and nephews. In another case, a staff member discovered that a profoundly retarded nonverbal male client had blood in his shorts. Physical examination later revealed that the injured man had severe anal lacerations and an asymptomatic gonorrhea infection of his throat.

Although direct care staff are often the first persons to discover or suspect that a sexual offense involving a person with mental retardation has occurred, few of them are trained observers, and few know how to differentiate an observation from an impression. Most behavioral incident report forms ask the person who fills out the form to record both: observations and impressions. A direct observation is information derived from using one of the five senses. It can be recorded by using the pronoun "I" followed by a verb reflecting one of the five senses followed by the information thus derived. For example, the sentence might read: "I saw George on top of Jerry in the bed"; or "I heard Jerry cry out"; or "I smelled smoke." By contrast, an impression can be recorded with the phrase, "I think that," as a prefix. Impressions based on these observations would be recorded as follows: "I think that George was trying to have sex with Jerry," or "I think that Jerry was calling for help," or "I think they had been smoking in bed."

Investigators are likely to discover that, in most behavioral incident reports, observations and impressions are jumbled together without clear distinction. Also, it is not unusual to find that the incident report contains impressions with no relevance to observations. For example, an incident report on the case example involving George and Jerry might well contain a statement such as, "George is sexually frustrated." Although this statement may reflect a deeply held belief on the part of the staff member, it is unlikely to be an impression based on an observation of the incident.

While an investigator may well choose to limit her or his record review to pertinent incident reports, a person who is asked to perform a clinical evaluation for sexual offense behavior in a person with mental retardation will wish to conduct a much more extensive record review. This may include reports of psychological testing, psychological evaluations, social summaries, medical reports, anecdotal log entries, and the like. In particular a clinical evaluation for sexual offense behavior should include a thorough review of all available written records, including incident reports over the person's lifetime.

To summarize, investigation of complaints of sexual abuse that involve persons with mental retardation (as suspected abusers or suspected victims, or both) should be painstaking and methodical. The following plan for performing investigative tasks is proposed. It is suggested that the tasks be performed in the order listed insofar as possible. By utilizing information elicited in the earlier tasks, the investigator can conduct the interviews with a minimum of leading yet stay focused on the complaint and the alleged sexual offense behavior.

Investigation and Evaluation Protocol

Preliminary Record Review

The investigator should examine all written records pertaining to the abuse complaint. These may include the written report to civil authorities who receive abuse complaints, a behavioral incident report, anecdotal records pertaining to the time when alleged abuse occurred, and the like. The purpose of reviewing these records first is obvious: the investigator needs a preliminary view of the observations and impressions of those who first had reason to suspect that sexual abuse may have occurred.

Interviewing the Complainant(s)

The complainant is defined as the person or persons who reported the suspected abuse. Often the complainant(s) supplied the information contained in the report to the civil authority or in the behavioral incident report. Investigators are likely to elicit additional information about the complaint if they conduct face-to-face interviews with complainants. In this way it may be possible to gather more detailed observations and impressions about the complaint and to derive an impression about the credibility of the complainant. Sometimes the complainant also will be able to serve as a bridge to facilitate communication between the investigator and the alleged victim or between the investigator and the alleged abuser. In other words, the complainant may be a person who already has a good relationship with the person(s) with mental retardation who should be interviewed next. If so, the complainant may assist the investigator to bring the interviewees to an appropriate interview site, make introductions, and encourage open communication during the interview.

Interviewing the Victim(s)

It is suggested that interviews with victims be conducted in neutral sites using nonleading interviewing techniques. Anatomically correct drawings, anatomically correct dolls, and free drawings are helpful aids during the interviewing. It is very helpful to ask a staff person or a family member of the person to be interviewed to perform introductions.

In the initial five minutes, the investigator should state that she or he wants to talk about the abuse complaint and communicate that the interview is voluntary in nature, perhaps by saying, "I'm going to ask some questions. You can answer me if you want, but you don't have to talk if you don't want to." Asking the complainant, a family member, or a staff person who knows the subject to remain while the interviewer explains that participation is voluntary will serve several purposes. First, the interview subject will have an opportunity to have this confusing issue (the voluntary nature of responding to the interviewer's questions) clarified by the familiar and (it is hoped) trusted caretaker. Second, the presence of another person in the initial stages of the interview provides a witness who can attest to the arrangements made for the interview. Third, having a familiar person present in the initial stages of the interview serves as an icebreaker for the subject and the interviewer. After all of the above have been accomplished, the interviewer can request that the other person leave so that the rest of the interview can be conducted in private.

Interviewing the Suspected Abuser

All of the points made in the preceding section should be underscored regarding an interview with a person with mental retardation who is suspected of committing sexual offense behavior. Nonleading techniques always should be used, and interviewing aids may be used as necessary. Every effort should be made to avoid coercion of the subject. Criminal investigators should take care to ensure that all of the subject's legal rights are respected. If there is any doubt about the latter issue, the subject's caretakers or guardian should request that an attorney for the subject be consulted before proceeding with the interview.

Collateral Interviews

Frequently it is necessary to perform a variety of collateral interviews in conducting an investigation or evaluation of sexual offense behavior involving a person with mental retardation. Witnesses to the abuse, other residents, family members, direct care staff, professional staff, educators, job coaches, and others who know the individuals involved in the complaint may be valuable sources of information. Each interview should be conducted in a neutral site with a minimum of distractions and a respect for the privacy of all concerned. Once again, nonleading interviewing techniques should be used. The interviewer should make a clear distinction in recording the observations versus the impressions of anyone who is interviewed.

Extensive Record Review

The investigation or evaluation should include an extensive review of all available records. These may include the following:

Behavioral incident reports.
Anecdotal records.

Psychological evaluations and testing.
Social summaries.
Educational records.
Employment history.
Medical records, including current medications.
Prior reports of offense behavior, including arrest records and complaints.

Although record review may be tedious and time-consuming, most investigators and evaluators will discover that it is fruitful. Reviewers should be alert for previously recorded information about sexual offense behaviors, aggressive behaviors, or reports of victimization by others. Any or all may have been recorded by persons who described them in other terms or perhaps did not recognize them as sexual offense behaviors or as incidents of victimization. Thorough record review is necessary to place the current situation in an appropriate historical perspective. The records are sometimes the best source of historical information about psychosexual development and previous victimization of persons with mental retardation. This is especially important when such persons lack the verbal capacity to share such information.

Writing the Report

Investigators and evaluators should list all of their assessment procedures with a careful description of the interviewing techniques used with persons with mental retardation. Historical background should be included, as well as a description of the current functioning level of any person with mental retardation under evaluation for sexual offense behaviors. Evaluators will wish to include a psychosexual history and a victimization history. An evaluation report should contain a detailed description of the alleged sexual offense behavior followed by a section explaining the evaluator's impressions of the individual who is the subject of the evaluation. A separate recommendations section should be at the close of the report. The list of recommendations should be as detailed as possible and should address the four major components of treatment: control, social intervention, therapy, and reeducation.

Patterns of Sexual Offense Behavior in Adults with Mental Retardation

Professionals who do not have the opportunity to respond to a variety of requests for evaluation may wonder if adults with mental retardation exhibit characteristic patterns of sexual offense behavior. Although it is not possible (or desirable) to formulate rigid categories at this time, here I describe some patterns that I have observed frequently when conducting evaluations.

Multiply Aggressive Adults with Mental Retardation

Although the chief complaint and stated reason for the evaluation may be sexual offense behavior, these persons actually exhibit a variety of aggressive behaviors—physical assault, sexual assault, property damage, theft, and the like. In this pattern, the sexual offense behavior is like to be violent in nature; the abuser carries out sexual interactions by threatening the other person with injury or by actual use of force. Often the abuser is a generally intimidating person who is viewed by others as someone to be avoided.

> Danny, a 25-year-old man with moderate mental retardation, required constant supervision because of his propensity for fighting. Although he occasionally engaged in a sudden outburst of breaking and hurling objects and punching and kicking others for no apparent reason, most of the violent outbursts seemed to occur when Danny could not "get his own way." Danny frequently attempted to thrust his hands inside the clothing of others, forcibly grabbing at women's breasts and attempting to fondle them in the genital area. On two recent occasions, the staff encountered Danny in the act of forcible intercourse with other residents, one male and one female. Each time the victim was screaming and attempting to get away. Danny's past history included multiple episodes of stealing money from the staff and from fellow clients. He also had punched holes in walls and windows and broken multiple objects, including television sets and radios belonging to himself and others. Danny's caretakers requested a psychosexual evaluation because Danny had committed an increased number of sexual assaults in the past year. Some staff members wondered if Danny's assaultive behavior might also be motivated by "sexual frustration."

Comment. This case example describes a man with a very poor impulse control and a pattern of violent acting-out behaviors, including but not limited to sexual behaviors. It is not unusual when this pattern of multiple aggression occurs in an adult male with mental retardation for someone to ask if sexual frustration might be motivating him to assault others. The answer is that sexual offense behavior is not an expression of pent-up sexual desire in persons with normal cognitive functioning or in persons with mental retardation. Instead, sexual offense behavior is a highly dysfunctional method of meeting one's need for feeling powerful and in control (Groth 1979, 13). It is unrealistic to hope that a program to enable Danny to have more frequent consenting sexual interactions will decrease his pattern of generalized aggression. We would not expect Danny to be less likely to steal money from others as a result of receiving a larger income or stipend. Danny's generalized aggression is unlikely to be occurring in response to a single causative factor. Instead there are probably multiple reasons for his generalized assaultiveness, including poor impulse control, a sense of powerlessness and inability to meet his needs, a lack of ability (and perhaps a lack of incentive) to learn and practice more constructive ways to meet his needs, and a lack of meaningful consequences for his aggressive behaviors.

Treatment Recommendations. Danny should receive a careful clinical evaluation, including a comprehensive medical evaluation. Underlying neurological and/or endocrinological causes for aggressive behavior should be ruled out. Thereafter, the four components of treatment should be addressed.

Control. Danny's access to weaker and more vulnerable persons should be carefully monitored. If possible he should be placed in a peer group comprised of assertive and communicative persons. He should occupy a private bedroom and should not be expected to share closet space or storage space for personal belongings. Staffing patterns must be planned so that Danny's assaultive behaviors can be controlled as much as possible. If he does assault another person, the staff must be capable of containing the physical violence as quickly as possible.

Social Intervention. Appropriate reports should be made to civil protective agencies if Danny abuses a member of any vulnerable population.

Therapy

Medication: Some multiply aggressive individuals become less violent if treated with psychotropic medications. If this is tried, careful medical supervision and frequent medication review will be required.

Behavior Modification: Danny's aggressive behaviors should be met with meaningfully negative consequences, and his positive behaviors should amply reinforced. This should include a thorough assessment with baseline data, analysis of environmental circumstances surrounding the aggressive behaviors, and a comprehensive and consistent plan to increase appropriate and reduce inappropriate behaviors. Critical to the success of any program is a monitoring evaluative system that enables appropriate modifications as needed.

Psychotherapy: If Danny has the necessary expressive and receptive capacities, he might benefit from long-term (minimum of one year) participation in peer group psychotherapy aimed at reducing assaultive behaviors. These groups are usually most effective when they have a strong educational thrust; serving as a milieu in which group members can practice social and communications skills.

Reeducation: Whether this is an aspect of peer group therapy or of a behavior modification program, Danny should receive intensive social skills training, including practicing how to communicate his own wants and needs to others (for example playing a game or dividing a task), being assertive without being aggressive, and anger management. Practice is an important concept in the area of social skills training. Danny needs between three and five years of social skills training, with daily opportunities for practice at home, at the worksite, in a recreational setting, and so on.

To summarize, Danny's sexual offense behavior occurred in a larger context of multiple aggression. Focusing on his sexual aggressiveness alone is unlikely to be helpful. Danny is not a candidate for sexual counseling or insight-oriented psychotherapy. Attempting to provide him with more opportunities for normal sexual relations with others is unlikely to reduce his sexual aggression. It is unlikely to be useful to label Danny as a sexual offender per se. However, no aspect of his multiple aggression should be ignored. Control may be the most important component of Danny's treatment in that he represents a serious physical danger to others. Treatment for persons who fit this pattern of behavior requires a careful balancing of their civil rights versus the rights of more vulnerable persons.

Rapist Behavior in Adults With Mental Retardation

For the purpose of this definition, a rapist is a person who uses threat of injury or use of force to engage another person in some type of interactive sexual behavior: sexual exposure, fondling, penetration, or simulated intercourse. Unlike the multiply aggressive person, the rapist generally uses physical aggression only when she or he is initiating a sexual interaction with someone else. This is not to say that a rapist necessarily always uses force or threat of injury in a sexual interaction; some rapist engage in consenting sexual interactions, as well as in sexually assaultive acts.

Martin, age 36 years, was a short, powerfully built man with profound mental retardation who had a history of sexually assaultive behavior beginning when he was 12 years old. Ordinarily quiet and tractable, Martin occasionally targeted a man or a woman in his environment for sexual interaction. Thereafter, Martin would follow that individual until an opportunity arose for him to grab both of the other person's hands and perform simulated intercourse by rubbing his penis against the victim's genital area. This often occurred in broad daylight with other people in the immediate area or within shouting distance. Although staff members often prevented him from following his target, they were unable to distract him as long as the targeted person was in sight. Martin also would arise from his own bed at night, climb into bed with another resident, and initiate a sexual interaction. If the other person resisted, Martin would forcibly sexually assault him or her. This aggressive sexual behavior was Martin's only type of acting-out behavior. He never damaged or stole property or money and was never physically assaultive toward others except in the process of committing a sexual assault. Martin was nonverbal and would not use signs expressively; however, he understood simple commands relating to all activities of daily living. He was considered a good worker and performed yard work and simple cleaning tasks well.

Comment. This case example describes a person with profound mental retardation who is capable of tremendous selectivity with regard to his targets for sexual assault. He is also selective with respect to using physical force; although capable of using his superior strength to take advantage of others in a variety of ways, he is generally not physically assaultive. The patterned and repetitive aspects of his sexual offense behavior began at a very early age (the onset of puberty). A careful record review would probably reveal that Martin was institutionalized at age 12 years because his parents and teachers could not control him in the community.

It is likely that at least some of Martin's caretakers will view his rapist behavior as a manifestation of frustration caused by inadequate opportunities for consenting sexual interactions. Some might hypothesize that Martin is unable to achieve relief from sexual tension because he is not masturbating effectively. I have encountered people who are ardent proponents of this theory and are convinced that teaching adult males with mental retardation to masturbate more effectively will reduce the frequency of their sexual assault behaviors. No evidence or results have ever been presented to support this hypothesis.

It is unlikely that anyone will be able to learn what motivates Martin to engage in patterned sexual assault behavior. Possibly he is reenacting a sexual assault that occurred early in his own life. Rapists who function in the normal range of measured intelligence also engage in patterned sexual assault behavior; insight into their motivations to rape is helpful to a limited extent. Careful observation may assist in determining what triggers Martin's sexual assault behavior. In turn, it may be possible to manipulate his environment so that the unwanted behavior is triggered less often. However, there is no reason to believe that helping Martin to gratify his sexual desires in other ways will reduce his sexual assaultiveness.

Treatment Recommendations

Control. Martin should not share a bedroom with anyone else. If it is not possible to monitor his whereabouts at night with awake staff outside his bedroom, equipping the exits (windows and doors) of his bedroom with alarms that will sound when he attempts to leave may be helpful. During the day, Martin will need line-of-sight supervision whenever he is in the presence of persons who are vulnerable to his assaults.

Social Intervention. Any member of a vulnerable population who is sexually victimized by Martin should be reported to the appropriate civil protective authority.

Therapy

> Medication: FDA-approved psychotropic medications are usually not effective in reducing rapist behavior when it does not occur in the context of multiply aggressive behavior. Martin is unlikely ever to be a candidate for an experimental medication to reduce sexual offense behavior because he is unable to understand the risks involved (and thus to give informed consent to receive it).

> Behavior Modification: To be effective, behavior modification to reduce Martin's rapist behavior will need to be consistently applied over his lifetime. It is unlikely that behavior modification by itself will permit a reduction of the control required to protect others from Martin's sexual advances.

> Psychotherapy: Martin is not a candidate for any form of verbal therapy. If he had a higher level of cognitive functioning, he might benefit from participation in peer group therapy with other rapists. The goals of peer group psychotherapy for adult rapists with mental retardation would be as follows: teaching members to recognize signs that they are at risk to commit a sexual assault, helping members to engage in avoidance behaviors when they are at risk for committing an offense, and helping members to learn to ask for help from others when they need it.

> Reeducation: For a profoundly retarded person such as Martin, the reeducation component of treatment should be directed toward helping him to be occupied mentally for as many waking hours as possible. These persons usually have many hours of waiting during their waking hours.

Waiting to be fed, waiting to be taken to work, waiting to go to bed, and so forth actually constitute different types of downtime, although they may be listed as free time in a daily schedule. If Martin is not engaged in some activity, the likelihood that his pattern of sexual offense behavior will be triggered is higher than if he is actively involved in some pursuit. Unfortunately, this usually requires a very high ratio of staff to clients and very comprehensive programming. Sadly, agencies or institutions that care for adults with mental retardation often wind up paying for huge amounts of overtime simply to assign a staff member to watch someone like Martin and keep him out of trouble. If the same amount of money were allocated for programming, there would be less downtime, a better service, and perhaps less "trouble."

Child Molester Behavior in Adults with Mental Retardation

Some adults with mental retardation are sexually attracted to children, just as some adults with normal cognitive functioning find that children are sexually appealing. There is no evidence to suggest that adults with mental retardation are more likely to molest children than adults who function within the normal range of measured intelligence (Groth 1978, 18). The term child molester in this definition refers to a person who uses a nonviolent method to engage a child in sexual behavior (Groth 1982, 215–216). By contrast, a person who uses force or threat of harm to initiate sexual behavior with a child would be described as a "child rapist" (Groth 1979, 141).

> David, age 39 years, was discovered under the stairwell in an elementary school by a janitor. When discovered, David was in the act of performing oral sex on a younger child. During his adolescence, David had been reported to the police on at least five different occasions by outraged parents; all of the reports involved nonforcible sexual assault of a prepubertal child (mostly male children). At age 19 years, David was sent to a large institution for adults with mental retardation where he resided for twelve years. Unlike many of the other residents in the institution, David had a verbal IQ of 74 and a full performance IQ of 69. He could read, write, do simple arithmetic, and had passed both written and road tests to obtain his driver's license. While in the large institution, David was never discovered to be engaged in sexual behavior with anyone. David had resided in a group home in the community for nearly one year before the offense with the 8-year-old boy.

Comment. This case example describes a man whose repeated sexual offense behavior with children fits the definition of a fixated child molester (Groth 1982, 215). That is, David's behavior indicates that he has a primary sexual orientation toward prepubertal children. (Readers are referred to chapter 12, which contains a description of fixated child molesters.)

It is noteworthy that David has a relatively high level of cognitive functioning; in some states he would not be considered eligible to receive tax-supported services for persons with mental retardation.

Probably David was institutionalized primarily as a result of his child molester behavior; otherwise, he might have been arrested for his offenses if he had remained in the community. Readers may wonder why David was finally placed in a group home located on the same block as an elementary school. Why indeed? Perhaps the original reason for David's institutionalization was overlooked when his community placement was being planned. It is also possible that since eleven years had passed with no further reports of child molester behavior (not surprising in view of the absence of children in his environment), the planners hoped or believed that David was "cured" or had "seen the error of his ways." Whatever the reason, David's placement in the group home again placed him in an environment where children were accessible to him. Since he was unsupervised much of the time (due to his high level of functioning), there were multiple daily opportunities for him to have contact with children apart from visiting the nearby elementary school.

Some may think that David's sexual behavior with children is actually a form of sexual exploration by a man who is developmentally delayed. Proponents of this hypothesis are likely to explain that David's sexual interest in children is occurring because he is too shy to interact with adults. This is an attractive hypothesis because it explains David's behavior on the basis of emotional immaturity and holds out a hope that he will "outgrow" a sexual interest in children in time. The hope is ill founded; David's sexual attraction toward children is likely to be of lifelong duration. If David develops enough confidence in another person to describe his sexual fantasies, he is likely to reveal that he has had frequent sexual fantasies about children since his adolescence. These are likely to be associated with a fantasy of himself as a big-brother figure who befriends, nurtures, and loves a boy who looks up to him and loves him in return. It is far more likely that David will be erotically stimulated by pictures of children than by pictures of attractive adults. Thus, his actual sexual interactions with children (when the opportunity had occurred) are augmented by multiple fantasies of encounters that never took place. David is likely to be shy; he is likely to be emotionally immature; he is likely to be intimidated by other adults. But his sexual interest in children is not likely to reflect a developmental phase of his sexuality or a stepping-stone to a sexual interest in older persons. Instead, it is more likely to reflect a sexual preference that he discovered years before and has acted upon periodically when the opportunity arose.

Treatment Recommendations. David's pattern of sexual offense behavior will require that many limitations be placed on him—to a far greater extent than those associated with his cognitive impairment.

Control. David should never permitted to have unsupervised contact with children. His movements in the community (such as travel from his home to his worksite) must be carefully monitored. Otherwise there is reason to fear that he will find an opportunity to engage another child in sexual behavior. It would be inappropriate to place David in a residence where there were children (for example, a group home supervised by a live-in couple with young children) or in a work placement involving children (for example, a school or day-care setting). Residing or working in less immediate proximity to children also involves some risk (for example, living on the same block as an elementary school or working in a store frequented by children). If David is placed in the latter situations, line-of-sight supervision would be necessary at all times. By contrast, placement in an institution that served adults only would be likely to entail little or no monitoring of David in that setting.

Social Intervention. The sexual abuse of David's 8-year-old victim must be reported to the statutory child protection agency.

Therapy

Medication: There is no evidence to suggest that any FDA-approved psychotropic medication will reduce David's emotional investment and sexual interest in children. Because it is unlikely that he would be considered competent to understand the risks involved, he would not be a candidate to receive a medication such as Depo-Provera, which has not received FDA approval for the treatment of such sexual offense behavior (Berlin 1985).

Behavior modification: Although it may be possible to demonstrate that aversive conditioning (Griffiths, Hingsburger, and Christian 1985) will reduce David's sexual arousal to children (as measured by his penile erectile response in the laboratory when presented with a photograph or drawing of a child), there is no evidence to suggest that aversive conditioning will decrease the risk that he would molest a child whom he encountered in the community.

Psychotherapy: Peer group psychotherapy with other child molesters might increase David's understanding of his problem and help him to recognize and avoid high-risk situations. However, even if he participates in long-term peer group psychotherapy, David is at high risk for reoffending unless he is also assisted by the types of controls described.

Reeducation: David is a candidate for a long-term reeducation program to improve his social skills, especially with regard to conducting meaningful relationships with adults. Although this will not reduce his sexual attraction to children, it may assist him to have more satisfying relationships with other adults. David needs intensive training to help him to meet his needs for affection, support, and affiliation with other adults. This is unlikely to be successful unless programmed over a time frame of at least five years, with frequent opportunities to practice and expand his social and communications skills.

Psychosis (with Recurrent Delusions of Sexual Assault) in Adults with Mental Retardation

This pattern is occasionally seen in adults who are dually diagnosed (mental illness and mental retardation). Although not frequently encountered, persons who manifest this pattern are highly memorable because of the difficulties they present in management.

Benjamin, age 40 years, was dually diagnosed in early adulthood as manifesting a thought disorder (with paranoid features) and moderate mental retardation. In addition to extensive paranoid ideation, Benjamin constantly verbalized his desire to have sexual interactions with persons of all ages, including children, especially with infants and toddlers. He talked incessantly about having anal intercourse with babies and about babies having anal intercourse with him. Benjamin's history included sporadic episodes of fighting with other residents and with staff members. On several occasions, other residents complained that Benjamin had forced them to engage in sexual intercourse with him.

Benjamin was considered to be a behavioral management problem primarily because the staff and other residents found it unpleasant to be in the presence of someone who constantly talked about sexual matters. Various regimens of psychotropic medications had been tried over the years, mostly for the purpose of attempting to reduce his physical aggression toward others. Various behavior modification programs were also used to try to reduce Benjamin's verbal torrent about sexuality and sexual assault. Neither medication nor behavior modification approaches proved to be successful.

Many of Benjamin's caretakers viewed him as an extremely manipulative person who talked incessantly about sexual matters as an attention-getting mechanism and as a method of getting his own way. Others viewed him as a "crazy" person who should be kept isolated from others and avoided contact with him whenever possible.

When Benjamin was independently evaluated in regard to his past history of sexual offense behaviors, he was found to be in an acute psychotic state with frequent visual, auditory, and tactile hallucinations. His speech was characterized by recurrent sexual fantasies and delusions. Benjamin was started on a trial of psychotropic medication aimed at reducing the frequency of his hallucinations and delusions. After six months of medication adjustment under careful psychiatric supervision, Benjamin manifested no hallucinations or delusional thinking. The sexualized content of his speech was greatly reduced, and he no longer talked about sexual assault or sexual relations with others. A long-awaited community placement in a group home was finally realized for Benjamin.

Comment. This case example of a man who was receiving inadequate psychotropic medication for a diagnosed thought disorder is instructive because it illustrates how peoples' emotional reaction to the sexual content of Benjamin's delusions interfered with their capacity to treat him. Although there was ample evidence that Benjamin had been both physically and sexually assaultive on occasion, his behavior did not appear to be that of a habitual sexual offender. However, his continued talking about sexual assault was understandably disturbing to those in his environment. Repeated behavioral interventions were not successful in reducing Benjamin's intrusive fantasies (and his verbal descriptions of them). Psychotropic medication was tried but without the benefit of careful psychiatric supervision based on information supplied by trained observers familiar with dealing with psychotic patients. As well, reduction of delusional ideation could not be used as a goal of the psychotropic medication regimen when some of Benjamin's caretakers regarded his delusional speech as an attempt to manipulate them.

Approximately two-thirds of patients who have an untreated thought disorder will be helped by some regimen of psychotropic medication; they will experience a decrease of their hallucinations and delusional ideation. When most of the content of the delusional ideation is sexual in nature, a decrease of the patient's verbal reports of her or his delusions is usually welcomed by the staff and other residents. Unfortunately professionals in the field of mental retardation are more accustomed to working with persons who receive psychotropic medication for the purpose of controlling acting-out behaviors rather than treatment of thought disorders. Accordingly, adults with mental retardation who manifest psychotic thinking about sexual assault or sexuality are more likely to be viewed as potential sexual offenders than as persons who are mentally ill.

Treatment Recommendations. A careful psychiatric evaluation must accompany the evaluation for sexual offense behavior. If an untreated or partially treated thought disorder is diagnosed, this should be treated first. Before deciding that the person is a sexual offender, she or he should be observed for a minimum of six to twelve months after the psychotropic medication has been adjusted to provide optimal treatment of the thought disorder.

Control. Benjamin should be monitored carefully at all times for self-injurious or aggressive behavior. He should not be permitted to have unsupervised contact with vulnerable persons unless or until his thought disorder is stabilized and he is no longer considered to be dangerous to others.

Social Intervention. If Benjamin has abused a member of a vulnerable population, the suspected abuse must be reported to the appropriate civil protective authority.

Therapy

Medication: Antipsychotic medication should be prescribed with careful psychiatric supervision, with the goal of reducing the frequency of Benjamin's hallucinations and delusions and restoring his capacity to live in the real world. Every effort should be made to avoid or minimize the risk of harmful side effects of the medication regimen. However, Benjamin should be given the opportunity to have his psychosis treated as well as is possible with antipsychotic drugs.

Behavior modification and psychotherapy: It will be unclear how much (if any) behavior modification or psychotherapy will be indicated until the optimal medication regimen for Benjamin is discovered and maintained.

Reeducation: It is highly likely that Benjamin's incompletely treated thought disorder has interfered with his capacity to learn and practice social skills and work skills. He should be reevaluated when his thought disorder has been stabilized and appropriate reeducation interventions can be planned at that time.

Sexually Promiscuous Adults with Mental Retardation

Some adults with mental retardation exhibit a high degree of interest in sexual interactions. Often they initiate sexual behavior with others in their residences or worksites or in the community. The sexual advances made by these men and women may be welcomed, tolerated, or experienced as intrusive by those in their environment.

> Betty, a 25-year-old woman with mild mental retardation, was constantly flirting with and clinging to several male staff members and two of the higher-functioning male residents in the group home. Most of her fellow residents avoided her, and she had no real friends, male or female. Betty talked constantly about dating and previous boyfriends. A year before, she had been sexually assaulted while on a date. Betty was referred for a psychosexual evaluation in the hopes that "sexual counseling" would be helpful for her.

Comment. Although the case example does not actually describe sexual offense behavior, Betty should receive a careful evaluation with regard to two issues: her possible offender status and her possible victim status. If Betty was an adult male (instead of an adult female) with mental retardation and was making sexual advances to female residents and female staff to the same degree as portrayed in the case example, the pattern described might well be viewed as sexual offense behavior and considered to be dangerous rather than annoying.

The other possibility should not be overlooked. Betty reported sexual assault of the date-rape type one year ago. There is also a strong possibility that she may have been sexually abused in childhood. Either situation could well be associated with unresolved emotional trauma resulting from sexual abuse. It is also possible that Betty may be reacting to present-day sexual victimizations (by a family member, staff person, fellow worker, or the like). Although it is not an invariable consequence, some females react to sexual victimization by becoming sexually promiscuous. It is speculated that their sexual promiscuity helps them to overcome the feelings of powerlessness and loss of control that they experienced during the sexual abuse; now, by initiating multiple sexual relationships, *they* are in charge, *they* feel in control, and so on.

Since Betty is described as a person with mild mental retardation, it is likely that her verbal capacity is high enough to make it feasible to perform nonleading interviewing with her and to explore all of the possibilities. It is possible that she will not reveal any recent or past episodes of sexual abuse, perhaps because none have occurred or perhaps because she is embarrassed or afraid to disclose right away. If the latter is true, she may report undisclosed abuse later.

It will be important to try to ascertain what Betty is looking for or wishing will occur when she initiates sexual behaviors with others. Is she seeking sexual gratification only? Is she looking for closeness, affection, affiliation, or intimacy? What are her fantasies before, during, and after she engages in sexual behavior? Does she have a favorite movie or television star? If so, can she imagine what an intimate relationship with that person would be like? If she could choose to have an intimate relationship with anyone in the world, who would it be, and what does she wish would occur? Obviously an evaluator needs to establish a trust relationship with Betty in order to elicit many answers to these questions. And Betty's level of cognitive functioning coupled with her expressive capacity will strongly influence her responses. However, if she is able to share her wishes and fantasies, the evaluator will be likely to discover that Betty is wishing for affection and intimacy, as well as sexual gratification. It is also likely that Betty flirts and makes sexual advances to others in a patterned and stylized fashion in part to conceal her anxiety, fear of rejection, and lack of social skills.

Treatment Recommendations

Control. It is unlikely that a psychosexual evaluation will elicit information that identifies Betty as a sexual offender. There will be little or no need for controls beyond the requirement that she conform to the rules for appropriate social behavior at home and at the worksite.

Social Intervention. If it is suspected that Betty is a victim of past or present sexual abuse, a report to the civil protective agency will be required.

Therapy

> Medication: Not indicated.
>
> Behavior modification: Not indicated.
>
> Psychotherapy: If Betty is a victim of sexual abuse, she may benefit from peer group therapy with other women to address victimization issues. (This will also depend on her cognitive and expressive capacities.) One-on-one sexual counseling is not indicated.
>
> Reeducation: Betty is a candidate for intensive social and communications skills training. This would be most effective if done in a peer group setting. To be helpful, it must be provided frequently (several times per week) over a period of two or three years. Betty and the others will need repeated opportunities to practice the skills in a safe and guided setting.

Summary

This chapter has presented a framework for evaluation and treatment of sexual offense behavior in adults with mental retardation. Because this field is in its infancy, present-day treatment emphasizes control and social intervention. For adults with mental retardation, reeducation is emphasized to a greater degree than therapy with regard to treatment of sexual offense behavior. Only by sharing information and expanding our pool of experience can more sophisticated and satisfactory treatment interventions be evolved.

References

Berlin, Fred. 1985. "Pedophilia." *Medical Aspects of Human Sexuality* 19:79–88.

Cage, Richard. 1988. "Criminal Investigation of Child Sexual Abuse." In S.M. Sgroi, ed., *Vulnerable Populations,* 1:187–227 Lexington, Mass.: Lexington Books.

DeLipsey, Jan, and James, Sue. 1988. "Videotaping the Sexually Abused Child: The Texas Experience, 1983–1987." In S.M. Sgroi, ed., *Vulnerable Populations,* 1:228–264. Lexington, Mass.: Lexington Books.

Griffiths, Dorothy; Hingsburger, David; and Christian, Ronald. 1985. "Treating Developmentally Handicapped Sexual Offenders: The York Behavior Management Services Treatment Program." *Psychiatric Aspects of Mental Retardation Reviews* 4:49–52.

Groth, A. Nicholas. 1982. In S.M. Sgroi, ed., *Handbook of Clinical Intervention in Child Sexual Abuse,* 215–216. Lexington, Mass.: Lexington Books.

Groth, A. Nicholas; with Burgess, Ann W.; Birnbaum, H. Jean; and Gary, Thomas S. 1978. "A Study of the Child Molester: Myths and Realities." *LAE Journal of the American Criminal Justice Association* 41:17–22.

Groth, A. Nicholas, with Birnbaum, H. Jean. 1979. *Men Who Rape: The Psychology of the Offender.* New York: Plenum Press.

Groth, A. Nicholas, with Stevenson, Thomas. 1984. *Anatomical Drawings for Use in the Investigation and Intervention of Child Sexual Abuse.* Newton Center, Mass.: Forensic Mental Health Associates.

Sgroi, Suzanne, with Porter, Frances, and Blick, Linda. 1982. "Validation of Child Sexual Abuse." In S.M. Sgroi, ed., *Handbook of Clinical Intervention in Child Sexual Abuse,* 39–79. Lexington, Mass.: Lexington Books.

11
The Chesapeake Institute

Linda Canfield Blick
Thomas S. Berg

The Chesapeake Institute is a private, not-for-profit program solely devoted to the study and treatment of child sexual abuse. It is located in Montgomery County, Maryland, a 496-square-mile, predominantly suburban area, directly north of and adjacent to the District of Columbia and approximately 40 miles southwest of Baltimore.

The Chesapeake Institute is geographically located in a tristate area and serves clients from Maryland, Virginia, and Washington, D.C. Founded by Linda Canfield Blick, LCSW, codirected by Thomas Berg, and incorporated in March 1982, the initial design for the program came as a result of professionals discussing a spectrum of needs. Advice and guidance came from Judith Server, LCSW, attorney Edwin O. Wenck, and attorney David Lloyd, all specialists in the field of child sexual abuse.

In 1982, there were no local facilities that treated child victims, juvenile and adult offenders, and adults molested as children in the same program. Government agencies' directives limited, compartmentalized, and separated the treatment of these interconnected populations. This compartmentalization led to skewed perspectives of each of the three populations. It is necessary to address identification, diagnosis, investigation, disposition, and treatment of cases in a coordinated fashion. Child and adult victims and juvenile and adult offenders need to be studied psychologically, legally, socially, and behaviorally.

The Chesapeake Institute was also developed to provide continuity and stability for the clients and staff. Nearly all of the originally developed child sexual abuse programs were funded by the federal government through the National Center on Child Abuse and Neglect (NCCAN). Grant funds fluctuate yearly based on budgetary changes. Entire programs that had been helpful, necessary, and well run were nevertheless closed because of budget cuts. This left clients abandoned once again and professional staff in a state of flux with regard to employment and career development.

The Chesapeake Institute is one example of a private alternative to this problem. Private programs have the ability to grow and expand rapidly, a necessary feature when their work addresses a pioneering field. Most bureaucracies have burdensome policies that either inhibit timely responsive changes or limit growth due to lack of funds to hire staff even as the demand for services soars. Additionally, the institute provides private sector representation to advocate for improved services for child sexual abuse clients.

Philosophical Orientation

Two vital aspects to The Chesapeake Institute's treatment philosophy are the importance of maintaining a comprehensive treatment program while always working from a "best interest of the child" perspective. A comprehensive treatment program provides evaluative and psychotherapeutic services to all individuals affected by child sexual victimization: intrafamilial and extrafamilial from young child victims to adults molested as children, from adolescent offenders to adult offenders, from siblings and parents of victims to spouses of abusers, from abusers with few victims to chronic pedophiles with large numbers of victims, male and female.

Professional staff of The Chesapeake Institute find that working with such a wide variety of situations and clients across the entire spectrum of child sexual victimization and within a program housed in one facility broadens their knowledge base and markedly increases their effectiveness. The staff members are aware, through direct personal contact, of the obvious and the more subtle difficulties experienced by a child who has been sexually abused. This enables them to assist parents to understand and support their children. The same staff members also understand the dynamics, motivations, and behaviors of offenders and because of their wider perceptions of the sexual abuse scenario, are better able to help both child and adult victims. Many other examples abound. The point is that awareness of the whole puzzle increases a clinician's overall effectiveness; lack of awareness decreases effectiveness.

The second philosophical cornerstone to the institute's approach is that, due to the nature of this work, therapists must serve a dual advocacy role: as advocates for the children with whom they work directly and for the entire community of children. Their obligation is to advocate that a child is not placed in a situation where abuse may reoccur. It is also their responsibility to ensure that a child is emotionally prepared for changes in family structure (such as family reunification) and that all family members are equally prepared to function in ways that will support the child and strengthen family life. Other professionals and agencies are usually involved, but as advocates for the child, The Chesapeake Institute staff base decisions and recommendations foremost on what is in the child's best interest. Good clinical decisions for the child and the family follow such considerations. Each individual and family situation is assessed carefully. A treatment plan is then developed and carried out based on the unique needs of each individual and family.

Equally important is our obligation to the community and to society. It would be irresponsible to neglect to consider the children who might become future victims by the offenders in treatment today. However, as clinicians, we also must develop appropriate supportive and therapeutic relationships with clients who have abused children. In response to what may appear to be a conflict of interest, staff of the Chesapeake Institute adhere to a victim's perspective approach to therapy with offenders. This approach allows staff to recommend incarceration when this is the only option to protect children yet allows for recommendations of probation and outpatient treatment when an offender is considered amenable to treatment in the community.

Incarceration is recommended as a protection measure to prevent the offender from further victimizing children and for their own safety. It is not a caring act to allow an individual to continue destructive behavior.

Thus, a therapist working with an offender can create a relationship in which empathy and understanding for the client's pain, confusion, and anger can be conveyed, while never losing sight of the offender's responsibility for sexually abusive behavior that must be the focus of therapy. The Chesapeake Institute staff members working with offenders encourage and direct therapeutic focus on the abusive behavior and related issues within an atmosphere that makes open discussion and disclosure possible because of the concern for the client's pain, which is also being communicated.

Clinical Program Description

Clinical Evaluations

When any client is initially referred or is self-referred for psychotherapeutic treatment, an evaluation and assessment process is initiated that lasts approximately five sessions for adults and may continue for as long as ten sessions for children. There are a number of reasons why evaluations are so lengthy. It is found universally that trust is a major issue; children who have been sexually victimized have little reason to trust anyone, much less another new person in their lives. Therefore, attempting to evaluate the extent of the sexual abuse experienced by the child and how that has affected him or her without first taking the time to develop rapport and trust is not only clinically unsound but also may be retraumatizing to the child.

Adults who have sexually abused children, nonabusing parents of sexually abused children, and adults who were molested as children bring similar difficulties concerning trust to their evaluations and therapy. Again, it is unreasonable to expect that they will quickly reveal and discuss events and issues that may be painful, frightening, and embarrassing and that they may never have discussed before. Only time and work with a skilled and experienced therapist will allow and encourage the development of trust and facilitate the process of disclosure. Evaluations may be more than incomplete without the comprehensive detail and understanding that comes during this extensive process. Brief and superficial evaluations may actually be misleading, and recommendations based on such evaluations may be counterproductive or even destructive.

Offender Evaluation

The Chesapeake Institute has developed strict guidelines for evaluating offenders, both juvenile and adult. Before beginning an evaluation, the following information must be provided:

1. A police report of the recent arrest and any prior arrests.
2. A victim's statement or account of the abuse.
3. Signed releases of information and signed waivers of confidentiality.
4. Copies of any available psychological or psychiatric reports.
5. Copies of pertinent medical reports.
6. Information on school performance (for juveniles) or work history (for adults).
7. Criminal record checks—local, state, national (Groth 1982, 236–237). Sexual offenders often lie about or conceal past and current offenses, and collecting as much outside data as possible will help to determine when the offender is misstating, rationalizing, or minimizing. A complete account of the victim's statement is especially useful. Victims of sexual abuse are often much more reliable reporters of these events than offenders. If the victim's account is inaccurate, it is usually that all incidents or details of their sexual victimization are not reported, often because of loyalty to the offender, their own embarrassment, or repressed memories. Other information, such as employment, military service, and criminal history, as well as results of psychological testing, is needed because it may be helpful in determining the offender's amenability to treatment and assist in formulating recommendations for disposition.

The Chesapeake Institute does not accept offenders for evaluation who have used extreme force, weapons, or violent, bizarre, or ritualistic behavior in the commission of their sexual crimes with children. By virtue of their actions, such individuals are unsafe to be treated on an outpatient basis and should not remain in the community. We are also aware that predominant among The Chesapeake Institute's daily client population are many adults and children who are vulnerable and for whom a safe environment must be maintained in our office. When time permits, The Chesapeake Institute has done and is willing to evaluate dangerous offenders at detention facilities, where all parties' safety can be ensured.

Following all evaluations, clinical impressions and recommendations for disposition and/or therapy are discussed with the client. All evaluation reports are written in a manner that can be understood by clients and are first shared with the client before being released to the appropriate courts, agencies, attorneys, and others. This alleviates any suspicion that we are reporting without the client's knowledge and thereby increases trust. This procedure also allows the client the opportunity to write an addendum to our reports and identify areas of disagreement with the findings or recommendations. These comments are attached and sent with The Chesapeake Institute reports, labeled clearly as the client's response and without comment. This procedure models appropriate forms of communication and assertive behavior. Additionally, judges have responded positively, commenting on "readable reports," openness, and honesty with clients.

Psychotherapy

Therapy at The Chesapeake Institute is generally long term, ranging from six months to four years or more. The average lengths of therapy are as follows:

Adult sexual offenders against children, three to five years

Adolescent sexual offender, one to two years

Child victims of sexual abuse by strangers or distant acquaintances, six to twelve months

Child victims of sexual abuse by family members or close acquaintances (varies based on age of child), one to three years

Adults molested as children, one to three years

Incest families, two to five years

Nonoffending spouses or mothers of victims, six months to three years

Therapy for each of these different groups of clients takes different paths, depending on the age of the client, the support and understanding available from parents, the behavioral patterns and functioning of the offender, and the complexity and functional level of the family, which encompasses parenting skills, financial stability, emotional strengths, and the like.

Treatment for Children

Victims of sexual abuse by nonfamily members and distant acquaintances often resolve their emotional difficulties and complete therapy within six to nine months, especially when their parents are supportive and cooperative. Since the child was not abused by someone who was emotionally close and in whom the child invested a major amount of trust, he or she usually experiences less confusion, self-blame, and guilt. These feelings can be dealt with in therapy and be resolved more quickly than if the abuser had been someone closer to the child. However, there are cases when parents are nonsupportive or overly negative and blaming of the child for the victimization experience or situations when the child had in fact developed a very close relationship with the abuser. Both scenarios are likely to result in greater trauma to the child, which intensifies and lengthens the course of treatment. Children who have been subjected to death threats (toward themselves or loved ones) are likely to suffer severe psychological trauma and require more extensive treatment also.

Therapy with young children focuses on play or art therapy, with discussions of the abuse, attendant feelings and cognitive distortions. Education and sexual abuse avoidance training are interspersed during sessions. Children will act out themes of fear, anger, sexual confusion, and protection in their play. These themes assist the therapist to understand the impact of the abuse and its meaning to the child. The therapist then helps the child to resolve those feelings by facilitating further play and developing positive variations on the themes presented. Over time, the child will begin to act out more positive themes and also develop positive endings to victimization themes expressed through play earlier in therapy.

It is extremely important to discuss the sexual abuse incidents more than once and in detail with children during the course of therapy. Even a very young child can speak about what happened and how he or she felt while the abuse was occurring. Children, whether quite young or adolescent, must learn that the therapist and other significant people in their lives believe that the abuse occurred. They need to hear that others do not blame them for what happened, are not disgusted by what occurred, and can withstand hearing about what a child may believe no one wishes to hear. These goals can be accomplished only by talking about what happened with the child. In many cases the therapist must attempt to direct treatment toward such discussions rather than waiting for the child to do so. The child's reactions to such attempts must be carefully monitored so that he or she is not pushed too quickly to discuss material that is threatening or frightening; to do so may cause harm by disrupting critical defense mechanisms.

Parents of these children are encouraged to become better observers of their child's behavior by filling out behavioral checklists developed for their child's age and developmental category (Blick 1982). They also become active participants in the treatment team. Parents are helped and encouraged to talk about the sexual abuse with the children, to answer their questions, to help them to learn about sexual abuse avoidance (through books, videotapes, and demonstrations), and to share with the therapists any new information or behaviors that may have surfaced or changed during the time between sessions.

Treatment For Adult Offenders

It is important to complete a thorough evaluation and assessment of offenders prior to beginning actual treatment. Determination should be made whether the client is an offender who has a primary sexual orientation toward adults—sometimes characterized as a "regressed offender" (Groth 1982, 216–218)—or as a situational offender (Lanning 1986) or a chronic pedophile with a more generalized and chronic attraction to children—sometimes characterized as a "fixated offender" (Groth 1982, 215—216) or preferential offender (Lanning 1986). Regressed offenders are more likely to abuse children within the family. We also assess the level of the offender's willingness or ability to acknowledge and accept responsibility for the abuse, the offender's motivation for ongoing treatment, the offender's capacity to understand the impact of the abuse on the victim, and the risk factors if outpatient treatment is undertaken.

Clients who deny allegations of child sexual abuse are offered a five-session evaluation. If, at the conclusion of the evaluation, the offender continues to deny the allegations, he or she is not accepted into The Chesapeake Institute's treatment program. We explain that our purpose is to provide help for actual child sexual abuse problems, and any client who does not believe her or she has such a problem is referred back to the court or to another clinician. The denial of the allegation is viewed by The Chesapeake Institute Staff as a legal matter, which should then be handled in the criminal justice system, since The Chesapeake Institute's purpose is to treat abusers, victims, or family members in cases of child sexual abuse.

Years ago, Linda Blick worked as the director of a child sexual abuse program for the Montgomery County Department of Social Services. Because it is a government agency, judges were able to order clients into treatment with it. Numerous denying offenders who were ordered to receive treatment in this way continued to deny their abusive behavior in therapy. The therapists worked with the offenders on other problem areas. Unfortunately, ignoring sexual offense issues does not resolve sexual offense behavior. Most of the offenders who fit into this category reoffended while in treatment. As a result of this experience, The Chesapeake Institute does not offer treatment to alleged abusers who deny that they committed sexual offense behavior.

Incest Offenders

We expect that treatment of incest offenders (who in our client population have been predominantly fathers and stepfathers) will progress through a series of identifiable phases that overlap to some degree. The term *incest offender* will be used for the sake of manageable reading. An incest offender can fit into a diagnostic continuum and could be a rapist, chronic pedophile who abuses children inside or outside the family, or someone who primarily targets his own children for sexual abuse. Progression in treatment can be identified by the predominant attitudes, issues, and growth associated with each phase. However, feelings, issues, and behaviors consistent with each phase may surface at a variety of times during the course of treatment.

Crisis Phase. Most incest offenders experience the disclosure of their behavior and the aftermath of such disclosure as highly stressful and frightening events. All offenders realize prior to being discovered that what they are doing is wrong, and disclosure brings to reality the enormity of their problems. Probable arrest, possible incarceration, public humiliation, loss of family, and loss of job are just a few of the immediate concerns precipitated by disclosure of the abuse. The crisis phase varies in length but usually lasts for weeks and is cyclical around critical events such as court hearings, unsupervised visits, and family reunifications.

Reactions to the crisis vary. Some type of denial is usually present, sometimes in the form of outright denial of all allegations, sometimes in partial denial of some allegations, sometimes in the form of admitting to the sexual abuse behavior but denying that the behavior was wrong or harmful. Other reactions include clinical depression, suicidal thoughts, suicide attempts, and overt or covert actions to manipulate therapists, the legal justice system, or the family.

During this phase, we use a careful combination of support and confrontation to help move the client through the crisis and assist him or her in coping. The therapist-evaluator provides support through direct questioning, clarification, honesty, understanding, and empathy. What is communicated is an acceptance of the individual but not of the behavior. Most offenders are surprised and relieved to discover that their therapists-evaluators do not treat them as ogres or monsters. This atmosphere of acceptance enables some offenders to acknowledge their sexually abusive behavior more fully. During the evaluation and initial phase of treatment, the offender is removed from the home for the safety of the children and to assist in reducing stress for all family members, as well as minimize the risk of reabuse. The Chesapeake Institute policy is that offenders must be out of the home, or they are not accepted for evaluation or treatment.

A client buddy, (Giaretto 1982, 21–32) can be assigned who provides immediate support and reduces potential suicidal risk. The client buddy can provide additional support by explaining the court process soon to be faced, by sharing his own feelings and reactions when he was experiencing the crisis phase, and by modeling that with honesty and hard work, things can get better. Many offenders will also diminish their denial after such discussions, sometimes disclosing abuse that was not even reported by the victim(s).

The term *voluntary referral* is solely used for clients who are not referred by the authorities. It is important to explore this because most such referrals are precipitated by a family member who threatens to report, get a divorce, or the like.

Narcissistic Guilt Phase. As an offender inevitably moves past the crisis stage and begins to accept more responsibility for the abuse, he will express what may appear to be sincere remorse for his behavior and concern for the victim and family; however, this is not true remorse or empathy. If the offender were capable of true empathy, he would not have engaged in sexual behavior with a child in order to meet his own needs.

What is actually being expressed in the narcissistic guilt phase are self-centered concerns (in many cases, understandable concerns) as to how the abuse and its disclosure will affect him "I know I was wrong; I never should have done what I did to my daughter," should be interpreted by the therapist as, "I feel badly about this because now my life is a mess, and I may go to jail." "I know what I did was wrong, and I've hurt my wife and family terribly," should be interpreted as, "I'm afraid they may not want me anymore, and I might lose my family." It is the therapist's task to focus on the underlying meaning of the client's concerns, empathizing with the pain and fear associated with this phase. It will require the development of trust within a long-term therapeutic relationship for the client to move beyond the narcissistic guilt phase.

Any major shift out of this self-centered phase takes an average of one year or more of intensive therapy. Emphasis during this phase should be on continued discussion of the abuse. Eliciting and clarifying details from the offender such as exactly what was said and done during the abuse, recollection of the child's reactions, exploration of the child's feelings, and describing his own fantasies before, during, and after the abuse should be discussed. In this way the offender's distortions can be challenged, and any genuine guilt can be amplified, encouraged, and built upon.

Police and social service reports of the offender's abuse of the child can serve to emphasize and highlight important aspects of the abuse from the child's perspective. Offenders should receive education about abuse through films such as *Incest, the Victim Nobody Believes* and books such as Katherine Brady's *Father's Days* and may participate in self-help and support groups such as Parents United/Adults Molested as Children United. During this phase of treatment, many other life issues will arise. They should not be ignored because they provide opportunities for the offender to develop greater self-awareness and insight, to learn new ways of coping with stress or adversity, to develop problem-solving skills, and to strengthen and deepen the therapeutic relationship.

Empathic Guilt Phase. As understanding of the potential impact of sexual abuse grows, along with a greater ability to explore and cope with the problems of living, so will the capacity for empathy with others. The offender will begin to demonstrate the ability truly to understand and empathize with his victim, his wife, and his family. With this growing empathy will come a greater ability to assess the needs of his victim and family and to assume more appropriate responsibility as a parent and a husband.

A much deeper feeling and more congruent expression of guilt, pain, and sadness also begin to surface. The development of greater empathy and the capacity to take responsibility bring greater awareness of the consequences and impact of past behavior. These feelings should be encouraged and focused upon as they arise.

It is normal at his point for the therapist to want to alleviate the pain associated with the client's increased awareness of the impact of his sexually abusive behavior. He must, however, be allowed and helped to experience these emotions deeply for two important reasons. First, these are the types of feelings that he has been too frightened to experience for most of his life. His fear of emotional pain and loneliness may have led him to dissociate himself from his own feelings and those of others. As he repeatedly confronts his fear and pain in therapy, he learns that he can face the feelings, experience them, survive, and recover. He grows in ability to be aware of and use his own feelings, especially as his feelings of self-esteem and self-worth are increased. Second, it is exactly the ability to experience true remorse, guilt, and empathy that most reduces the risk of further abuse.

During the empathic guilt phase, the focus of therapy is on greater awareness and expression of feelings of guilt associated with the abuse, development of further understanding and responsibility taking, and, finally, further development of self-esteem and self-worth.

Integration Phase. As the feelings of understanding and empathy that were encouraged during the previous stage take root, clients will begin more fully to integrate these new skills and discoveries into their daily lives. With help from his therapist, the offender will develop new patterns of behavior and relating to others in many areas of his life: at work, especially with authority figures; in the development of new friendships; and in intimate relationships, whether with his wife or in a new relationship.

Another indication of movement into this integration phase is the offender's ability to see now that there were warning signs prior to committing the abuse that could have alerted him to his stress and emotional difficulties. During the integration phase of his therapy, he must now develop a list of his personal warning signs, along with a healthy and positive plan for how to address and cope with the problems they signal.

During this phase offenders who were themselves sexually abused as children begin the major portion of therapeutic work on this issue. Although some work is done previously, it is unrealistic, and usually unhelpful, to direct therapy toward the offender's own victimization prior to this time. The reasons for this position are both practical and clinical.

First, at the initiation of therapy following disclosure of sexual abuse, an offending parent's first obligation is to attempt to become an appropriate parent and adult, a goal that becomes self-evident when the child's best interest in the major consideration. Hence the emphasis during the early stages in treatment on the development of empathy and attending to the impact of his behavior on all family members. Second, experience has shown that the feelings of shame, embarrassment, and guilt associated with being discovered in sexually abusing a child are less emotionally threatening to address and confront than are the lifelong feelings and self-doubts resultant from being sexually abused as a child and keeping it secret for so many years. An individual may be forced to deal with his abusive behavior because he was actually caught, but he is usually unprepared emotionally to address his own abuse when beginning therapy.

Treatment for the Nonoffending Spouse

The nonoffending spouse (referred to in this section as the mother although abusers and nonoffending parents are from both genders) may not have been aware of the sexual abuse of her child, or her level of awareness may fit anywhere along a continuum that ends with mothers who actively colluded in the child's abuse. Dissociation may play an important role in the life of mothers who were abused as children and who report no knowledge of their own child's abuse. In any case, it is the mother's ability following public disclosure to respond to her child and demonstrate support, belief, understanding, and appropriate parenting thereafter that is the real key to her child's recovery. The mother's response is also a central factor in assessing the child's safety should the family desire to reunite.

Early assessment of the mother in an incestuous family focuses on her capacity to believe that the abuse occurred, the level of blame she directs at her child, and her ability to protect her child. Beyond assessment, the initial goals of treatment are to help her understand what her child has experienced, to help her learn appropriately to parent a child who may manifest behavioral and emotional problems as a result of having been abused, and to provide support as she tries to navigate the storm of far-reaching effects of a disclosure of sexual abuse.

These are all vital aspects related to her child's and her family's recovery, yet because mothers in incestuous families are often the most difficult of family members to engage in treatment, accomplishing these goals can be agonizingly frustrating.

The following points are helpful to keep in mind when working with mothers and will help in maintaining patience while developing a working relationship:

1. A mother's initial reactions may not be what is expected, by they are usually very normal reactions to a crisis situation and should be understood in this way. A disclosure of child abuse creates a crisis for different reasons in each individual of the incestuous family. She may be angry at the system or at the therapist, and she may employ one or more forms of denial. These should be viewed as attempts to keep her emotions and being intact (holding back the tide so the dam does not burst) and can be responded to with understanding, concern, and practical support. As she begins to accept the reality of her family life and her situation, her initial coping mechanisms should drop away, and depression may begin to set in. Crisis phases last four to six weeks and involve shock, denial, anger, grief, and depression.

2. Underlying their immediate presentation, most mothers feel tremendously guilty and responsible for the abuse and believe others hold the same opinion. (This is true whether or not they were aware of the abuse before public disclosure.) Often their thoughts are, "If I had been a better mother . . ." or "I must not have been the wife he needed." Sometimes this guilt takes a year or longer to surface. A mother's need to hide from that sense of guilt, and especially her fears that others blame her, creates a tremendous obstacle to developing an open, trusting therapeutic relationship.

3. There is an intergenerational pattern to child sexual abuse; many mothers were themselves sexually abused as children. Ironically, rather than increasing her awareness and understanding of the harm her child has experienced, a personal history of childhood sexual abuse often makes it even more difficult for a mother to understand and accept her child's

victimization. Few of the mothers who were sexually abused as children were afforded the opportunity to deal with their abuse in a straightforward manner because sexual abuse treatment programs did not exist when they were young. These mothers usually maintain the secret of their own abuse well beyond the initial stages of therapy following their child's disclosure. In order for mothers who themselves were sexually abused to acknowledge the fear, shame, confusion, pain, or sadness their children experience, they must force themselves to acknowledge their own similar feelings. They were not able or helped to do so in the past and, like offenders who were also abused as children, they have not chosen to enter therapy for themselves. Many mothers are court ordered into evaluations and treatment by juvenile court petitions. Often this is the only technique that ensures their initial cooperation.

Mothers in most incestuous families present in therapy with a history of focusing on their social roles in life—as somebody's mother, wife, or child and possibly as a PTA member or church group participant—giving little attention to their own needs, desires, and goals. While the early phases of treatment with a mother must focus on how she helps and protects her child and how she may develop a healthier relationship with her children, the long-term goals are much different.

These goals center on helping mothers better understand themselves as individuals. They must begin to see that they have been influenced by their past. As mothers become successful in treatment, they become more aware of their own needs and explore positive ways to fulfill those needs. They also become aware that they have, and deserve, options in their lives: who they choose to live with or remain married to; how they will relate to their children and other family members; if they choose to have a career inside or outside the home; and how they will cope with all the varied problems of day-to-day living.

Family Therapy and the Reunification Process with Incest Families

Many families enter treatment at The Chesapeake Institute predetermined to survive intact as a unified family. Others are undecided as to their family goals, and still others have clearly decided to separate.

When providing therapy and case management to families in which parent-child sexual abuse has occurred and who are undecided or who wish to reunite following the disclosure, the emotional and physical reunification of the family is viewed as a long, arduous decision-making process. It is a process that should always first be predicated upon both the physical and emotional safety of the child(ren). As treatment progresses and that safety is ensured, the decision to reunite or permanently separate is one that rightly belongs to the family rather than to the agencies and professionals involved. How such reunification takes place is a treatment and safety concern that must, however, be handled with sensitivity and caution.

The decision to reunite during the early stages of treatment—following disclosure and beginning therapy—is not a static one that must remain as if carved in stone. As the parents, particularly the nonoffending spouse, increase their understanding and emotional strength, the initial decision to reunite should and does endure hard and close scrutiny. Under the intense emotional stress and pressure that accompanies initial disclosure, most people understandably are not capable of thoroughly examining their own feelings, needs, options, and concerns. However, with time, support, and guidance, questions will begin to arise in the wife's mind. "Can I ever really trust him again?" "How could I have not known?" "Will we ever be able to make love again without mental pictures of the abuse entering my mind?" "Do I really want to accept so little closeness and communication in my marriage?"

For therapy to be successful, all family members must feel free to express whatever doubts, anxieties, angers, fears, or other feelings they may have without undue concern that expressing these feelings will stop the process of therapy. That expression is the process, and without a safe arena in which to address those feelings, informed and useful decisions about reunification cannot be made.

A careful, well-planned, step-by-step process of therapy and visitation is most productive in helping family members make informed decisions and progress in therapy. Such a program allows all individual family members a sense of safety and control as changes in contact, visitation, and therapy are made in a thoughtful and cautious manner. Flexibility is also built in; these changes are the result of observable progress and the express participation by family members. No specific timetable based on arbitrary time limits is used to force decisions. Families and individuals advance at their own pace, based on clinical assessment of observable progress.

Following is an outline of the step-by-step reunification process in use at The Chesapeake Institute, with a brief clinical rationale for each step. For convenience, the outline will refer to father-daughter sexual abuse. However, the information is equally applicable whether the offender is male of female, a natural parent or a step-parent, and whether the child is male or female.

Step 1: The offender lives out of the family home, with court-ordered "no contact" (physical, verbal, and visual) with the children. No visitation between the offender and any child in the family should take place during an initial five-week assessment period.

The family's natural tendency is toward homeostasis, that is, an attempt to restore the family to types of functioning similar to, if not exactly the same as, the old familiar patterns of relating and living. Creating strong, artificial boundaries and limits, necessarily controlled by forces outside the family (the courts, child protective services, and the therapists), initiates the process of helping the family learn new dynamics of interaction, communication, and personal boundaries. This is true whether the family ultimately reunites or permanently separates.

Having the offender live outside the family home provides a safe environment for the victim, minimizing the risk of reabuse and the potential for recanting or minimizing by the victim due to pressure from the offender. The nonoffending spouse, usually the mother, has an opportunity to begin viewing herself separately from the offender, thus decreasing the strength of her emotional alignment with the offending father, to her child's detriment. No contact between the victim and offender facilitates the assessment of the child's ability to demonstrate and/or articulate feelings (both positive and negative) concerning the offender, the abuse, the level of self-blame, and her relationship with her mother.

The father has already demonstrated his lack of control. Forced separation from the family provides the distance and control he may not otherwise maintain. At the same time, his strong desire to return home to the environment in which he is most comfortable is a powerful motivating force to pursue and actively work in therapy. Siblings are included in this moratorium in order to avoid further stigmatization and isolation of the victim, as well as to provide for their own safety.

The power of the family's drive "to get back together and be a normal family" is often an accurate diagnostic measure of the family's level of enmeshment, boundlessness, and minimization. Incestuous families have some level of ability to ignore or minimize immediate and diverse concerns such as the risk of reabuse, the injury done to the victim(s), other family members, and the marital relationship, and the seriousness with which society regards such behaviour. An assessment of that need to do so can be a useful indication of family dynamics and their initial ability to trust and utilize the advice and guidance of professionals.

Step 2: All family members attend regularly scheduled (weekly or biweekly) family visits at child protective services, supervised by a CPS worker or professional trained in child sexual abuse and child development.

Assessment of family members should take place on an individual basis. Little or no purpose is served by seeing the whole family together at this time and could be quite destructive to a child whose father is observably distraught and/or who is not yet able to assume appropriate responsibility for his behavior. If the child clearly does not want to see the father, visitation should not be scheduled until the issue is more fully explored. During his first weeks in treatment, the father's capacity to understand and take responsibility for his behavior, to control his impulses, and to emphasize with other persons are being evaluated. Until he is able to demonstrate growth and change in these important areas, he continues to represent risk of emotional and/or sexual harm to his child. Continued controlled separation from the family also emphasizes the father's responsibility for the abuse. The mother should attend the visits because she is the person on whom the victimized child must now depend. Her ability to support, protect, and relate to her child can continue to be assessed, as well as her level of minimization, or lack therof.

Visits permit the child to see her father and verify that he is physically well and has not disappeared. The visits may also dissipate any distortion of the father the child may have. ("He's so wonderful" or "He's such a monster.") Risk of reabuse in an unsupervised setting is still a real possibility. The child is also emotionally vulnerable to father's self-centered narcissistic tendencies, such as "poor me" looks and statements, as well as possible verbal threats to change her story or stop talking. We find that the level of safety and control that these supervised visits provide is essential for child victims to make progress in therapy, to trust the process and to deal openly about the abuse.

The following clinical indicators are signs that the family is prepared to advance beyond supervised visits:

1. All parties must place appropriate responsibility for the sexual abuse on the father.

2. The siblings of the victim must have participated in the therapeutic process to some degree. This may include individual evaluation and treatment if needed.

3. There should be total elimination of major behavioral symptoms on the part of the child victim in therapy sessions and in her general environment.

4. Mother-daughter therapy sessions have demonstrated open communication, including negative feelings expressed by the child to the mother, discussion of a structured list of any concerns that the child needs to raise with her mother, and discussion of the sexual abuse itself, including what actually happened and the child's feelings about it.

5. The mother is prepared and, through her own individual therapy, is able to respond to her child's questions and issues.

6. Father-daughter therapy sessions have demonstrated open communication (including a list of questions written by the child for the father

regarding any issues and especially regarding the sexual abuse. This technique was first communicated to us by Lucy Berliner, Harborview Sexual Assault Center, Seattle, Washington. This technique also includes a letter written by the child about her feelings that is given to the offender and his therapist).

7. The father is prepared through his own individual therapy to respond to his child's questions, issues, and feelings.

8. The father can discuss the sexual abuse without minimizing his responsibility for its occurrence and has some knowledge of the impact of the abuse on the child.

9. Family therapy meeting(s) have occurred to discuss the conditions of visits by the father with family members that will take place outside the home and be supervised by the mother.

10. Conjoint parental therapy sessions have been initiated.

Step 3: Weekly visits, supervised by the mother, to take place outside the family home in a public place.

The father may not yet have advanced to the point where he fully empathizes with the hurt, anger, sadness, and confusion that he has caused his child, wife, and family. He may not yet have developed a full understanding of why he initiated a sexual relationship with his daughter, nor does he understand the environmental and emotional warning signs that preceded and endured during his initial loss of control and his continued abusive behavior. Some minimization of his behavior and its impact usually continues; however, he has developed some understanding of the hurt he has caused.

Through father-daughter therapy sessions, he has given his daughter permission to experience whatever negative feelings she may have about him and the abuse. He has attempted to answer appropriately some of her questions about the abuse, and he also has attempted to help her shift the blame and responsibility for the abuse from her shoulders to his. At the same time, the mother has demonstrated her ability to support and protect her daughter, as well as her ability to be emotionally accessible to her.

The family is ready to meet without outside intervenors present. Family visits in a public place rather than in the family home are recommended at this time for the following reasons:

Safety: Meeting in a public place provides an added measure of safety and control for all family members. Because the possibility of finding herself alone with her father (either inadvertently or in some arranged way) is diminished, the daughter's anxiety level is also diminished. Risk of abuse while meeting in a public place is much lower than meeting at home allowing the family to be more relaxed together.

Family interaction: The family is encouraged to find activities that facilitate social family interaction. Going to the movies would not be appropriate, for instance; a trip to the zoo or a museum or a family picnic would. Activities outside the family home allow the family to reexperience normal family time together without rushing the family into reunification.

Safety: During this process, the family home has remained a place where the daughter has been free of risk of abuse and the emotional pressure of needing to subjugate her needs and feelings to protect her father. Family visits outside the home allow her to retain that comfortable environment while still working on abuse-related issues in therapy. Simultaneously the mother-daughter bond continues to be strengthened, and the family reexperiences being together again.

Indicators that the family is prepared to advance beyond out-of-home visits are the following:

1. The father can clearly and fully describe his sexual behavior with his daughter and accepts full responsibility for this behavior. There should be no minimization of the behaviors or responsibility.

2. The father can clearly identify the life stressors and unique aspects of his sexual paraphilia(s) that contributed to his abusive behavior and has learned skills to cope with stress and any inappropriate impulses that may arise.

3. The father can articulate the impact of the abuse on his daughter. He should be able to discuss the impact as it relates to her personally as a child, to her relationship with her mother, to her relationship with her siblings, to her relationship with him, and to other aspects of her life. He should demonstrate a sense of empathy and remorse regarding the negative effects of his behavior on his child, wife, and family.

4. The mother demonstrates that she has developed a greater sense of autonomy and independence.

5. The mother demonstrates that she is readily available to protect her daughter and meet her emotional needs and is unlikely to be influenced by or attuned to her husband's needs at the expense of her daughter's.

6. The daughter's behavior continues to stabilize.

7. The father and daughter show continued improvement in their relationship during conjoint sessions.

8. The mother, father, and daughter are able to discuss the abuse in their own therapy with less negative impact on ego and functioning.

9. The husband and wife begin work on relationship issues, past and present, and discuss the effect of the abuse on their marriage in marital therapy sessions.

10. The daughter indicates approval and readiness for advancement beyond out-of-home family visits.

11. The mother indicates similar approval and readiness.

12. The father indicates similar approval and readiness.

13. The family is engaged in family therapy session(s) in which beginning in-home visits have been fully discussed. The family should be able to present a plan for ensuring that the father will not be alone with the daughter or siblings who may be uncomfortable and should be able to negotiate a contract covering physical contact between father and daughter (only at the daughter's initiation), discipline (the mother is to handle discipline problems), and conflict resolution.

Step 4: Time-limited weekly visits in the family home, supervised by the mother (no overnight visits).

Although most families at this stage, are quite anxious to advance more quickly, the continuation of this process in small and careful increments is vital. The family now has lived separately for approximately twelve to twenty-four months, and spending time together in the family home is more anxiety producing than might be anticipated. The control and safety provided by such limited visits allows each family member to assess his or her feelings about reunification without the fear that the process is moving so quickly that it has a momentum of its own and cannot be slowed or stopped. Additionally, there is always a noted honeymoon period when everyone tends to be on his or her best behavior.

Step 5: An increase in the number of time-limited visits in the family home (usually three times per week with no overnight visits).

The family should demonstrate the ability to bring to individual and family therapy any problems that arise as a result of being together more frequently. It is expected that problems and difficulties will arise. Whether family members are willing to acknowledge and confront their problems is a diagnostic indicator of their level of functioning. Issues likely to arise include (though are not limited to) an amplification of the mother's anger at and distrust of her husband, an increased acting out by all children, parental problems in cooperative parenting, a variety of struggles in the marital relationship and, a fear of reabuse.

There should be continued progress in all treatment and behavioral areas. Finally, the parents should increasingly focus on their own families of origin and on childhood issues, including their own possible sexual victimization.

Step 6: Indicators that the family is prepared for beginning overnight visitation (one night per week only).

1. The victim provides positive and realistic responses to detailed discussions of risk situations in the home.
2. The mother and father have realistic discussions in marital therapy of potential risk situations in the home.
3. The parents can discuss their own sexual expectations.
4. The family openly discusses fears previously discussed in individual sessions.
5. The family continues to progress in all areas of treatment, including individual therapy, marital therapy, and family sessions.
6. The family has been successful in previous stages of reunification. Although any of the phases can precipitate a crisis, this phase is most likely to do so. This is the first time the mother is faced with the loss of total control. Since she must sleep at some point, both parents have to confront the safety issue at a deeper level.

Step 7: Indicators that the family is prepared for an increased number of overnight visits:

1. The family has been successful in the previous stage of reunification.
2. The family as a unit and its individual members continue to progress in all areas of therapy.
3. Family functioning continues to be monitored through regular family and individual therapy sessions.
4. The mother and father continue to participate in marital therapy.

Step 8: Full-time reunification on a time-limited basis.

Full-time reunification is reevaluated after a one-month trial period. All family members, therapists, CPS workers, and probation officers should be involved in this reevaluation. This should include feedback through individual therapy, as well as a family discussion of reunification during regular family therapy sessions.

Following a successful reevaluation, a continued plan of therapy can be developed as the needs of the family dictate. Some continued family therapy is usually indicated. There are often good reasons—legal and therapeutic—for the father to continue individual therapy. Parents also are usually eager to continue marital therapy into the future. Once the family is completely reunited, the monitoring phase should gradually diminish over a six-month period to family sessions every other week, once every third week, and so forth.

The success of the process of therapy and family reunification should not be judged simply by completion of all the prescribed steps. Each advance through the process is an opportunity to evaluate the family and each family member's progress, as well as an opportunity for each family member to assess her or his feelings, comfort level, and needs—thus strengthening an informed decision-making process.

The reunification process is a success if it facilitates the safety of the child, if it helps determine that a father does or does not have the ability to become an appropriate parent, and if a couple decides during the process to reunite or to separate and divorce.

Experience has shown that it is the norm rather than the exception for problems to arise during the stages of reunification. The process rarely proceeds smoothly. Families willing and able to struggle with these problems in therapy, rather than pretending that problems do not exist, are the families whose level of functioning increases and in which risk of reabuse diminishes. In some instances, inappropriate behaviors or actual reabuse do occur, regardless of the caution and care of clinicians. However, the step-by-step reunification process provides the best structure for sound and thorough clinical assessment of all family members and an arena in which each family member may recover and progress to her or his greatest potential.

Staff Support and Development

Maintaining consistently high levels of morale, experience, advanced knowledge, and expertise is an integral part of managing any child sexual abuse treatment program. While initial motivation to work in this field may arise from its current high visibility or from a truly altruistic concern for those who have been abused, the burn-out rate is high. Facing clients each day and hearing painful, depressing, and even frightening accounts of abuse, tackling the misinformation of the uneducated or inexperienced, remaining optimistic while confronting the enormity of the problem society faces, spending as much as an hour on telephone calls, case consultation, coordination, and court appearances for each hour spent in actual client contacts—

these are all integral parts of clinical life at The Chesapeake Institute and other such programs.

Three specific avenues of support are addressed at the institute in an effort to revitalize, positively stimulate, and support staff members.

First, the executive director and supervisors possess significantly advanced knowledge and experience related directly to child sexual abuse. Their general guidance and specific direction impart a concrete sense of confidence and assurance that helps to counterbalance the inevitable feelings of becoming overwhelmed that naturally occur when doing daily clinical work in this field.

Second, staff cohesion is vital to a continued positive morale. The Chesapeake Institute's multi-disciplinary staff presents a variety of perspectives to treatment that stimulate diverse ideas, invigorating discussions, and sometimes outright arguments. Central to such interactions are mutual respect and open, honest working relationships. Great care is given to hiring staff who are not only capable clinicians but have the ability to work in and help develop such an environment. The shared support and personal comfort and satisfaction derived from those working relationships helps to provide the type of stable foundation necessary to continued work in child sexual abuse treatment over a long period of time.

Third, continued professional training, especially with those who are at the forefront of this field, helps to stimulate intellectual and clinical growth and to increase specific expertise. Inservice training is provided on topics such as multiple personalities, human sexuality, and assessment in divorce and custody situations. Whenever possible, these trainings are arranged with nationally known colleagues who are visiting the Washington, D.C., area. Additionally The Chesapeake Institute staff go on retreats annually. This gives the staff an opportunity to advance work on a given aspect of this specialty.

Experience at The Chesapeake Institute (reinforced by similar programs around the United States) has shown that to work in isolation or in a setting that provides little support is inadequate at best. The risks of providing less than competent services and growing stale or burning out are significant. Great care and attention must be given to the overall support and clinical well-being of all staff members.

The field of child sexual abuse is difficult, exciting, and rewarding to work in. Knowledge of trauma studies is allowing us to rethink psychiatric interventions and revolutionize client care and achieve successful recovery previously thought to be impossible.

References

Berliner, Lucy. Personal communication.

Blick, L. 1982. Preschool, Schoolage and Teenage Assessment Forms. Unpublished checklists used at The Chesapeake Institute.

Giaretto, H. 1982. *Integrated Treatment of Child Sexual Abuse: A Treatment and Training Manual.* Palo Alto, Calif.: Science and Behavior Books.

Groth, A. Nicholas. 1982. "The Incest Offender." In S.M. Sgroi, ed. *Handbook of Clinical Intervention in Child Sexual Abuse,* 215–240. Lexington, Mass.: Lexington Books.

Lanning, K. 1986. *Child Molesters: A Behavioral Analysis for Law Enforcement.* Quantico, Virginia: U.S. Department of Justice, F.B.I.

12

Understanding Sexual Offense Behavior and Differentiating among Sexual Abusers: Basic Conceptual Issues

A. Nicholas Groth
Frank J. Oliveri

O ver the past decade we have become increasingly aware of sexual victimization and abuse. Sexual assault is a complex and multi-determined problem that does not fall exclusively within the province of any single discipline. It is a cultural issue, a social issue, a political issue, an economic issue, a legal issue, a medical issue, a psychological issue, an educational issue, and a spiritual issue. As such, it requires a multidisciplinary approach in order to be effectively combated. In addition, sexual abuse behavior can be regarded from a number of perspectives: moral (Is such behavior good or bad, moral or immoral?), legal (Is such behavior legal or illegal?), social (Is such behavior harmful or harmless?), clinical (Is such behavior indicative of psychopathology?), and sexual (Is such behavior sexually gratifying?). These are separate, if not always distinct, issues that overlap and often become intermeshed when addressing sexual abuse. Intervenors therefore, need to be clear about their roles and identify from what perspective they are approaching this problem. Sexual abuse behavior is characterized by blurred role boundaries between offenders and victims, and we must be careful not to increase confusion by blurring professional role boundaries in our interventions.

One of the major obstacles encountered in addressing the problem of sexual victimization is the limited information available with regard to persons who commit such offenses. Where factual data are absent, biased attitudes and misconceptions tend to prevail. Given the serious and intimidating

This chapter contains some material that was originally published in the form of a quiz on sexual assault in *Medical Aspects of Human Sexuality*, 22 (3): 127–130, and is reprinted through the kind permission of Hospital Publications, Inc. We wish to acknowledge the contribution of Fred S. Berlin, M.D., Ph.D., director of the Sexual Disorders Clinic at the Johns Hopkins Hospital, whose ideas and conceptualization of paraphilic sexual offense behavior has influenced our writing in this chapter.

nature of rape and child molestation, the prevailing emotional response on the part of the public toward such offenders is one of anger and fear—emotions that do not facilitate clear thinking and rational judgment. The predominant societal response to such individuals is punishment rather than treatment, and consequently the majority of offenders do not identify themselves or seek assistance for their problems since they realize the adverse social and legal consequences that will ensue. Accordingly data collection has been sparse and limited, for the most part, to populations of convicted offenders.

This chapter addresses several questions about sexual assault that repeatedly emerge with regard to the motivations of the offender and the dynamics of the offense. Our responses reflect observations, conceptualizations, and understanding of these issues derived from our combined experience of twenty-five years of clinical work with identified offenders and victims. Since the majority of offenders we have worked with have been males, we have chosen, for ease of narration, to use a masculine pronoun when referring to the perpetrator in the text of this chapter, although we recognize that sexual abuse may also be perpetrated by females.

What Is the Difference between a Sexual Offense and a Sexual Deviation, and How Are These Terms Related to the Concept of Sexual Abuse?

Sexual offense is a legal concept; sexual deviation is a psychological one. A sexual offense is any sexual behavior prohibited by law. The term *sexual deviation* generally refers to a persistent, predominant, and unconventional sexual interest on the part of an individual either in regard to a particular type of sexual activity or toward a particular type of sexual object or individual. *Sexual abuse* refers to any form of nonconsenting interpersonal sexual behavior that poses some risk of harm to the other individual. These concepts are not synonymous. For example, in some states, oral-genital sexual acts are prohibited by law, and therefore such activity would constitute a sexual offense; however, such activity would not in itself be regarded as psychopathological and, when engaged in voluntarily and through mutual consent, would not constitute sexual abuse. On the other hand, there are sexual activities (for example, habitual cross-dressing or transvestism) that are not against the law and therefore are not sexual offenses. Because of its repetitive and unconventional nature, however, transvestism is classified by mental health practitioners as a psychosexual disorder, or paraphilia. (The latter term has come to replace words such as *deviation* or *perversion* which have acquired unfortunate and condemnatory connotations.) Finally, some forms of sexual abuse may not constitute either sexual offenses or sexual deviations. For example, some states incorporate a marital exclusion clause in their statutes defining rape so that forcible sexual assault of one's spouse is not a crime; and when such behavior is not persistent or a precursor for sexual satisfaction in the psychology of the perpetrator, it would not be considered to be a paraphilia.

Although the terms *sexual offense* and *sexual deviation* are not identical, neither are they mutually exclusive. For example, sexual activity by an adult with a child constitutes a sexual offense; when it reflects the perpetrator's sexual orientation, it constitutes a sexual deviation or paraphilia; and since it poses some risk of harm to the victim, it constitutes sexual abuse. The legal concept of sexual offense, then, addresses the manifest sexual behavior in regard to the law; the psychological concept of sexual deviation relates to an individual's sexual nature or orientation; and the clinical concept of sexual abuse has reference to the impact on the victim of involuntary and nonconsenting sexual activity.

When working with someone whom you have reason to believe has sexually victimized someone else it is important to differentiate properly among a number of issues. First, was the person convicted of a sexual offense? If so, then he is an identified sexual offender. If he was not convicted or if he has plea-bargained to a nonsexual crime, then in the strictest legal sense, he is not a sexual offender. This fact needs to be taken into consideration in anticipating what influence it will have on the likelihood that the person will recognize and acknowledge his problem as opposed to maintaining denial about the offense. It will also affect the treatment approach used with such a client.

Second, since you have reason to believe that this individual did in fact sexually victimize someone, you may understand this to constitute sexual abuse. However, the client may not appreciate that what he did was harmful even though he knows that what he did was against the law and therefore regarded as a crime. Often the client did not act out of any malicious intent, and there may have been no immediately apparent adverse consequences for his victim. Some clients may simply be unaware of or ignorant of the potential such victimization has for immediate and/or future traumatic effect on the victim. On the other hand, you may be dealing with a client who, whether or not he admits to his offense, does recognize its abusive nature. Such abuse may be intentional on the perpetrator's part, or he simply may be indifferent to the consequences of the abuse; or he may be troubled or remorseful about what he did. Obviously, what you learn about the foregoing will influence what you will incorporate into the treatment plan for each client, especially with regard to recommending outpatient or inpatient treatment, and what emphasis you may place, for example, on such goals of treatment as attitude change, re-education, restitution, and the like.

Third, regardless of whether your client is a convicted offender or not, or whether or not he appreciates the abusive nature of his sexual behavior, it is important to determine if his sexual offense behavior is the result of and reflective of a paraphilic sexual nature or is due to other causes. Not every instance of sexual abuse reflects a sexual deviation on the part of the abuser anymore than every instance of intoxication indicates a condition of alcoholism. Just as there are a number of different issues underlying why people get drunk—one of which may be alcohol addiction—so too are there a number of different reasons why individuals commit sexual abuses—one of which may be a psychosexual disorder or paraphilic inclination. Only through ascertaining what prompts such behavior on the part of a given individual will you know how to deal with him effectively. In the assessment of your client, a differential diagnosis in regard to the etiology of his sexually abusive behavior is essential, for it will have both legal and clinical implications. It will shape how we regard his behavior. It will influence our thinking in deciding, among other things, to what degree is a given individual to be held responsible for his misdeeds; in understanding to what extent free-choice operates in such behavior; in determining the respective roles of treatment and punishment in intervention with such clients; and in formulating a treatment plan and deciding what is indicated: medically, psychologically, educationally, behaviorally, and the like.

Do Sexual Offenders Have a Specific Personality Profile That Can Be Detected through Psychological Evaluation and Testing?

Sexual offenders differ from nonoffenders only in regard to certain aspects of their unconventional sexual interests or activities. Knowledge of a person's sexual interests, desires, and behavior does not in itself reveal the nature of his character or personality. There is a great deal of sexual diversity among human beings, and people differ from each other in several basic ways with regard to their sexuality.

Sexual Orientation

One way in which people differ is in regard to their sexual orientation. Who is sexually appealing to them? One man may be sexually attracted to women his own age, whereas another man may be sexually attracted to other men, and a third may find he is sexually attracted to both men and women. Some adults are sexually drawn toward children exclusively, whereas others find that both age-mates and children are sexually appealing. People differ from each other, then, in regard to the objects of their sexual attraction, whom they find sexually appealing, and who arouses sexual desire in them.

Types of Sexual Behavior

A second way in which people differ is in regard to the types of sexual behaviors in which they find pleasure or excitement and the kinds of sexual activities in which they engage. One person may report that he finds masturbation to be the most pleasurable sexual act, whereas another person may report a preference for intercourse. One person may highly enjoy performing oral sex, whereas another person might not, and a third might be repulsed by such an act. Some people find unconventional behaviors sexually arousing or exciting. Some men cross-dress as part of their masturbatory ritual because they find this enhances their sexual excitement or pleasure, whereas most men do not experience cross-dressing as sexually arousing and would not consider engaging in such behavior. Some men are aroused by sexually exposing themselves to children, whereas most men do not behave in this way—not simply because it is against the law but because they do not experience any urge or inclination to do so; it is not part of their sexuality. Some men experience coercive sexual interactions as more exciting or arousing than consenting sexual interactions.

Frequency of Sexual Behaviors

People also fall along a continuum in regard to the frequency and intensity of their sexual needs or drives. At one extreme, someone reports wanting to perform sexual acts several times a day, and at the other extreme, someone else may report that he seldom experiences any desire for sexual acts. One individual may experience sexual urges as very strong or compelling, whereas another individual may not. With reference to sexual abuse, some persons will be compulsive, repetitive offenders and others will be more occasional or episodic.

Attitudes toward Sexuality

There is a great deal of diversity among individuals regarding their attitudes about sexuality, their sexual interests, desires, and activities. Some people are reasonably comfortable with their own sexual preferences and behavior, whereas others are conflicted or troubled in some respect with theirs. One man may report being comfortable with masturbation, whereas another man may feel guilty about such behavior. Some sexual abusers will not be at all troubled by their abusive inclinations or by engaging in abusive acts; others may be so distressed by having these unwanted desires or inclinations or by committing such acts that they commit suicide.

Capacity for Self-Control

The fifth way in which people differ is in their ability to control unwanted sexual urges or to resist unwanted sexual temptations. Here, we are referring to self-control—not whether a person refrains from some inappropriate behavior in the presence of external authority or control (no offender will molest a child in front of a police officer). Rather we are referring to a situation in which there is nothing to stop inappropriate behavior except the person's self-control or willpower. People do not possess an equal ability to inhibit inappropriate behaviors or suppress unwanted desires. Although individuals may recognize that their sexual inclinations are inappropriate or harmful, this does not mean that they are always able to deny their expression. Some sexual offenders experience their offenses as irresistible impulses, as sexual compulsions. For them, it is not a matter of "won't stop" but a matter of "can't stop."

People differ then in regard to their sexuality with respect to the kinds of partners they find sexually appealing, the kinds of activities they find erotically exciting, the frequency or intensity of their sexual desires, their attitudes toward their sexuality, and their abilities to control unwanted sexual desires. It is important to appreciate, in this respect, that none of us *chooses* our sexual preferences, we *discover* them as we grow up. As we sexually mature, we discover whom we find sexually appealing, what acts we find sexually pleasurable, and so on. The heterosexual man, for example, did not decide, when he began to enter puberty, that he would become sexually attracted to females; he found that females were sexually appealing to him. The homosexual man did not decide, "When I grow up, I will be sexually attracted to other males"; he discovered as he grew up that other males were sexually appealing to him. Neither do persons decide to be sexually drawn to children or to experience coercive sexual acts as arousing; they discover this at some point in their lives. Whatever the determinants of our sexuality, it is not volitional. Sexuality is rooted in our biological makeup and shaped to some extent by events that transpired during the developmental years of our childhood. Neither biological nor developmental influences can be consciously chosen or controlled by the developing child. However we arrived at our particular sexual makeup, it was not through a conscious, decision-making process. We may have some choice—and even here some persons have more limited choices than others—when it comes to how we actually behave sexually—whether we pursue our sexual interests, whether we engage in particular sexual activities—but we did not choose what would be sexually stimulating to us.

Even more important, knowing a person's sexual preferences or nature does not in and of itself reveal anything to us about that individual's personality or character. To know, for example, that a particular individual is a heterosexual male who engages in sexual intercourse on a regular basis with women his own age may tell us something about his sexuality but does not tell us anything about what he is like as a person: whether he is kind or cruel, law abiding or criminal, generous or selfish, hard-working or lazy, honest or dishonest, bright or dumb. Personality traits and character traits are separate and distinct from sexual orientation and sexual interests. Unfortunately, many persons (including some clinicians) mistakenly believe that an individual who exhibits an unusual or unconventional sexual behavior or orientation will also differ in other ways from persons who exhibit more traditional patterns of sexual interests or behaviors. This is not so.

Not all persons who behave in similar ways do so for the same reasons, nor are they all the same "type" of person. It is obvious, for example, that not all men who are sexually attracted to women are similar in all other respects. Men who commit sexual offenses differ from men who do not commit sexual offenses only in regard to the specific offense behavior. There is as wide a variety of individual differences, for example, among men who are sexually attracted to children as there is among men who are not sexually attracted to children. All sexual offenders are not the same. They do not all do the same thing in the same way for the same reasons. Knowing that a person has sexually abused a child gives us little information about what he is like as a person. Conversely, knowing what a person is like with respect to his personality or character tells us little about whether he is sexually attracted to children or whether he has ever engaged in sexual acts with a child.

A variety of psychological tests can be employed to help assess an individual's personality, intelligence, character, abilities, values, achievements, adjustments, aptitudes, and interests, but the validity of such instruments depends on the cooperation and truthfulness of the respondent. Furthermore, there are no sets of test responses unique to sexual offenders. Unless a particular individual chooses to disclose an interest in sexual behavior with children, no clinical questions, probes, or batteries of psychological tests will reveal whether he is sexually attracted to children or has sexually molested a child. Furthermore, there is no set of test responses unique to sexual offenders. For example, given only the test responses of fifty men, a psychologist would be unable to determine reliably which, if any, of the subjects were men who found children sexually appealing or found coercive sexual acts erotically stimulating. We might, through clinical assessment, determine that a given individual is one of the nicest, friendliest, and most admirable persons we have ever met. He might, for example, be a clergyman who is genuinely devoted to his church and parish. This does not mean that he has not molested a child. Many such individuals—kind, good, caring persons—unfortunately, are child molesters. Or we might find that a given individual is one of the most awful, uncaring, and reprehensible persons we have ever encountered—a religious bigot, for example—but this does not mean that he has molested a child. Many such individuals, despicable though they appear, are not sexually attracted to children. There is no personality profile that differentiates sexual abusers from nonabusers, nor is there any battery of psychological tests that will identify if an individual is or is not a sexual offender.

This is not to say that identified sexual offenders do not have psychological traits or features in common. They often do. For example, we commonly find that offenders present with low self-esteem, feelings of inadequacy or vulnerability, and difficulties in interpersonal relationships. But such features are neither specific nor unique to sexual abusers. We might find the same traits, for example, in persons who are victims of traumatic sexual abuse.

Retrospectively we can find common problem areas or personality defects among sexual offenders, but we cannot conclude that if we find such traits in a particular individual, he is more likely than not to be a sexual offender. For example, one of the common behavioral traits we have noticed among sexual offenders with whom we have worked is that the large majority of them smoke. We would never assume that because a person smokes, he is more likely to be a sexual offender than a person who does not. It is also true that a person may exhibit a characteristic trait across many areas of his life. For example, a given individual may be a dishonest person: dishonest in his work, dishonest in his social relationships, and dishonest in his sexual behavior. But to reach such a conclusion, we would first need to ascertain his dishonesty in each of these areas of his life.

Therefore, in assessing sexual offenders, we need to determine the nature of each individual's sexuality, as well as the nature of each individual's character and personality. We need to identify the person's strengths and weaknesses, resources and limitations, conflict-free areas of functioning and problem areas. We are assessing what kind of a person he is, as well as what type of offender he is. We cannot know the former simply by knowing the latter, and vice-versa.

What Contributes to a Person's Developing a Sexual Orientation to Children? Are Such Persons Born That Way and, If Not, How Do They Come to Develop Such an Interest?

We do not yet know all the factors (biological, psychological, and social) that need to occur, in what combinations or relationship to each other, at what critical points in development, with what intensities, and in what contexts, for the outcome to be the development of a proclivity toward sexual molestation or assault. However, work with identified abusers has indicated the presence of two major types of risk factors in the etiology of erotic interests toward children or inclinations to assault others sexually: biological flaws and unresolved sexual trauma.

From the work of the Sexual Disorders Clinic at the Johns Hopkins Hospital in Baltimore, Maryland (Berlin 1983), a higher incidence of biological defects (such as genetic variations or defects, chromosomal abnormalities, brain insult/dysfunction, hormonal imbalances, and the like) has been noted in clients treated for sexual abuse problems than in clients being treated for other types of psychological problems. This does not mean that any one factor alone is sufficient to produce a sexual orientation toward children or an eroticization of coercive sex; rather, it indicates that biological factors may contribute toward the development of such paraphilic sexual disorders in some persons. Just as we are now discovering that some people may be more genetically predisposed toward alcoholism than others, so too early work appears to indicate that some people may be more biologically predisposed toward sexually abusive behavior than others. It is important to recognize, however, that "predisposed" does not mean "predestined."

From a developmental rather than a biological perspective, it has been our observation that the majority of sexual abusers were themselves sexually victimized during the formative years of their childhood (Groth and Hobson 1983). Such victimization occurred in the form of direct sexual abuse or other types of sexual trauma, such as witnessing inappropriate sexual behavior on the part of their parent(s), being sexually humiliated by significant persons in their lives, or growing up in a family environment characterized by excessively strict, punitive, and negative attitudes toward ordinary and natural childhood sexual curiosities, interests, and activities. The trauma was not a single, exceptional event in the life history of the offender; rather, we found such victimization to be repetitive or ongoing in a context in which the individual felt alone and abandoned with this problem. There was no one in his life whom he could tell, no one who would listen to him, believe him, and help him. Either he did not dare disclose the event; or if he did, he was not believed; or if he was, *he* was blamed and/or punished. Whatever the case, he had to come to terms with this experience on his own, and it appears that his way of dealing with such a traumatic event was to move from the more helpless role of victim into the more powerful role of victimizer.

Ultimately it may be that there are as many different reasons that sexual abuse occurs as there are persons who commit sexual abuse, and such propensity may derive from a combination of biological, developmental, psychological, and social influences. It appears that sexual abusers are not born as such but develop abusive behaviors as a result of forces and events over which they have no choice or control. Biological flaws and childhood sexual traumas have been identified clinically as significant risk factors in such development. A risk factor is something that appears to contribute to a particular outcome but of itself may not be sufficient to produce the particular result. For example, if a person smokes, he is more at risk of developing lung cancer than if he does not smoke, but this does not mean that all or even most people who smoke will develop lung cancer.

Certain biological flaws and childhood sexual traumas seem to pose the risk of interfering with a person's psychosexual development, perhaps resulting in a paraphilic sexual disorder. It must be kept in mind, however, that the presence or absence of these factors does not raise, validate, or invalidate a suspicion of sexual abuse behavior. Although most sexual offenders were themselves sexually victimized as children, most children who were sexually abused do not become sexual offenders. Furthermore, even when such etiology exists, an explanation is not an excuse. Each person is accountable for what he or she has done. Understanding the etiology of sexual abuse does not diminish its seriousness or its harmfulness, but such understanding may help lead the way to the abuser's recovery and prevention of repeated abuse.

The diagnostic evaluation should assess the extent to which biological factors may contribute to such behavior on the part of an individual in order to determine what medical treatment might be indicated. Similarly, when the offender himself was sexually abused as a child, treatment will need to encompass the type of assistance adult survivors need to recover from such trauma, for in this case, we are dealing with an adult who has survived by moving into the maladaptive role of an abuser.

Is a Man Who Sexually Molests a Boy a Homosexual? Are Gay People More Likely to Abuse Children Sexually than Straight People?

In approaching these questions, one has to realize that a number of factors determine what type of partner one will find sexually appealing: the person's sex, age, physical appearance, and so forth. When an individual finds that he or she is sexually attracted, exclusively or predominantly, to other persons of the same sex, he or she is described as having a homosexual orientation; if an individual is attracted to persons of the opposite sex, he or she is described as having a heterosexual orientation. In identifying a person as either heterosexual or homosexual, the implicit assumption is that the persons he or she finds sexually desirable are peers, age-mates, or sexually matured individuals. In other words, it is assumed that the primary determinant of sexual arousal is the sex of the partner. For some persons, however, what appears to be critical in eliciting their sexual interest is the age of their partner; these persons are sexually drawn to prepubertal children. Such individuals are properly described as having a pedophilic sexual orientation; they are predominantly or exclusively drawn to presexual or sexually immature children. Some pedophilic individuals are drawn exclusively or predominantly to boys, others to girls, and some to both boys and girls. Also just as some persons might be bisexual and find they are sexually attracted to both males and females, so too are some persons cross-generational and are sexually attracted to both other adults and children. When an adult is exclusively or predominantly sexually oriented toward children, that adult is described as fixated; the offender whose primary orientation is toward age-mates but who turns to children when such age-mate relationships become disrupted is described as regressed. In other words, some persons are sexually fixated on or consistently drawn to children; other persons regress from adult partners and become sexually involved with children only when such adult relationships are no longer psychologically available (Groth 1978).

When an adult male has sexually victimized a young boy, we need to ask a number of questions:

- To what extent is his sexual offense due to a sexual orientation on his part to children? Is such an orientation primary (a fixation), or does his offense represent a departure from a more conventional orientation toward age-mates (a regression)?

- How exclusive is his sexual involvement with children? Is this man sexually active with adults as well or only with children? Which is primary?

- If he is also sexually active with adults, is he attracted predominantly to other adult males or to adult females or to both?

- How focused is he on boys or girls in his sexual attraction to children? Is he drawn predominantly to male children or to female children, or is he drawn equally to both?

Answers to these questions indicate that men who sexually abuse boys fall into three primary categories on the basis of their sexual orientation or preference.

The category of exclusive fixation includes men who essentially are not sexually oriented to other adults, male or female, but are sexually oriented exclusively to children. Some fixated men may be drawn only to boys; others to both boys and girls; and some, although primarily drawn to girls, may approach a boy sexually on occasion.

The category of nonexclusive fixation is comprised of men who are primarily sexually oriented to children but have a secondary sexual orientation to adults. These persons find that they can enjoy sexual activities with some adult partners but are aroused more by their desires for children than for other adults. And, as with the person who has an exclusive fixation, some of these men will be exclusively or predominantly sexually oriented to boys; others equally to boys and girls; and still others predominantly to girls but will sexually approach boys on occasion.

In both of these categories a secondary sexual interest in adults may be directed toward other men exclusively, toward both men and women, or toward adult women primarily. On occasion the last-described individual may become sexually active with another man.

The third category, regression, describes men who are primarily sexually oriented to other adults but have a secondary sexual orientation to children. Although these persons may experience some children as sexually arousing in certain situations or life contexts, generally they are sexually attracted to other adults. Some men who are described as regressed may be primarily oriented exclusively to either men or women as sexual partners, and others will be attracted sexually to both men and women. In turn, each may be drawn exclusively or nonexclusively to boys in regard to his secondary sexual orientation.

To summarize, in our clinical work we have found that adult male sexual offenders who have targeted prepubertal boys as their victims have been (in descending order of incidence) (1) exclusively fixated on children and are not oriented to or interested in other adults sexually (an exclusive fixation); (2) primarily fixated on children but under certain circumstances have been sexually active with adults (a nonexclusive fixation); or (3) primarily oriented to adult partners sexually but have turned or regressed to children when their adult relationships became unmanageable and/or adults became psychologically unavailable as partners (a regression). When one also realizes that victim-selection in some instances is determined more by external, situational factors than internal, psychological dynamics, one can appreciate the variety of determinants and the diversity of factors involved in the sexual abuse.

How, then, we answer the question, "Are men who are sexually attracted to pre-adolescent boys homosexuals?" depends on the definition of homosexual. We choose to confine the use of this term to persons who are attracted to other sexually matured persons of the same sex as themselves. Although one might describe sexual involvement between men and boys as homosexual activity in a literal sense (that is, sexual activity between persons of the same sex), the sexual orientation of such adults is more accurately described as pedophilic or cross-generational. The latter designations apply to men in the first two categories, exclusive fixation and nonexclusive fixation.

The exclusively fixated male has no significant age-mate sexual relationships. When we consider the two groups of sexual offenders against boys who have had some sexual involvement with other adults, the nonexclusively fixated group and the regressed group, it is our observation that in the majority of cases, the offender's adult partner was much more likely to be a woman than a man. Interestingly, in over two decades of work with over three thousand perpetrators of child sexual abuse, we have yet to encounter a single case in which a gay man regressed from sexual relationships with adult male partners to sexual relationships with prepubertal boys. On the contrary, the men we have seen who have been identified as sexual molesters of boys have either been primarily sexually orientated towards boys or have regressed to having sexual relationships with boys from adult heterosexual relationships (Groth and Birnbaum 1978).

To understand this, one must appreciate the fact that exclusively fixated offenders tend to be homophobic, and therefore it is important to them that the young boy victim has not sexually matured. In fact, as the boy victim begins to mature sexually, such an offender often loses sexual interest in him. This perpetrator describes the sexual appeal of a young boy's body as "soft and smooth with no body hair; he doesn't have a big penis, he doesn't ejaculate"; in other words, adult sexual characteristics are absent. The offender would interpret another adult male's sexual interest in him as an indication that the other man was a homosexual, but typically the sexual offender against boys does not regard his victims as gay or homosexual. Psychologically, it appears that this offender identifies with the boy. He finds the prospect of sex with another *adult* male to be unappealing or even threatening and finds the *young* boy erotically stimulating. The boy appears to represent what the offender feels himself to be sexually and/or psychologically: an immature male. Boyhood may represent an escape from the burdens of adulthood, a return to a developmental stage of unfinished business, or a point of arrested development. Whatever the sexual involvement with a prepubertal boy may mean, it does not appear that sexual involvements with boys on the part of the offender are simply extensions of sexual attractions to other men. Men who are sexually drawn to boys may have had little or no meaningful involvement in peer-age or adult sexual relationships and do not experience any strong desire for them or they may have regressed to boys from a primarily adult heterosexual orientation. The psychological nature of their sexual involvement with boys is better described as narcissistic rather than homosexual. Rather than reflecting an unadmitted desire for sexual involvements with adult males, such offenses seem to constitute an identification with being a boy. The homophobic character of many such offenders may in part be an aftermath of having been sexually abused themselves when they were children by adult male perpetrators. In this context, adult sexuality may have been perceived as confusing or threatening and avoided thereafter. Or they may have misidentified their perpetrators as homosexual and carried over and displaced their resentments for being victimized onto gay men. In any case, such offenders are not homosexuals. Gay men pose no more risk of sexually abusing children than straight men do—in fact, perhaps less so.

The blurring of homosexuality with pedophilia reflects an erroneous understanding of the nature of sexuality. Unfortunately, one of the arguments often used to prohibit gay men from occupying roles as teachers, foster parents, scout leaders, and the like is the mistaken belief that they pose more of a risk for sexually molesting children than do heterosexual people. Even if, contrary to our experience, some gay men should sexually victimize a child, prohibiting all homosexuals males from holding such positions because some might sexually exploit children makes as much sense as prohibiting all heterosexual males from becoming fathers because some commit incest.

Does Explicit, Hard-core Pornography Encourage Sexual Offenders against Children to Commit Their Offenses? What Role Does It Play in Regard to Child Sexual Abuse?

Not all sexual offenders are alike nor do they respond in the same fashion to pornography. First of all, offenders differ in regard to the types of visual material they find erotically stimulating. For example, men who are sexually attracted to young children usually do not find sexually explicit, hard-core pictures of adults arousing. Also, what may be perceived by some offenders as erotic may not even be generally regarded as pornographic. For example, some pedophiles may find underwear advertisements for children in mail-order catalogs sexually stimulating, and some rapists may be sexually aroused by the covers of detective magazines. Secondly, as with any other group of persons, there will be a wide range of individual differences among sexual offenders in regard to the interest they demonstrate in such material. At one extreme are sexual offenders who exhibit practically no interest in any pornography. At the other end of the continuum are some offenders who report being obsessed with such material. In general, however, there is no evidence that men who sexually assault children are more preoccupied with or more exposed to hard-core pornography in their lives than men who do not commit sexual offenses.

Nevertheless, we might ask in regard to those sexual offenders who do acknowledge being interested or fascinated by pornography, "What is the relationship for you between looking at pornography and committing a sexual offense?" There are some offenders who report that viewing pornography at times stimulates their sexual fantasies, arouses their urge to assault someone, and activates their offense behavior, much as another person might find that the sight or smell of food cooking has focused his attention on food, stimulated his appetite, and activated his inclination to eat. Other sexual offenders describe pornography as serving to diminish and inhibit their inclinations to commit an offense. For these persons, using pornography may be a safe outlet through which they discharge unacceptable and/or unwanted sexual inclinations, much as a person who has just eaten loses his appetite. The majority of sexual offenders with whom we have worked, however, report that pornography neither elicited nor inhibited such proclivities. Nor did we find that pornorgraphic material played a significant role in the lives of most sexual abusers of children either as something to which they were exposed during their childhood or as something that played a role in the activation of their sexual assaults. It may be that pornography reflects an individual's erotic interests, but it does not appear to play a significant role in creating such interests.

From a clinical perspective, the role pornography plays in regard to sexual offenses should be assessed on a case-by-case basis. Questions to ask might be: What type of pornographic material interests this person? To what extent is he obsessed with such material? What relationship does this material have to his offense behavior? Obviously, since we are seeing someone who has been identified as having committed a sexual offense, we are less likely to be seeing someone for whom pornography has been a successful and dependable means of safely discharging such inclinations. Exploring the content of such material may help us understand the underlying dynamics of his offense. Furthermore, some offenders do come to understand that acquiring pornography may constitute a lapse in their recovery and in the control of a problem that, unchecked, can lead to relapse and reoffense. When there is a clear connection between the use of pornography and the commission of a sexual offense in the case of a particular offender, we should instruct him to dispose of all such materials in his possession and to be on guard against exposing himself to pornography in the future. For him, pornography constitutes a risk factor in maintaining self-control. Pornography disinhibits this offender, putting him at risk of further offense, much as drinking or being intoxicated increases the risk of reoffense for a different offender.

Pornography may also play a role in the actual commission of sexual abuse. Some offenders entice or seduce their victims by showing them sexually explicit material. For example, some offenders show adolescent boys pornographic films and videos to arouse the boys and then approach them sexually. Other offenders show young children photographs of sexual activities involving other young children to instruct them in specific sexual activities and to demonstrate that "it's all right. Other kids do this too." Some offenders photograph their victims to blackmail them into keeping the offense secret. Still others use such photographs to document and remember the sexual involvements. Such offenders may use the photographs and videos that they take of their victims to fantasize about and relive the experience or to incorporate into their masturbatory practices. For some offenders, such material reflects a strong voyeuristic aspect of their sexuality; for others it may be the means by which they fantasize about sexual abuse, thus constituting a scenario that becomes part of their offense behavior. For still others, photographing and selling such material becomes a means of income or financial gain.

In other words, sexual offenders may become involved with pornography for a variety of reasons, and the sexually explicit materials themselves may have diverse meanings. Anyone who works with sexual abusers must realize that pornography might play a part in the lives and crimes of some offenders, as it does in the lives of some nonoffenders. It is also apparent, however, that there are many more sexual offenders for whom pornography plays no such role.

Although it is essentially impossible to identify definitively what is pornographic and what is not, there is sexually explicit material about which one may object for a number of reasons. It does not appear, however, to be a valid argument that pornography is objectionable because it promotes sexual abuse. Furthermore, it would seem that the best way to combat pornography would be to "put out a better product": good sexual information and education beginning in early childhood. Censorship and prohibition are not the solution; they seem instead to enhance curiosity, preoccupation, and interest in the forbidden.

Can Men Who Commit Sexual Assaults against Children Be Treated Successfully?

To a large extent the notion prevails both among mental health professionals and the public at large that sexual offenders against children are largely untreatable. As a result, little effort is made to establish treatment services for such clients. Thus the majority of such abusers go untreated. But this does not mean that they are untreatable. Contrary to popular opinion, where treatment services have been established for such persons, most offenders are found to be amenable to treatment, and their rate of recidivism is significantly reduced.

Proper treatment depends on a careful assessment and differential diagnosis in regard to the etiological factors involved in the sexual abuse behavior in each individual case. There are three major modalities of treatment that can help sexual abusers to curb their inclinations.

The first is pharmacological treatment. Certain drugs or medications such as Depo-Provera (medroxyprogesterone acetate) can be used to lower testosterone levels in selected male sexual offenders, resulting in a corresponding decrease in the intensity of their sexual thoughts, urges, or drives. Such medication does not change the nature of a person's sexual orientation; rather it enables him better to resist unwanted pedophilic temptations or inclinations toward coercive sexual behavior. Pharmacological treatment is indicated where the sexual offender experiences his offense behavior as unwanted but irresistible. Such treatment may have significant medical side effects and is feasible only when careful medical supervision is available.

Second, behavioral modification techniques, such as aversive conditioning, masturbatory satiation, covert sensitization, and the like, can be used to diminish an offender's inappropriate sexual arousal patterns to children or to coercive sexual behaviors. Such treatment is symptom specific. It provides a person with techniques to counter unwanted sexual inclinations.

The third category is psychological treatment. Psychotherapy and counseling (individual, group, marital, family, and the like) may be used to help an offender discover, through reflection and introspection, the underlying meanings to his sexual offense behaviors and identify the unhealthy or traumatic early life experiences in which they originated. Due to such understanding, he will be better able to recognize the early warning signs, to identify risk factors associated with his offense behavior, and to control such inclinations.

Since there is a wide range of individual differences among men who sexually assault children, it is not surprising that no single modality constitutes the treatment of choice for all offenders. Treatment services must be tailored to the individual client for maximum effectiveness; the more modalities a treatment program has to offer, the wider range of clients it can treat effectively. The formulation of a treatment plan depends on a good diagnostic assessment to determine the extent to which the sexual abuse reflects a pedophilic sexual disorder, diminished intellectual capacity, psychiatric illness, post-traumatic stress disorder, an antisocial personality, or the like. Treatment is a collaborative effort; it is helping persons to help themselves. It is not that men who sexually assault are untreatable but that we have not created a social climate in which they feel safe to come forward and know they will be helped. The prevailing social attitude is that offenders are undeserving of help and should be punished for their wickedness and misdeeds. While public outcry demands more stringent penalties and more severe punishments for offenders, there is very little advocacy for their treatment. It is often mistakenly believed that sexual abusers do not want help, do not deserve help, or cannot be helped. Given the adverse social and legal consequences of disclosure or discovery, it is not surprising that few offenders come forward seeking assistance. However, this does not mean that they are untreatable. We would argue that sexual offenders against children should receive treatment and deserve help both for their own sakes and in order to make our community safer.

The public wish for more punitive responses toward perpetrators has the unintended effect of creating a climate in which fewer offenders are held accountable for their crimes. For example, in states where there is mandatory incarceration for sexual abuse, offenders are deterred from pleading guilty to such crimes, necessitating victims to testify to their sexual victimization in court. This intimidates some victims to the extent that they refuse to cooperate with the prosecution, or they recant their allegations. In a milieu of harsh penalties, child victims may be deterred from reporting their victimization lest the abuser, a person about whom they care on some level, be sent to prison for a long period of time. When the offender is a violence-prone person, then the more severe the penalty for the crime, the greater the jeopardy to the life of the victim.

Men who sexually abuse children are troubled persons. They need to be held accountable for what they do, but they also need to be helped to change. Incarceration or institutionalization is necessary in some cases, but exercising control by incarceration is insufficient to address the problem. Children who are sexually victimized deserved treatment to recover from such abuse, but it is equally important to provide help to offenders; only if known abusers are treated can other children be protected from being victimized.

Most sexual offenders have probably committed more offenses than they have been charged with, and most victims probably remain silent about their victimization. Therefore, although help is available for some children who are identified victims of sexual abuse, most victims go untreated. By advocating offender treatment, we hope to increase the number of people who are spared the trauma of sexual abuse. No program for the prevention of sexual abuse is complete if it does not encompass the treatment of the perpetrator.

Treatment does not mean cure. A sexual offender must remain vigilant to the risks of reoffending in the same fashion that a recovered alcoholic must remain alert to the risks of relapse. With proper help, in a variety of settings varying from institutional to community based, we may ultimately be able to treat sexual offenders against children with the same success with which we are able to help alcoholics to recover from alcohol abuse. Where treatment programs for sexual abusers have been established, the rate of offender recidivism has significantly diminished. It has been our clinical experience that the majority of sexual abusers we have seen have benefited significantly from treatment (Groth 1983).

These are the questions we repeatedly encounter in teaching and supervising others with regard to working with sexual offenders and combating sexual abuse. Our responses reflect our thinking on these issues derived from clinical work and experience, not from methodologically strict, formal research. In this field, much remains unknown, and much of what we believe we know remains untested. This happens to be the state of affairs at this point. What we have shared in this chapter constitutes opinion—hopefully expert opinion arrived at through careful exploration and thoughtful scrutiny of over two decades of work.

Suggested Reading

Berlin, Fred S., and Krout, Edgar. 1986. "Pedophilia: Diagnostic Concepts, Treatment, and Ethnical Considerations." *American Journal of Forensic Psychiatry* 7(1):13–30.

Burgess, Ann W.; Groth, A. Nicholas; Holmstrom, Lynda L.; and Sgroi, Suzanne M. *Sexual Assault of Children and Adolescents*. Lexington, Mass: Lexington Books.

Carnes, Patrick. 1983. *Out of the Shadows: Treating Sexual Addiction*. Minneapolis: Compcare Publications.

Groth, A. Nicholas, with Birnbaum, H. Jean. 1979. *Men Who Rape: The Psychology of the Offender*. New York: Plenum Press.

Knopp, Fay Honey. 1984. *Retraining Adult Sex Offenders: Methods and Models*. New York: Safer Society Press.

Sgroi, Suzanne M. 1982. *Handbook of Clinical Intervention in Childhood Sexual Abuse*. Lexington, Mass: Lexington Books.

References

Berlin, Fred S. 1983. "Sex Offenders: A Biomedical Perspective and a Status Report on Biomedical Treatment." In Joanne G. Greer and Irving R. Stuart, eds., *The Sexual Aggressor: Current Perspective on Treatment*, 83–123. New York: Van Nostrand Reinhold.

Groth, A. Nicholas, 1978. "Patterns of Sexual Assault Against Children and Adolescents." In Ann W. Burgess et al. *Sexual Assault of Children and Adolescents*, 3–24, Lexington, Mass.: Lexington Books.

Groth, A. Nicholas. 1983. "Treatment of the Sexual Offender in a Correctional Institution." In Joanne G. Greer and Irving R. Stuart, eds, *The Sexual Aggressor: Current Perspectives on Treatment*, 160–176, New York: Van Nostrand Reinhold.

Groth, A. Nicholas, and Birnbaum, H. Jean. 1978. "Adult Sexual Orientation and the Attraction to Underage Persons." *Archives of Sexual Behavior*, 7 (3):175–181.

Groth, A. Nicholas,and Hobson, William F. 1983. "The Dynamics of Sexual Assault." In L.B. Schlesinger and E. Revitch, eds., *Sexual Dynamics of Antisocial Behavior*, 159–172. Springfield Ill.: Charles C. Thomas. 159–172.

13
Sexual Offenders as Victims: Implications for Treatment and the Therapeutic Relationship

Margaret C. Vasington

S ince 1982 I have volunteered at Connecticut Correctional Institution–Somers, a maximum security prison for men. Doing individual and group therapy in the Sexual Offenders Program started by Dr. A. Nicholas Groth, I have worked with men who have molested, raped, and murdered. Some have been designated incorrigible; some have been institutionalized from the time they were 6 or 7 years old; some have been substance abusers since their early teens. Most have been poor, coming from dysfunctional families, and having serious school problems. As their life stories emerged, it became apparent that all of the men whose histories I knew had been victims of neglect and physical, emotional, and sexual abuse—often so pervasive that it is difficult to distinguish where the effects of one form of abuse begins and another ends.

Although it is not always necessary to separate the forms of abuse, since this book focuses on child sexual abuse it may be helpful to be aware of two elements in sexual abuse that I believe are particularly significant. First, sexual abuse is an assault on the body that invades a person's entire being—her or his whole sense of self—and may deeply traumatize that person emotionally, intellectually, and spiritually. The body never forgets. Although the mind may deny the invasion, the bodily responses are ever present and affect the victim's life in ways often incomprehensible to others. Second, there exists within society an enormous confusion regarding sexuality and sexual roles. Sex too often is combined with violence, shame, control, and exploitation. The sexual assault victim's misery often is exacerbated by the reaction of family, friends, and helping professionals who reflect the societal confusion. Thus, the victim may experience an acute sense of invasion in vicious combination with powerlessness and degradation.

Groth and Birnbaum (1979, 101) report that 30 percent of sex offenders admit being sexually abused in contrast to 10 percent of the remaining prison population. This percentage of admitted victims is almost certainly a low figure since it is doubly difficult for male inmates to acknowledge their own victimization. In society in general, it is more difficult for men than women to admit to being sexually abused, and in the prison population this difficulty is compounded because an admission of victimization may be used by others as an invitation for more sexual abuse. Further, it may require as much as five or six years of group therapy before an inmate remembers his own sexual abuse or recognizes the childhood incident as abusive. It is probable that the majority of sexual offenders have witnessed sexual abuse or have been sexually abused in their own homes, in foster homes, or in the institutions in which many were housed.

All of this is written as an explanation of, not as an excuse for, the behavior. I believe that understanding the reasons for the offensive behavior helps both therapist and client perceive that the behavior developed as a result of a series of circumstances in the client's life and therefore that it is open to change. This possibility enables them to work toward changing the offender's behavior, for the sake of the individual and for the sake of potential future victims.

In this chapter, I discuss some of the therapeutic issues I have found to be most important in working with offenders in the prison setting. These correspond with the ten impact and treatment issues listed by Porter, Blick, and Sgroi (1982, 109), but for the purposes of this discussion will be dealt with somewhat differently. I am writing about therapeutic issues and the therapeutic relationship rather than describing programs of case management. That is, I am suggesting means by which the therapist can connect some of the underlying issues that contributed to the behavior for which the inmate was incarcerated. Some of these means involve recalling and reworking past traumas (especially of childhood), offering insights, and reframing and connecting to the inner child. This description has worked for me and suits my style. It is not suggested to be the only way to practice therapy nor is it a manual for therapy. Rather, it is meant to suggest areas in which clinicians might newly consider or explore in working with sexual offenders. No intervention, however fitting, substitutes for the therapeutic relationship in psychotherapy; it is this that enables most of the client's growth. The relationship with the therapist may be the first opportunity for sexual offenders to have an experience of being known and accepted as they are. Several hypotheses seem crucial in establishing a healthy therapeutic relationship:

> Human beings innately seek to fulfill their needs, achieving autonomy and their fullest potential in cooperative and harmonious interactions with other humans and with the world around them.

> Behavior contrary to this principle results from organic or environmental damage to the organism.

There is an undertandable reason for any behavior however bizarre, though the clues are often hidden in our genetic, environmental, and evolutionary history.

All humans do the best they can, given their unique history.

Blame and condemnation in contrast to justifiable consequences for behavior impede growth and encourage evasion of responsibility.

These basic premises are particularly important in working with offenders. Their crimes frequently repel the therapist so thoroughly that it becomes difficult to separate "the sinner from the sin." Society at large does not distinguish between the person and the action, labeling those who commit bad actions as "bad" people. (Even a newborn is labeled "good" if he or she does not fuss much. Little mention is made of the pain the child might be expressing by acting "bad," that is, fussy.) Society clings to an illusion of child victims quietly hanging their heads in shame and fails to remember that the angry, spitting, biting child is suffering as well. We call these "bad" children "delinquents." It seems more accurate and more therapeutically fitting to recognize the hurt child within and see the fully human person hidden behind the dysfunctional defenses and the brutal behavior. The offender is in prison for his offense; it is not the therapist's job to inflict further blame or guilt. In my experience, blame or guilt interfere with the offender's taking full responsibility and feeling fully remorseful for his crimes. And both responsibility and remorse play key roles in preventing repetition.

It is helpful to wait to read the file that documents the offenses until after the relationship has begun to be established. The child is seen first as a human being rather than as someone defined by his crimes. Listening and following the client's process rather then plying him with the questions necessary for crisis intervention usually puts the therapeutic relationship on a more mutual basis. A barrage of inquiries often upsets the balance and paradoxically interferes with the authentic self-disclosure that is the heart of the therapeutic relationship.

To establish an atmosphere conducive to self-disclosure, it is helpful to understand the issues that inmate-clients are likely to bring to therapy, issues resulting chiefly from their victimization as children. I do not wish to imply that these men are only victims. They are also victimizers; they are incarcerated for crimes, some for committing heinous crimes. But in focusing on these men solely as victimizers, most people forget that they were victims first. I have no desire to minimize the victimizations for which these men are responsible, nor in any way do I diminish the anguish of the victims and their loved ones. As a victim myself, I know that anguish all too well. I do believe that problems usually are solved by exploring, understanding, and dealing with the causes rather than simply by deploring the symptoms, as deplorable as they often are. The issues of inmates differ little from the issues of the populace at large and still less from the issues of any other victim of abuse and neglect. What does differ is that these men have acted out their issues through violent antisocial behavior, and they have been sentenced to serve prison terms. By "acting out" I mean the manner in which a person externalizes a feeling by expressing it overtly and physically rather than internalizing it, verbalizing it to others when appropriate, and experiencing it as a feeling, not as an action. For example, a person expects a raise but is denied it. He becomes silent and withdrawn rather than admitting that he is angry and speaking to the boss. Or instead of speaking to the boss, he takes a gun and shoots the boss. Both actions are acting-out anger. To contain the feeling rather than repress it or act it out, he would need to recognize the feeling as anger and allow himself to feel the anger as fully as possible (for example, by breathing deeply so he can feel fully and acknowledging that he is angry rather than pushing the anger away). Then he would need to decide whether it would be productive to confront his boss by saying, "I'm angry you did that," or wait to address the problem later. Containing a feeling—not repressing or acting it out— gives one control of the experience and frees one from being either a victim or a victimizer in this situation. This is not easy to do and is especially difficult for those with histories such as these men have.

This chapter focuses on sexual offenders who are also victims of child sexual abuse. I will discuss impact and treatment issues, frequent acting out behaviors, and the effect these behaviors and treatment issues have on therapy and the therapeutic relationship. Since I am describing my work with males, I will refer to the client as "he" and to the therapist as "she" throughout the chapter.

Impact and Treatment Issues

Manipulation

The first question directed toward anyone treating offenders is, "What do you do about manipulation?" My reaction is to relax and treat it as I would treat any other defense. Everyone manipulates; mass media advertising is an extreme example of socially approved manipulation, for instance. If a child cannot express needs or realities openly by saying "I need appreciation," or "Your yelling scares me," she or he finds some other way to get what is needed; that is, she or he manipulates others in an effort to have present needs met. In order to be appreciated, he will stuff himself with fourteen pancakes so that he will hear, "What a good boy you are, eating up all my cooking!" Or she will lie about where she has been to keep her parent from screaming at her. The more unresponsive, dysfunctional, and dangerous the environment, the more manipulation is exacted.

On the other hand, a therapist does not have to be manipulated; it takes at least two people for manipulation to work: one to manipulate and the other to collude. Instead a therapist can recognize the manipulation, use it as information about the client's needs, and appreciate the manipulation as an attempt to protect the self, as are all other defenses. It helps to abandon stereotypes—in this case "all inmates are con artists"—and meet the individual wherever he is. If the inmate proves to be a master manipulator—and some certainly are—this is an issue for therapy.

> X's reputation as manipulator extraordinaire was such that several of his friends warned the therapist before therapy started. She videotaped a session and asked him to notice how he tried to control the session, noting the most blatant instances for special attention. She carefully offered this as an observation rather than a judgment, recognizing that the control was a manipulative device that had protected him while growing up. (It had obviously worked!) The therapist's request that he review the tape infuriated him, but she refused to withdraw her observation or to enter into control issues of her own by insisting that he had to do this. She offered it to him as a choice: if he wanted to learn as he said he did, then he could. It was his choice. Fuming, he listened to the tapes. Fuming, he defended his actions. The therapist listened, nodded acceptance of his feelings, and repeated her observations and request that he continue to view tapes of their sessions.
>
> They repeated this interaction for several sessions until the client began to recognize the ways in which he used manipulation to gain control and why he did this. He and the therapist traced its origins back to a childhood of such neglect and random violence that his only protection seemed to be to gain complete control. Since his parents were not in control, someone else had to be. There was no one left but him. With continuing therapy he learned to recognize when he was controlling, and the manipulative behavior lessened.

Implications for Treatment and the Therapeutic Relationship. When the therapist becomes indignant or judgmental about any defense—and all therapists will at times—the client has two main choices: to maintain a false sense of power by digging in his heels and resisting the therapist's attempt to change him or attempt to change (adjust) in accordance with the therapist's evaluations and demands. Either choice repeats the dynamics of earlier relationships in which the client was compelled to rebel or conform. Since neither achieves autonomy and both tend to breed resentment, it seems more conducive to growth to assist the client with defenses, such as manipulation, in the following ways:

1. To regard the defense as the most effective and safest way the child could devise to get his needs met.
2. To appreciate the defense for serving this purpose and accept the necessity of the defense as a survival mechanism.
3. To investigate the feelings and needs the defense is masking.
4. To offer more appropriate ways for handling feelings and meeting needs than the acting out of the defense.

A major part of therapy is working with defenses—those behaviors we have learned to help us adjust and survive when the environment does not meet our needs in any other way. If an infant's cries are met with indifference or rage, even a 2 month old will begin to withdraw or add the screams of indignation to the cries of hunger, discomfort, or boredom. In X's case, the attempts to control imparted a feeling of security against the random chaos of his family. If felt better to try to control rather than feel the terror of being at the mercy of two parents who themselves were confused and unstable.

The client begins to appreciate these qualities as devices that saved the child from further harm rather than regard them as weaknesses. The therapist helps the client investigate the feelings masked by defenses and then suggests rather than imposes alternative behavior that may work more effectively. Only then comes the deep and permanent restructuring of the personality.

Relationship sessions with X and his wife proved the most effective way to reach X's feelings buried so deeply under his defenses. He had come into therapy because "I can't feel anything for anyone, not for my victim, not for myself, not for anyone." In sessions when he began to control his wife, the therapist probed for his feelings. This required persistence; he was well defended. At times he became angry. Slowly he became aware of the helplessness and powerlessness for which he attempted to compensate by controlling behavior. Rather than trying not to feel the helplessness and powerlessness, he was encouraged by his wife and therapist to allow himself to feel these emotions and express them. "When you have problems at home, I feel helpless since I'm not there, and I feel powerless to do anything for you." Once he could say this, he could give up trying to tell his wife what to do, which left her feeling helpless, powerless to reach her own solutions, and hopeless that he would ever be able to listen in a way beneficial to her. She did not want him to do anything about her problems except listen to her. He began to state his needs clearly, to listen empathically, and to trust his wife to be capable of solving the problems herself. Slowly both relinquished some of their defenses and began to communicate their needs more directly. The need for manipulation decreased on both their parts.

This process takes time, especially when people are invested in not experiencing emotions, as these men usually are. It is hard for them to identify emotions, to experience them, to allow themselves to have feelings without judging themselves, and finally to admit the emotions openly to another person. Men admitting to fear, sadness, or tenderness, for example, are seen as less manly for having such emotions—and men in prison guard their manliness zealously. A personal history of child sexual abuse tends to heighten this fear. It takes delicacy and persistence to assist the men in accepting and expressing their emotions, but it is fundamental to treatment and building a therapeutic relationship.

Paranoia

Paranoia may be the second most conspicuous characteristic of inmates. These men often have been victims of continual and, sometimes, horrendous mistreatment by caretakers. The fear described by Porter, Blick, and Sgroi exists in full measure (1982, 117–118). Many of these men have acted out in socially unacceptable ways since they were young, and neighbors and teachers often misunderstood and joined in the mistreatment. Thus, no place was safe. In turn, these inmates committed invasive and fearful crimes, so, "Who should know better than me that these things happen?" Added to this, society labels them the "dregs of humanity," "subhumans," and "animals"; the other inmates call them "tree jumpers" and "rippers"; some of the guards and staff dub them "scumbags." Prisons breed paranoia, and trust is almost nonexistent.

Implications for Treatment and the Therapeutic Relationship. The inmate is more connected to a world that assaults, shames, ridicules, and betrays than to one that supports, encourages, and trusts. He twists the present to fit a reality that belongs neither to the therapist nor to the present situation. Paranoia lurks under every interaction. The therapist must expect the possibility of having every facial expression, every body posture, every verbal expression misconstrued. It is vital to establish early in the therapeutic relationship an atmosphere of mutual give-and-take that encourages the client to offer his reactions to the therapist for a reality check. This is particularly necessary when the issues of trust, betrayal, safety, and fear loom as large as they do with victims of child sexual abuse. The therapist must invite such checking rather than be annoyed by it. The therapist must be aware of her reactions and open to sharing them honestly. A primary task of therapy is sorting old reality from new, (paranoia being an old, once-understandable fear carried over and mistakenly seen as existing in the present). The therapeutic relationship affords a splendid opportunity for unraveling the paranoia.

> Y's childhood was filled with persecution. His father deliberately took away anything positive in his life—and there was little enough that was positive. Y found refuge curling up in a toy box. It was his only safe place. As soon as his father discovered this, he whipped Y and smashed the toy box. A stray dog became his best beloved and only friend, the only creature he ever felt love from. His father shot the dog. Y's classmates teased him, his teachers humiliated him, and the one neighbor who "befriended" him sexually abused him. No one in his life had accepted him or showed caring for him. Those he trusted betrayed him. Life for him was creeping through a thickly planted mine field. So was therapy.

Implications for Treatment and the Therapeutic Relationship. As the trust built in the therapy, Y could express his perceptions of the therapist. The following are illustrative: "You didn't speak to me when I said 'hello' this morning. You seem angry with me today. What did I do wrong? You didn't call me down Friday, so you don't care about me. Why don't we just cancel the therapy if you don't want to see me?" The therapist could tell him she did not hear him; yes, she was angry but not with him; she did call him Friday, and the guard said he was not there. The therapist's patient step-by-step response serves as a reality check. The present is not the same as the past. When the therapist is angry with the client, it is important to say she is and why, so they can work it through. We teach best by modeling. Thus, the client has a chance to express his feelings and the therapist hers in a clear, contained, and humane manner. This process is unlikely to be within the inmate's experience. When the therapist can accept the client's paranoia, reframe it into accurate reality, and reassure him she neither rejects nor scorns him for having such fears, the client takes a step into reality and toward increased self-esteem.

The next step can use the paranoia for tracing the fears to the sources, usually early childhood, and working with them from there. Again, the therapist's acceptance of the paranoia as reasonable given the client's history and the use of it to create a learning situation strengthens the therapy and the therapeutic relationship. It requires many such checks and much patience to diminish the paranoia and develop truat.

Trust

Folk wisdom designates trust as the cornerstone of any relationship. As one offender asked, "Without trust, what is there?" Victims of sexual abuse seldom trust anyone: not parents, not therapists, not the system. This lack of trust manifests itself in devious ways that test the therapeutic relationship to the limit.

The first step in developing trust is to accept what the client says, especially about the sexual abuse. The amazingly strong denial system around child sexual abuse can envelop therapists as well as clilents. In my experience, clients tend to minimize rather than make up or exaggerate the abuse. Other victims accuse themselves of wallowing in self-pity or block the trauma completely. It is essential to accept the client's story, no matter how bizarre, until it is proved beyond doubt to be wrong. Then the distortion becomes an issue for therapy, not a reason for rejection. Sometimes as protection against seeming gullible, therapists save their pride at the expense of the client. In this instance, the cost to the client is too great to risk making a mistake. If the therapist does not believe the client's story, often shared with much fear of humiliation and disbelief, the therapeutic relationship may suffer an irrevocable blow if the story later proves to be true.

Working with inmates, the therapist may be less likely to believe the client or have a greater need to avoid "being taken in." I have found this fear unsupported by experience. It is important for the therapist to believe the clients in this population as in any other. (There are a few psychopathetic inmates who cannot be trusted in any way. They are beyond the limits of this chapter. They are probably far fewer in number than one would estimate and seldom present themselves for therapy. Most therapists would sense the presence of a psychopathic personality). The therapist's trust in and respect for the client as a human being is perhaps the key element in the relationship.

Implications for Treatment and the Therapeutic Relationship. There are many ways of building trust, and each therapist has a personal style of doing this. The following guidelines may help:

Respecting the person and accepting where he or she is at any moment, as an expression of his or her unique history.

Acknowledging his or her feelings and accepting these feelings as appropriate for the client's past rather than the present.

Separating the person from the act (judging the act, not the person).

Supporting the small "child within" while setting limits on behavior.

Being honest with and aware of oneself and sharing that with the client when appropriate.

This population will have little or no experience with anyone effectively and consistently relating to him in this way. Trust builds slowly in such relationships. Trust in people and in society has been betrayed again and again. They learn to trust by testing the therapeutic relationship again and again and yet again.

Low Self-Esteem

The extremely low self-esteem of these men intensifies the lack of trust. They lack self-esteem for several reasons. Victims of child sexual abuse generally suffer low self-esteem. They feel responsible for the abuse. As victims they feel helpless and weak. They feel an immense amount of shame surrounding the abuse. They feel "weird," abnormal, different, evil, contaminated, "rotten to the core." These issues are likely to affect every victim of sexual abuse. This is the "damaged goods syndrome" (Porter, Blick & Sgroi 1982, 109). If a victim later becomes the victimizer and commits one or a series of attacks, he is then labeled a criminal, ostracized by society, and banished to prison, thereby proving his worthlessness beyond doubt.

> Speaking of his family, one offender explained, "They thought I was bad; they wanted bad so I gave them bad." Each act increased in seriousness until he received a fifteen-year-sentence for being "bad." He fulfilled the role assigned to him in the family very well by being bad; that is, to be "good" for him in his family was to be "bad."

This "bad" side of us, the "shadow side" as Jung (1933) terms it, is universally unacceptable. People try to hide it completely. To allow others to see it runs the risk of shame, abandonment, and rejection by those others. To allow oneself to see it risks shame, abandonment, and rejection of self. To avoid these unbearable emotions, human beings assume various poses: an air of invincible bravado or unyielding "niceness" or such anger that no one comes near. The sexual offender lives in dread lest anyone discover his dark side, yet at the same time he yearns for closeness to ease the pain and loneliness. A basic disbelief that anyone could value him combines with the elemental need to be valued. This gives the therapy a yo-yo quality; at times the client says, "come close—get away!" and utters a wail of abandonment if the therapist steps back.

Implications for Treatment and the Therapeutic Relationship. One of the most powerful methods of dealing with this shadow side, of exposing the source of the damaged goods syndrome, is to work with the client's victimizer—the source of the assaults, putdowns, abuse, and hurt the abused child experienced. The therapists asks the client to role play the victimizer (the person, persons, or force that hurt him as a child) either by imagining it or with a chair or pillow representing himself as a child, adolescent, adult. As the client speaks with the voice of the victimizer, the hidden assaults surface. "What a selfish child you are!" "I wish you'd never been born." "You never do anything right." With the therapist's guidance, the client identifies the original victimizer: parents, peers, relatives, teachers. Eventually he perceives more clearly the hurt and humiliation he experienced as a child. Slowly he forms a more sympathetic relationship with himself. His self-loathing diminishes. He begins to place the anger where it belongs: on the original victimizer. He learns to express it clearly rather than acting out the anger by committing more crimes.

Meanwhile, the most effective antidote to this same syndrome, yet perhaps the most subtle, is the therapist's ability to regard the inmate-client as a human being, finding empathy for the hurt child within while hating the crimes he committed. There are no techniques to communicate this, but the client will sense it nevertheless. Therapists who regard the client as an evil person or as a case study probably will not reach their clients very deeply. This factor, plus the quantities of time and energy needed, may account for the low success rate reported for treating convicted sexual offenders. In other words, these are not incorrigible or untreatable clients. It is we who may lack the capacity to perform therapy with them in an effective manner.

Twisted Reality and Confusion

The client's lack of trust in his own reality complicates building trust in the relationship. Human beings seem to be born with an innate, though unformed, knowledge of what is best for them. We intuitively sense that we need to be held tenderly for long periods of time, to be fed when hungry, warmed when cold, comforted when fearful. As children, we sense that we are intended to be completely accepted and unconditionally loved simply because we are. When this does not happen, we are perhaps surprised, disappointed, frustrated, enraged, or terrified. Few, if any, of us experience fulfillment of all our needs or bask in unconditional love. Through ignorance, poor modeling, and their own unfulfilled needs, adults (and society) fail, over and over, to provide for the children in their care. To the child, these adults are all powerful and all knowing. The child also knows that he or she must stay connected to the primary caretaker or perish.

If the world around the child is not congruent with the intuitive expectations of the child, the child must begin to twist internal reality to fit external reality. The child begins to relinquish, bit by bit, his or her own sense of reality, chipping away at the core trust in one's own sense of self. The child cries, "My finger hurts!" The adult says, "Oh, that's a little cut; it can't hurt." The child reports, "Grandpa did this to me." The adult rebukes, "You bad little boy to say a thing like that! Grandpa would never do that that." Slowly the child surrenders his belief in his own experience to the all-powerful adult. Without trusting oneself, trusting anyone else is likely to be difficult.

The inmate in therapy tends to be more connected to a world that invades, hurts, ignores, shames, and betrays him than a world that respects, supports, encourages, and trusts. The therapist must be prepared for her best efforts to be twisted to fit a reality that is not hers, in the same way the client's inner reality was distorted at a critical age.

Lack of trust in oneself is far more damaging than the inability to trust others. Without a solid sense of one's own reality, there is no reliable way to be in touch with one's inner self and emotions, no way to check out what is happening inside. These clients question every move, every choice, every idea, every action because they are never sure of the parameters of inner or external reality. "Did I do this right—or wrong? Do they like me—or hate me? Do they think I'm smart—or stupid?" Life is a frantic leaping about on a hot griddle, with no safe place to light, no way to stop the macabre dance. There is no way to ground oneself in a trustworthy reality.

The abused child similarly loses a clear way of choosing what is right and what is wrong. This is one of the factors leading to the confusion suffered by victims of child sexual abuse that Gelinas notes (1983, 327). The sexual behavior does not correspond to the child's intuitive sense of what is appropriate. The sexual abuse is developmentally out of synchronization and disrupts the developmental steps that follow (Sgroi and Bunk 1988, 143–144; Erikson 1950). In many dysfunctional families, boundaries are unclear, and there are so many double binds that confusion multiplies, leaving the child to feel that there is no safe, clear way to be. Given his family history, the issues of confusion and wrong are almost overwhelming to many inmate-clients. Multiple factors in their lives may cause them to act out aggressively from an early age. This socially unacceptable behavior often causes adults around them to react by shaming, labeling, and rejecting the client. This exacerbates his feeling of being wrong or bad. He is in the wrong place at the wrong time doing the wrong things. Often lacking the social skills or parental guidance to extricate himself from the quagmire, every new twist and turn sinks him further in, until he feels "wrong all over."

Implications for Treatment and the Therapeutic Relationship. The client will need to make the therapist's interventions wrong in order to fit his now-twisted inner reality. It will be less threatening initially for the therapist to be wrong than for him to be wrong. He may be defensive and accusatory to protect himself from the devastation of feeling "wrong all over." On the other hand, he may not be able to voice a different opinion or hear anyone else's if it is different. His need to be right may be so strong that he resists any attempts to give him responsibility for his actions. The therapist must avoid getting into a power struggle over who is right and who is wrong. Such a power struggle will result in blaming and put the relationship on a win-lose basis, and any relationship so based is already lost. Such dynamics would repeat the hurts that underlie the actions that led him to prison. The therapist models a more productive approach by being nondefensive, by acknowledging her own mistakes, and by refraining from blaming or humiliating either her client or herself for mistakes that are made.

At the same time, it is equally critical to hold the client and oneself responsible and accountable for inappropriate actions. It is not helpful to refrain from confronting inappropriate actions to protect the client or the therapist from the uncomfortable feelings that may arise as a result of the confrontation. By repeatedly dealing with mistakes in a nonjudgmental way—which means that the therapist responsibly acknowledges her own frustration, anger, and hurt, when appropriate—the client will begin, only then, to experience that making mistakes is an expected, acceptable characteristic of being human. He no longer interprets his mistakes as proof that "I'm stupid, inadequate, unlovable, worthless, and deserve to die" but instead recognizes that "I'm human, and therefore, likely to make mistakes, and I can learn from this." Then at last it becomes possible for the client to say: "I made a mistake. I'm sorry, and I'll try to do it differently next time." If the therapist is to model this experience, then she too must have worked on her own reactions to being wrong. Confusion about the "all rightness" of being wrong manifests itself in indecision, "spaciness," misunderstanding, lying, vagueness, and more. In therapy sessions, the therapist may find it as difficult to say in touch with herself as the client does. Such reactions on the therapist's part can be used very effectively as a diagnostic tool to promote learning and growth rather than as an impediment to therapy. I find this to be one of the most helpful tools in the therapeutic relationship.

Obviously part of the therapist's reaction to the inmate-client may be her own unfinished issues. Unless the therapist has a similar and consistent reaction of confusion (or any other emotion) with most of her clients, then something in this client at this moment contributes to the therapist's reaction. The therapist is fusing with some of the client's feelings at the moment. In turn, the way the client feels at this time provides clues as to how he felt in the past under similar circumstances.

Y's childhood left seasoned case workers numb with disbelief. The unrelieved disasters of childhood persisted into adult life. Any one of them was enough to stagger the ordinary human being; collectively they defied the law of random selection. As a result he continually misheard and misunderstood what the therapist said, trying to turn her into his sadistic mother. He could not accept any clarification of his misperceptions (if he did, then he would be "wrong"). He manipulated, lied hurled untrue accusations of cruelty at her, and tried to make her as "all bad" as his mother had tried to make him.

Using the dynamics of the interactions as a diagnostic tool helped the therapist stay separate—and sane. Rather than getting pulled into the old dynamics and reacting as the victim of these onslaughts, as Y had been as a child, or victimizing the client by blaming or rejecting him, as his mother had done, the therapist used her emotional reactions to guide the process into a learning experience for both parties. She used these steps:

Step 1: With her feelings of frustration, anger, helplessness, and hopelessness as clues, she assumed that since she rarely, if ever, felt this way with any other client, at least some of the feelings were not only the understandable results of facing such a barrage but she was picking up the client's feelings as well.

Step 2: Making this assumption, she shared her feelings with the client: "When you do this, I feel helpless, unappreciated, unfairly treated, misunderstood, angry," and then she added, "I imagine this is how you must have felt as a child when your mother did this to you. I see you are doing to me what your mother did to you. And you could never say to her, 'I am angry that you are doing this to me.!' Each time the client accused her, the therapist quietly repeated the same theme. "I see you need to make me 'Little Y' so you won't have to feel the way he did." "I see you're being your mother now." "I feel blamed just the way 'Little Y' must have felt." "What do you feel underneath all this?"

Step 3: When the therapist recognized but refused to accept the client's feelings as her own, the client eventually had to acknowledge them as his own feelings and experience the loneliness, rage, and helplessness that he tried to bury in the tirades.

Step 4: After allowing him time to ventilate these emotions and to reassure him that, despite her feelings, she was not going to abandon him, the therapist began to guide the client to less destructive, more effective ways to handle his emotions. In time, he began to express anger and hurt more directly and more responsibly.

These steps are crucial with all clients but particularly with inmates because such dynamics have contributed so heavily to their crimes. The victim becomes a victimizer. The beaten child wrenches away the stick and beats whomever comes near. Caught in the cross fire between transference and countertransference, the therapist nevertheless, must respond with interventions that interrupt the cycle of hurt, refusing to become a victim or the victimizer of the client.

Neediness

The neediness often found in such a population intensifies the confusion for therapist and client alike. The degree of neediness is proportional to the extent of the deprivation, and most sexual offenders have been extremely deprived. Their needs were unrecognized, ignored, denied, or assaulted. Perhaps the parent(s) were so needy the child existed solely to fill the parent's needs, an unnatural and impossible task. The child's unconscious concluded: "I deserve to live only if I take care of my parents. No matter how hard I try, I can't do this. Therefore, I have no right to exist." Other children are unwanted for any reason and sense this; some are told quite clearly. No victim of child sexual abuse has had his or her needs considered, let alone met. Many adult victims have so little sense of their right to exist that they "walk in the world begging pardon of the molecules of air for parting them," as one victim described herself.

The resulting pain and frustration teaches the child to withhold requests for meeting his needs. When the withholding becomes too painful, the child begins to deny that his needs exist. Rarely do these clients know how to state clearly and simply, "I need." They have disconnected from the need so thoroughly they are unaware that they have any. When one is not aware of her or his feelings, those feelings cannot be clearly experienced. When that person cannot experience them clearly and fully, she or he acts out.

> When Y learned his therapist injured herself seriously in a skiing accident, he angrily burst out, "She had no right to go skiing!" He regarded her leisure activity as irresponsible and her absence as deliberate abandonment and uncaring. He remained angry for months, did not want therapy with her, demanded another therapist, and reminded her at every opportunity of her absence, that is, neglect. The next season, he pleaded with her not to ski again. It took some stormy sessions to unearth and work on his deep terror of losing the therapist as he had lost everyone else he had ever cared about in his life. Unable to connect with and express his need, he believed that he could only act out wildly.

Implications for Treatment and the Therapeutic Relationship. Here again it is vital for the therapist to recognize and accept the dynamics implicit in the client's history and to use these as catalysts for growth rather than reasons for blame. Since therapy is a relationship, we recognize that the dynamics are a good portion of the therapist's history as well. Human beings often feel compelled to reenact the damage of their childhood until they learn a way to "redo" it better. When the client acts out the neediness of childhood by making inappropriate demands of adult relationships, it can be too easy to forget that at this moment, this therapeutic relationship involves one adult and one adult acting as a child. It is the therapist's job to remain adult, to model the "good enough" parent the client never had or did not have in the particular situation he is remembering. Sometimes this leads to an initial but temporary display of excessive dependence on the therapist, mirroring the parent's excessive demands on the child (Bettleheim 1987). It may help the therapist to remember that as the client clings so tightly, the therapist feels strangled; he is clinging while dangling over what he feels is the dark abyss of nonexistence. Such clients frantically demand, invade, cajole, wheedle, and threaten in order to get what they need, testing the limits of any therapist. This is one of the times it may be helpful to the therapy to have the client behind bars; the therapist can risk having the client angry in relative safety.

Therapy, like most other human endeavors, is partly science and partly art—that is, partly based on research and logic and partly on intuition. The therapist needs to trust this intuition bolstered by experience in order to engage effectively in the myriad facets of the therapeutic relationship. One of the most bewildering of these facets centers on the therapeutic dilemma between helping a client fulfill a need and encouraging responsibility. If we do this for him, how is he to learn responsibility? This is a valid question. The well of unmet needs is dark and deep with victims of child sexual abuse. Many exhibit all the symptoms of posttraumatic stress syndrome and arrested development (American Psychiatric Association 1980, 198). They are exceedingly needy because they have had so many needs unmet. Much of the therapist's work will be reparenting these adult children or giving the small, hurt child within examples of "good enough" parenting—not to meet the needs, not to comfort, not to assist the client, too often merely duplicates the hurt and neglect of his childhood instead of teaching responsibility. George Rogers, a director of Hartford Family Institute, explained "It makes as much sense as telling the hungry infant to go to the refrigerator and get his own bottle." People who were asked to be responsible before they were able to be responsible, or who have been labeled so incompetent that they can never be responsible for anything, have to learn step by step what being responsible is, what their needs are, and how to fill them responsibly.

No one who has been a victim escapes feelings of helplessness and powerlessness. The therapist helps the client take steps, sometimes small steps, toward responsibility. Developmentally, the first step into reclaiming power is asking for what one needs and having the experience of its being lovingly delivered. Sometimes the therapist provides the first experience of that all-important step. If we refuse to respond to the client's legitimate therapeutic requests as the parents refused to respond to the child's legitimate needs, then we reenact the negative experiences, reinforcing the neediness and despair. "Why ask, if it won't be met? If my therapist can't help, no one can." The inner rage and powerlessness that led to the offenses intensify.

The art lies in distinguishing between fulfilling a client's need in order to repattern the past in a new and productive way and denying a client's demands as necessary for the client's progress. After all, one way to build muscles is through resistance. At times the client needs to ask, and the therapist needs to say, "No." Sometimes she refuses because she cannot fulfill a legitimate need. A client may understandably request extra therapy time because a sister died, but the therapist may be too ill to come in. On the other hand, the client may have a chronic need for attention that he acts out by waiting until the last few minutes of the session to bring up the issue. Then the therapist may rightfully say, "We need to leave this until next time," and wait until the next session to deal with the feelings that arise from setting limits. This allows the client an opportunity to feel the grief or rage or whatever other emotion he felt as a child when he did not get what he needed rather than have the therapist collude with his insatiable attempts to manipulate "getting" as a way to deny the emptiness of "not getting." It is also necessary for the therapist to differentiate needs from wants. At such times, it helps to have the security of the prison setting as back up. The therapist can say "No" in a way that accepts the client's needs and feelings, reassures the client that the refusal is neither rejection nor abandonment, and, if fitting, shares what it feels like to have such demands made on her.

Much dependency stems from helplessness and powerlessness, from a sense of inadequacy and hopelessness. Sexual abuse in childhood can create these emotions for the victim in large doses. Most prison systems in the United States offer few opportunities to contradict such responses. If the client has not learned organizational and decision-making skills before his incarceration, then it is appropriate to give him the opportunity to learn these vital skills within the therapeutic relationship. In therapy with inmates, it becomes even more important for the client to have occasions for choice, for inclusion in the decision-making process, for a chance to exercise judgment and power under the guidance of the therapist. Others may regard this process as coddling the client or view it as indecisiveness on the part of the therapist; however, when we are impatient with the client's awkward ways of expressing his neediness or with his indecision and disorganization and yet we offer no remedies for these deficiencies, it is likely to prevent him from taking the next step toward independence.

My philosophy about psychotherapy views true healing as ultimate empowerment for the client, not as adjusting to adverse conditions. It is not about sacrificing one's own well-being to the demands of a disappointed parent or spouse or bowing to meet the obligations required by a maladaptive society. It is about restoring autonomy and helping the client to find the resources and power to fulfill his potential in ways appropriate to him.

Therefore when the inmate-client resists my interventions or openly or verbally expresses anger toward me in an inappropriate manner, I usually welcome and support these actions as the client's steps toward empowerment. These actions or words are what the client needed to be able to express to his caretakers in childhood but could not. In therapy, the client has a chance to redo that step in a way that gives him back his power. As a therapist, I accept that step toward autonomy without blaming, humiliating, or rejecting him. If a therapist has unresolved issues about being wrong, rejected, resisted, or humiliated, she may be threatened by the client's behavior and have trouble accepting it. Through a personal therapy process, it is crucial for the therapist to have her own issues well in hand. In this way, she can be aware of her personal conflicts, acknowledge them whenever appropriate, and offer clear, honest communication to the client, offering another example of good-enough parenting.

Humiliation and Shame

Humiliation and shame are unbearable emotions. Inmates suffer from large amounts of both. Most come from dysfunctional families of overwhelmed mothers and absent or brutal fathers. Their family lives were usually rife with substance abuse and violence; often there was desperate poverty; always there was abysmal ignorance of human needs. Many inmate clients also suffered from physical or sexual abuse and often from severe neglect. To these traumas are added the shame of their crimes and trial(s) and the dehumanizing nature of the institution to which they are sentenced.

Most prison systems consciously or unconsciously, avoidably or unavoidably, humiliate inmates. Strip searches and shackles, sometimes considered necessary for security, are humiliating. Lack of privacy humiliates. Lack of autonomy humiliates. The pecking order among inmates reduces sex offenders against children to the lowest of the low. Humiliation and shame are hidden issues that, tragically often, are too painful for the inmate to bring up or to discuss.

Implications for Treatment and the Therapeutic Relationship. The therapist who is aware of these issues is sensitive that her own actions and interventions may be mistakenly perceived as intentions to humiliate. The inmate may have experienced so much shame in his life that this distorts his perceptions of the world. But often the client cannot identify the shame easily or is too ashamed to admit it. It is humiliating to feel humiliated. The therapist helps by identifying the feeling and warning the client that it may surface in therapy. In addition to asking the client to tell her when he feels humiliated, she can be sensitive to body posture, facial expression, tone of voice, and words in either herself or the client that might touch shame. Sometimes a simple explanation is helpful. The therapist might say, "I'm smiling because this reminds me of another incident; I'm not laughing at you." Or the therapist might comment. "You seem upset by what I just said. What's that all about?" In turn, the client needs to be able to say, "You didn't speak to me in the hall." He needs to hear the therapist say, "I didn't do that to shame you. I was preoccupied." This is not the client "being a baby" or the therapist "holding his hand." Rather, it is another experience in separating the old reality from the new. In this new reality, the therapist is not "out to get the client as others were before her." The client needs to test this new reality over and over again before being sure. A trusting, non-judgmental, accepting relationship fosters such exchanges.

Boundaries

Such clients call for a feather-light awareness and a firm hand. No rigid rules apply. Yet sometimes therapists set up rigid rules to compensate for the client's lack of boundaries and his lack of responsibility in setting his own limits. Certainly molestation, rape, and murder are among the ultimate examples of lack of respect for boundaries. People learn to form boundaries, in part, from the experience of being recognized, respected, and accepted as a separate, autonomous being. Such experiences were not common in the lives of most convicted sexual offenders. The therapist's modeling teaches best. Setting limits may infuriate the client. He may consider it rejection, abandonment, uncaring, but the therapist offers an example of setting boundaries without hurting another person; this is a new experience for the client.

> When the therapist kept Y waiting ten minutes (ironically because she was attending an emergency staff meeting concerning the client), he had a temper tantrum. This proved she did not care, was mistreating him, was unreliable, couldn't possibly be the right therapist for him, and on and on. He repeated these tirades whenever a busy schedule meant that she did not have a full hour for him, though he knew he received more attention than anyone else in the program.

Implications for Treatment and the Therapeutic Relationship. Clients with such overwhelming needs and so little sense of boundaries are likely to harass, complain, and demand more from the therapist than she can give. Their demanding behavior is a reversal of the impossible demands made on them when they were children. It would not be in the best interests of the client to supply everything the client insisted on in any case. The therapist's refusal to try to fulfill these excessive demands is something the client was unable to do as a child—and usually still cannot. Sometimes the therapist can say what the child could not: "I'm sorry, but that's too much to ask. I can't do it." She can also say, "I understand you're angry, but I was late because we were concerned about you. It had nothing to do with rejecting you, though you may think it did." When the therapist leaves on vacation, she can say, "I realize you're angry, but I'm going on vacation. I'm not rejecting you. I imagine you wanted to tell your father how angry you were when he went away so much and how it felt like rejection to you." Step by step, the interactions of the therapeutic relationship afford opportunities for new and healthier ways to relate.

By now the role the therapeutic relationship plays in healing and growing is evident. The therapeutic relationship is often the only experience the client has had in which human feelings have been acknowledged and accepted nonjudgmentally, and limits have been set nonpunitively, while he has been respected and valued as a human being. In any setting, a male client may confuse the therapeutic relationship with a female therapist with a romantic fantasy. In a prison setting, such confusion is even more likely. It does not necessarily mean the therapist is leading the client on. Nor does it mean she should not develop a therapeutic relationship in the first place, out of fear it will lead to this. The therapist simply acknowledges and respects these feelings as she would any others, helps the client express them, explains what is happening in the client's process, and firmly sets her boundaries. This is another important learning experience for the client. The prison setting undoubtedly makes it a safer learning experience for both the client and the therapist, since external controls imposed by the setting mean that the therapist effectively set limits and maintain the boundaries.

Those familiar with Gestalt therapy will recognize its influence in this discussion. Throughout this chapter I have mentioned the concept of the small child within which forms an important part of Gestalt therapy and proves to be enormously helpful with inmates, as it is with other clients. The child within is still there waiting for someone to see how hurt he was, explain the confusion, comfort him, and eventually return to get him out of that difficult place. Each time the small child had to disconnect from himself to survive, he betrayed himself. Each time the adult abuses himself, he betrays himself and the small child. On the extreme end of the continuum, some people have been so hurt they have had to disconnect completely. They feel no connection with themselves; they are filled with rage. Rape and murder are terrible ways to act out the rage of total abandonment.

When the client begins to reconnect with that small child within, not by victimizing him but by conversing with him, caring for him, and reparenting him in a new and positive way, the reconnection with oneself begins. Self-abuse diminishes as the self-esteem grows.

Realities of Working in a Prison Setting

Being a therapist for male sex offenders in a maximum security prison is not the easiest assignment. To all the interpersonal difficulties are added the difficulties of conducting therapy in a prison setting. Therapy for inmates is not the primary goal of our correction system; in some prisons, it is not a goal at all. The correctional system is often indifferent or hostile to the concept of therapy for inmates and, sometimes, to the therapist in person. Therapy usually takes place in ugly settings, in uncomfortable chairs, under the watchful eyes of the guard, with loudspeakers blaring. When the clients leave the session, described by many as "the only place I can feel and act human," to return to the prison at large, they need to put back the mask. The whole system, usually authoritarian and oppressive, is counterproductive to growth and learning and all too often a source of more hurt, confusion, and fear.

Prison regulations often impede therapy. The client usually cannot call the therapist in an emergency. Some guards "forget" to call inmates to the mental hygiene unit for therapy sessions or call with remarks intended to humiliate. Touching is taboo. Inmates are transferred to other prison settings without warning with no termination process possible either for individual or group therapy. And, of course, there is always too much to do with too few to do it.

Society at large offers little support for those working with such vulnerable populations. People often consider that the therapist is either wasting time, is not good enough to work elsewhere, or, if female, is "looking for a man."

Despite the many obstacles, providing therapy in a prison setting can be highly rewarding work. It challenges the therapist tremendously, and therein lies the learning. It affords an opportunity to redress some basic social and individual injustices. It provides a chance to be with men who have molested, raped, and murdered in encounters where neither the therapist nor inmates are victims or victimizers but human beings engaged in a mutual healing process. It satisfies a deep place within that never denies the horror of the crimes yet reaches beyond blame, rejection, abandonment, and banishment of these victims turned victimizers, and remembers that they are human also. It helps men whose lives have been so wracked with pain that, as one inmate wrote, "Death represents peace and safety. Though to most people, death is ugly and something to be feared and avoided, to me, at times in my past, the prospect of death has been my only source of comfort and my only means of escape and safety. In many ways, death had protected me and offered the only promise of peace, beauty and contentment."

If therapy for inmates who are sexual offenders can help that person "find other ways to survive troubles, problems and sadness," it may also help prevent him from raping again. This, then, gives life to two people: the inmate and the person no longer about to be victim. For me, that has made it worth the difficulties.

References

Alpert, S., and Bressette, N. 1988. *Reclaiming Aliveness: A Matter of Heart*. Private monograph.

American Psychiatric Association. 1980. *Diagnostic and Statistical Manual of Mental Disorders* 3d ed. Washington, D.C: APA.

Bettelheim, Bruno. 1987. "Importance of Play" *Atlantic Monthly* (March): 35–46.

Erikson, E.H. 1950. *Childhood and Society*. New York: W.W. Norton.

Gelinas, Denise. 1983. "The Persisting Negative Effects of Incest." *Psychiatry* 46:312–332

Groth, A. Nicholas, and Birnbaum, J.H. 1979 *Men Who Rape: The Psychology of the Offender*. New York: Plenum Press.

Jung, C.J. 1933. *Modern Man in Search of a Soul*. New York: Harcourt Brace Jovanovich.

Miller, A. 1983. *For Your Own Good*. New York: Farrar, Strauss, & Giroux.

Miller, A. 1984. *Thou Shalt Not be Aware*. New York: Farrar, Straus & Giroux.

Porter, F.S.; Blick, L.C.; and Sgroi, S.M. 1982. "Treatment of the Sexually Abused Child." In S.M. Sgroi, ed. *Handbook of Clinical Intervention in Child Sexual Abuse*, 109–45. Lexington, Mass.: Lexington Books.

Rogers, George. 1987. Private conversation with the author.

Sgroi, Suzanne M., and Bunk, Barbara S. 1988. "A Clinical Approach to Adult Survivors of Child Sexual Abuse." In S.M. Sgroi, ed., *Vulnerable Populations: Evaluation and Treatment of Sexually Abused Children and Adult Survivors*, 1:136–186. Lexington, Mass.: Lexington Books.

14
Community-Based Treatment for Sexual Offenders against Children

Suzanne M. Sgroi

The complexities and challenges inherent in treating sexual offenders against children in the community are legion. It is clear that, as a society, we want to punish people who sexually abuse children—humiliate them, lock them up, send them away forever, or at least for a long time. Paradoxically, child victims of sexual abuse are rarely so punitive toward the relatives, teachers, clergy, helping professionals, neighbors, and family friends who are most likely to be their abusers. While they are still children, the victims, for the most part, just want the sexual abuse to stop. They also want the attendant burdens of secrecy, confusion, sense of violation, powerlessness, guilt, and shame to disappear. As adult survivors of child sexual abuse, most wish for an opportunity to confront their abusers and hold them accountable for the wrongness of their behavior and the damage that it caused. But as children yearning for safety, affection, affiliation, and acceptance, a public trial is a high price to pay to exact accountability from an abuser who denies that he or she committed a crime.

Sexual abusers of children rarely stop their offense behavior voluntarily. In 1985, Dr. Richard Gelles, a sociologist who has made distinguished contributions to our knowledge of family violence, addressed a meeting of the American College of Obstetrics and Gynecology on the topic of spouse abuse. He told the gathering that he was often asked, as a sociologist, to explain why men batter their wives. "There is a simple answer," said Dr. Gelles. "They do it because they can. No one stops them, and they do it because they can."

A similar dynamic also exists for child sexual abuse. People sexually abuse children because they can. And if no one stops them, the abuse continues. Some clinicians believe that at least some abusers realize that they need help to stop their sexual offense behavior. It is argued, however, that offenders are afraid to seek help because they fear the sanctions that will probably result if they come forward and admit to criminal behavior. Others believe that few offenders would voluntarily seek help to stop their sexual offense behavior even if criminal sanctions were absent. Be that as it may, no one would responsibly suggest the decriminalization of sexual offense behavior against children. What is possible in some states, however, is to negotiate by a plea-bargaining process for some offenders to receive short sentences or suspended sentences for incarceration and also to be sentenced to a long probationary period with community-based treatment as a condition of probation.

Will the latter be an effective way to stop abusers from committing more sexual crimes against children? We do not know. It depends a great deal on the individual characteristics of the abuser and the shape of the treatment program. What we do know is that many child molesters also have ample reasons to wish to avoid the time, expense, and publicity associated with prosecution for a sexual crime against a child. However, pleading guilty to a felony charge is no small matter for an otherwise law-abiding person. Many child molesters have no history of any other type of criminal behavior. What is the most reliable incentive, therefore, to induce a child molester to plead guilty? The answer is simple: avoiding incarceration altogether or receiving a short prison sentence. Secondary benefits to pleading guilty can include a speedier disposition of the criminal matter and associated court proceedings, lower legal fees, less time devoted to one's defense (and thereby lost to other pursuits), and a generally shorter period of public exposure and stigmatization. For some abusers, the act of taking responsibility for their crimes and avoiding the possibility that their victims will need to testify in court has the effect of both increasing their self-respect and the respect of others. In intrafamily abuse when the abuser admits to the crime, her or his willingness to take responsibility for what occurred may be a stepping-stone to repairing damaged relationships with other family members. However, there is no question that the greatest incentive for any child molester to admit to her or his crimes is the hope of avoiding incarceration.

In jurisdictions where judicial and prosecutorial discretion make it possible, plea-bargaining to avoid incarceration can be a powerful tool to increase the accountability exacted against persons who have committed sexual crimes against children. It enables a careful assessment of the offender's treatment needs during the period of presentence investigation. Whenever it is possible to present the court with a comprehensive list of treatment recommendations for sexual offenders against children, the odds are high that the judge will agree to make those recommendations the conditions of probation. With good case management, the result will be that a high degree of accountability is placed on the abuser while she or he remains in the community.

Will this ensure that the abuser will not commit another sexual offense against a child? No. Would it not be preferable to prosecute the offender and sentence her or him to a long period of incarceration in a prison where there is no access to children whatsoever? Perhaps. What is the problem, then, with using imprisonment of abusers as a means to protect children?

The answer is that there are numerous barriers to prosecuting and convicting sexual offenders against children when a trial by jury takes place and the defendant's guilt must be proved beyond a reasonable doubt. It would be extremely difficult for most child victims to sustain their allegations over a period of one to three years and then to testify against their abusers and undergo cross-examination in open court. Some children can be supported through this process, but it is arduous and costly in terms of time, money, and emotional expense.

Prosecutions and jury trials are arduous and expensive for everyone. The citizens and taxpayers of most states have demonstrated again and again through their elected representatives that they do not wish to pay the staggering price required by tax-supported law enforcement and judicial systems that bring every person accused of a crime to a trial. Child sexual abuse cases require meticulous police investigation (Cage 1988) and extensive preparation for court (DeLipsey and James 1988). The longer the time that elapses between the reporting of the crime and a trial of a person accused of the sexual abuse, the greater the likelihood that the charges will be dropped because the child victim is unavailable to testify. The child is less likely to withdraw of her or his own accord and more likely to be responding to pressure from older family members who are unable to endure the increasing stress of a prolonged wait for the trial to take place. Efforts to decrease the waiting period or to make it easier to present the child's testimony to the court (by videotape or closed circuit television) are problematic in that they may interfere with constitutional freedoms that all thoughtful citizens wish to protect and maintain. A relatively small proportion of abusers will be prevented from committing future sexual crimes against children as a result of receiving long prison sentences following prosecution and conviction. Of the small proportion of abusers who do receive prison sentences, the likelihood is that their periods of incarceration will be well under five years. What will happen, we may ask, when they are released back into the community? If their treatment consists of incarceration only, the odds of recidivism are unfortunately high.

One approach to the problem is to focus society's limited capacity to prosecute, convict, and incarcerate sexual offenders against children on the particular offenders who are likely to require the greatest amount of control. This would require a clinical assessment of the offender's treatment needs with an emphasis on her or his amenability to control in the community. Many helping professionals and laypersons do not realize that there is a tremendous amount of discretion involved at each step of the process, which begins with a report to the police and can end at many points prior to a trial by jury. Few people besides police officers, attorneys, judges, and court personnel appreciate fully that between an arrest and a criminal trial, there are numerous opportunities for negotiation and bargaining. When a clinical assessment culminates in a finding that the abuser appears to be a good candidate for community-based treatment, it can be used as a tool by both the defense and the prosecution to avoid a trial. In most cases, prosecutors will be interested in obtaining a guilty plea (even to a lesser charge) from the accused without having to go to the trouble and expense of a trial for which their principal witness is a child. Prosecutors and judges also have a legitimate concern about subsequent offense behavior by a child molester who is permitted to remain in the community. Knowing if the accused is considered to be a good candidate for community-based treatment by a reputable agency (preferably an office that sponsors an ongoing treatment program for sexual offenders against children) helps the prosecutor and the judge to decide which defendants are likely to need the level of control afforded by a prison setting. (A list of contraindications for community-based treatment is presented later in the chapter.)

Treatment for Sexual Offense Behavior: A Definition

What do we mean by treatment for sexual offense behavior? At New England Clinical Associates, we have found it helpful to define treatment as having four separate components—control, social intervention, therapy, and reeducation. Each component is necessary, we believe, for effective treatment of abusers. In intrafamily cases, an application of all four components is necessary to enable the child victim to receive appropriate treatment as well.

Control

It seems to be necessary to impose external controls on abusers in order to stop their sexual offense behavior. The most effective control is incarceration or fear of incarceration. Child rapists (abusers who use force or threat of force to engage children in interactive sexual behaviors) appear to need the level of control afforded by being incarcerated in a prison setting. Otherwise treatment providers may legitimately fear that if the offender becomes angered by their interventions, she or he may act out violently against them or against a vulnerable person at home or in the community. Repeat offenders (persons who have sexually abused a child subsequent to being convicted for a previous sexual offense) have communicated by their behavior that they require the control afforded by incarceration. Offenders with large numbers of victims (often a person who works with children and has sexually abused multiple children over a long period of time) have demonstrated that they have poor impulse control and need to be in an environment where no children are accessible.

By contrast, child molesters (abusers who use a nonviolent method such as enticement or entrapment to engage a child in interactive sexual behavior) appear to present fewer risks if they are treated in the community. This is more likely to be true for child molesters who have a general history of law-abiding behavior with no history of other criminal offenses or convictions and who have reportedly abused a smaller number of children.

When the offender has an untreated psychosis, a life-threatening depression with suicide attempts, or an untreated substance abuse problem, she or he has also demonstrated a need for more controls than can be imposed in the community. Sometimes it is possible to arrange inpatient treatment in a psychiatric hospital or a substance abuse treatment center to stabilize the conditions. In other words, the controls needed in such cases may be available in settings other than a prison setting. This is not to say that psychiatric stabilization of a psychosis or residential treatment for substance abuse will "cure" the offender with regard to her or his sexual offense behavior; it will not. However, some child molesters with these problems can be treated in the community for their sexual offense behavior, following inpatient or residential treatment for psychosis or substance abuse. It should be noted that these individuals will need outpatient psychiatric and substance abuse treatment in addition to community-based treatment for sexual offense behavior against children.

Child molesters who do not need the level of control afforded by incarceration do need controls notwithstanding. We recommend a probationary period of five years that includes the following conditions: participation in a treatment program for sexual offenders against children; living apart from children until the treatment providers are willing to approve a closely monitored plan to live with children once again; and avoiding jobs or social situations that allow the offender to exercise authority over children or to have unsupervised contact with them. These conditions of probation are necessary controls for all sexual offenders against children. Additional controls may be necessary for some offenders. For example, an offender with a substance abuse problem may need the additional control of being required to attend a certain number of Alcoholics Anonymous meetings each week.

It is extremely expensive and therefore impractical (since sexual offense behavior against children is so common) to impose external controls on offenders over a lifetime. In very few states will an offender be sentenced to a probationary period of greater than five years. Accordingly, an important goal of treatment for sexual offense behavior is to help the offender to substitute internal controls for external ones. It is the other components of treatment that assist offenders to acquire internal controls, to monitor their own behavior, and to meet their intimacy needs with adults instead of children. However, it is the control component of treatment that enables the other components to take place.

Social Intervention

Whenever we have reason to suspect that a child has been sexually abused, a report to the statutory child protection agency must be made. The latter is a civil authority empowered to investigate reports of suspected child abuse. Child protective services also has a mandate to ensure the safety of children who have been neglected or physically, sexually, or emotionally abused. Unfortunately, the statutory child protection agency has little or no authority over adult abusers or parents of child victims. Child protective services interventions usually have little effect on the adults upon whom the abused children must depend.

Treatment for child sexual abuse victims, offenders, and their families is usually most effective when there is coordination between the control and social intervention components. When there is little or no cooperation between criminal justice personnel and child welfare staff, child victims and their families tend to suffer, and little effective treatment can take place. In general, administrators underestimate the need to take leadership in fostering cooperation between the control and social intervention components of treatment. The unfortunate result is that, too often, opportunities are missed to use the control component of treatment to improve the lot of child victims of sexual abuse. To cite a few examples, most judges are willing to require the offender to pay for the victim's treatment as a condition of probation. However, this will rarely occur in the absence of input from a child advocate. Or the offender can be required to participate in (and pay for) family therapy as a prerequisite to reuniting the family. Once again the requirement to live apart from the family (and the child victim) in intrafamily abuse situations is unlikely to be imposed without a child advocate. If the child protective services agency (which has no direct authority over the abuser) works cooperatively with criminal justice personnel, it may be possible to facilitate treatment for the child victim and other family members that would not occur otherwise.

Therapy

Medication. Psychotropic medications are sometimes prescribed for sexual offenders against children who are clinically depressed or suffer from severe anxiety. Little effort has been made by drug manufacturers to discover and produce psychotropic medications that will safely diminish sexually aggressive behavior (without causing unwanted sedation) or will inhibit the intrusive and recurrent sexual fantasies about children that some offenders report. A medication that is being used experimentally and without approval by the Food and Drug Administration (FDA) for these purposes with male sexual offenders is Depo-Provera (medroxyprogesterone acetate). This medication is an injectable slow-release preparation of a synthetic female hormone. When administered to men, Depo-Provera may reduce sexually aggressive behavior and repetitive unwanted sexual fantasies (Berlin 1985). It can also cause a host of dangerous side effects in men, including testicular atrophy, damaged sperm, lowered sperm count, impaired sexual functioning, breast development and other forms of feminization, diabetes mellitus, and hypertension, (Meyer et al. 1985). No one knows what might be the long-term consequences of treating significant numbers of male sexual offenders with a female sexual hormone. An alternative would be a medication that would directly inhibit the body's capacity to produce male sexual hormones or else block them chemically. Thus far, such drugs (although available elsewhere) cannot be obtained in the United States.

A grave concern about using female sexual hormones to treat male sexual offense behavior has received little attention. The men receive amounts of synthetic progesterone by depot or slow-release injection, which can cause testicular atrophy and damaged sperm, yet often allows them to maintain erections and to have sexual intercourse. Patients are cautioned to avoid impregnating a woman while they are receiving the medication. It should come as no great surprise to readers that mistakes happen and pregnancies do sometimes occur. Needless to say, the risk of spontaneous abortions resulting from such impregnations is high. However, the consequences may be even more serious if women carry such pregnancies to term—the risk of serious congenital defects in their babies is unacceptably high also.

It would be beneficial to have more and safer drugs available to use in treatment of sexual offense behavior. To date, manufacturers have had little incentive to develop such drugs. Also, clinicians have made little effort to perform controlled studies on sexual offenders with the host of FDA-approved psychotropic drugs currently available to treat thought disorders and affective disorders. Many other drugs used primarily in the treatment of hypertension and heart disease have the side effects of diminishing anxiety and ameliorating the body's response to stress. A field trial of such drugs (all of which have acceptable margins of safety with regard to unwanted and dangerous side effects) might demonstrate a beneficial effect on aggressiveness and intrusive recurrent sexual fantasies. Designing and carrying out controlled studies would be difficult and challenging but might also yield unexpectedly helpful results. (Skeptics are reminded that a drug that was originally developed in pill form to treat hypertension was recalled after several years, was retested, and has now been rereleased in the form of a cream to treat male baldness!)

Behavior Modification. Most sexual offender treatment programs that use behavior modification techniques focus their attention on the male sexual offender's arousal pattern. An instrument known as a penile plethysmograph (a strain gauge attached to the penis that can record erectile response) is used to measure the offender's physical reaction to various stimuli. For example, a person who is being treated for sexual offense behavior against children may be presented with a photograph or a slide of a naked child, while his penis is attached to a penile plethysmograph. The instrument records his degree of sexual arousal (as measured by his penile erectile response) when presented with this stimulus. Other measuring devices are also used, including a balloon that is inflated around the penis and is equipped to measure increases in penile volume when the man is presented with a similar stimulus. Regardless of the nature of the measuring and recording process, such instruments all have the same underlying purpose: to generate data that can be examined comparatively when different aversive or deconditioning approaches are used.

There are two major difficulties with monitoring the sexual offender's response to treatment in this fashion. First, there are numerous factors that influence any man's penile erectile response, among them, fear, pain, cold, over-the-counter drugs, alcohol, commonly prescribed medications for hypertension and heart disease, and medical conditions such as diabetes mellitus and alcoholism. It is necessary to be certain that all of these factors remain constant in order to compare penile erectile responses before, during, and after behavior modification interventions take place. The second difficulty is that no one has demonstrated how the degree of a man's penile erectile response when presented with a picture of a naked child in the laboratory compares with or predicts what his behavior will be if he meets a child in the street on in a private place. In other words, following aversive conditioning, some sexual offenders against children may have an absent or greatly diminished penile erectile response to a photograph of a naked child. However, after leaving the laboratory, that same sexual offender may encounter a child on the street who appears lonely and looks shabby and neglected. If the offender succumbs to an impulse to befriend that child, what is likely to happen next? If he is a child molester, the odds are high that he will become emotionally invested in that child first and sexually aroused later. It is impossible to know if the behavior modification approach that changed his penile erectile response in the laboratory will interfere with the child molester's pattern of enticing or entrapping a child whom he encounters at home or in the community into interactive sexual behavior.

Proponents of medication and behavior modification therapy for sexual offenders usually require that they be combined with psychotherapy and reeducation for best results. Of course, when more than one form of therapy is utilized, it is difficult (if not impossible) to isolate and measure the effects of the different therapy interventions. None of this is to say that behavior modification cannot be useful in treating sexual offense behavior. Rather, it is to challenge the premise that measuring the effectiveness of behavior modification with the penile plethysmograph is a useful predictor of the offender's progress in treatment for sexual offense behavior.

Psychotherapy. Psychotherapy for sexual offense behavior against children has a nontraditional goal: to help offenders to manage their lives in a way that will enable them to avoid sexually abusing a child again. No single psychotherapeutic approach is appropriate; most clinicians find that utilizing a variety of methods is necessary. Traditional one-on-one insight-oriented psychotherapy certainly has been ineffective. At new England Clinical Associates, we use time-limited cycles of peer group psychotherapy as the primary therapy modality for sexual offenders against children, with individual and family therapy being used adjunctively with the group therapy. Coupled with reeducation, peer group psychotherapy seems to be the most effective milieu in which offenders can work on the skills that are the stepping-stones to accomplishing the long-term goal of refraining from future sexual offense behavior against children.

Reeducation

Sexual offenders against children usually need many types of reeducation as an integral part of treatment. Some may need job retraining, especially if they have heretofore earned a living by working with children. Most offenders need extensive reeducation in the area of social skills, especially communications skills. This is true despite the fact the many adults who sexually abuse children are well educated (some with graduate as well as undergraduate degrees), and many work in positions of authority that require them to be articulate and communicative. Nevertheless, we find that most sexual offenders against children lack the basic interpersonal communications skills to enable them to tell another person how they are feeling or what they want or need. It follows that they also have great difficulty in asking for help from others or in setting limits for themselves and others with regard to interpersonal interactions.

The best way to teach basic interpersonal skills is within the peer group therapy milieu. In order to be effective, the training must include repeated opportunities for the men to practice the skills in the peer group setting.

Evaluation Methodology

There have been a number of comprehensive evaluation protocols (Groth 1978, 1979) and descriptions of evaluation procedures (Salter 1988, 182–205) for sexual offenders against children. Chapter 11 in this volume describes how another private office conducts evaluation and treatment for persons who sexually abuse children within the family. The evaluation methodology described in this chapter has been formulated in a trial-and-error fashion at New England Clinical Associates. Its primary purpose is to determine if an adult who has committed sexual offense behavior against children (intrafamily or extrafamily abuse) appears to be suitable for treatment in the community. In other words, the evaluation procedures are designed to address two questions:

1. Can we reasonably expect to help this person with the therapy and reeducation resources available in our program and in the community?
2. Does this person thus far demonstrate that she or he is likely to cooperate with the control measures that the program and the community can provide?

Few, if any, programs or communities will be able to provide a full range of the control, social intervention, therapy, and reeducation modalities needed to treat a broad range of sexual offense behavior against children. Professionals who work with sexually abused children, abusers, and their families have a responsibility to advocate more and better community resources for offender treatment. And, professionals who direct offender treatment programs have a responsibility to determine insofar as is possible, if prospective candidates are suitable for treatment in that particular program. It is advisable to screen prospective clients prior to beginning a formal evaluation process; in this way, time, effort, and money can be conserved by eliminating from consideration persons who need treatment resources which are not provided by the program or elsewhere in the community.

Screening Considerations

Danger to Others. Child rapists are not good candidates for community-based treatment because of their tendency to threaten to use violence or to be violent in other areas of interpersonal relationships. In a secure treatment setting, one can confront such persons without fear of precipitating a violent response. In community-based treatment programs, such controls are lacking, and treatment providers may reasonably fear that the child rapist who becomes angry or threatened by a treatment intervention may strike out against them or may act out against a child or against some other vulnerable person in the family or in the community. Accordingly, a history of rapist behavior is reason to screen out a prospective candidate for community-based treatment unless the offender had received treatment in a secure setting first.

Impulse Control. Persons who have committed large numbers of offenses with large numbers of victims have demonstrated that they have poor impulse control. That is, when presented with multiple opportunities to abuse children, they acted on their impulse to commit sexual offenses with accessible children. This person is very likely to be someone who works with children (perhaps as a teacher or as a child care worker) and may have sexually abused tens or even hundreds of children over a period of years. Such offenders are more appropriate candidates for treatment in a secure setting because their previous pattern of sexual offense behavior suggests that the risk of reoffending will be high if they remain in a setting in which children are easily accessible to them.

In addition, offenders who fit this description may also have become well known in the community because of publicity regarding their multiple offenses. Such notoriety may place these offenders at risk of injury from angry friends, relatives, or neighbors of some of their victims. For all of these reasons, a plan for treatment in the community is inadvisable.

Danger to Self. Some offenders are severely depressed, even suicidal, after their sexual offense behavior against children has been discovered. Some engage in suicide attempts or other forms of self-injurious behavior. Others may become psychotic or have serious impairment of reality testing (usually a temporary phenomenon). Offenders who present a significant danger to themselves or an inability to care for themselves may need residential care. Sometimes this can be arranged in a psychiatric treatment center; for offenders who have an active substance abuse problem, residential treatment for drug or alcohol abuse is an option. It is important to remember that these treatment options will not by themselves address the abuser's needs for therapy and reeducation. Instead, they should be viewed as a means of stabilizing a separate problem (suicidal or self-injurious behavior, drug or alcohol abuse), which must be brought under control before the person's sexual offense behavior can be addressed in the community.

To summarize, the following conditions require treatment in a secure setting:

Rapist behavior (sexual abuse of a child by force or threat of injury).

Repetitive sexual offense behavior, especially when a history of prior convictions exists.

Large numbers of victims (thereby indicating poor impulse control).

Untreated substance abuse.

Severe affective disorders, untreated thought disorders, or suicidal or self-injurious behavior.

Inability to care for oneself.

When any of these are present by history, a community-based treatment program would be wise to advise those who are seeking an evaluation that the offender will require treatment in a secure setting.

Requirements for Evaluation

We have found it helpful to insist that persons seeking an evaluation for sexual offense behavior against children comply with certain requirements. Since some of the requirements have legal implications for the offender, it saves a great deal of time and energy to talk to the person's attorney first so that she or he fully understands what is being required. If the abuser makes the first contact with the office, it is useful to make her or him responsible for having the attorney call the clinician. Then the clinician can explain directly to the attorney that the purpose of the evaluation will be to determine if the person is suitable for community-based treatment for sexual offense behavior against children.

It is essential to dispel the notion that a clinical evaluation can demonstrate that a person did not commit a sexual offense. Deciding if a complaint of child sexual abuse is valid or determining if probable cause exists to believe that a particular person committed a sexual offense against a child are investigative processes. There is no method of clinical assessment that can determine if a person did or did not commit a sexual offense. (See also Chapter 12 for a discussion of this issue). Also, there is no combination of psychological tests that can be used to determine guilt or innocence. A clinician who evaluates a person accused of sexually abusing a child depends on collateral sources of information such as the statement of the child victim, and the subject's own truthfulness when deciding if the abuse actually occurred. There is no diagnostic profile of abusers to consult or apply in order to assess the likelihood that the person might or might not have committed a sexual offense against a child.

Sadly, many attorneys (and many clinicians) do not agree. Accordingly, in the initial conversation with the attorney, the clinician must take care to avoid being hired by an attorney who wishes to purchase an evaluation to uphold or reinforce a client's denial that she or he committed a sexual offense against a child. At the same time, it will be important to communicate to the attorney the real purpose of the evaluation, as well as the requirements with which the client must comply. These include:

1. Furnishing the clinician with copies of the arrest record, statements made by victims, statements made by the accused, and so forth. These must be supplied prior to the first visit.

2. Providing the office with summaries by other clinicians and treatment providers.

3. Signing two-way releases (permission to receive information and to give information) for the district attorney's office, the statutory child protection agency, other treatment providers, and the defense attorney. These must be signed no later than the beginning of the initial visit.

4. Supplying the clinician with a list of previous arrests and prior criminal convictions.

5. Establishing a residence apart from the victim and any other children and refraining from working with or caring for children.

6. Acknowledging responsibility for the abuse.

The reasons are obvious for most of the requirements. The clinician needs to review the complaint and the arrest record to decide if she or he believes that the sexual abuse took place. As well, it is important to know the impressions and plans of other clinicians and treatment providers who may have worked with (or still be treating) the offender. Permission to receive information from and share information with the other professionals named in item 3 is essential. Otherwise the clinician may find herself or himself grappling with the ethical issue of breaching confidentiality if she or he discovers information that should be shared with one or more of these other parties but lacks permission to do so. In addition, the clinician will wish to avoid a situation that permits the offender and her or his attorney to prevent an unfavorable report from reaching the attention of the court.

No one is likely to question the appropriateness of a requirement to supply the evaluator with a list of previous arrests and convictions, but many offenders and their attorneys balk at fulfilling the next requirement. Living apart from one's victim and any other children entails much effort and inconvenience, as well as expense and sometimes actual hardship. Some mistakenly believe that this requirement is solely to prevent future sexual abuse of children. However, there is another important reason for this requirement: living apart from the victim and any child usually does require the offender to move to another residence. This is both a structural and strategic intervention that clearly establishes that the offender is responsible for the sexual abuse and needs to make significant life changes. The change in residence may be temporary or permanent. Refraining from working with or caring for children will definitely be a permanent requirement. No one who has sexually abused a child should be employed as a teacher or a child care worker or be in a position of authority over children for the rest of her or his life. This last requirement always entails hardship for a person who has heretofore worked with children; however, no compromise is possible in this matter. If we believe that the person sexually abused a child, he or she needs this level of control, whether the offense took place in an intrafamily setting or elsewhere in the community or in the workplace. To permit a sexual offender against children ever to be employed as a schoolteacher or to do volunteer work with children would be analogous to hiring an alcoholic to work as a bartender or to permit a recovered drug addict to work as a pharmacist's assistant. A person who has already demonstrated that she or he could set aside personal and societal inhibitions to commit a sexual offense against a child should never be employed or permitted to volunteer in a position that permits unsupervised access to children. Such employment and/or access to children would place too much stress on the individual's internal controls and entail an unacceptable risk of another offense. (The last requirement, acknowledging responsibility for the sexual abuse, will be discussed thoroughly under evaluation procedures.)

When prospective candidates for community-based treatment refuse to comply with these requirements, they are demonstrating by their behavior that they are unlikely to abide by the rules and/or fulfill the requirements of the treatment program. Willingness (or lack thereof) to cooperate with these requirements is part of the evaluation. In other words, observing if the person will abide by the requirements is a test built into the evaluation process. Cooperation during the evaluation is *not* a guarantee that the offender will continue to cooperate with treatment requirements after being admitted to the treatment program; however, refusal to cooperate with evaluation requirements during the time between arrest and prosecution or between arrest and sentencing (if a guilty plea is entered) is an ominous predictor of lack of cooperation thereafter.

Community-based treatment provides no direct controls and is dependent on the offender's willingness and ability to comply with rules and requirements in a context of minimal oversight provided by the treatment program and the probation officer. Therefore, compliance with all five requirements is an important test of the offender's suitability for treatment in the community. When the offender refuses to cooperate with any or all of the requirements, clinicians are well advised to recommend treatment in a secure setting first.

Evaluation Procedures

Interviewing the Offender. Several interviews with the offender are necessary to establish a relationship and assess level of functioning and specific treatment needs. The clinician will wish to obtain a comprehensive social history, personal victimization history, and psychosexual history. As well, it will be important to ask many questions about the person's sexual offense behavior, both in regard to the instant offense and in relation to other offenses (possibly not yet reported). Whenever indicated, a mental status examination should be performed.

Every clinician has a personal style of establishing a relationship with a client. In working with sexual offenders against children, it is usually helpful to convey warmth and genuine concern for the person's human needs and feelings while at the same time communicating a belief that the sexual abuse with which she or he is charged did in fact take place. In other words, the evaluator is demonstrating an ability to respect and care about a person who has committed a sexual offense against a child. It is impossible to fake this capacity. A clinician who is personally threatened by sexual offenders against children or has unresolved anger, fear, and loathing for abusers will be unable to communicate an ability to separate the offender from the offense. What is likely to be perceived by most offenders as helpful is an implicit message that the clinician accepts her or him as a human being worthy of respect and caring. This is not to say that it is appropriate or necessary for the clinician to deprecate or minimize the seriousness of the offense. But a person under evaluation for sexual offense behavior against children desperately needs to receive a message of hope and affirmation from a potential treatment provider. Hope and affirmation from people who also insist that the offender be responsible and accountable for committing acts of child sexual abuse are essential. The offender is likely to be depressed, frightened, and confused and to have very low self-esteem at the time of the evaluation. She or he may not communicate appreciation at this time for receiving realistic hope for recovery and affirmation as a worthwhile human being; however, the hope and affirmation, if received, will be powerful messages with a significant long-term effect.

More than anything else, the clinician must demonstrate that she or he can hear the offender describe the sexual offense behavior without being punitive and blaming in return. Prior to the first interview, the clinician should tell the attorney that it will be necessary to discuss the instant offense and that the offender is expected to be honest about what occurred. The clinician should ask the attorney to advise the offender about the legal implications of this process prior to the first interview. If the attorney says that she or he will advise the client to refrain from admitting to or discussing the offense behavior because it will be incriminating, there is no point in conducting an evaluation to determine suitability for community-based treatment. It is impossible to treat a person in the community for something that she or he denies completely. Persistent and total unwillingness to admit that she or he committed sexual acts with a child is therefore a condition that precludes a recommendation for community-based treatment. Both the offender and the attorney must be made aware of this before the first evaluation interview—thus the importance of raising the issue again early in the first session.

If the offender is still hesitant to discuss the sexual abuse and expresses concern about the potential for legal liability in doing so, the clinician can advise her or him to consult the attorney before the next evaluation appointment so that the issue can be clarified. The clinician can then state that it will be necessary to discuss the sexual abuse in detail in the next session and that a decision by the offender and/or the attorney to refuse to do so will be viewed as a reason to stop the evaluation process. After giving the offender an opportunity to respond and to ask questions, the clinician can move to another topic. As soon as possible after the session, the clinician should call the attorney, report the offender's concerns about disclosure, repeat again that acknowledging and accepting responsibility for the sexual abuse is a prerequisite for community-based treatment, and ask the attorney to clarify this with the client and address the person's legitimate concerns about the legal implications of compliance.

This discussion illustrates the importance of skilled and consistent case management in working with sexual offenders against children. Few clinicians have received training or experience in case management skills of this type. The process outlined is an illustration of the type of negotiation and bargaining necessitated in a "customer approach to patienthood" (Burgess and Lazare 1976). This approach and the techniques involved are based on a premise that the clinician has something to sell and needs to convince the patient that she or he wishes to buy it. In turn, the patient or client needs a service and can exercise some discretion in regard to the type of service he wants or needs, how much he is able or willing to pay, and so forth. What is taking place between them is therefore a business negotiation involving salesmanship, bargaining, and "consumership." The service being sold by the clinician is an evaluation to determine suitability for community-based treatment; the product the offender wishes to buy is an evaluation report that will assist him or her to avoid incarceration and avoid punitive sanctions.

The clinician who has the requirements for evaluation is setting a high price in human as well as in financial terms upon the service. If the offender (and the attorney) believe that a comparable service can be bought elsewhere at a less exacting price, enlightened "consumership" will be likely to encourage them to look elsewhere. On the other hand, the clinician can increase the likelihood that they will "buy" the service offered by exercising planning and negotiating skills. Interestingly, a willingness to pay the "price" of the service makes the offender a much more attractive candidate for community-based treatment. Therefore, the effort expended by the clinician in "selling" the service is likely to be rewarded later.

Meanwhile, it is also necessary for the "clinician-seller" to communicate ethical, consistent, and caring behavior. She or he must model honesty, firmness, compassion, and absolute integrity in regard to keeping promises coupled with a quiet insistence that the "patient-buyer" also be honest and also keep promises. To tell the attorney and the patient that certain requirements are nonnegotiable is to make a promise: I will not see the patient or complete the evaluation if these requirements are not fulfilled. It would be breaking the promise if the clinician agreed to proceed when one of the requirements is not fulfilled.

Some clinicians see themselves solely as therapists, not as therapists and case managers. They are likely to believe that it is someone else's job to require the offender to admit responsibility for the offense, to live apart from children, and the like. But if the therapy and reeducation components of treatment are expected to assist the client to manage her or his life so that future sexual offense behavior against children is avoided, it seems reasonable to expect that the clinician will exercise comparably effective case management skills.

When clinicians lack both experience and confidence, it is difficult to perform the case management tasks outlined without appearing to be inflexible and punitive. Yet the essential ingredients of the service being offered are fairness, caring, a willingness to be accountable, and a capacity to require accountability from others in a nonpunitive and nonblaming fashion. In the absence of experience, a sincere desire to learn, good supervision, or consultation from someone who is more experienced and a willingness to practice are essential.

The clinician's ability to "sell" is tested extensively by the offender's denial of the sexual abuse. It is helpful to anticipate that the offender will be somewhere on a continuum of denial at the time of the first interview. If total denial that the abuse took place represents one end of the continuum, the other end will be represented by a total willingness to acknowledge every incident of sexual offense behavior over a lifetime. Most offenders who were willing to comply with all of the other requirements for the evaluation will present at the initial interview with a measure of denial that places them somewhere in the middle of the continuum. For example, an offender might acknowledge that the abuse took place but state that he cannot remember how it happened or even what happened. Some offenders say that they were under the influence of alcohol or drugs and therefore are unable to remember. Others will admit to one or two incidents of abuse but deny responsibility for as many incidents as were reported by the victim. Still others will admit to some, but not all, of the types of behavior reported by the child; for example, they will admit to committing acts of sexual fondling but will deny that they performed oral sex on the victim. And other abusers will admit to committing sexual offense behavior against one child but will deny that they abused another child who is also believed to be a victim.

Other variations of denial might be to acknowledge that sexual acts with a child took place but to relabel the behavior. For example, some offenders may describe what they did as a form of sex education. One man claimed that his reason for touching his daughters' breasts repeatedly was a sincere desire to teach them to perform breast self-examinations for early detection of cancer. Another man acknowledged that he had fondled his 11-year-old stepdaughter and performed simulated intercourse with her, but also claimed that she, not he, initiated the sexual behavior.

Although all degrees of denial are frustrating, clinicians usually discover that offenders who are willing to acknowledge that the abuse occurred at all (even if they relabel the behavior) are people who can be worked with. To put it differently, acknowledgment that at least some of the sexual behavior reported by the child did in fact occur is a movement toward the right end of the continuum of denial. If the abuser now acknowledges sexual offenses for which he has not yet been charged, he can legitimately fear that he will be charged with more crimes and that the outcome will be greater sanctions and more punishment. If the abuser now is ready to take total responsibility for all aspects of her or his sexual offense behavior, then most of the work of treatment has already been accomplished. It is unreasonable to expect either to occur during an initial evaluation session.

The clinician's response to the offender's degree of denial will influence greatly how much denial is maintained. An angry response—such as "You must think I'm pretty stupid if you think I'll believe that!" is disrespectful and likely to increase denial, not reduce it. If the clinician finds it necessary to challenge the distortions of reality inherent in relabeling the behavior as sex education, the offender may respond by refusing to disclose anything else. It would be preferable to explore further each incident that the offender describes and defer challenges. At most, a quiet comment could be made, such as, "Not everyone would agree with you about that," or "Children do sometimes bring up the idea of having sex first, especially if they have been taught that some people will reward them." As far as expressing anger is concerned, the clinician should ask herself or himself, "Why am I getting angry right now?" and "How is it going to help if I make an angry response?" The answer to the latter question is that it will not help at all to make an angry comment and may well make it much harder to work with the offender.

It is usually helpful to plan to spend part of each interview session with the offender in discussing the sexual offense behavior. Thus one session could focus on describing the details of the behavior itself, another could address the fantasies about the sexual abuse experienced by the offender before, during, and after each episode, another might explore other episodes of abuse prior to or after the instant offense, and so on. Meanwhile, each session should also address another aspect of the history taking: social history, victimization history, psychosexual history, and the like. It is useful to obtain this information in association with stages in the person's life: preschool years, early primary school years, later primary school years, junior high, and so on. For example, the clinician might ask, "What can you remember about what was going on for your family before you were old enough to go to school? What kind of work did your parents do? Did you have any special chores or responsibilities at that time?" In regard to the victimization history, all types of victimization should be addressed: physical abuse, excessive discipline, neglect, sexual abuse, and so forth. Many men deny that they were abused *per se;* it is preferable to avoid the word *abuse* and ask questions such as, "Did anyone ever trick you or trap you or force you to perform any type of sexual behavior while you were in grade school?" Another useful probe question is, "Did anyone ever take advantage of you when you were a teenager [or in college or in grade school]?"

In taking a psychosexual history, the clinician is gathering information to try to determine the offender's sexual preference, fantasies during sexual behavior, ideas about human sexuality in general, and her or his own sexuality in particular. As well, this is a good opportunity to get a sense of the person's ideas and rules about intimacy, closeness in human relationships, wishes to be cared about by others, and so on. One may begin by asking about masturbation. When does the person remember a first episode of masturbation? How did the parents treat this behavior? What did the person think or feel while masturbating? The clinician can then ask when and from whom the person learned about menstruation, wet dreams, "jerking off," vaginal sexual intercourse, oral sex, and the like. The clinician will wish to explore the person's attitudes about males and females at each stage of development. Same-sex recreational or group experiences, mixed-sex parties or activities, dating, and so on should be explored methodically. The clinician wants to derive an impression of the quality of the offender's peer relationships and relationships with persons of the same sex and of the opposite sex at each stage of development. This will obviously include asking about interactive sexual experiences with others, male and female. At intervals, the clinician should continue to ask, "What was that like for you then?" and "What do you think about that now?"

This historical information can be supplemented by asking the offender about favorite movie stars, favorite books, and favorite television stars. The clinician explores what the offender likes or does not like about all of the above. Least favorite movie stars and television shows (and why they are not enjoyed) are useful probes also. The offender should be asked questions such as, "When you first became interested in your spouse, what was it that attracted you? Did anything about that person put you off? How about now?"

At the time of the last evaluation interview, the offender should be informed if there are discrepancies in the information he or she has supplied in comparison to information supplied by others. In a nonblaming way, the clinician should ask the offender to explain the discrepancies. During each session, the offender should be given an opportunity to ask questions of the clinician. While assessing the person's current functioning, the clinician should address issues such as where the offender is residing, whom he or she talks to, how she or he is sleeping, what is her or his state of health, and the like. Particular attention should be paid to issues such as communication with spouse and children. Is communication taking place? How? Do they visit? Has the abuser seen the children? What was the visit like? If the offender has not seen family members and wishes to do so, the clinician might offer to help to schedule a supervised visit in the office. (Visiting with the victim is an important issue and will be addressed later in the chapter). It is unrealistic to expect that there will be no communication or contact between family members. When a clinician offers to facilitate contact early, she or he may be performing a much-needed service, as well as preventing later difficulties.

Lastly, the clinician should consider offering the offender an opportunity for peer contact. In other words, a visit in the office with an offender who has more experience of treatment (and agrees to the visit) could be arranged. A rule for the visit is to maintain confidentiality. The "veteran" client agrees to answer questions posed by the person under evaluation. It may also be desirable for the offender who is being evaluated to visit a therapy group. Again, confidentiality would be maintained, and the person could ask questions of others who have more experience of treatment. Such peer contacts are invaluable because they convey hope to the person under evaluation that it is possible to move beyond the pain and anxiety in the presentence period.

Collateral Interviews. The clinician will wish to interview the offender's spouse or sexual partner, the offender's children, and the victim, if possible. The clinician should call the spouse and request an interview; if this is refused, the offender or the attorney may be able to persuade the spouse to be interviewed. It is preferable to ask the spouse during a face-to-face interview for permission to interview minor children.

Each family member should be asked in a separate interview what she or he thinks or understands about the sexual abuse complaint. In addition, the clinician should explore their reactions to the disclosure, the arrest, and the family separations that have taken place. Each should be asked how she or he views the offender, including strengths, weaknesses, good and bad points, and so forth. Each should be asked about hopes, fears, wishes, requests, and so on. The clinician should give each family member an opportunity to ask questions also and then answer those questions as honestly as possible without violating confidentiality.

In addition, the clinician should conduct face-to-face or telephone interviews with the child protective services worker, the probation officer performing the presentence investigation (if the offender does enter a guilty plea), and other treatment providers who may be working with the offender and the family. Written permission must have been obtained prior to these interviews. Talking to the offender's clergyperson or spiritual adviser is also advisable. Each of these collateral interviews has a dual purpose:

1. To obtain more information about the offender and the family.
2. To try to enlist that person's cooperation in the treatment plan.

Although sometimes very time-consuming, these collateral interviews with other professionals are likely to be beneficial later.

Intensive Record Review. All of the arrest records, reports of other offenses, reports of psychological testing (if available), and other clinical evaluations must be reviewed thoroughly. Again, the clinician should be alert to any discrepancies that may be present between history supplied by the offender and history supplied by others. Discrepancies should be thoroughly explored with the offender and with others if necessary.

Writing the Report. The evaluation report should begin with a list of evaluation procedures, including the dates of all interviews (face-to-face and telephone), conferences (with whom and for what purpose), and the like. The report should contain a recounting of all of the historical information that was elicited, including a history of sexual offense behavior, social and employment history, victimization history, and psychosexual history. The report concludes with the clinician's impressions and recommendations. Sometimes the clinician can say that the offender's behavior fits the pattern of behavior frequently seen in fixated molesters or regressed molesters or rapists (Groth 1982). Often there is insufficient information about the offender's psychosexual history to decide if the behavior is more similar to that of a fixated molester or a regressed molester. If so, this should be stated.

The most important part of the impressions section of the report is the clinician's statements about the offender's suitability (or lack of suitability) for community-based treatment. The impressions section should conclude with a discussion of the offender's treatment needs and the clinician's requirements if the offender is accepted into the treatment program. Each requirement should be explained: the need to reside apart from children, the need to participate in peer group therapy, the benefits expected, and so on. If there are special requirements, these should be explained also. For example, an offender who has a reading problem might be very dependent on family members in this regard. One such offender depended on his child victim to read all of his correspondence, interpret bills sent to the house, and so on. This man was required to participate in a literacy program so that he could learn to read and be less dependent on others. Another offender might have an inadequately treated drinking problem and be required to attend a minimum number of Alcoholics Anonymous meetings each week.

The last page of the report should be a list of the requirements for treatment. These should address control, social intervention, therapy, and reeducation and be as directly stated and explicit as possible. Clinicians frequently discover that probation officers who conduct presentence investigations will pass on these recommendations to the judge. In turn, at the time of sentencing, the judge is likely to order that the clinician's recommendations become the conditions of probation.

Recommendations. Typical recommendations for a person considered to be a suitable candidate for treatment in the community might be as follows:

1. Reside apart from children for a minimum of one year; refrain from unsupervised contact with children; do not work with children. The recommendation to live apart from children will be reviewed after one year. Active participation in family therapy will be a prerequisite to recommending a return to living with children.

2. Participate in treatment for sexual offense behavior for five years, including weekly peer group therapy and individual or family therapy at least as often as once a month.

3. Pay for one's own treatment and that of one's victim and one's family.

4. Maintain continuous employment and maintain sobriety.

These are the basic requirements for all sexual offenders against children. Those with additional treatment needs have additional requirements—for example, attend Alcoholics Anonymous.

Some community-based treatment programs are subsidized, and therefore, no fees are charged for offender treatment. This is unfortunate, because free treatment tends to be devalued by many of its recipients. For offenders, paying for one's own treatment and for the victim's treatment is a way of being accountable for the offenses; paying for the victim's treatment can also be viewed as an expiatory process. Clinicians who work in subsidized programs may be able to devise another form of payment, perhaps in the form of paying into a fund to help victims. If offenders are indigent, the fee could be very small. However, a token payment is better than no payment.

The clinician should plan a time in which the offender can review the report in the office and then be available to answer any questions that may arise. It is courteous to offer the offender an opportunity to comment on the report and the recommendations and to agree or disagree with any aspect of the report. Adding an addendum page for this purpose is useful.

Long-Term Treatment

Initial Reaction to Treatment

Immediately after the sentencing, offenders are likely to appear depressed, perhaps for the first time or perhaps with an intensification of previous signs and symptoms of depression. It is normal for the period of relief that follows a sentence that did not require incarceration to be followed by a period of letdown and sadness. The crisis of facing a sentence to prison is over. A period of taking stock of the damages that have been incurred is likely to follow soon. It is also likely that the offender will feel bruised by the court appearances, not to mention the probable impact of the cost of legal representation. All of the previous family problems and worries will still be present. The offender is likely now to focus on his living situation and job situation and be intensely dissatisfied. As well, the requirements for treatment, although considerably less stringent than a prison sentence, are likely to be viewed now as onerous and unjust.

The odds are very high that the offender will now displace much of his anger and resentment on the treatment providers who helped him to avoid incarceration. Some clinicians may be wounded by this response to their sincere effort (entailing a degree of risk taking) to help the offender to remain in the community. Whatever the offender's style of being angry (it may range from exaggerated politeness coupled with seemingly offhand passive-aggressive remarks to outright expressions of hostility), the clinicians and the other clients in the treatment program will soon begin to feel its effects.

During this period, it is desirable for the offender to be seen individually by a clinician each week, even if time constraints or financial constraints require that the visits be brief. In the individual sessions, the clinician can anticipate the letdown, depression, and anger experienced by many other offenders at this time. She or he can suggest that this is a predictable reaction and offer some practical suggestions for getting through this period, including a suggestion that the offender bring it up in the group. Some offenders will do so at once; others will need to be encouraged to do so while group sessions are taking place. This will be an appropriate matter for the offender to process individually and in peer group therapy. Other members can let the offender know that they had a similar experience when they were beginning treatment and perhaps offer practical suggestions as well.

Again, it should be emphasized that clinicians must train themselves to expect that offender-clients will often be angry and resentful or, at best, unenthusiastic about the treatment process. This is a normal and understandable human reaction. Most human beings fear change; most become disorriented when their living arrangements are disrupted; being the subject of a criminal proceeding is intensely threatening to citizens who are generally law abiding; it is incredibly discomforting to be separated from one's family, even if there was much stress within the family system and the home; and it is humiliating and frustrating to have controls and limits set upon oneself by others. The offender may have little previous experience in having controls and limits set upon herself or himself in a nonpunitive fashion by others. However, none of the interventions by the treatment program are likely to feel good to the offender at this time; instead, it feels intrusive and perhaps oppressive to be required to attend weekly sessions of peer group therapy and frequent individual sessions as well.

Clinicians must be prepared to receive angry feedback in some form from the offender *and train themselves to avoid responding angrily in return*. This may well be a time when some of the previous contacts with other treatment providers that were part of the evaluation process can be utilized. Clergy or spiritual advisors, an Alcoholics Anonymous sponsor, the child protective services worker, and the probation officer all should be advised when the offender is depressed and angry and their help enlisted in various ways. It may not be necessary for them to make interventions, but it will be helpful if they are alerted to what is taking place and are available for support if needed. Once again, all treatment providers must remind themselves that offenders do not necessarily acknowledge that others are being supportive. Positive feedback indicating awareness of and appreciation for the support (or other interventions) may not be forthcoming. This does not mean that the support or other interventions are useless or counterproductive. It does mean that help does not always feel like help. It may also mean that one is dealing with a person who has not learned or does not practice the interpersonal communications skills that enable others to know that support or help has been received and is being acknowledged.

Stages of Recovery

Identifying a recovery process for persons who receive treatment for sexual offense behavior against children presupposes that offenders were in some way impaired or even ill (from a psychosocial perspective) at the time that they committed their crimes. This formulation has advantages and disadvantages. The principal advantage is that the concept of recovery is a dynamic one, enabling offenders who are in treatment to see themselves as moving (or having moved) toward a state of improvement in which they can take justifiable pride. The disadvantage is that some offenders already see themselves as victims; for them, the concept that they can be helped by a recovery process may reinforce their firmly held belief that they were not responsible for their crimes and should not be held accountable.

Since "treatment" in itself, implies a goal of improvement or "getting better," we have found the concept of going through a recovery process to be useful in treating sexual offenders against children. The offender treatment program at the New England Clinical Associates office has consistently stressed that clients are responsible for utilizing the various components of treatment as they strive for self-improvement. Therefore, treatment providers have a responsibility to provide the tools (the components of treatment) with which the clients themselves perform the work necessary for their own recovery. We can thus acknowledge that many sexual offenders against children were impaired or deprived in a variety of ways by unhappy or abusive childhoods and the stresses and vicissitudes of living as adolescents and adults in a world that is often characterized by unfairness and a lack of caring. At the same time, offenders are also reminded that they committed sexual acts with children because they mistakenly believed that it was justifiable for them to meet personal needs for affection, affiliation, power, and control in this way. Most offenders also mistakenly believed that they would not be held accountable for their criminal behavior. Full recovery therefore means that they have taken total responsibility for their past as well as their present behavior; in the present, they are actively working to manage their lives in a way that will enable them to avoid committing sexual acts with children in the future.

The following stages of recovery for sexual offenders against children have been identified.

Acknowledging Fully the Sexual Offense Behavior. This is actually a stage of overcoming numerous layers of denial, including denial of the abuse itself, denial of its impact, and denial about why it occurred. Thus we can identify several components:

Admission that sexual acts with a child occurred.

Acceptance of full responsibility for the sexual behavior, even if the child apparently agreed to it or perhaps initially, suggested it.

Acknowledgment and understanding that the sexual abuse was harmful for the child.

Admission that the sexual abuse met many needs for the offender.

Acknowledgment that sexual abuse of a child was a selfish and wrongful act brought on by many distortions of thinking.

Experiencing Appropriate Guilt and Shame for Committing the Abuse. This is an incredibly painful process. (See also the description of empathic guilt in chapter 11.) Many offenders move from the depression about their new life circumstances following a sentence that includes stringent conditions of probation to becoming depressed for different reasons as they become more fully aware of the damage caused by their selfishness and lack of caring. Support from peers in group therapy has been essential for offenders to endure this emotional pain and move beyond it to the next stages. Clinicians must be alert to signs such as self-destructive behaviors, risk taking, diminished capacity for self-care, and suicidal behavior at this time. Paradoxically, at this stage when the offender is experiencing the greatest amount of emotional pain associated with the sexual offense behavior, she or he may also be at greatest risk for reoffending. Turning to a child to meet one's emotional needs at a time of great vulnerability and stress may be a deeply ingrained behavior. To be caught committing another sexual crime while one is on probation will likely result in harsh punishment. Although reoffending is a self-defeating behavior, it is understandable in the context of the offender's belief that she or he is deserving of punishment at this time.

Exploring Fully What Needs Were Met by the Sexual Offense and Identifying Danger Signals. In this stage of recovery, offenders begin to come to terms with the needs that were met (albeit dysfunctionally) by their decision to commit sexual acts with a child. This means acknowledging that one was scared, hopeless, and in some degree of emotional pain at the time that the offenses occurred. One man recalled that he always wept while he was performing sexual acts with his victim and that he let the boy see some of his emotional pain and sadness. For this offender, the victim's concern for him and caring for him could be expressed most effectively by cooperating with interactive sexual behaviors at the offender's request. Compliance with sexual acts for this offender was an important way of receiving acceptance and caring from another human being. The symbolic meaning of the sexual abuse varies for each offender. The task of recognizing the symbolic meaning and what needs were being met for her or for him is appropriate and necessary for each offender.

The clinicians who are directing the offender's treatment must be sure that she or he also explores the danger signals that were present before, during, and after the instant offenses. Many offenders, for example, will say truthfully, "I didn't know that I was scared. I didn't know that I was angry at that time." The offender who wept in front of his victim and for whom the child's sympathy and concern were so important said, "I didn't ever realize that I was hurting so badly except when I was with Jerry. When I was with him, it would all just come over me, like a wave." These offenders need encouragement to review painstakingly the events of their lives while the abuse was taking place. Another group member might say, "There were probably plenty of danger signals at the time. What were you thinking about when you were driving to work? Or when you were in bed, just before you went to sleep?" Again, peer group therapy is a highly effective milieu for exploring past and present danger signals. It will also be important for the offender to explore how she or he is meeting emotional needs now. In the next section of this chapter, a discussion of a methodology for accomplishing this exploration will be presented.

Learning More Effective Coping Skills. Sexual offenders against children need to learn safe and effective coping skills in order to reduce their risk of sexually abusing another child. Although each client's needs are different, most offenders have significant deficits in several areas.

Identifying Emotions Correctly. It is not unusual for these clients to have great difficulty in identifying their own emotional responses to other people and to various situations. This is particularly likely when the offender's emotional response is one of fear or sadness. The latter are likely to be suppressed immediately and be replaced by anger. In its turn, anger may also be denied or suppressed.

The difficulty inherent in these common patterns of suppressing dysphoric responses lies in the offender's history of meeting emotional needs by turning to children for comfort, acceptance, affection, reassurance, sympathy, and the like. As well, many offenders have a history of displacing their anger (which may be disavowed or unrecognized) on others. Either of these patterns is especially risky for sexual offenders against children to continue to demonstrate. Correctly identifying one's emotional response when it occurs is a necessary first step in the process of learning safer methods of meeting emotional needs.

The reciprocal may also be true: the offender may believe that she or he can correctly guess another person's emotional response, sometimes with disastrous results. For example, an offender might way, "My victim never complained; that's how I knew she must have liked what we were doing." This is not just an example of a self-serving distortion of thinking; it is also an example of the offender's capacity to misinterpret the child's response based on a mistaken belief that one's guesses (or wishes) about another person's feelings are accurate. It is also essential for offenders to learn that they must be open to receiving information about what is actually occurring on an emotional level for others. Not only is it inappropriate to believe that one can guess what someone else is thinking or feeling, it is also inappropriate (and may even be dangerous) to refuse to hear (or appreciate) what another person is trying to communicate. This is especially true if the communication that is not being received is influencing the course of a a close interpersonal relationship. Some molesters said to their victims, "You like this, don't you." (in reference to the sexual behavior). The victim is likely to report, "I tried to tell him that I didn't like it, but he didn't hear me." The odds are high that the child's perception is accurate: the offender probably was not paying attention to the child's reply at that time because he believed that his guess that the child was enjoying the sexual behavior was accurate and because he had a powerful emotional investment in ignoring any response by the child that might contradict his dearly held belief. Again, it is obvious that offenders with these deficits need much practice not just in identifying their own emotions, but also in being sensitive to the emotional responses of others.

Expressing Feelings Directly and Honestly. Offenders usually need to learn that it is possible and appropriate to tell others with whom they are closely connected about what they (the offenders) are experiencing emotionally. It is not unusual for offenders to expect to be able to bypass that process and to expect others to guess what they are feeling. The closer the relationship is, the more likely the offender is to expect that a spouse, a child, a sibling, a boss, a subordinate, or a clinician will guess correctly. And probably the offender couples this unrealistic expectation with a strong sense of entitlement: others *ought* to know, appreciate, and be concerned about what the offender is feeling or thinking. These expectations interfere markedly with open and honest communication with others. They also interfere with the offender's capacity to receive attention, caring, affection, and nurturance from others, If another person does not know what the offender is feeling, it is hard to respond appropriately. By the same token, a consistent refusal to communicate one's feelings directly can result in a consistent experience of believing that others are indifferent; this may reinforce the offender's deeply held belief that she or he is constantly being victimized by other adults, and therefore it is permissible and appropriate to turn to children for emotional support.

Many clients find that to practice expressing one's emotional response is onerous and uncomfortable. They may initially go through a process of hurling verbal reports of their feelings at others in a challenging or blaming fashion. Most people find it easier to report positive feelings rather than negative ones; however, it may not even occur to offenders that verbalizing positive emotional responses is as important as reporting negative ones. Again, practice in peer group therapy is safest and can be particularly effective.

Making and Receiving Requests After learning to express feelings, it is a logical next step to verbalize one's wishes in the form of requests—logical, perhaps, but difficult to accomplish for many offenders, who may fear (sometimes with justifiable historical basis) that expressing their wishes and requests is an invitation for others to refuse them.

Be that as it may, offenders need practice in communicating requests to others in a direct fashion. Otherwise they are likely to continue to be locked into a pattern of communicating requests indirectly to those few people whom they expect will be able to understand and meet their needs. For example, one offender would say to his wife at the breakfast table, "I'm going to be home late tonight." If she did not reply, he would repeat the statement, usually in a louder voice, until she finally made a reply such as, "I'll keep your supper warm until you do get home." This man expected that his wife would guess that he wanted something from her and offer to supply it without being asked directly. Yet the statement, "I'll be home late tonight," could just as easily have been interpreted as a message that he would eat dinner elsewhere and that it would not be necessary to save food for his evening meal at home. Frequently disappointed by his wife's apparent indifference to his wishes and needs, this offender found it easy to justify his six-year sexual relationship with his adolescent daughter. By use of an entrapment strategy (communicating to his daughter that, because he was her father and her caretaker, she was obligated to engage in sexual acts with him), he was able to avoid the necessity of asking his wife to have sexual relations and risking her refusal.

Again, a peer group therapy milieu affords an excellent opportunity for offenders to practice making (and receiving) requests. Offenders can thereby learn from each other how important it is to be clear about what is being asked of another person.

Giving and Receiving Help. Being able to make a direct request of another person is a necessary antecedent to receiving attention and help. In addition to asking for help, offenders must learn to receive help from others. The reciprocal processes are also pertinent to treatment of sexual offense behavior against children. To have a satisfying intimate relationship with another adult, reciprocity and mutuality are important. One must not only receive help, nurturance, and affection; one must also be prepared to reciprocate all of the above. Many men are as uncomfortable about receiving help as they are about asking for it. The peer group therapy milieu, once again, is an ideal setting in which offenders can practice these skills.

Setting Limits and Maintaining Boundaries. If a person is to maintain an identity as an individual or as a self, it is necessary to be able to set limits on that which will be given or received, regardless of the expectations and demands of others. To avoid enmeshment in an intimate relationship, each adult must have the capacity to refuse to accept at some times that which is proffered by the partner and to refuse at times to give that which one's partner may request or demand. It is difficult to learn to do this without also communicating anger and blame. Without a capacity for open and direct communication, it is impossible for partners in an intimate relationship to avoid hurting one another and threatening the relationship. In peer group therapy, offenders can also practice saying "no" to another member's request or to another member's offer of help. Setting limits and maintaining boundaries in an assertive but nonangry fashion is definitely an acquired skill. The capacity to do this is necessary if one is to meet emotional needs by intimacy with another adult. Sexual offenders against children have already learned that they could meet their intimacy needs with a child without feeling "swallowed up" by that relationship or by the child. If the offender believes that she or he will be swallowed up in a relationship with another adult, the choices are to avoid intimacy altogether or to relapse into sexual offense behavior against children once again. Practicing limit setting in a peer group therapy milieu as a stepping-stone to nonthreatening intimacy with adults affords a more realistic (and acceptable) choice.

Substituting Internal Controls. In the last stage of recovery, the offender has developed all of the internal controls that were heretofore externally applied. The offender is now capable of avoiding high-risk situations in which she or he might turn to a child to meet emotional needs. These include periods of unsupervised access to children, periods in which uninterrupted fantasizing about children might take place, and periods in which the offender is avoiding the effort required to meet intimacy needs with adults. All of these situations and their attendant warning signals are now well known to the offender, and she or he has developed a capacity to recognize them early and take remedial action. A large measure of an internal control process involves managing one's life so that high-risk situations are avoided.

Instead of being compelled to participate in treatment, an offender who has substituted internal controls will recognize that she or he has a lifelong need for treatment and that periodic returns to a clinician or to the treatment program will be necessary. Meanwhile, the offender is able to take responsibility for directing her or his treatment and knows when to seek outside help. Recognizing a need for further therapy should be regarded by offender and clinician alike as a sign of health, not as a sign of weakness or relapse.

When the treatment plan has required the offender to live apart from the family, there is always keen interest focused on when it will be permissible for the family to reunite. For some families, it will not be appropriate for the offender to return to the home while minor children are living there. In other cases, the marital couple decides to separate permanently and divorce. In still other cases, the parents wish to maintain their marriage and to live together once again and the children wish for a reunification also.

Chapter 11 contains an excellent description of a step-by-step reunification process when the intrafamily offender, the child victim, and other family members wish to do so and are ready to do so. O'Connell (1986) has also provided a comprehensive and helpful discussion of this process.

It is difficult to know when an offender has reached the last stage of recovery. Often it is a matter of the expiration of probation and a cessation of external controls for that reason only. Salter (1988 171–181) offers a number of criteria to help determine the offender's progress in treatment. Rowan (1988) does also and acknowledges that there are no proven ways to predict when reoffense behavior is likely to occur. In fact, the goal of treatment is predicated on a negative behavioral outcome: repeated sexual abuse of children will not occur. It is, of course, possible to devise various scales or measurements to assess the offender's progress in accomplishing the step-wise treatment goals for each stage of recovery. However, we do not *know* if these stages of recovery are operationally valid with regard to avoidance of future sexual offense behavior. Only prospective longitudinal studies will reveal if any treatment approaches are more effective than no treatment and our largely subjective assessment of progress in treatment was accurate.

Using Time-Limited Cycles of Peer Group Therapy for Sexual Offenders against Children

Since so much emphasis has been placed on the benefits to offenders of participating in peer group therapy, a methodology for conducting this modality will be presented. At New England Clinical Associates, we have found it helpful to conduct peer group therapy for sexual offenders against children in time-limited cycles. All of our clients have been adult male child molesters. The majority were never incarcerated but have participated in the treatment program as a condition of probation. Only one man was never arrested for his offenses; in this case, he signed an affidavit in which he promised to participate in the program until he was discharged; family members, in turn, agreed to defer prosecution unless he dropped out of treatment against advice. A few of the men were incarcerated for a period of fifteen months to thirty six months and then joined the treatment program after being released from prison. All of the men have resided apart from their victims upon initiating treatment; some of these have since been reunited with their families with our knowledge and permission. The majority of the men abused a child inside the family, but some of the offenders committed extrafamily child sexual abuse. The majority of the offenders abused girls and fit the pattern of regressed molesters; however, some of the clients abused boys and fit the pattern of fixated molesters. No child rapists have been treated in the program to date. The men have ranged in age from 18 years to 78 years at the time when they began treatment. Most of the men, however, have been in their 30s when they entered the program.

All of the offenders treated at the New England Clinical Associates office thus far fulfilled all of the requirements outlined in the section on evaluation methodology, with one exception: a few offenders were admitted to the program with much shorter periods of probation (one to two years). These men consistently dropped out of the program as soon as their period of probation expired. Consequently subsequent admissions to the treatment program have been persons who were serving longer periods of probation (three to five years).

Each of the cycles of time-limited peer group therapy has been coled by a male and a female therapist. It has seemed important for the men to have an opportunity to relate to therapists of both sexes. In addition, the co-therapists are able to rolemodel appropriate male-female adult working relationships in their interactions with each other as the sessions are conducted. Three men and three women have rotated as cotherapists; thus, group members have had an opportunity to relate to several different male-female co-therapy teams.

All but the first cycle of time-limited peer group therapy for sexual offenders against children have had a theme. We tried to choose themes for the cycles that would enable the men to explore what needs were met by their sexual offense behavior and to practice more effective communications and coping skills. The themes utilized have included "Coping with Pain," "Dealing with Fear," "Identifying Self-Deceiving Behaviors," "Meeting My Needs" and others. A description of the way in which the theme is used will follow shortly.

Each client is required to pay for his own treatment in the program; this includes paying for all group sessions, even if it is necessary occasionally to miss a session because of illness or a work requirement. All of the men are employed; most have health insurance that reimburses them for part of the cost of therapy. Some men have declined to bill their health insurance company for the therapy, probably because they were unwilling to reveal that they were receiving therapy for sexual offense behavior against children. All of the men are required to participate in individual or family therapy, as recommended by the office, at least as often as once per month. Some are seen as often as weekly or biweekly for individual or family therapy. The content of individual sessions frequently involves processing what happened for that offender in a recent group session.

One requirement of the program has been that each group therapy session is videotaped. Anyone who refuses permission to videotape the group therapy session in which he participates is not admitted to the program. The videotapes are used for study and treatment planning by the clinicians; the videotape of the previous week is reviewed routinely in planning for the next session. Members are promised that the videotapes will be treated with the same respect and confidentiality as afforded to all patient records. We frequently assign offenders to view all or part of the videotape of a session whenever that seems appropriate for the individual. As well, offenders are asked to view the videotapes of any session they miss. We have found that the videotape can be a powerful tool to help the offender to understand his own behavior especially in regard to his interactions with peers and with the clinicians.

Each cycle of peer group therapy is scheduled to last for ten to fourteen weeks. The offenders are notified prior to each cycle of the dates for beginning and ending. In practical terms, the spring and fall cycles are longer (thirteen to fourteen weeks), and the summer cycle is shorter (ten to twelve weeks). There is usually a four-week hiatus between the cycles. During this time, each offender is seen at least once, to review his progress individually with one of the clinicians. Reports to probation officers are routinely filed at the end of each cycle, with a copy sent to the offender. Each man's progress, apparent level of commitment to treatment, gains, losses, strengths, and weaknesses are included in the report. When necessary, additional communications (during a cycle) to probation officers take place, as part of case management procedures.

Benefits of Time-Limited Peer Group Therapy

Three types of therapeutic opportunities are afforded by peer group therapy. (See also Chapter 6). They are as follows.

Identification with Peers. Offenders have an opportunity to see other men who have also committed sexual offenses against children and to identify with them. George might say to himself, "Joe is really a lot like me. We both abused our daughters and now we are both having trouble with our wives." What George may not be aware of is that he can learn a great deal from Joe's recovery process that is applicable to his own. As the men practice self-disclosure in the opening session of each cycle of peer group therapy, they tell the other members about their offenses and about themselves. As a gradual process of identification with others takes place, they can also demonstrate support and acceptance for each other. Joe can say to George, "I don't approve of what you did with your daughter, but I think I can understand it. A lot of what you did is very much like my offenses. And I'll bet we had many of the same reasons for sexually abusing our daughters."

Another subtle process is taking place: men who are further along in their recovery process can model that all-important first stage of recovery (acknowledging fully the sexual offense behavior) for newer members who are just beginning treatment. A new member can observe a "veteran" member describing his offense in detail, without relabeling it, without blaming someone else, and accepting full responsibility and think that this is a human being who is worthy of respect, despite his crime. In turn, the new member can consider the possibility that others can separate *his* offense from *him* and can view him as a worthwhile human being even as he describes his crime with a minimum of denial.

Members are encouraged to perform self-disclosure also on the level of feelings and wishes. While telling others, "This is who I am," and "This is what I did," offenders are also encouraged to reveal, "This is what I am thinking or feeling," and "This is what I want." It is the task of the therapists to see to it that each man performs self-disclosure frequently in the group. Clinicians also frequently facilitate group process by directing members to ask each other questions such as, "What do you mean by that?" or "What is going on for you right now?" The greater the self-disclosure practiced by each member, the greater the opportunity for each person to find common ground on which to identify with others.

Challenge by Peers. Each group member can issue and receive challenges with peers in peer group therapy. What is challenged are the distortions of thinking that are common to all sexual offenders against children. All of the men, to a greater or lesser degree, begin treatment with an internal justification and self-serving explanation for their offenses. Some men believe that their victims enjoyed or at least were not harmed by the sexual abuse; some believe that the abuse was justifiable because they felt betrayed or abandoned by their own parents or by spouses; some believe that they do not need court-mandated treatment. Each member is likely to be able to recognize such distortions in thinking when expressed by others, even while he clings to similar distortions in regard to himself. The therapists should always encourage the members to challenge each others' distortions of thinking. Challenge by peers is significantly more effective than challenge by an authority figure.

This therapeutic opportunity is also pertinent to the offender's exploration of the emotional needs that were met by his sexual offenses. Roger, a man who had abused his daughter, consistently claimed, "I just did it when I had the chance. I wasn't thinking of anything special." The other men would then urge him to recall a single incident of abuse. A minute exploration followed of what preceded the abuse, what Roger was thinking before, during, and after the sexual behavior with his daughter, what occurred after the abuse and the like. By slow steps, Roger finally admitted that he had turned to his daughter on that particular day because he was feeling bruised and lonely following a fight with his wife the night before. Before they were finished, his peers were able to press him to acknowledge how warm and safe and accepting it had been to receive attention from his daughter in that context.

The therapists must guard against any tendency for the challenges to be hostile, blaming, or deprecatory of any individual. It is never productive for the group to gang up on any member. Nor is it appropriate or helpful to communicate to any member that he, as an individual, is disliked or despised. Confrontation need not be hostile and dramatic; it can be quietly assertive or even humorous.

Practicing Communications Skills with Peers. This third therapeutic opportunity afforded by peer group therapy has already been discussed to some degree. Disclosing oneself to others (and receiving self-disclosure by others) and challenging distortions of thinking in a reciprocal manner in the group involve communications skills. The clinicians who are leading the group have a responsibility to ensure that all of the members are practicing open and direct communication. The verb practicing implies that a person can learn, by repeated efforts, by being praised for good performance and by having mistakes pointed out and corrected. The cotherapists must be careful to role model direct and open communications skills themselves in the group. To be most effective, the clinicians must create opportunities for the members to report their emotional reactions, to identify wishes or needs, to make requests of others, to give and receive help, and the like. Therefore, the job of the cotherapists is to see to it that the clients do most of the talking and communicating in the weekly sessions. It is, alas, tempting for the clinicians to do most of the talking and monopolize most of the "air-time," instead of directing group members to respond to each other. It is also easy to fall into a pattern in which a clinician does individual therapy with one member of the group while the others listen and look on. This is not only counterproductive; it is a misuse of the group therapy milieu.

Selecting a theme for a cycle of peer group therapy for sexual offenders against children and utilizing the theme to help group members to practice communications skills with each other has proved useful at the New England Clinical Associates Office. Use of a theme helps to focus the discussion each week and provides a practical way for the members to set personal goals for themselves during each cycle of group therapy. The theme for each cycle is selected by the cotherapists and announced to the members at the opening session. The theme must relate to some aspect of managing one's life in a manner that diminishes the risk of committing sexual crimes against children in the future. For example, if "Coping with Pain" is selected as a theme, the underlying premise is that an adult who chose to engage in sexual acts with a child did so, at least in part, because the sexual relationship with the victim somehow helped her or him to cope with emotional pain at that time.

In using the theme, the therapists first should encourage group members to think deeply about how they were coping with emotional pain during the time when they were committing sexual offenses against children. The offenders should be encouraged, then, to give each other feedback as each speaks about his own crimes. It might take several sessions in a group comprised of eight to ten members to explore this issue thoroughly for each individual. Exploring this subject can be a painful and time-consuming process in itself. First, it requires the offenders to recall and describe often depressing and frustrating events in their past lives. Second, some offenders can readily acknowledge that they were experiencing emotional pain in the past, but others will have more difficulty. Third, not all offenders will immediately recognize that behaviors such as distancing from spouses or other family members or being angry or irritable most of the time are methods of coping with emotional pain. The cotherapists must see to it that the group members assist each other to come to these realizations. It is a stepwise process for the offenders next to conclude that the methods they were using to cope with pain at the time of their sexual offenses were inadequate and dysfunctional. In all probability, all of them were lonely, frightened, desperate, and hurting. Unable to satisfy their wishes for affection, affirmation, and nurturance in satisfactory intimate relationships with other adults, they turned instead to children to satisfy their intimacy needs. Again, it is important to remember that each group member is an individual. For some, the stepwise process of learning to view their sexual offense behavior against children as a dysfunctional way of meeting intimacy needs will be lengthy and problematic; for others it is a brief and straightforward process. Group members who are in later stages of their recovery can take leadership in this area; others will require much support and prodding.

The next step is a difficult one for most offenders. The therapists will now be asking, "How are you coping with pain right now? What current methods are you using to try to cope with pain?" Once again, the odds are high that at least some of the members will still be engaging in self-defeating and destructive behaviors, including blaming others and distancing from others in some ways. More experienced group members are likely to be more aware of the methods they use to cope with emotional pain.

> During a group therapy session for adult offenders, one man remarked, "I always know that I am close to getting into trouble again when I start thinking about my brother." Another group member asked, "What kinds of thoughts do you have about your brother?" The first man replied, "Oh, I think about spending time with him and showing him how to play baseball and taking him to games. In one of my fantasies, he's watching me while I'm playing baseball and I even hit a home run!" Another man commented, "I don't see what's wrong with that. I didn't even know you had a brother. I

haven't heard very much about him." The first man, Al, replied, "That's just it; I don't have a younger brother! But I always wanted to have one, so when I was a teenager, I just made one up! And for the rest of my life, whenever I have wanted to reward myself or whenever I'm lonely or scared, I think about that brother a lot. In my fantasy, I'm always taking care of him, just like I wanted someone to take care of me."

At this point, one of the therapists said, "George, what's the problem with Al's fantasy? After all, he's not fantasizing about having sex with his brother! By the way, Al, I'm glad you brought this up."

"I'm not sure," replied George. "Does it have anything to do with it being a fantasy about a child"

"I think so," put in Al. "Part of the problem is that I'm putting energy into wishing for something I can't ever have!"

"That's right, " said the therapist. "And what's wrong with wishing for something that you can't ever have as a method of coping with pain?"

"Is the fantasy too close to reality?" Roger (another group member) asked. "Wishing to have a younger brother is a lot like wishing you could be close to any child who might happen to be handy."

"Yes," said George and Al together.

"What does the fantasy interfere with, Al?" asked the therapist.

"I think it gets in the way of my being close to other people," Al replied. "If I'm putting all of my energy into dreaming about a brother who doesn't exist, it gets in the way of my adult relationships. For one thing, it doesn't leave me much time or energy to work on them."

The foregoing case example illustrates how group members can help each other both in working on the theme and in exploring all aspects of their sexual offense behavior. If Al receives praise for sharing a frequently used method for coping with pain, George and other group members will be encouraged to reveal their coping methods as well. It is noteworthy that the therapist chose to ask other group members to help Al to explore his fantasy. If the therapist had offered an interpretation of the fantasy right away, the probable result would have been a cut-off of the discussion.

After each man shares information about how he is currently coping with pain, the therapists are now ready to ask group members to set a goal for working on some aspect of coping with pain for the rest of the cycle. Each man is also asked how others can help him to work on the goal selected. If Al, for example, decides to work on his pattern of coping with pain by fantasizing about a nonexistent younger brother, it is important that

Al be asked, "What can we do to help you in the group?" If Al can identify a request, that will be very helpful. If not, others may help him by making suggestions. For example, George might offer to ask Al each week during the group session if he has been fantasizing about having a brother. If Al refuses to accept this offer of help, he can then be asked to articulate a request for a type of help that he will accept. On the other hand, if he agrees to George's initial offer, Al might then be asked, "What else can we do to help you to cope with pain besides asking you each week to tell us how much it has been necessary for you to use that old method of fantasizing about a younger brother?"

The point is for Al to make a commitment to work during the cycle on a realistic short-term or stepwise goal related to coping with pain. The initial part of that process involves identifying past and present methods of coping with pain and comparing them. Are Al's present-day methods of coping with pain safer than the methods he was using when he was committing his offenses? If so, how can he strengthen or expand them? If not, what current method of coping with pain could he try? Setting a goal for the rest of the cycle and asking one's peers for help is the next phase of working on the theme within the group. It is extremely useful for offenders to practice asking others for help in a direct manner. It is also instructive, to practice refusing help from others within the context of being encouraged then to verbalize a different request. In a reciprocal fashion, it is helpful to practice refusing someone's request in a direct but nonhostile fashion, especially when one will immediately be asked, "Okay, Roger, if you are not willing to agree to George's request, how would you be willing to help him to work on his goal?"

Once again, it is the job of the cotherapists to monitor group process while seeing to it that each member's individual needs are addressed. Some members will find it easy to set goals but much harder to ask for help. Other group members will have less difficulty in asking for help than they will have in setting limits on what they will accept. Still others will need feedback from the group to help them realize how they are currently coping with pain. For example, one man consistently described himself as doing well and having no need to cope with pain because life was so good for him at that time. Over the next several sessions, his peers, were able to give him direct feedback about several methods of coping with pain that they observed him using in the group, including frequent denial, constant joking about difficult matters, and consistently arriving late for group meetings. Again, the cotherapists must be vigilant to ensure that such feedback is offered in a constructive and nonhostile manner.

To summarize, participating in peer group therapy enables the offenders to identify with peers, experience challenge by peers, and practice the communications skills that are the building blocks for intimacy. All of the above can be performed in a safe and guided setting in the peer group therapy milieu. Use of themes in time-limited cycles of peer group therapy has several advantages: (1) the theme promotes a framework in which the offenders can work; (2) it enables members to make connections between past and present behaviors; and (3) it affords opportunities for the members to practice interpersonal skills that will assist them in managing their everyday lives. We have seen offenders make significant gains in these areas as they participate in multiple cycles of peer group therapy. Participating in one cycle of group therapy or even in one year of group therapy has not appeared to be sufficient for offenders treated at the New England Clinical Associates Office. Thus far, we have seen gradual improvement for offenders in the second year and marked improvement in the third year. We are currently recommending a five-year treatment plan for sexual offenders against children, with participation in peer group therapy for a minimum of three years.

Case Management Considerations

A community-based treatment program for sexual offenders against children requires a large case management component! The first part of this chapter addressed the significant amounts of coordination and maneuvering that must take place after a clinician receives a request to perform an evaluation. Since most offenders are at best ambivalent about participating in any kind of substantive treatment, cases are likely to continue to require extensive attention to case management during the first year of treatment. Thereafter, clinicians who direct treatment programs for offenders may not need to expend quite as much energy on case management. However, regular reports to probation officers and regular collateral contacts with other treatment providers will still be necessary.

Clinicians must be alert to the probability that each case will periodically require intensive case management at intervals during the second through the fifth years of offender treatment. This is a sober but realistic prospect since offenders (and their families) may go into crisis during the later stages of recovery as well as during the earlier stages. Some of these crises are bound to be situational as marriages go through evolutionary stages, children get older and have different needs, job situations change, aging parents or other members of offenders' families of origin become ill or die, and so forth. Thus, in addition to moving through stages of recovery with regard to sexual offense behavior against children, offender-clients are also going through life stages, family crises, and external stresses, all of which impact on their treatment and many of which will require the community treatment program to step up its case management interventions.

It can be dangerous as well as unrealistic to have a formula approach to community-based treatment of sexual offenders against children. Not all offenders are alike; each is an individual and will have individual treatment needs. When the community treatment program has limited resources, it may depend on other treatment providers to address the offender's needs for individual or family therapy. The latter arrangement is feasible only if the community treatment program acts as case manager for the offender, takes leadership in coordinating the services, and insists that all of the treatment providers communicate frequently with each other. Sometimes the energy required for the last is equivalent (in staff time) to providing the individual and family therapy oneself (from the perspective of the community treatment program).

It is not necessary to subsidize community-based treatment for offenders, nevertheless, if the clients are permitted to work and earn wages to support their families and to pay for their own treatment. It may be tempting for agencies (such as the Department of Adult Probation) that refer offenders for treatment to put pressure on private treatment providers to keep the fees unrealistically low. An unfortunate result is that some community-based treatment programs may skimp on case management, which is a cost of providing treatment that is rarely reimbursed directly by third-party payers. Another way for the community treatment program to try to keep its fees lower is to sponsor therapy groups with twelve to twenty members. Sadly, it is not possible for clinicians to identify individual treatment needs, monitor each member's progress and plan and facilitate therapy interventions in groups of that size. Our experience at New England Clinical Associates has been that experienced cotherapists must work very hard to accomplish their goals in groups with a maximum of eight to ten members.

A few other case management considerations deserve special mention.

Liability

When a clincian evaluates a sexual offender and recommends community-based treatment, she or he is offering a professional judgment that the offender does not need the level of control afforded by incarceration. Stated differently, a recommendation for community-based treatment is bound to be viewed by others as a reflection of the clinician's belief that the offender presents an acceptably low risk for reoffending if allowed to remain in the community.

If the person commits another offense while in treatment or after being discharged for treatment, there is always the possibility of an attempt (perhaps by a victim's parents) to prove liability on the part of the clinician or the treatment program. Little attention has been paid to this issue to date, and if civil liability suits have been filed in some locations, there has been little national publicity about them. It is likely that more attention will be paid to this issue in the future. Private community-based treatment programs and the clinicians who service them need adequate professional liability coverage. In turn, private programs are justified in being selective about the types of sexual offenders they will accept into treatment. If a community or a state is not willing to fund treatment programs in prisons or in halfway houses, it may be necessary for it to subsidize from public funds a community-based treatment program for high-risk offenders.

Resistance to Treatment

Few client groups display as extensive and prolonged resistance to treatment as is true for many sexual offenders against children. In earlier sections of this chapter, the mind-set needed to perform effective treatment was discussed. In addition to displaying firmness, patience, caring, nurturance, and consistency, clinicians must avoid being punitive, judgmental and inconsistent. It is extremely difficult to maintain the necessary mind-set, which also includes a willingness to forego expressions of appreciation from one's clients. Clinicians who work in community-based treatment programs will be likely to be most effective if they are part of an in-house team that shares responsibility for offenders treated by the program. This enables them to share the burden of responsibility while maintaining some perspective on the ever-present resistance and occasional rewards of working in such programs.

Displacement of Anger

Part of the experience of working with the resistance described above involves absorbing the anger displaced by most offenders upon their treatment providers. As Margaret Vasington points out very movingly in chapter 13, most sexual offenders have had a lifetime of experiences about which they can be legitimately angry. Many sexual offenders against children were abused themselves in childhood; lacking safe opportunities to learn to express anger directly and deal effectively with frustration as children, they need to learn these skills as adults.

Despite all of the drawbacks of a prison setting for treatment, it can be a safe place for a clinician to work with a violent client. The outpatient setting of community-based treatment affords little safety when clients have a potential for acting out violently when they become angry. Since most sexual offenders against children are child molesters, their style of expressing anger (displaced or direct) is likely to be passive-aggressive rather than violent. Since most offenders displace their anger on the treatment program and its staff, this is fortunate! Child rapists, on the other hand, are more likely to have a history of violence in their interpersonal relationships with other adults, as well as in their patterns of engaging children in sexual behaviors by force or by threat of injury. Accordingly, the recommendation that child rapists receive treatment in a secure setting first before they are treated in the community is based on two considerations:

1. Child rapists represent a greater potential for physical danger to the staff of the treatment program as well as to vulnerable persons in the community.
2. A secure setting such as a prison-based treatment program may be the only safe place in which a child rapist can learn to express anger and deal with frustration in nonviolent and more constructive ways.

Besides looking at the method by which the offender engaged children in sexual behaviors (violent versus nonviolent), clinicians should also be alert to other indicators that offenders might express displaced anger in a violent fashion. These include a history of poor impulse control, a history of substance abuse, a history of self-mutilation or suicide attempts and a history of emotional investment or preoccupation with guns or weapons. Careful evaluation procedures will enable most clients who have a high potential for violence to be eliminated before they are admitted to the treatment program. If, however, a pattern of escalating potential for violence is revealed after the offender begins treatment, it may be necessary to revise the treatment recommendations and to present them to the court. This is not likely to occur often, but it may be necessary as the treatment program accepts more clients and clinicians gain additional experience.

Conclusion

Community-based treatment for selected sexual offenders against children is an alternative to prison-based treatment. There are few community-based programs in the United States that have been in continuous operation for more than five years and have performed careful data collection and monitoring. This chapter presents a model for evaluating and treating sexual offenders against children in a community-based treatment program that stresses time-limited cycles of peer group therapy as a primary treatment modality. Chapter 11 in this volume, "The Chesapeake Institute," describes a community-based program in which long-term individual therapy is the primary treatment modality. Few reliable methodologies for evaluating progress in treatment have been published to date. On the other hand, great strides have been made in the last decade in learning feasible methods of providing community-based treatment for sexual offenders against children.

References

Berlin, Fred. 1985. "Pedophilia." *Medical Aspects of Human Sexuality* 19:79–88.

Burgess, Ann, and Lazare, Aaron, ed. 1976. "The Customer Approach to Patient-hood." In *Community Mental Health: Target Populations,* 35–54. Englewood Cliffs, N.J.: Prentice-Hall.

Cage, Richard. 1988. "Criminal Investigation of Child Sexual Abuse." In S.M. Sgroi, ed., *Vulnerable Populations,* 1:187–227. Lexington, Mass.: Lexington Books.

DeLipsey, Jan, and James, Sue. 1988. "Videotaping the Sexually Abused Child: The Texas Experience, 1983–1987." In S.M. Sgroi, ed., *Vulnerable Populations* 1:228–264. Lexington, Mass.: Lexington Books.

Groth, A. Nicholas. 1978. "Guidelines for the Assessment and Management of the Offender." In A. Burgess, ed., *Sexual Assault of Children and Adolescents,* 25–42. Lexington, Mass.: Lexington Books.

Groth, A. Nicholas. 1982. In S.M. Sgroi, ed., *Handbook of Clinical Intervention in Child Sexual Abuse,* 215–239. Lexington, Mass.: Lexington Books.

Groth, A. Nicholas, with Birnbaum, H. Jean. 1979. *Men Who Rape: The Psychology of the Offender.* New York: Plenum Press.

Meyer, Walter et al. 1985. "Physical, Metabolic and Hormonal Effects on Men of Long-Term Therapy with Medroxyprogesterone Acetate." *Fertility and Sterility* 43:102–109.

O'Connell, Michael. 1986. "Reuniting Incest Offenders with Their Families." *Journal of Interpersonal Violence* 1:374–386.

Rowan, Edward. 1988. "Predicting the Effectiveness of Treatment for Pedophilia." *Journal of Forensic Science* 33:204–209.

Salter, Anna. 1988. *Treating Sex Offenders and Their Victims.* Newbury Park, Calif.: Sage Publications.

Index

About the Contributors

Thomas S. Berg, M.S.W., is executive director for clinical services at The Chesapeake Institute, Inc., in Wheaton, Maryland, where he supervises a multidisciplinary staff providing treatment for sexually abused children and their families, adult and juvenile offenders, and adults molested as children. Mr. Berg also serves as clinical director of the Montgomery County chapter of Parents United. He received his M.S.W. from the University of Maryland with a focus on marriage and family therapy. Mr. Berg has previously worked with child sexual-abuse victims and offenders at the Prince George's County General Hospital and Medical Center and The Sexual Abuse Unit of Montgomery County Protective Services.

Linda Canfield Blick, M.S.W., is the founder and executive director of The Chesapeake Institute, Inc., a not-for-profit program in Wheaton, Maryland solely devoted to the study, treatment, and research of child sexual abuse. Ms. Blick also serves as executive administrator of The National Resource Center on Child Sexual Abuse, a program supported by a grant from the National Center on Child Abuse and Neglect. A licensed social worker in Maryland, Ms. Blick received her M.S.W. from the University of Connecticut. She is a nationally recognized teacher and lecturer and has co-authored several articles on child sexual-abuse intervention. She is the recipient of the 1986 Victims' Service Award from the United States Department of Justice.

Judith A. Carey, RSM, Ph.D., received her Ph.D. in educational psychology from the University of Connecticut. She is a former special education consultant for the Connecticut State Department of Education, and was director of the Gengras Center for Children and associate professor of special education at Saint Joseph College in West Hartford, Connecticut. Dr. Carey participated in the development and implementation of the sexual-abuse avoidance curriculum for adults with mental retardation described in this book. She maintains a private consulting practice in Manchester, Connecticut.

A. Nicholas Groth, Ph.D., is the founder and executive director of Forensic Mental Health Associates (FMHA) in Webster, Massachusetts, and Orlando, Florida. FMHA is a private enterprise providing education, consultation, and training in regard to sexual assault. He is a consultant for New England Clinical Associates and the Saint Joseph College Institute for Child Sexual Abuse Intervention in West Hartford, Connecticut, and for the sex offender treatment program at the Wyoming State Honor Farm in Riverton, Wyoming. He is also the founder and former director of the sex offender program at the Connecticut Correctional Institution in Somers, Connecticut. Dr. Groth received his Ph.D. in clinical psychology from Boston University. He has worked with both victims and perpetrators of sexual assault in institutional and community-based settings since 1966, and is the author of *Men Who Rape: The Psychology of the Offender* and co-author of *Sexual Assault of Children and Adolescents*.

Kerry Christensen Homstead, Ed.D., completed her doctorate in 1985 with research on group therapy with adolescent victims of sexual abuse. She is currently a group therapy supervisor at Sojourn, Inc., a nonprofit agency in Northampton, Massachusetts, where she focuses on individual and group work with adolescents and women. Dr. Homstead also maintains a private clinical practice. In addition to direct work with clients, she provides consultation to other practitioners.

David Hussey, LISW, CCDC, is the program manager of Adolescent Services at St. Vincent Charity Hospital-Woodruff Pavilion in Cleveland, Ohio. He is a graduate of John Carroll University and received his practice degree from Case Western Reserve University School of Applied Social Sciences. In addition to his inpatient work, Mr. Hussey also maintains a private practice in the Cleveland area.

Jamshid A. Marvasti, M.D., is a child and adult psychiatrist specializing in the treatment of sexual abuse victims, offenders, and their families. He has been the director of the Sexual Trauma Center in Manchester, Connecticut since 1981 and consultant at New England Clinical Associates since 1985. Dr. Marvasti is a faculty member of the Saint Joseph College Institute for Child Sexual Abuse Intervention in West Hartford, Connecticut. He is a fellow of the American College of Forensic Psychiatry and the author of several papers on child sexual-abuse topics.

Frank J. Oliveri, B.A., received his degree in counseling psychology from Columbia Pacific University in San Rafael, California. He was a resident counselor for the Wyoming State Honor Farm in Riverton and has worked with both victims and offenders in institutional settings. Mr. Oliveri is a contributor to the book, *It Happens to Boys Too,* and to a forthcoming text on male sexual victimization. He has co-authored a journal article with Dr. Groth on sexual assault and has presented at Forensic Mental Health Associates training seminars.

Francis J. Pescosolido, M.Ed., M.S.W., M.P.H., is clinical director at the East Side Center in Providence, Rhode Island, a private diagnostic and treatment center specializing in child/adult victimization and psychological trauma. He is a faculty member of the Boston University School of Social Work's postgraduate certificate program in child psychotherapy where he teaches assessment and treatment of child and family psychological trauma. He is a consultant to numerous mental health centers and child and family agencies and to the Massachusetts Department of Social Services and the Sexual Abuse Assessment Unit of the Rhode Island Department for Children and their Families. He received his M.Ed. in counseling psychology from Springfield College, his M.S.W. from Simmons College, and his M.P.H. from Harvard University.

Norah M. Sargent, M.A., received her degree in counseling in ministry from Fairfield University, Fairfield, Connecticut and is now a doctoral student in clinical psychology at the University of Rhode Island. Ms. Sargent is also a therapist and consultant on spirituality at New England Clinical Associates in West Hartford, Connecticut where she has gained extensive experience in working with adult survivors of child sexual abuse. Along with a background in retreat work, she has sixteen years of experience in education at the primary, secondary, and adult education levels. Between 1984 and 1988, she was the director of the counseling department at the Academy of Our Lady of Peace in San Diego, California.

Mark I. Singer, Ph.D., is associate professor of social work at the Mandel School of Applied Social Sciences, and assistant professor of pediatrics at the School of Medicine, Case Western Reserve University. Dr. Singer has spent over twenty years in clinical practice with adolescents and has published numerous articles on youth-related problems and issues. He is presently involved in a two-year follow-up study of psychiatrically hospitalized adolescents that will address the ongoing behavioral effects of victimization in this population.

Margaret C. Vasington, M.A., is a psychotherapist in private practice in Storrs, Connecticut. She also serves as a volunteer counselor for the sex offender program at the Connecticut Correctional Institution in Somers, Connecticut. Ms. Vasington received a master's degree in counseling psychology from Antioch/New England Graduate School and is also a graduate of Hartford Family Institute. She has conducted numerous workshops in the United States, Canada, and Europe.

Lynn A. Werthamer, M.S.W., has been working in sexual-abuse treatment and adolescent therapy since 1981. She is currently an individual and group therapist for adult survivors of child sexual abuse at Franklin-Hampshire Community Mental Health Center in Northampton, Massachusetts. Ms. Werthamer also works directly with these client populations in private practice and provides consultation for other practitioners.

Amy B. Wheaton, Ph.D., has served as commissioner of the Connecticut Department of Children and Youth Services since March 1987. Between 1984 and 1986, she served as acting commissioner and as deputy commissioner of administrative and support services for the Connecticut Department of Mental Retardation. Dr. Wheaton holds a Ph.D. in foundations of education from Trinity College. Her previous experience includes developing and implementing remedial psychoeducational programs for children and adolescents and writing and implementing practicums for mental health workers in a variety of clinical settings.

About the Author

Suzanne M. Sgroi, M.D., is executive director of New England Clinical Associates, a private treatment center for child sexual abuse. She is director of the Saint Joseph College Institute for Child Sexual Abuse Intervention in West Hartford, Connecticut. Dr. Sgroi served as program developer of the Connecticut Department of Children and Youth Services' Sexual Trauma Treatment Program from 1977 to 1979 and is a teacher and consultant on child sexual abuse for child protective services and the Municipal Police Training Council.

A physician in private practice in Suffield, Connecticut, Dr. Sgroi is also actively involved in teaching and consulting on child sexual abuse. She is the author of *A Handbook of Clinical Intervention in Child Sexual Abuse* (Lexington Books, 1982), which received the American Journal of Nursing Book of the Year Award in 1983.

A native of Fulton, New York, Dr. Sgroi received her A.B. in liberal arts from Syracuse University, and her M.D. from the State University of New York at Buffalo. Her internship was served at the Millard Fillmore Hospital, Buffalo, New York, and residency in internal medicine at the Rochester General Hospital, Rochester, New York. Before moving to Connecticut in 1972, she served as a rotating physician, Internal Medicine, on the Hospital Ship Hope mission to Natal, Brazil.